The Basics of Artistic Painting

THE COMPLETE COURSE ON PAINTING AND DRAWING

The Basics of Artistic Painting

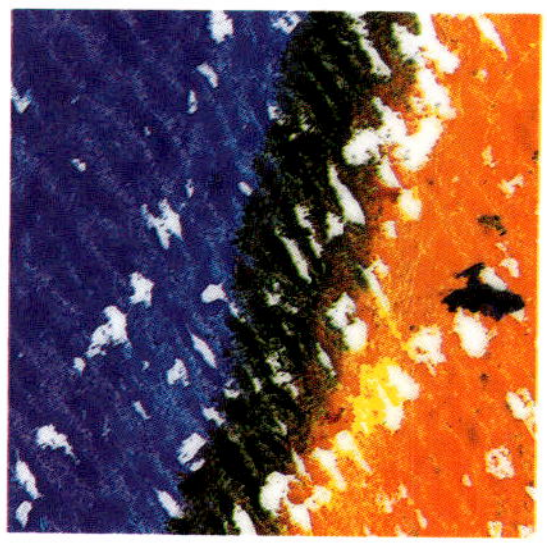

BARRON'S

Original title of the book in Spanish is "Las Bases de la Pintura Artistica"

Published by Parramón Ediciones, S.A., Barcelona, Spain
First edition, January 1992

Author: Parramón Ediciones Editorial Team
Illustrators: Parramón Ediciones Editorial Team

All inquiries should be addressed to:
Barron's Educational Series, Inc.
250 Wireless Boulevard
Hauppauge, New York 11788

Library of Congress Catalog Card No. 93-20837
International Standard Book No. 0-8120-1928-8

Library of Congress Cataloging-in-Publication Data
The basics of artistic painting.
p. cm. — (The complete course in drawing and painting)
Includes index.
ISBN 0-8120-1928-8
1. Art—Technique. I. Barron's Educational Series, Inc.
II. Series.
N7430.B315 1994
751.4—dc20 93-20837
CIP

Printed in Spain
4567 9960 987654321

Contents

The theory of color

First Isaac Newton established a principle that all artists today accept as indisputable fact: Light is color. Newton reached this conclusion by shutting himself in a dark room and allowing just a little light to filter in through a window. Then he placed a triangular glass prism in the ray of light; the result was that the glass split the white light into the six colors of the spectrum, which became visible when they fell on an adjacent wall.

Some years later, Thomas Young, an English physicist, carried out the same experiment in reverse. First, through his investigations he established that the six colors of the spectrum can be reduced to three basic colors: Green, red, and deep blue. Then he took three lamps and projected the beams of light through filters of these three colors, focusing them on the same spot; the green, red, and blue beams became white. In other words, Young *recreated* light.

So white light, the light that surrounds us, is made up of six different colors of light; when these fall on any object, that object absorbs some of the colors and reflects others. Let's emphasize this point:

All opaque objects, when illuminated, reflect all or part of the light directed at them

To understand this phenomenon more easily, let's say that, for example, a red tomato absorbs green and blue light and reflects red and that a yellow banana absorbs blue and reflects the colors red and green which, added together, allow us to see the color yellow.

We are going to devote a few pages to studying the theory of color, and we are going to do it as artists; that is to say, *not painting with light* (with colored light) but *painting light* with colored substances that we call pigments. Using the popular medium of colored pencils, we will show you how to study a wide range of colors based on the theories of Newton and Young, but applying them from the artist's point of view.

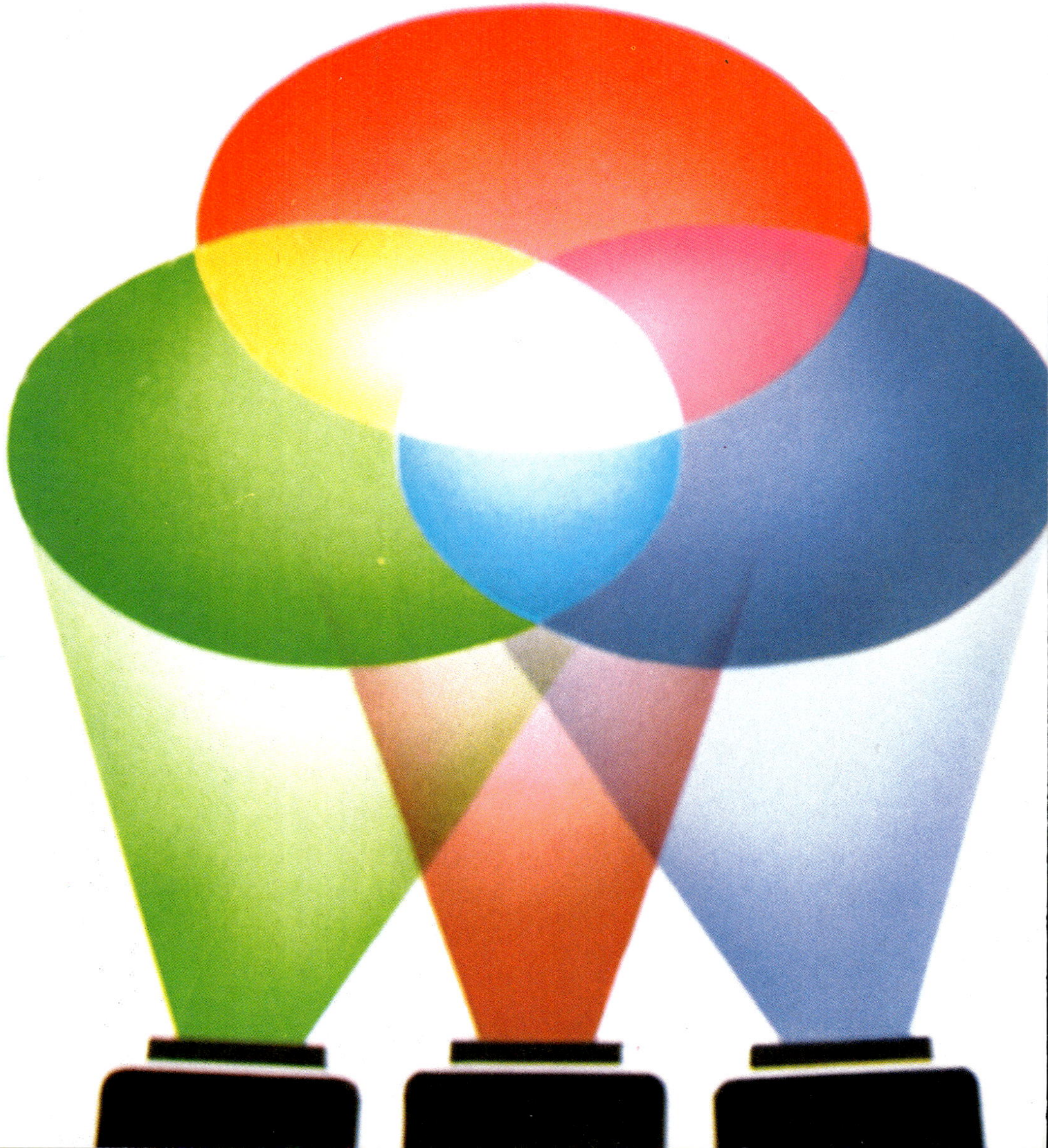

Three beams of light, passing through green, red, and bright blue filters—the primary colors of light—recreate white light. By projecting them two at a time, you obtain the three secondary colors of light—yellow, cyan blue, and magenta.

Colors of light and pigment colors

RANGE OF SPECTRUM COLORS

Newton broke down the colors of light and established the six colors of the spectrum. Young recreated light and classified the colors of the spectrum as primaries and secondaries.

PRIMARY colors of light:
red, green, deep blue
SECONDARY colors of light:
Blue light + green light = cyan blue
Red light + blue light = magenta
Green light + red light = yellow

So a complementary color is a secondary color that only requires a primary color to complement it to recreate white light, or vice versa.

COMPLEMENTARY colors of light:
Deep blue complements yellow
Red complements cyan blue
Green complements magenta

PIGMENT COLORS

Primaries:
Yellow
Cyan blue*
Magenta

Secondaries:
Green
Red
Deep blue

Tertiaries:
Orange
Carmine
Violet
Ultramarine blue
Emerald green
Light green

In the chromatic circle, or color table, which appears below left, the primary colors have been indicated with a P and the secondaries with an S. Everything we have said up until now has pointed to certain conclusions:

• Artists paint using pigments with which they can reproduce the colors of light, or spectrum colors.
• Given that colors of light and palette colors coincide, it is easy for the artist to imitate the effect of light on objects and, therefore, to reproduce exactly all natural colors.
• Theories of light and color show us that the artist can paint all natural colors using only the three primary colors which, as pigments, are yellow, cyan blue*, and magenta.
• However, an understanding of the use of complementary colors considerably broadens the expressive potential of the artist's "palette" when capturing shades and quality of light and color and, as we shall see later on, when trying to achieve perfect harmony in a picture.

*Cyan blue does not exist in artists' color charts. It is mainly used in graphic design and color photography. The term has been used in the theory of color to define primary blue (very similar to Prussian blue oil paint mixed with a little white).

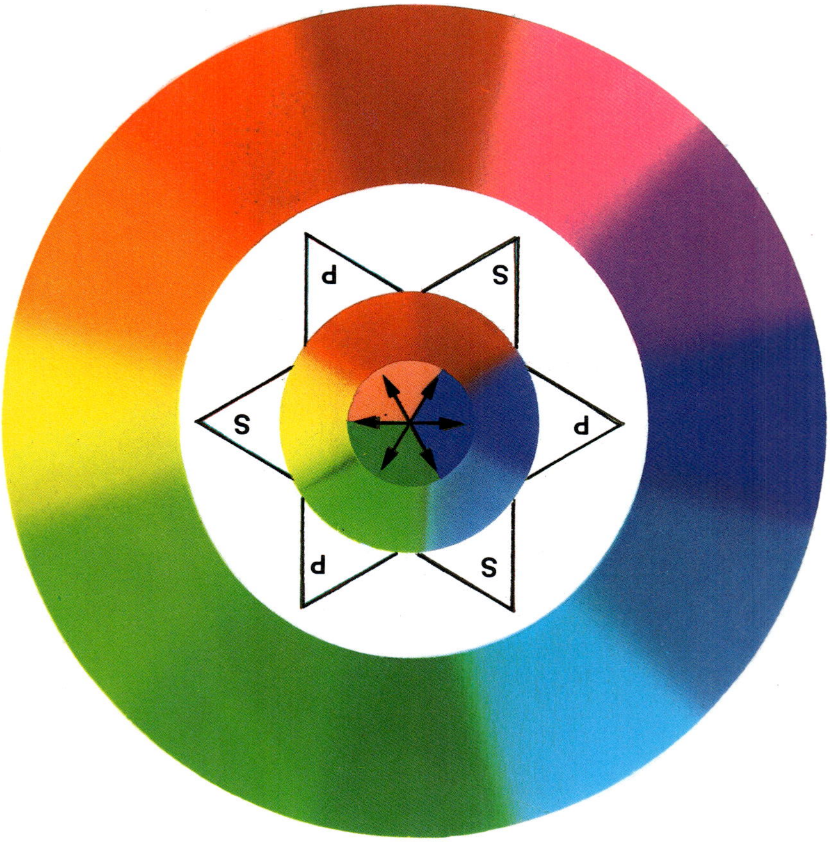

Green, red, and blue, primary light colors.

Cadmium yellow, cyan, and magenta, primary pigment colors.

LIGHT COLORS

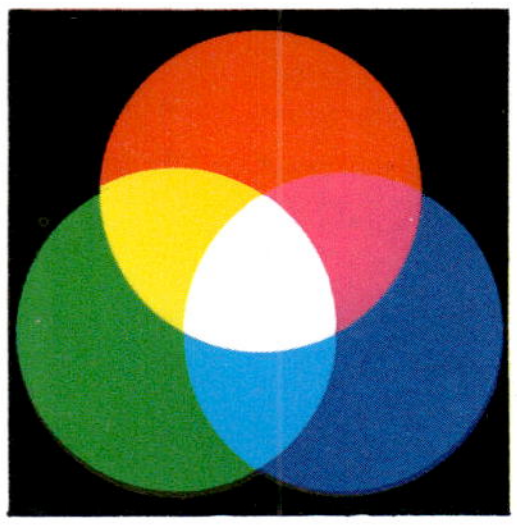

PIGMENT COLORS

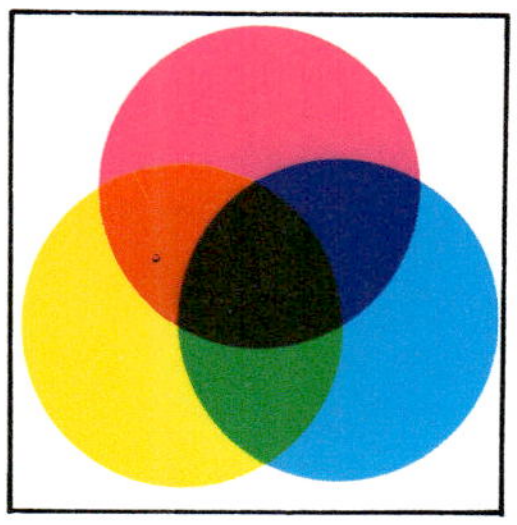

Complementary colors

As we can see in the chromatic circle on the previous page, complementary colors are pairs situated opposite one another. Using this principle, we can find the complementary pairs of tertiary colors. For example:

Orange	**Ultramarine blue**
Carmine	**Emerald green**
Light green	**Violet**

It is easy to demonstrate (see the examples at the bottom of the page) that complementary colors are those that offer the greatest contrast. Carmine and emerald green, for instance, have an extraordinary impact side by side in a painting—and look at deep blue next to yellow!

Once the theory and practical application of complementary colors have been mastered, the rendering of shade and shadows will hold no secrets for the painter. In shade portions of the object itself, or in its projected shadow, you will always find the color complementary to that of the object. An example will illustrate this point more clearly: In a green melon's shadow—which is a dark green such as tertiary emerald green—the complementary color carmine will appear.

Great Post-Impressionist painters such as Matisse, Derain, Vlaminck, Dufy, Braque, and Friesz adopted the use of complementary colors as a style of painting in its own right, called *fauvism*. There could be no more useful and definitive lesson than studying paintings by these masters of the palette; the colors of their paintings are veritable explosions of light, intensity, and contrast. The examples offered on this page and the next five have been produced using colored pencils, but they could just as easily have been created in oils or any other medium. The theory of color applies to them all.

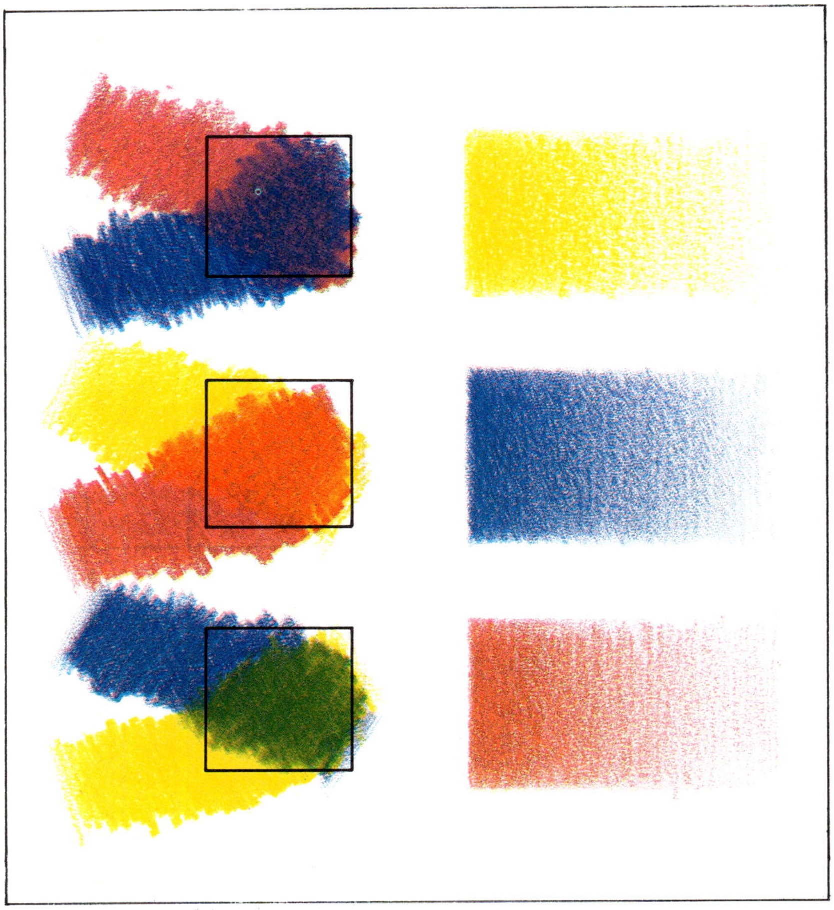

Above. ***Above.*** *The secondary deep blue—a mixture of the primaries blue and magenta—is the complement of primary yellow, and vice versa.*

The secondary red—a mixture of the yellow and magenta primaries—is the complement of primary blue, and vice versa.

The secondary green—a mixture of the primaries blue and yellow—is the complement of primary magenta, and vice versa.

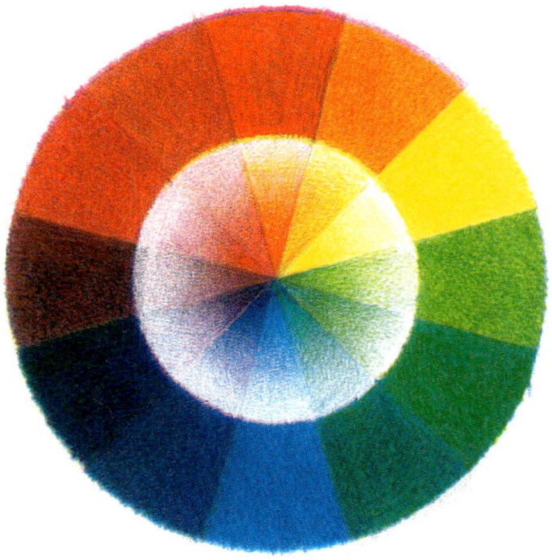

In this chromatic circle we have shown only the primary and secondary colors, the central arrows indicating complementary colors.

Below, *a small sample of the effect achieved by juxtaposing complementary colors to create maximum contrast.*

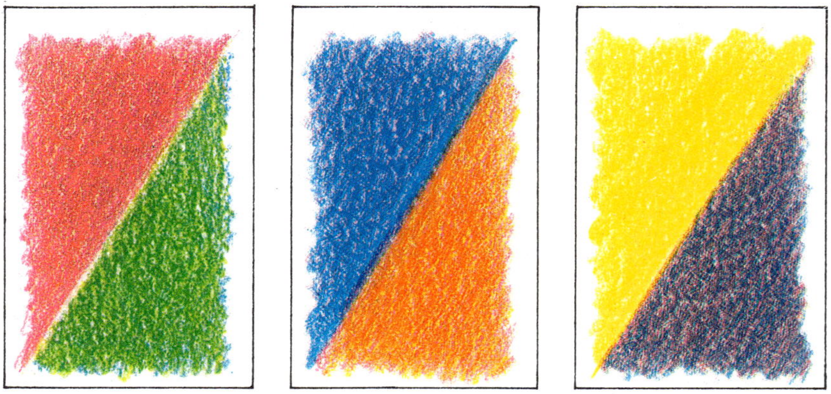

Creating colors by mixing primaries

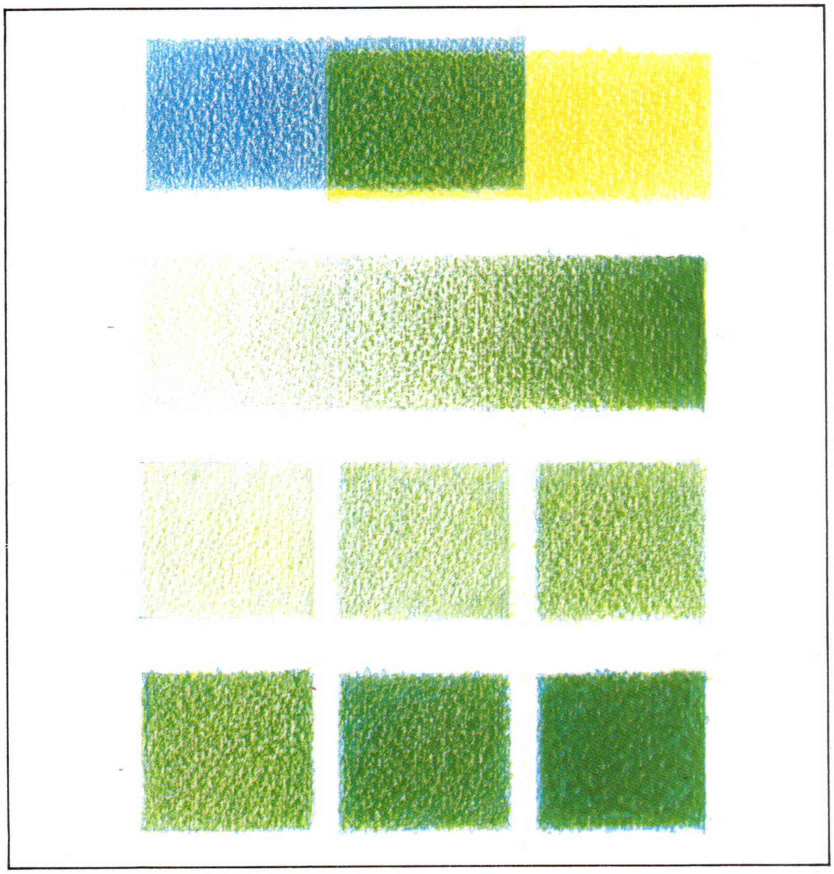

We suggest that you discover for yourself how to obtain any color using only blue, magenta, and yellow—that is, the primary colors. You will need only three colored pencils (one of each primary color) and a good quality, semi-rough watercolor paper, ideal for our goal of creating a color chart of 36 colors, obtained by superimposing two or three primary colors.

But let's take it stage by stage. Start by individually coloring the different color ranges that will make up the complete chart. Using pieces of paper no larger than the boxes containing our examples, and good quality pencils, do the following:

Creating the green color range

Greens are made by mixing blue and yellow. The first color you should apply is blue, yellow being added later. Try to achieve a smooth gradation starting with the palest tint and moving towards the final, darkest tones.

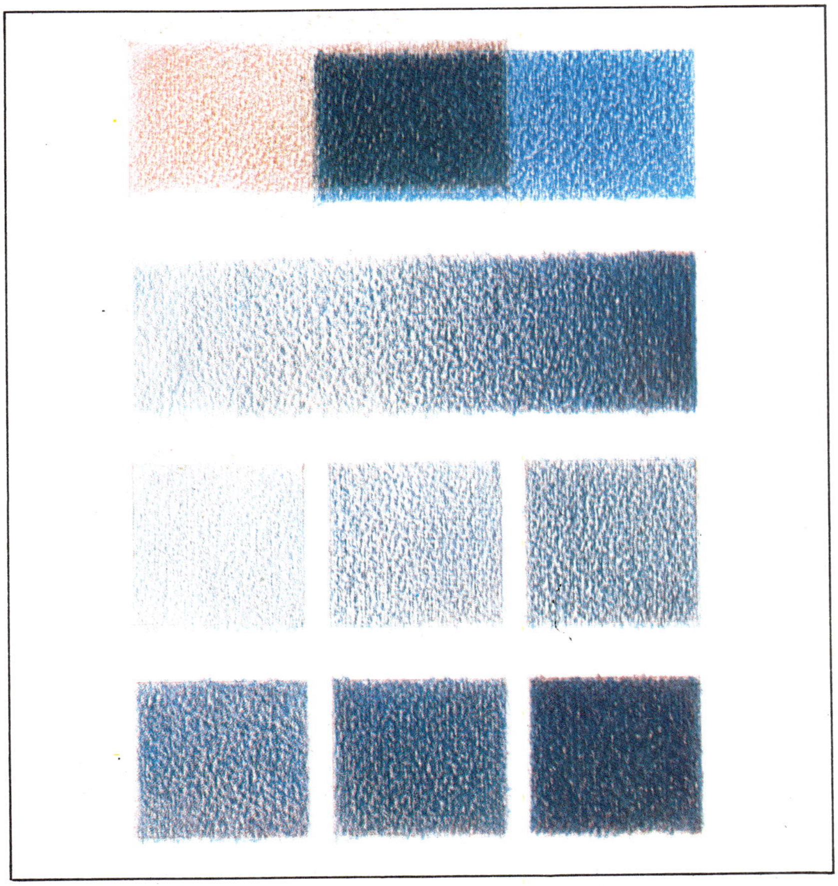

The blue range

Note that the darkest blues have been obtained by mixing magenta and blue, the magenta being laid down first.

Be careful with magenta. It is a very intense color and it should be used sparingly.

To make these dark blues, blue has been laid on top of magenta. You can really take the plunge with both these primaries and experiment, changing the order in which you apply the color, superimposing magenta onto blue. This way can be useful if you want to darken a blue-colored area; notice the intensity of the color in the bottom righthand corner.

The orange-red range

If yellow is added to an area of deep magenta (see the upper example), you get a deep red. However, if your objective is to achieve colors in the orange-red scale, the quantity of both magenta and yellow must be carefully controlled. In our examples you can see a gradation produced with the magenta pencil, on which we have superimposed another gradation in yellow. This has created, from left to right, the transition from the white of the paper to a deep red, passing through orange-reds of increasing intensity.

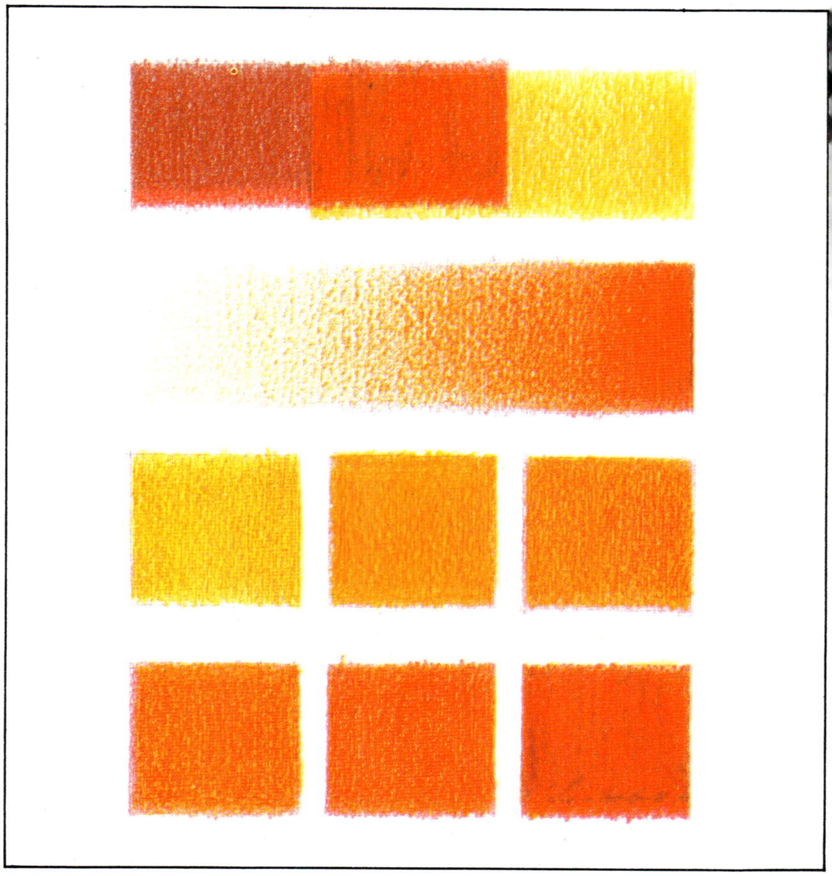

The range of ochres and earth colors

Using a medium violet made from magenta and blue (see the top example), it is possible to achieve an extensive range of colors ranging from yellow ochre, through the siennas, to burnt ochre. To do this, you add yellow to the different violets created from the other two primaries. As always, you must practice altering the quantity of each color according to the result you wish to achieve. It is obvious, for instance, that in the first three examples of the range, there is much less blue than in the three samples underneath, in which magenta and blue dominate the yellow.

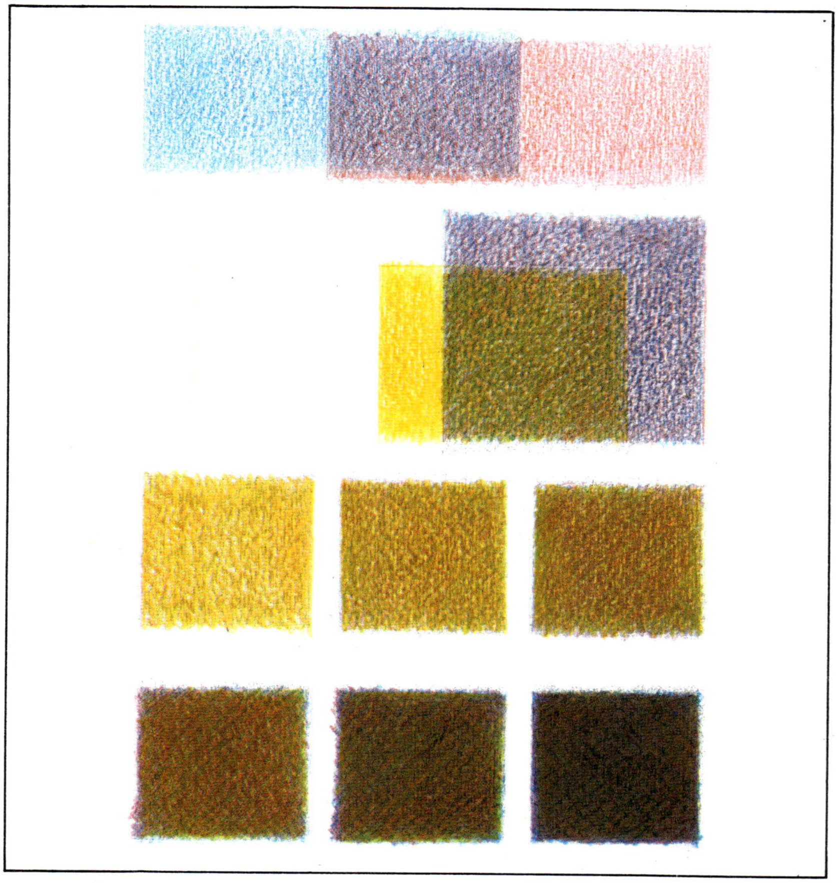

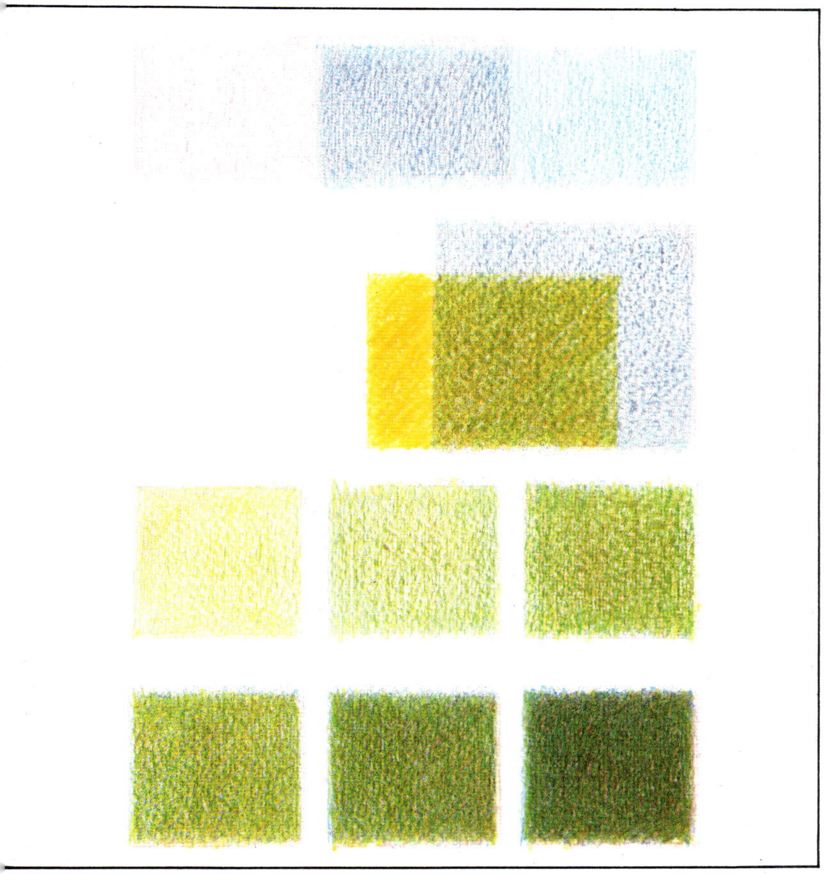

The "neutral" green range

This is a series of greens of increasing intensity, in which there is some magenta. They may be described as "neutral" because they are subdued by the presence of a third color that alters the pure green which consists only of blue and yellow. These greens can be regarded as being produced by yellow when added to a violet base, as opposed to a base of blue. Study the amounts of each color required to achieve the same shades as those appearing in our six examples.

The bluish-gray range

You now will have the opportunity to find out the extent to which the greater or lesser presence of a primary in a mixture affects the final color. We are going to create a range of bluish-grays.

The initial mixture of blue and magenta will give us more or less the same violets produced in the blue range as in the section above, and that, in the previous example, led us to neutral greens. To this violet mixture we will add a moderate amount of yellow, without intensifying the color too much. The difference between these mixtures and the neutral greens results entirely from the lesser amount of yellow applied.

Now we are going to combine in a single chart of 36 colors the information we have accumulated through studying each range separately. Bear in mind the following tips:

• Use a sheet of good quality, semi-rough watercolor paper.
• Assuming that your pencil box contains two blues and two reds, use only the bright blue (cyan) and the magenta or carmine, in addition to the yellow.
• Keep a protective sheet of paper under your drawing hand.
• Hold the pencil in the usual way, but slightly higher than for writing.
• Before starting on the definitive version, practice on separate pieces of paper of the type you will be using for the exercise.
• To produce the first set of gradations, start on the left (or on the right if you are left-handed). Without exerting pressure with the pencil, and keeping the lead at a bevelled angle, apply the color with vertical strokes, shifting your hand to the right as necessary, making the strokes stronger and closer together as you go, trying to achieve a regular gradation.
• Finally it is possible that parts of the scale might require some touching up; by all means do this, but without losing sight of the color range as a whole.

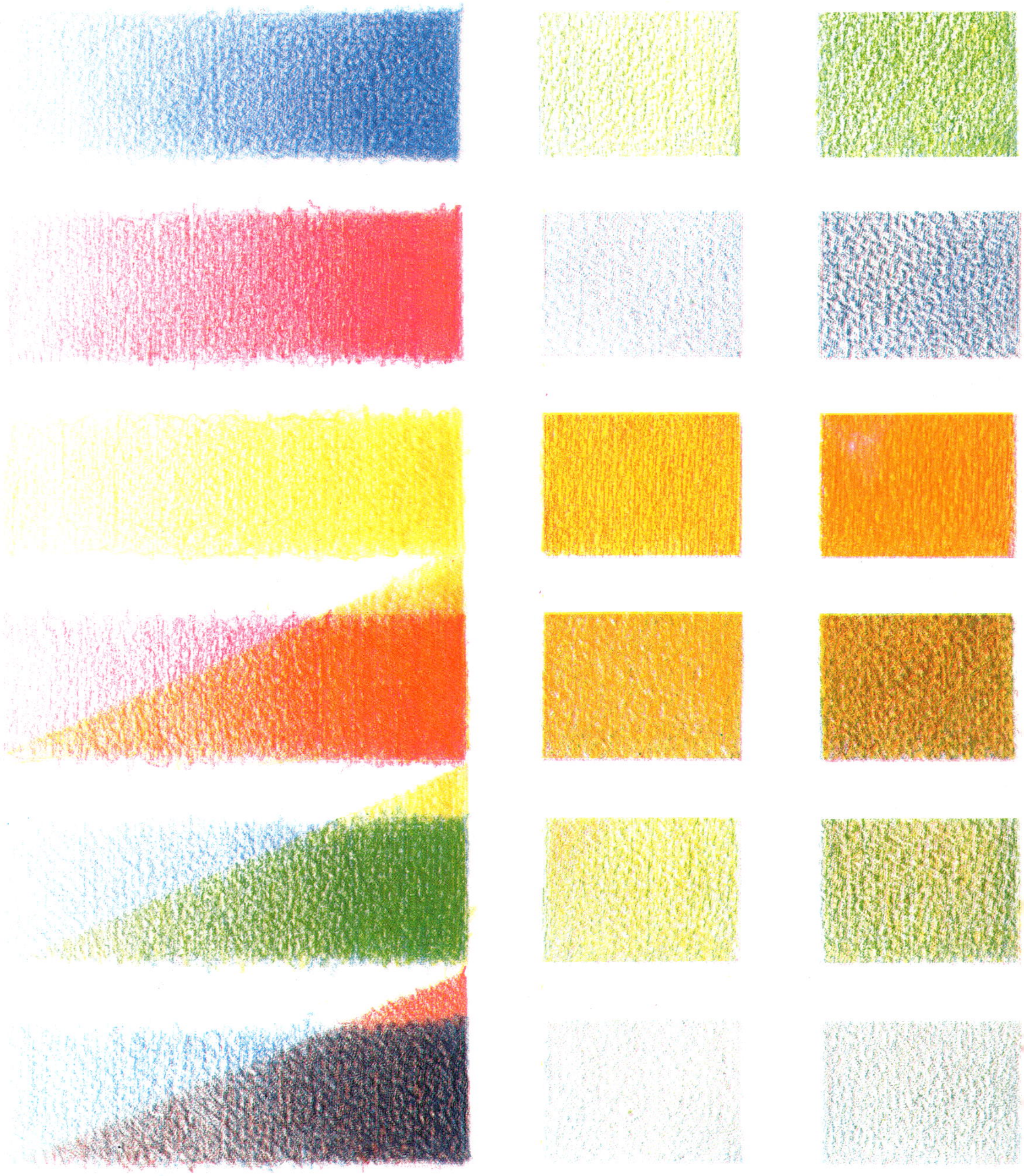

Binary mixtures. Notice how mixing two of the primaries together gives us reds, greens, and violets.

Consider, alongside the binary mixtures, the chart of 36 different colors you have to create, using just three colors: Blue, carmine or magenta, and yellow.

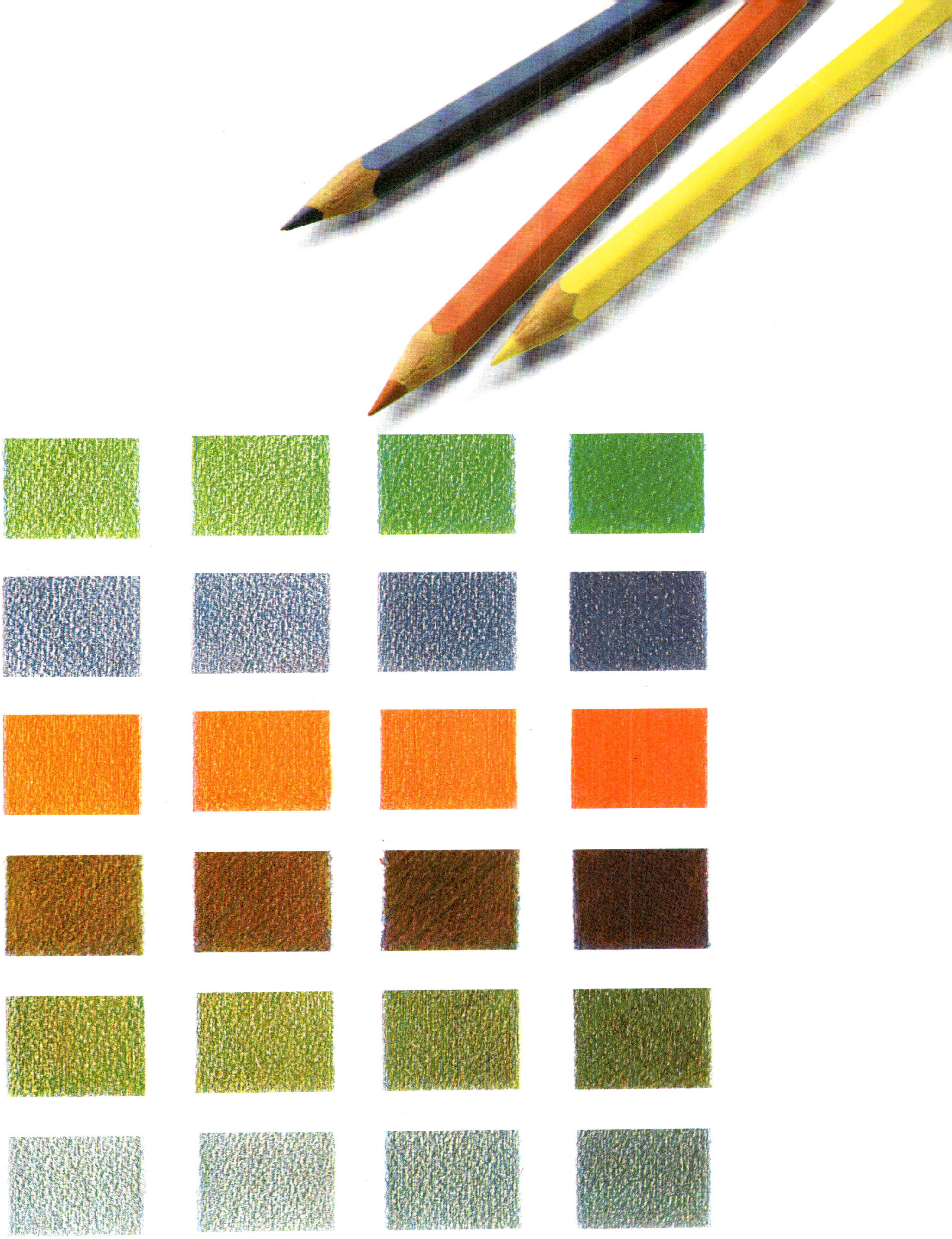

Colored pencil techniques

The following points are a summary of what we have learned in the preceding pages:

- White light consists of all the colors of the spectrum.
- Those individual colors are produced by the three primary light colors, blue, green, and red.
- By mixing the primary colors of light two at a time, you can obtain three lighter tones, which are the secondary colors of light, cyan blue, magenta, and yellow.
- If you mix the primary colors of light you get white light.
- Objects reflect all or part of the light focused on them.
- Light gives color to objects by means of the *additive synthesis* (adding together of light colors) of the primaries blue, green, and red.
- The artist uses pigment colors, the mixing of which subtracts light (*subtractive synthesis*). If you mix the primary pigment colors, cyan blue, magenta, and yellow, you produce black—that is, the total absence of all the primaries of light.
- Basically, light and the artist "paint" with the same colors: Those of the spectrum. The primary colors of light are red, green, and dark blue; the primary pigment colors are cyan blue, magenta, and yellow. The secondary colors of light are cyan blue, magenta, and yellow, while the secondary pigments are red, green, and dark blue.
- This correlation allows the artist to reflect in his work the effect of light on objects and to reproduce natural colors with accuracy.

In the next few pages we will continue to use colored pencils, showing different pieces of work in this medium and also giving you a practical exercise. This will consist of the step-by-step creation of a seascape, following the example offered to us by the artist Miquel Ferrón. This exercise will be carried out using the three primary colors, plus black.

Why, at the beginning of a book on painting, have we decided to use colored pencils? Mainly because with colored pencils you sketch and use tonal variations and shading at the same time as applying color, the theory of which we have summarized in the first pages of this volume. Besides this, colored pencils are an ideal introduction to the art of painting and the techniques of mixing, contrasting, and experimenting with color. Apart from this, the colored pencil is a medium that offers ample opportunity for artistic expression.

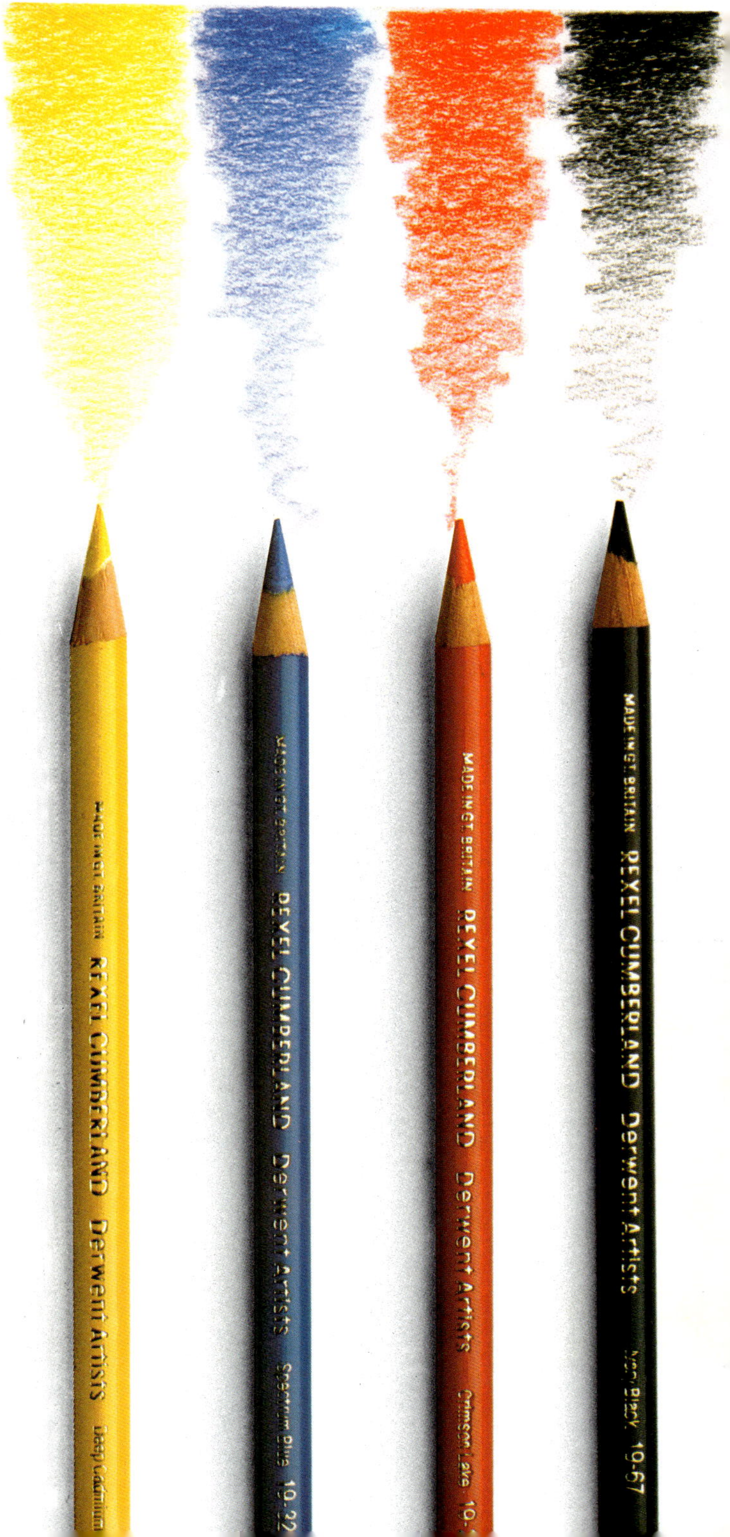

In theory, cadmium yellow, blue, magenta, and black, in varying combinations, are all you need to create all the colors of the spectrum.

Presentation boxes and brand names

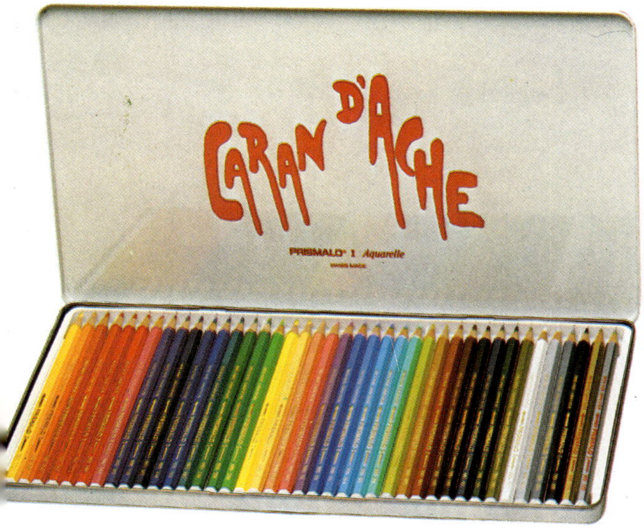

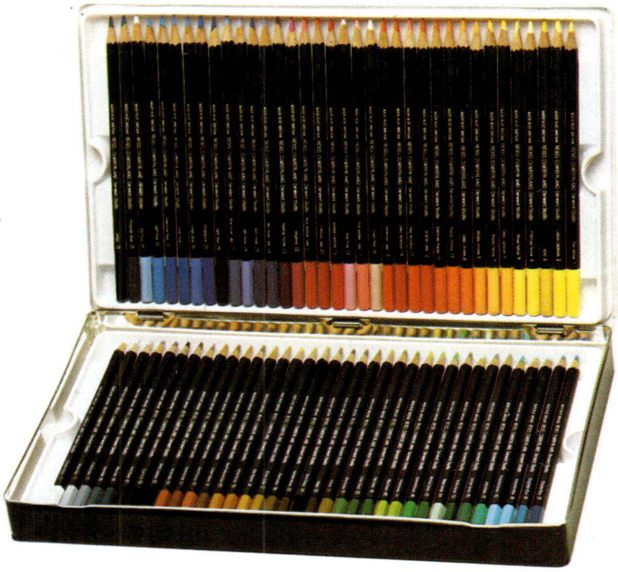

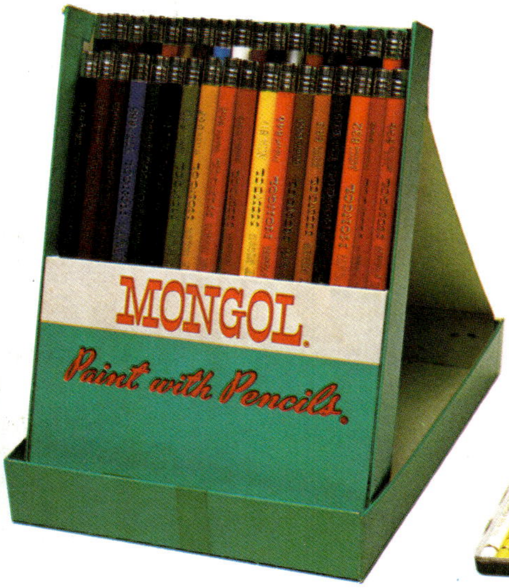

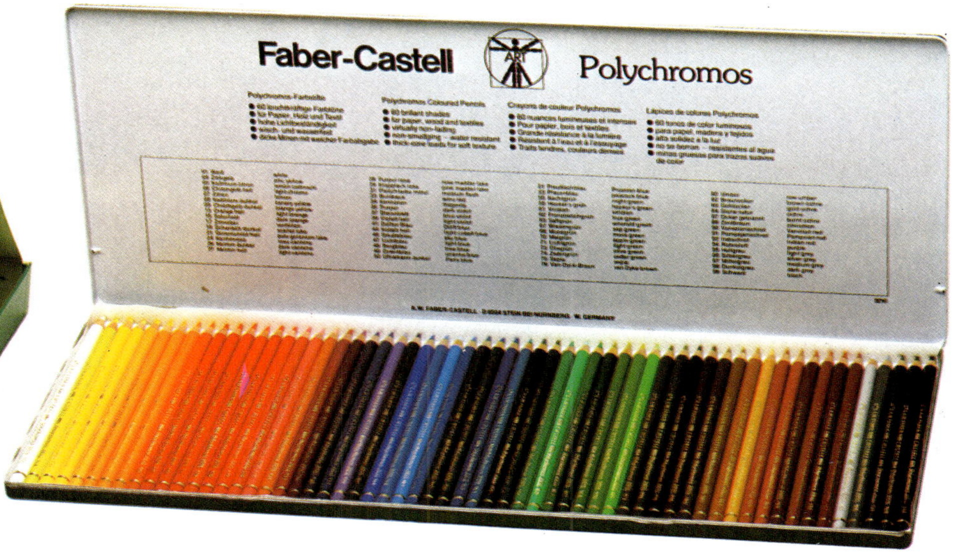

PRINCIPAL MAKES OF COLORED PENCILS		
Make	**Manufacturer**	**Country**
Derwent Studio	Rexel Cumberland	Great Britain
Polychromos	Faber-Castell	Germany
Staedtler	Staedtler	Germany
Prismalo I and II	Caran d'Ache	Switzerland
Lyra	Rembrandt	Germany
Albrecht Dürer	Faber-Castell	Germany
Mongol	Faber	United States

Above.
Colored pencils of high quality. They come in metal boxes containing 12, 24, 36, 60, or 72 pencils, corresponding to the various tones of each color. Colored pencils of student quality are available in boxes of 12 colors.

Exercise using the three primary colors and black

Van Gogh, in one of his famous *Letters* to his brother Theo, explained in detail all the theories we have outlined on the subject of color. He emphasized that by mixing two complementary colors in unequal proportions, you can create a neutral tone that appears as a kind of gray. This theory is easy to put to the test using colored pencils or watercolor, where the white is that of the paper.

The artist Miquel Ferrón now proposes that you try out these theories, following his step-by-step execution of a seascape, in which he will only use four colored pencils: The three primary colors plus black.

Before this, study the illustrations on this page, which demonstrate, yet again, the principle that with just three colors (and black) it is possible to reproduce all nature's colors.

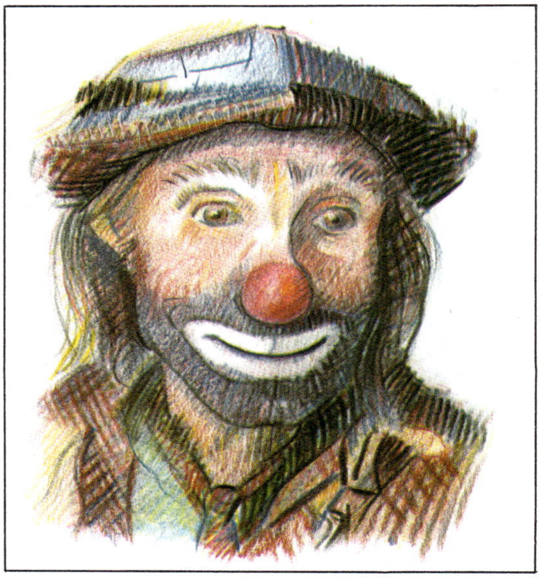

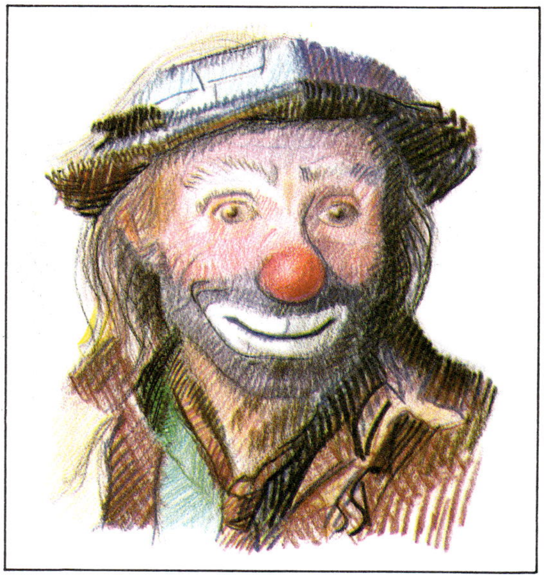

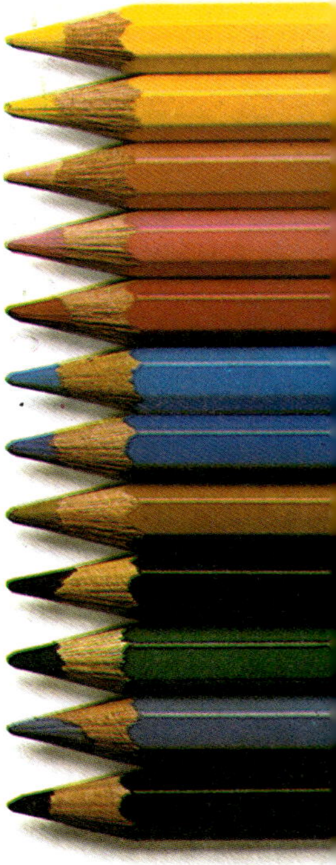

Right.
Two illustrations that appear identical but that have been carried out using different methods: With the three primary colors plus black (above) and with all the colors of the spectrum (below). The result is not exactly the same but is certainly very similar. It is a good example of the application of the theory of color.

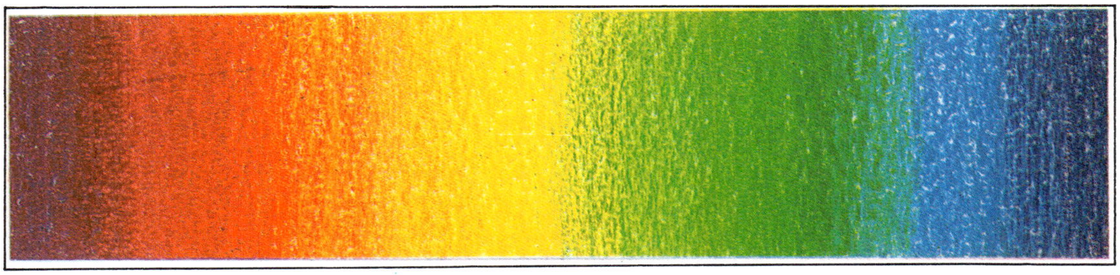

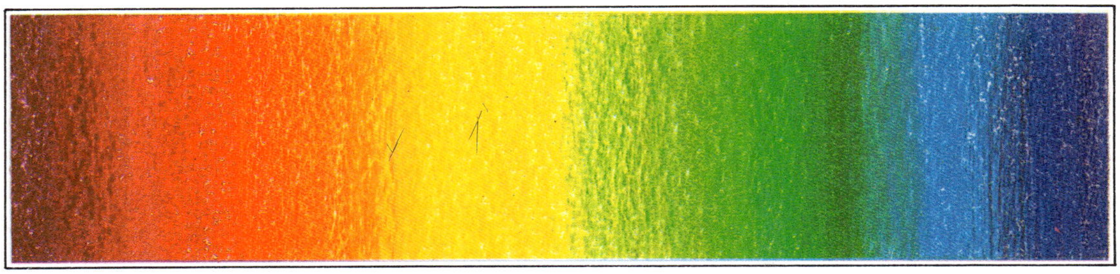

Left.
A scale showing the colors of the spectrum produced using the three primary colors (above) and another using all the colors (below).

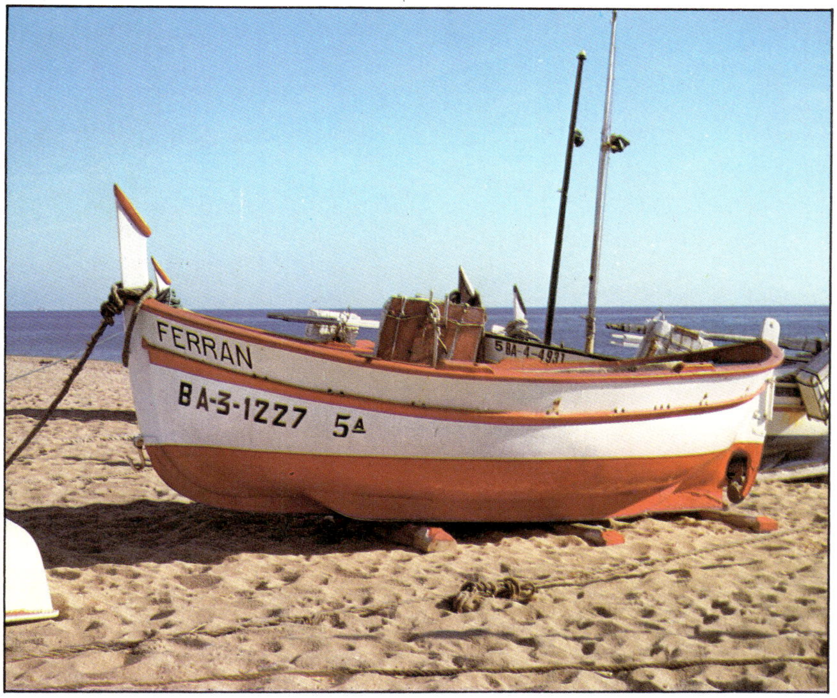

Any subject will do

Seascapes, landscapes, cityscapes—any subject can be represented on paper using colored pencils. These four photographs, put forward as a sample of the enormous variety of subject-matter to be found all around us, might inspire you to begin. But remember that you must use only the three primary colors along with black. Difficult? On the following pages you will see how, with these apparently limited resources, Ferrón has created a picture of undeniable quality that you will now attempt to imitate. A final word of advice: Whenever possible, work directly from nature.

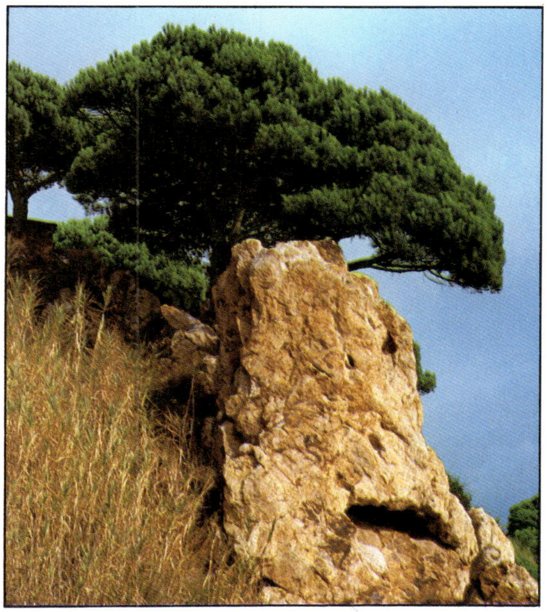

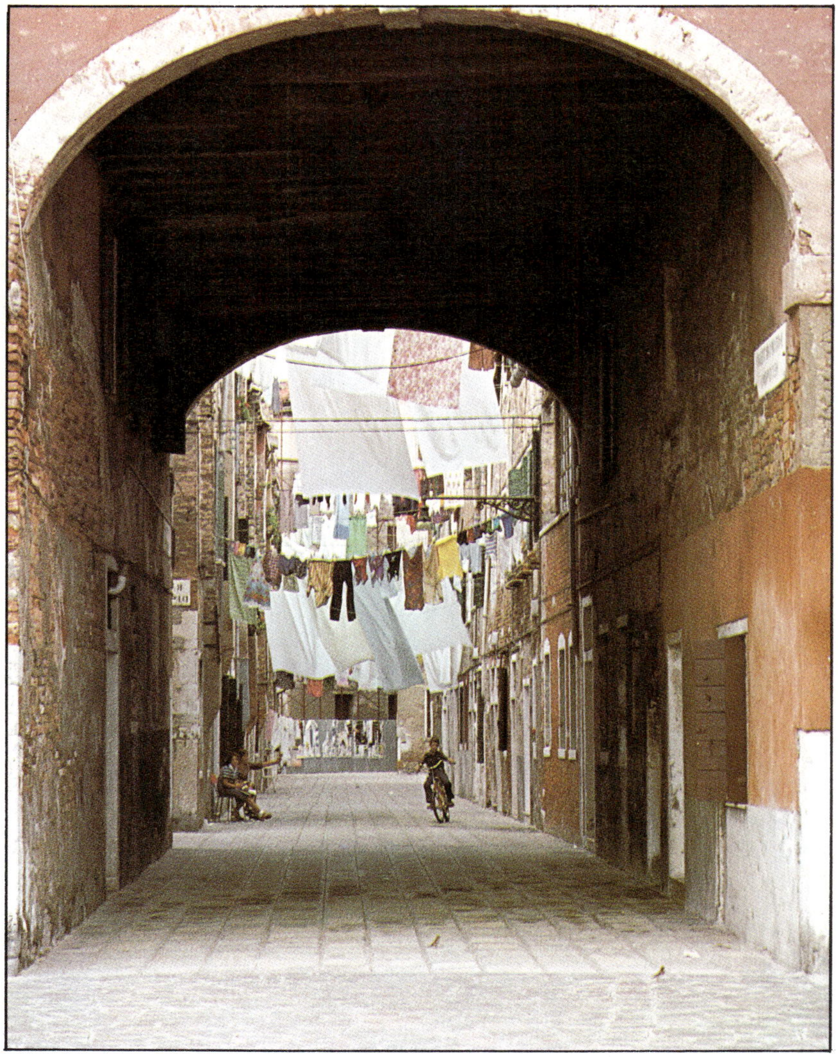

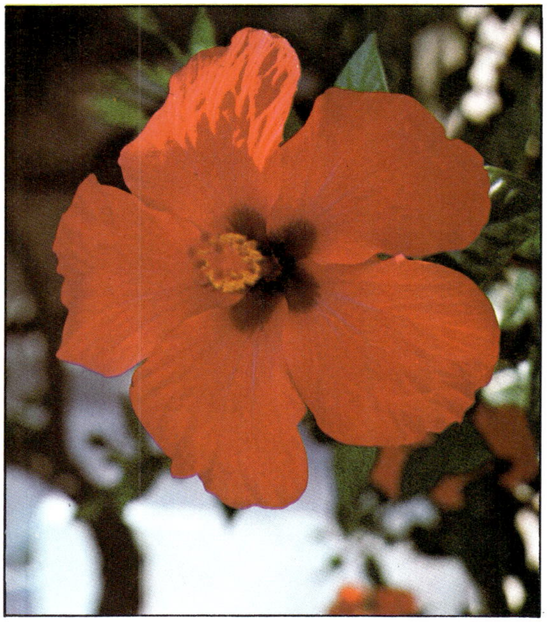

Initial construction

You are going to copy a seascape from the work of Miquel Ferrón (see page 20) using just three colors and black. In this first stage, creating the initial outline, a blue pencil is used to build up the subject. Use light strokes so you can rub them out if you make a mistake. Keep the surface of the paper clean and in good condition, and erase as little as possible. It helps if you produce a perfect outline sketch with as much detail as possible so that later you can work on the picture without having to worry about size and proportion.

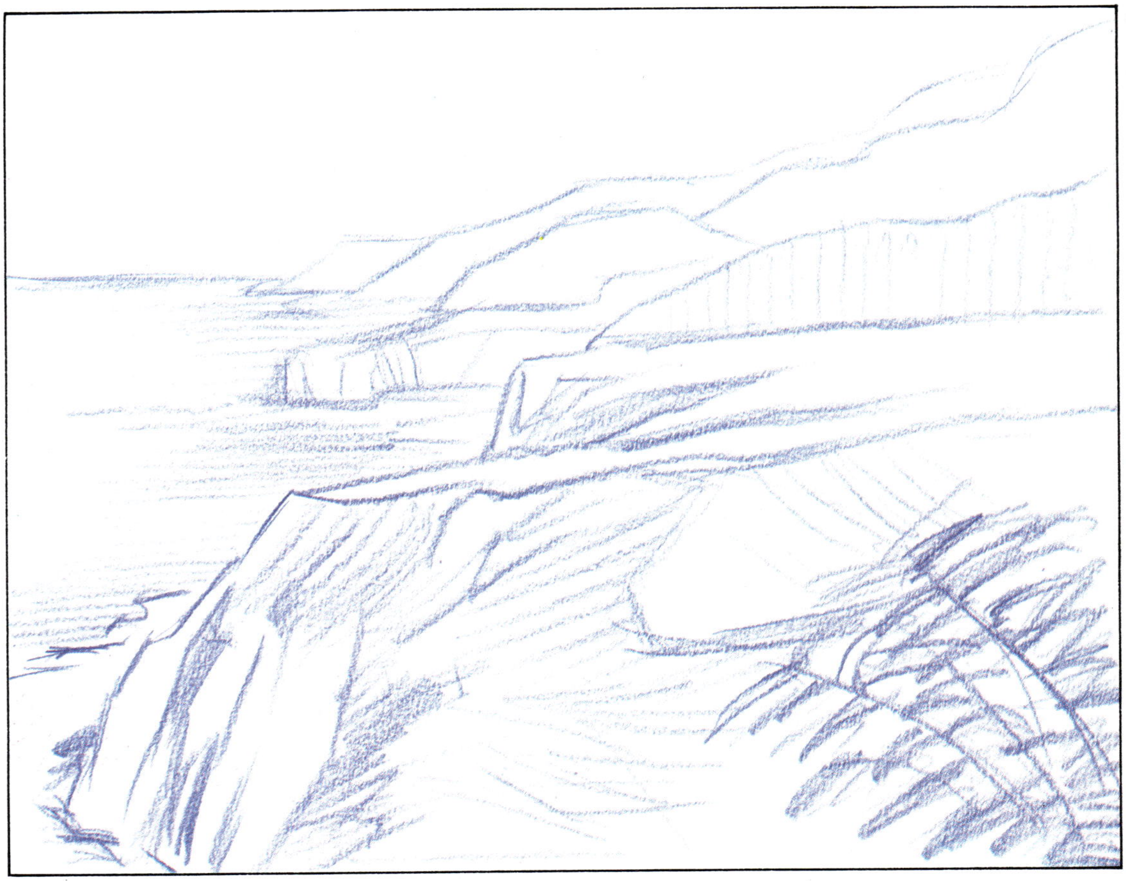

First stage: Blue

When drawing with the three primary-colored pencils, with or without black, you normally begin with blue. This makes it easier to mix the other two colors later—magenta and yellow—in order to achieve the desired tones. Notice the areas in which blue has been applied more heavily: In the sea, in the rocky foreground and in the sheer cliff-faces, which will remain in shade in the final picture. Note also the direction of the pencil strokes in each area of the drawing.

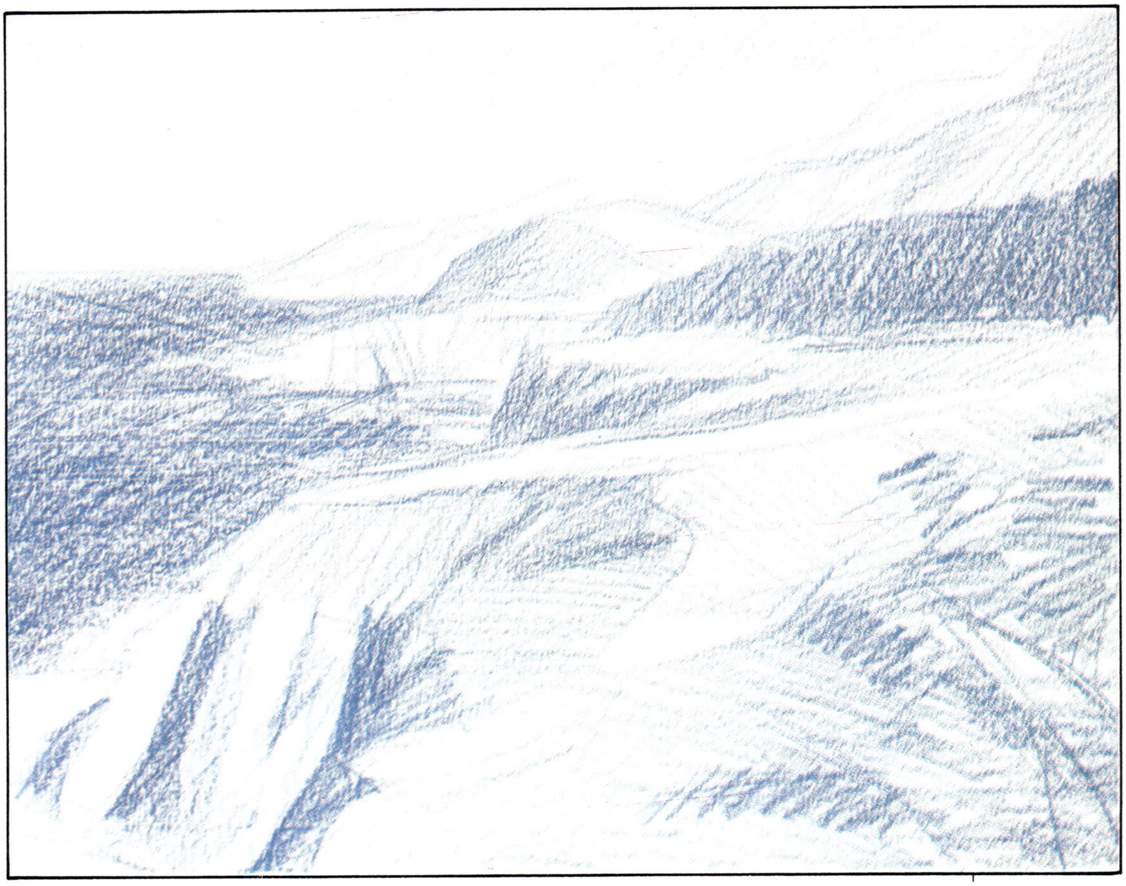

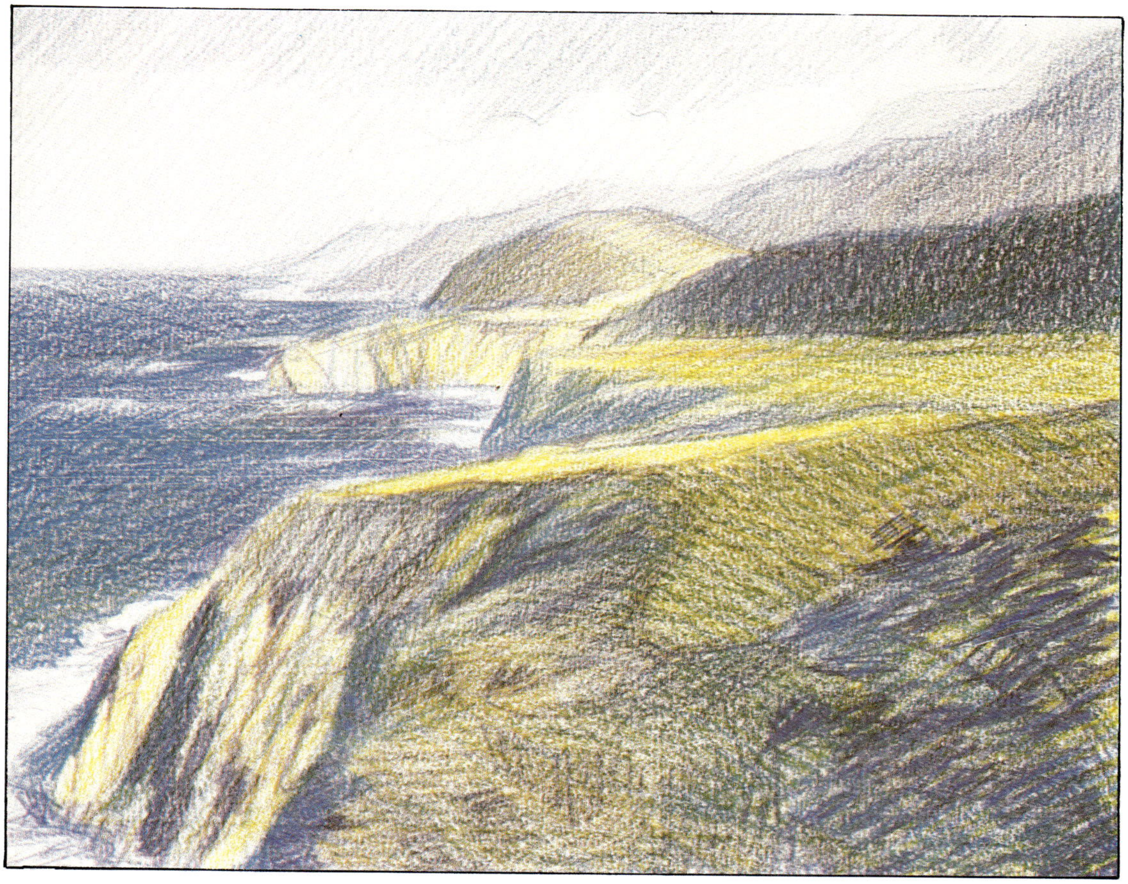

Second stage: Yellow

Notice how the appearance of the picture changes dramatically with the addition of yellow. The subject really begins to take shape and it already looks similar to the finished work. Foreground greens appear, along with a few subtle violets in the background where the yellow has just "caressed" the blue. The whole scene has taken on depth and the first contrasts are visible. At the beginning, the artist reserved some white areas in the sea and clouds. Using this method, even the white of the paper becomes a color.

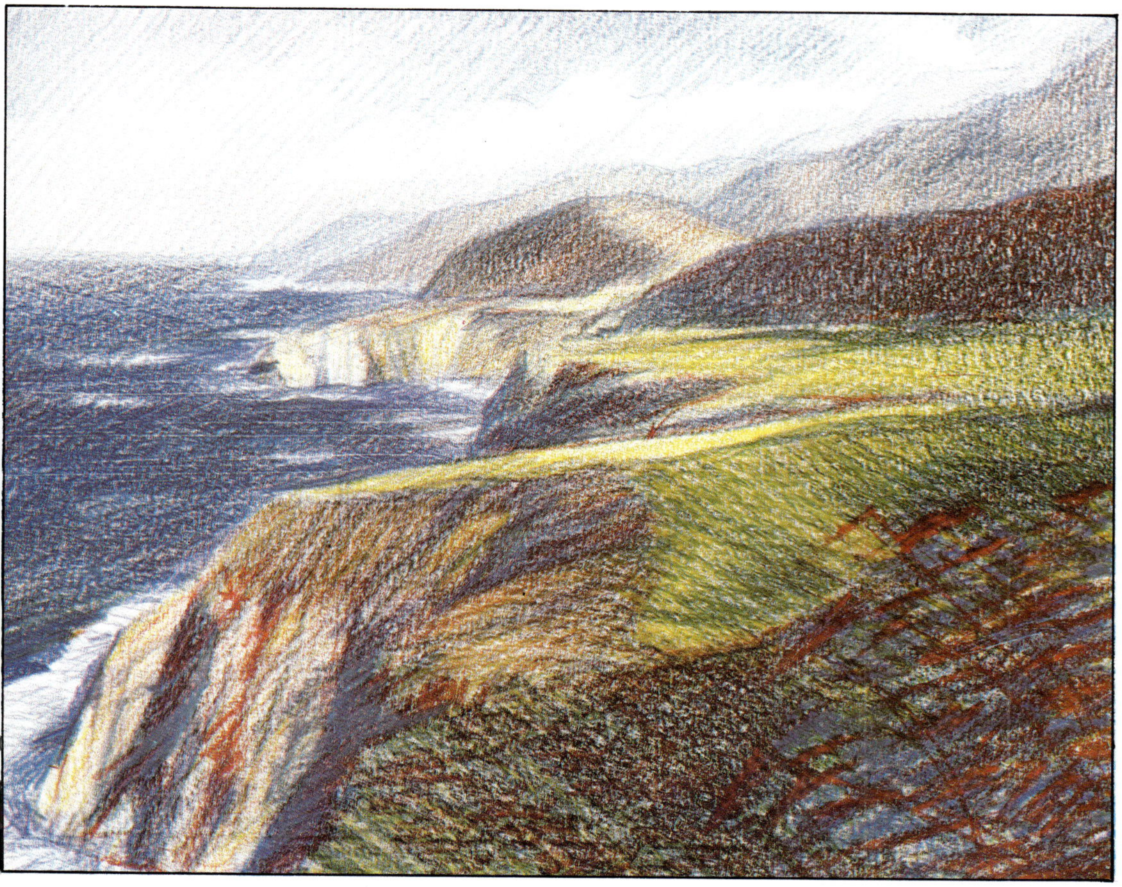

Third stage: Magenta

Now we come to lively, intense magenta, the third of the primary colors to be used in this exercise. The artist warns us: "With magenta we must be especially careful how we apply the pencil strokes, softly in some areas and forcefully in others. For example, the vegetation in the foreground and the shadow on the cliffs need a lot of pressure from the pencil. On the other hand, on the distant hilltops you can only just make out a few subtle pencil strokes."

Final stage: The finished picture

Before achieving this definitive result, Ferrón used the black pencil in the areas where the tone needed to be brought out, as with the foreground vegetation. But take care: It is easy to get carried away with black. Start by just touching up something here, by reinforcing that outline there, by adding a little shading, and the work ends up looking dusky and dirty. Besides the black, a few last touches of color were applied to enhance the feeling of depth and contrast in the finished illustration. Finally, the strips of adhesive tape around the picture were removed; these ensured that the edges were crisp and clean. Now it's up to you; either copy this seascape, or find a subject of your own and make a picture using three colors with black.

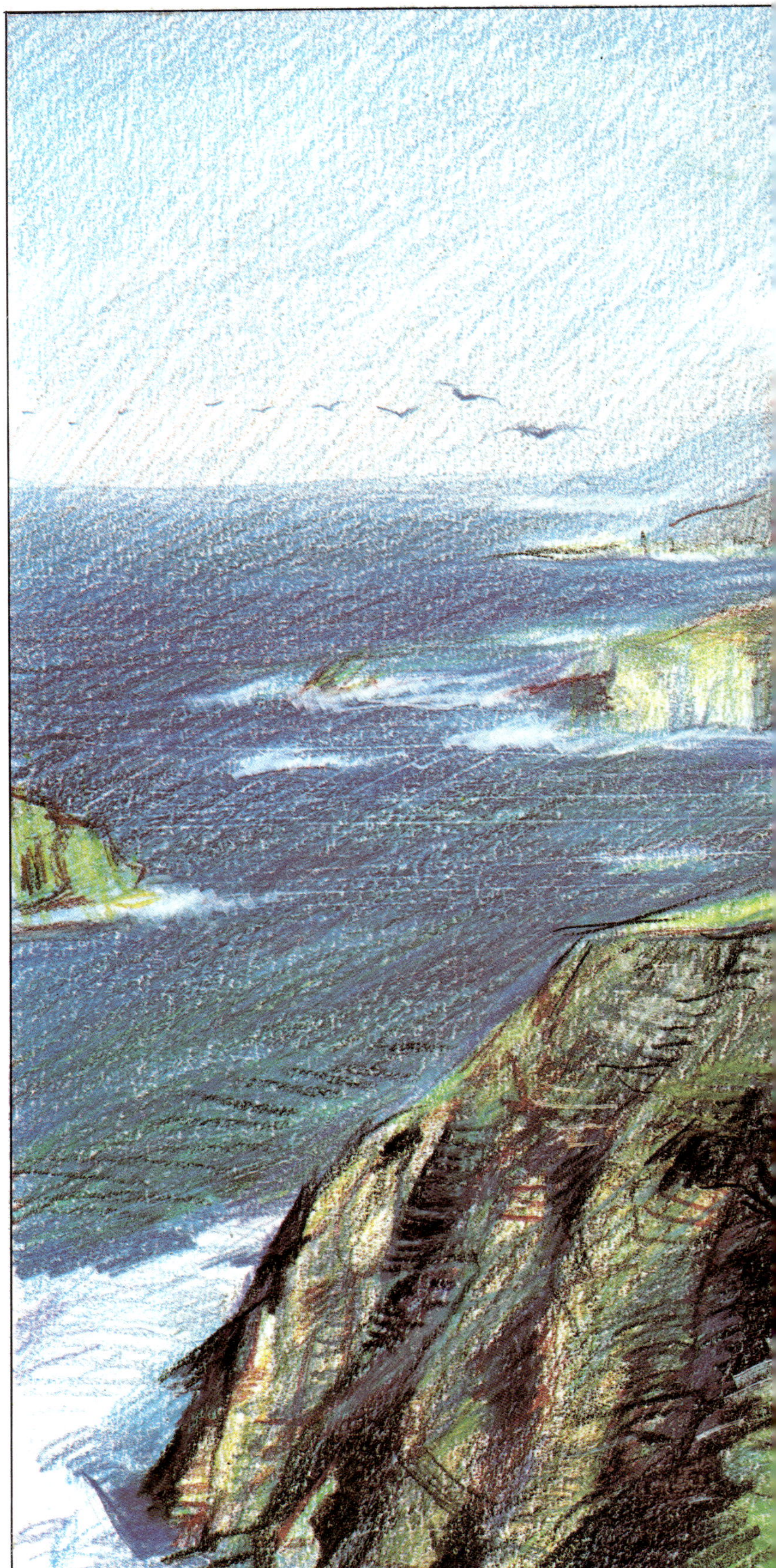

Definitive result of the seascape in pencil in which Ferrón shows us how natural colors can be created using primary colors along with black.

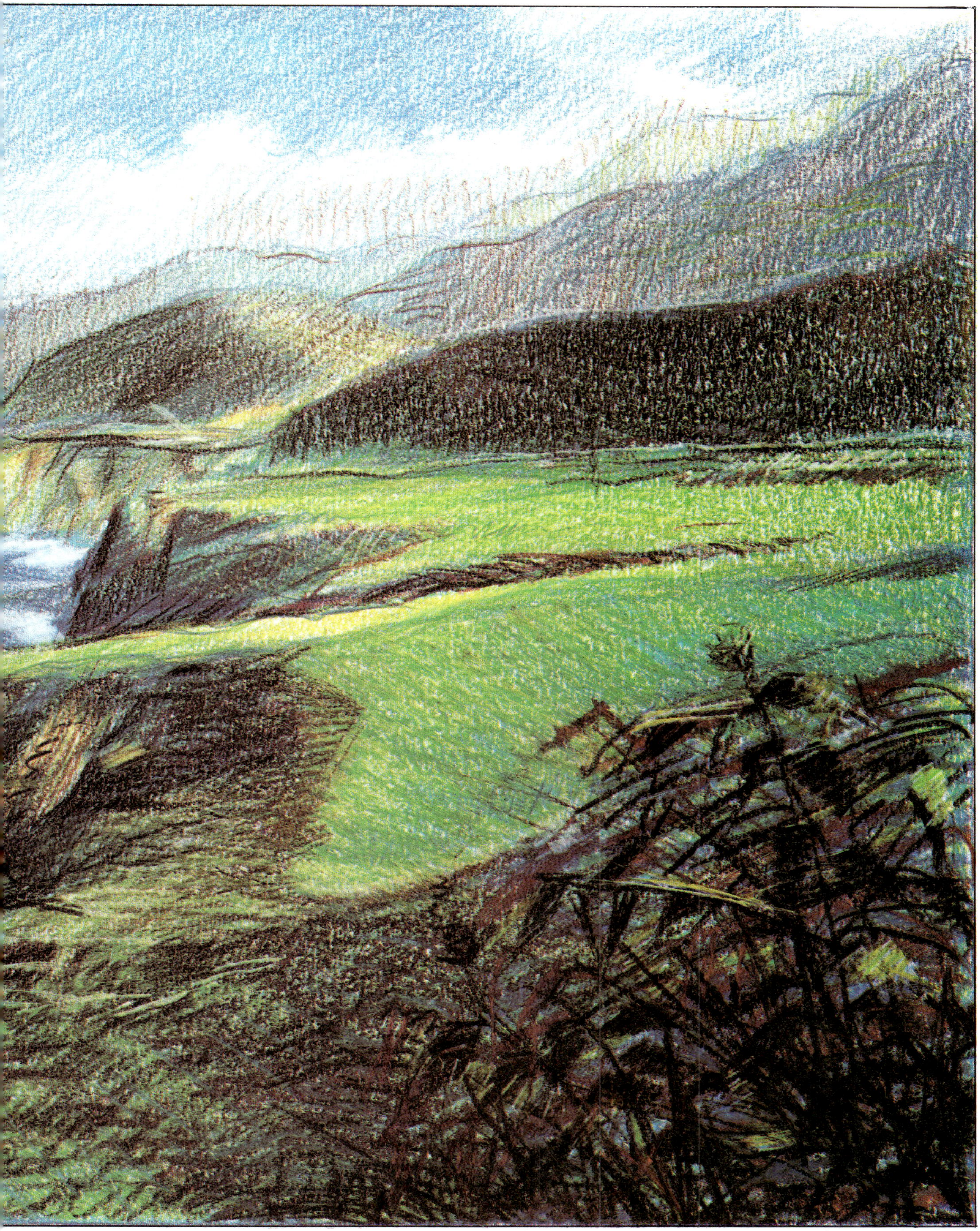

Tools and techniques

Everybody has used colored pencils. It is difficult to imagine meeting anyone who has not used them, even if it was only in their school days. Of course what we have in mind here is more serious: We intend to elevate what were our modest colored drawing pencils to the status of a pictorial medium. Our objective, simply stated, is to be able to paint with colored pencils. Let's begin by getting to know a little more about the tool we will be using.

First, we had better make it clear that when we refer to colored pencils at this level of artistic activity, we mean pencils of a very high quality. The "classroom" type of pencil is of no use to us. We need pencils made of American cedar, exceptionally soft (very easy to sharpen to a good point), but durable enough to provide solid protection for the lead and to withstand pressure from the artist's hand. The lead must be hard and strong, but able to produce an intense color when required, and pale tonal values when attempting half-tones and gradations. An inferior quality lead is easily spotted: It produces little depth of color, its lead feels rough, and it breaks easily.

Colored pencils, when used as part of the picture-making process, have the one drawback that they can only produce a single line; they cannot cover vast areas as a paintbrush can and are therefore not suitable for large works. However, for works on a small scale, whatever the subject matter, they offer a wealth of possibilities and are capable of producing sophisticated pictures.

All manufacturers of graphite pencils (or almost all) also make colored pencils. Usually they offer an extensive color range and sell pencils individually and in boxed sets of varying degrees of luxuriousness containing 12, 24, 48, or 72 pencils.

The most normal color range, for a box of 12 pencils, consists of two blues, two greens, two reds, two siennas, a yellow, a violet, black, and white; more than enough for the majority of requirements.

As for brand names, it is difficult to recommend one in particular. The big brands all offer high-quality products. Personal tastes and circumstances generally lead an artist to opt for one brand or another. Here are a few of the best-known names: Castell (Faber), Caran d'Ache, Lyra, Staedtler, Stabilo, and Jovi. Finally, we should mention paper. Except for shiny or coated papers, on which the pencil lead slips and can hardly make a mark, almost any matt paper is suitable for drawing on with colored pencils. However, for any special projects, the best choice would be a high-quality, semi-rough watercolor paper.

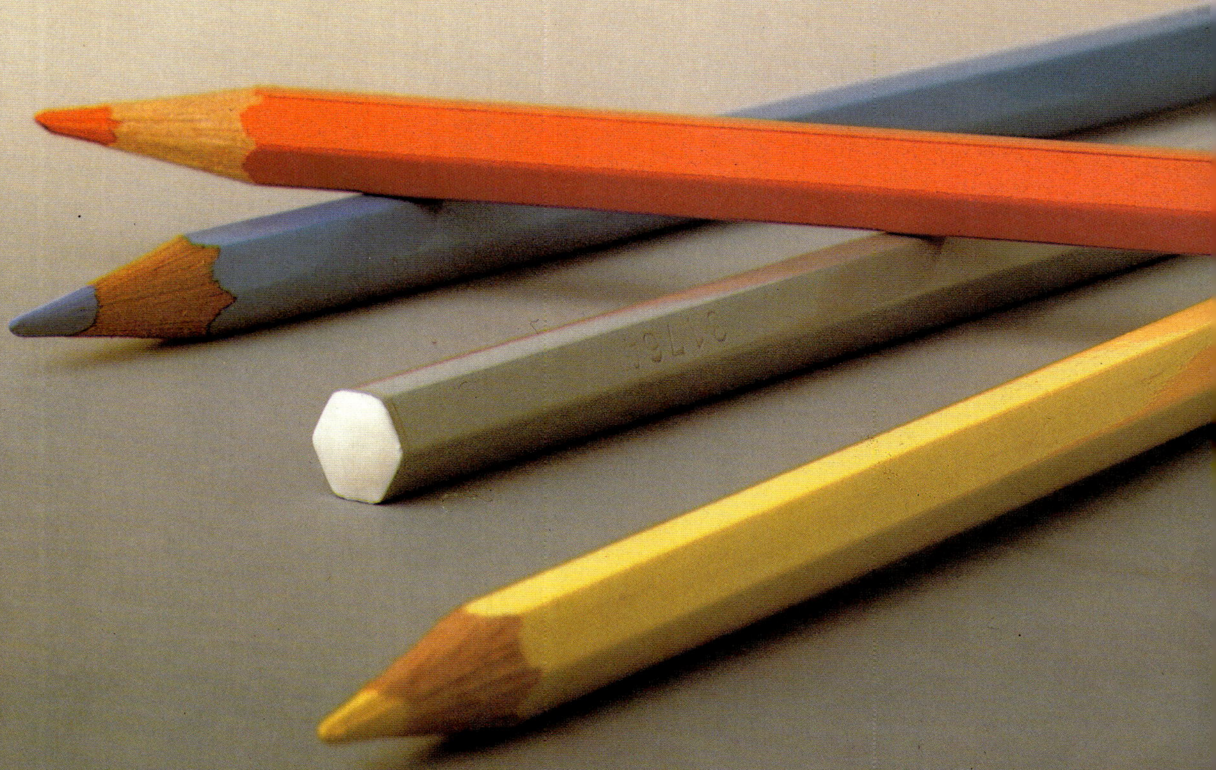

Three examples from a master of the medium

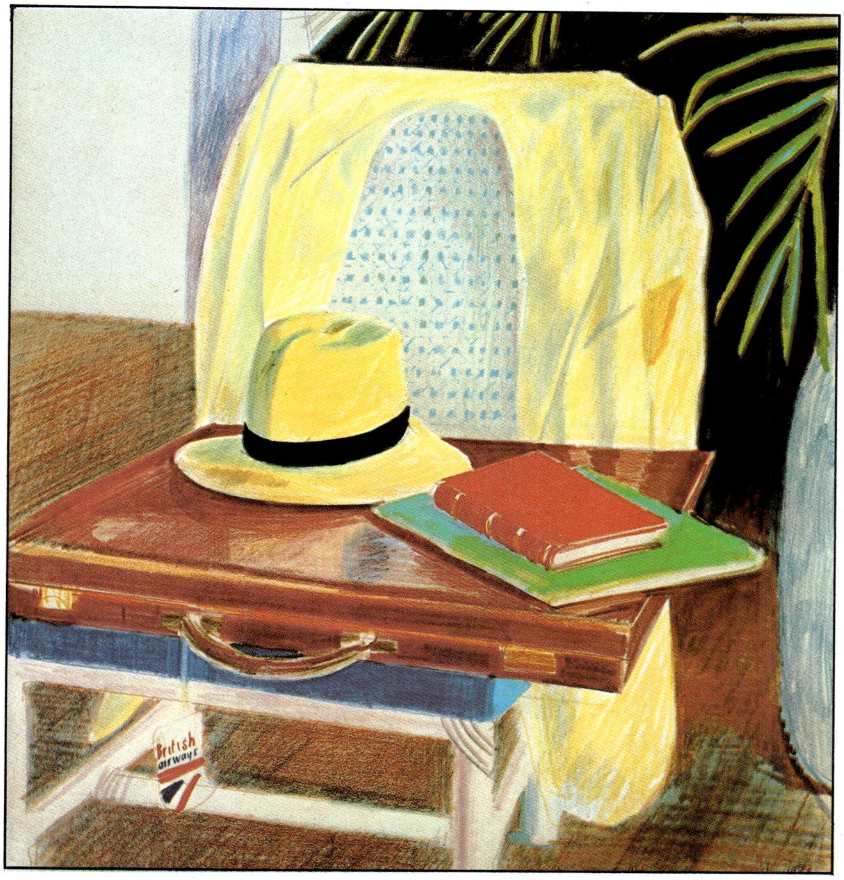

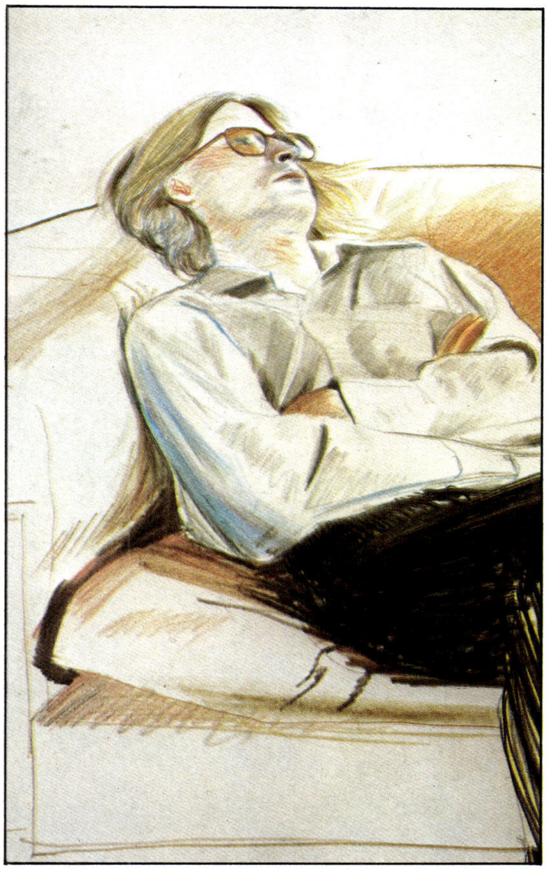

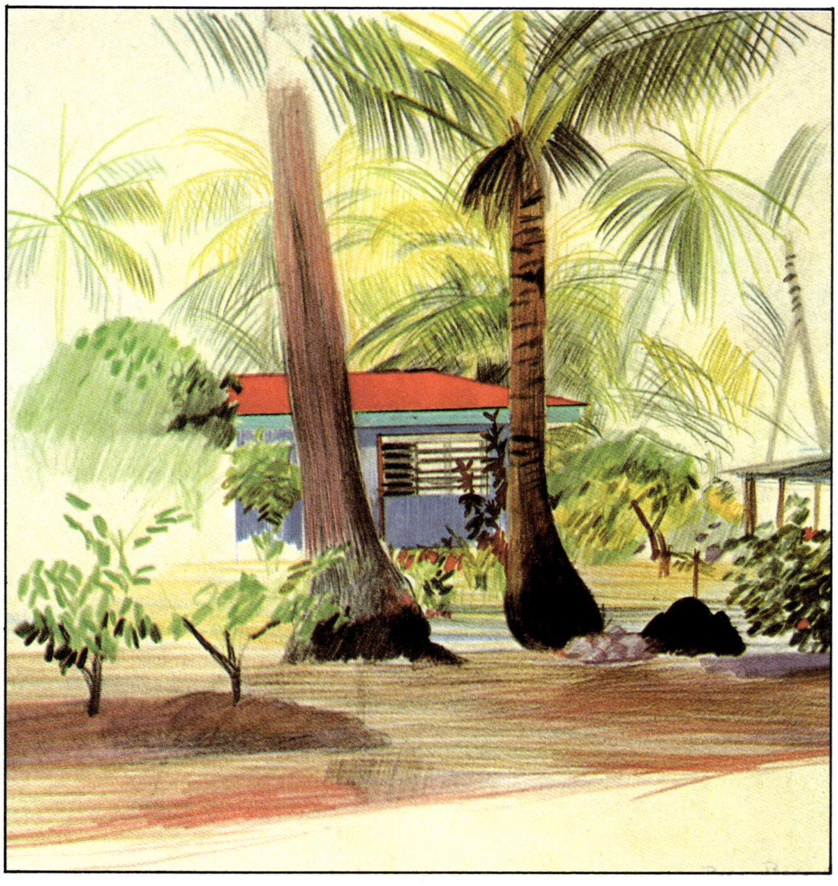

David Hockney, a British painter and engraver (b. 1937), famous for his etchings, his portraits, and his illustrations, frequently uses colored pencils in small-scale works and in making studies for future pictures. On this page we offer three examples showing Hockney's mastery of this medium. He loves contrasts and bright, luminous colors. Look at the play between complementary colors and the radiance of color in the first picture. The second illustration is a masterly example of what a colored pencil study should be. This sketch contains all the essential ingredients of a finished picture. In the landscape study (with a distinctly tropical atmosphere), his love of contrast can be seen again. Note the simplicity with which he has treated the leaves of the palm trees. We think it could be a useful experiment to try to imitate the methods of a master like Hockney to appreciate how difficult it is to "say so much with so little."

Tools and techniques

The point

To get a good point on the pencil, use a sharpener (it must have a large aperture) when you want a sharp point for detailed work and outlines. Use a penknife if a longer or bevelled tip is required for thicker strokes, such as shading an area or going over a color.

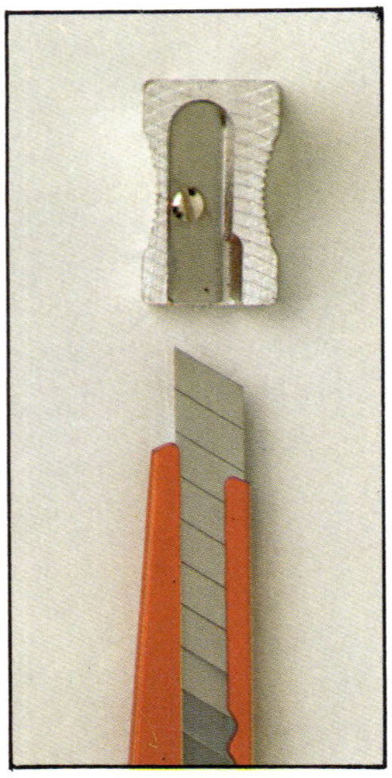

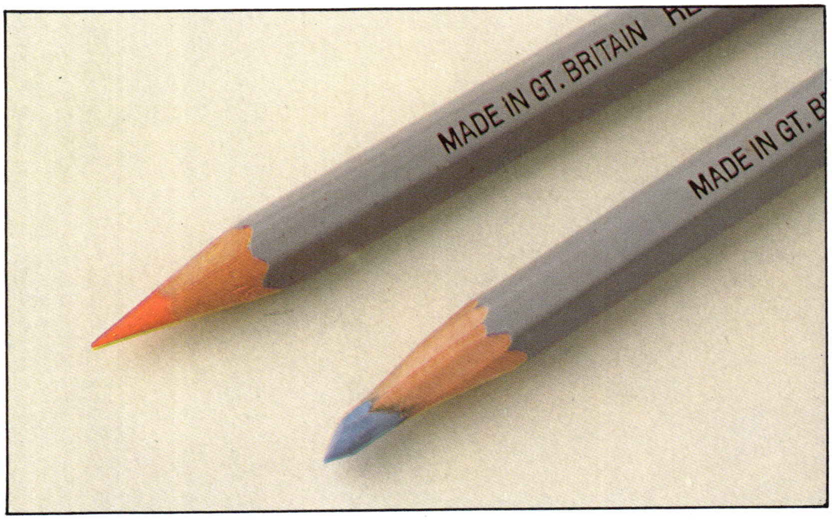

Pencil position

Try not to work with the pencil at too much of an angle. It should be at about 45 degrees from the paper. This decreases the risk of the lead breaking.

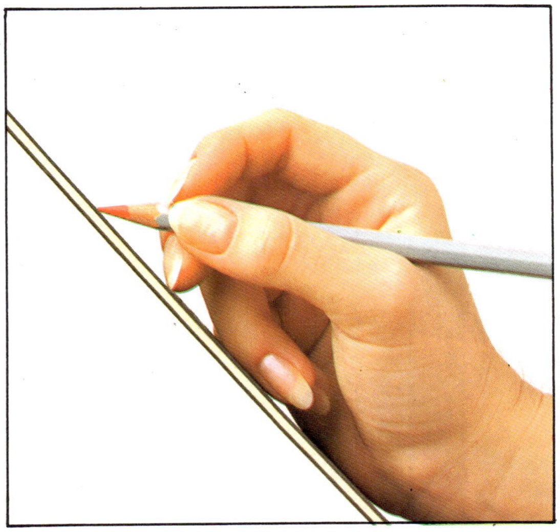

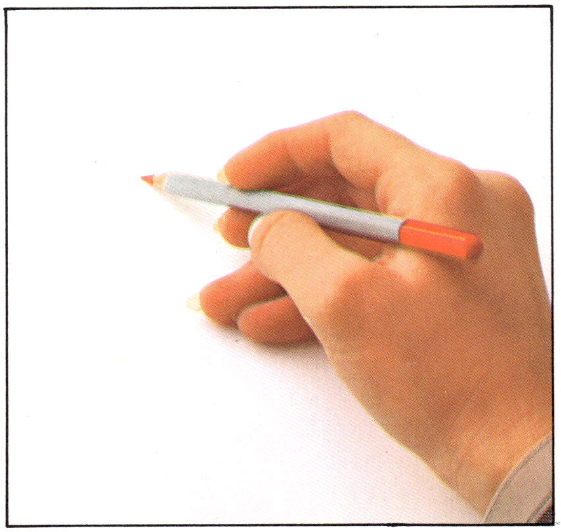

A practical tip

When using colored pencils do not keep taking them in and out of their box or leaving them on the worktop. That is a waste of time, and also exposes them to knocks that can result in broken leads. The best idea is to keep all the colors you intend to use in your left hand or, as in our photograph, to use two containers, one for the warm and one for the cool ranges of colors. It is a practical system and makes it easy to find in an instant the color you need.

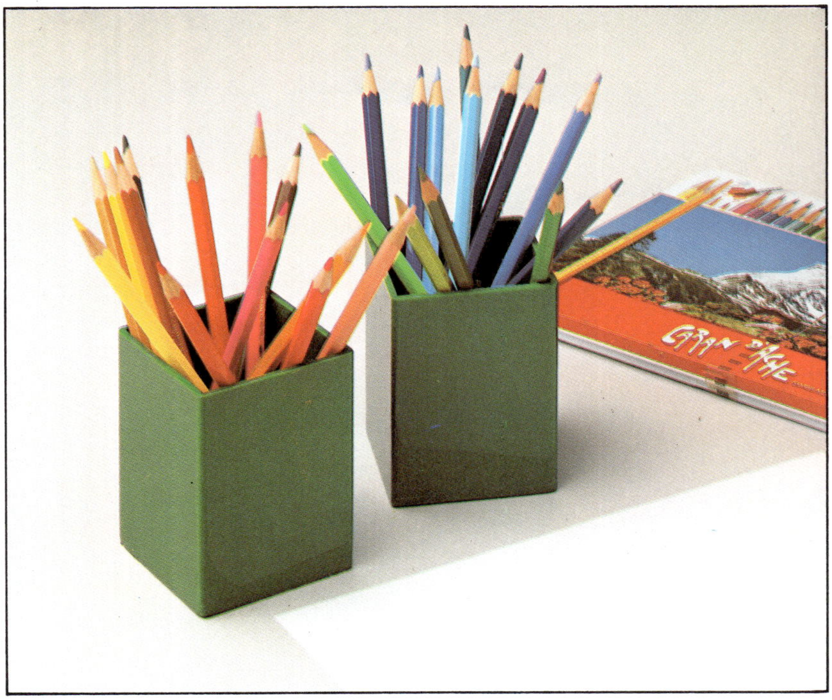

Color mixing

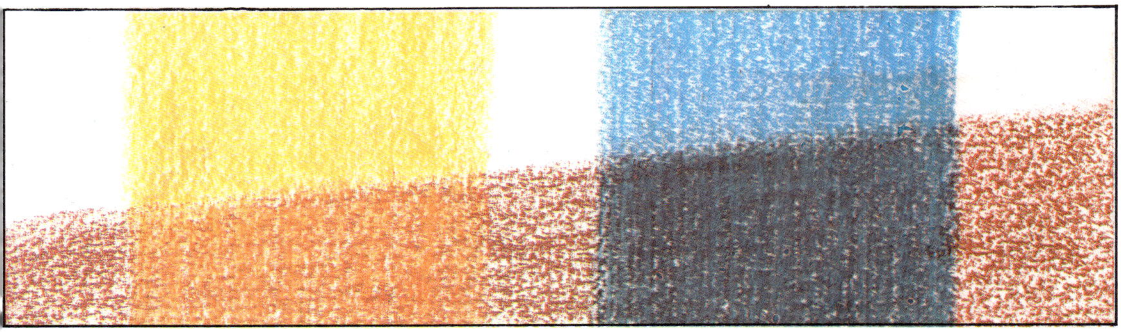

Color mixes with colored pencils are always optical, obtained by superimposing transparent colors. They are not homogeneous mixes of pigment as, for example, with oils and watercolors.

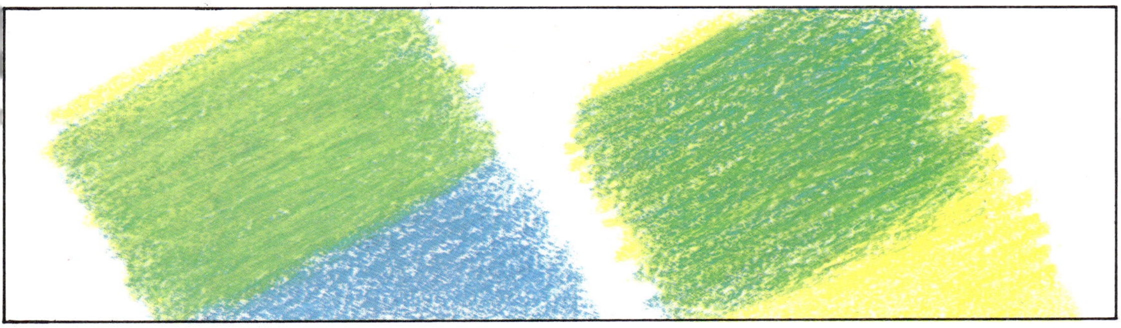

When mixing two colors, it is important to remember that the order in which they are applied will affect the result. Applying blue on top of yellow is not the same as applying yellow on top of blue.

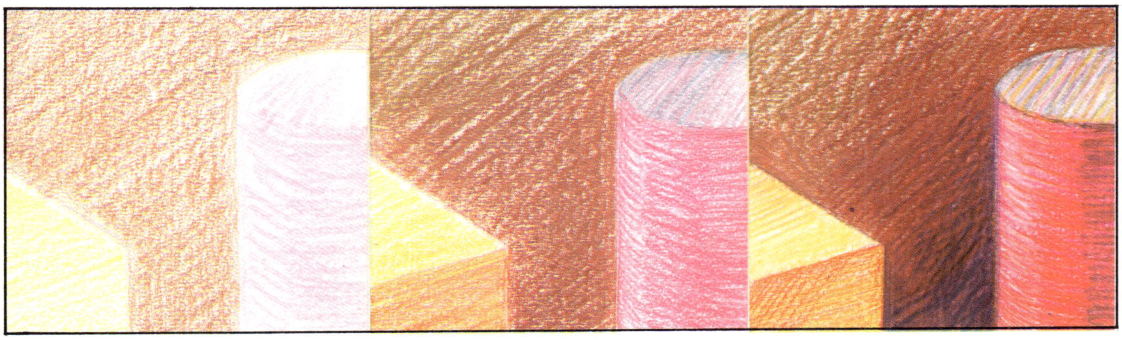

As shown in this short progression, with colored pencils you should work "from light to dark." In other words, intensify color by means of successive layers that build up tonal and chromatic values.

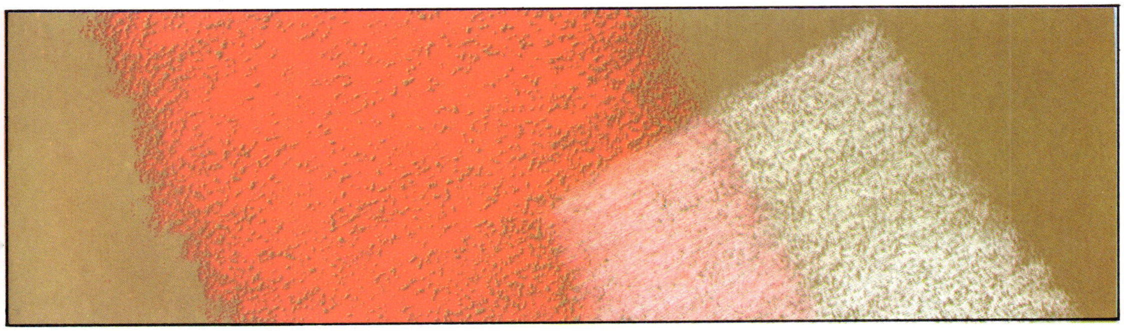

Tinted papers such as cream, pale blue, gray, salmon-pink, and others, provide a good support for colored-pencil work. They provide a tonal base that can harmonize a color scheme and also make it possible to use white.

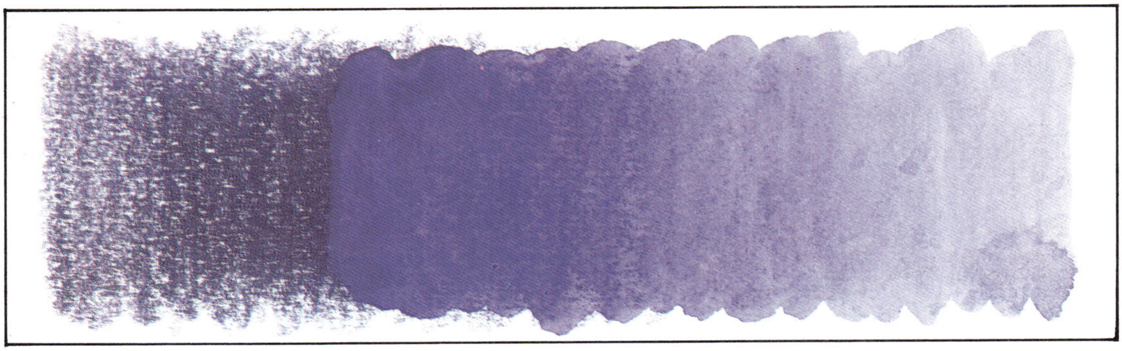

Water-soluble pencils allow you to produce gradations using a paintbrush. The colors come to life and you can create some really striking transparent effects. However, something of the original pencil mark always remains on the paper.

Exercise with water-soluble pencils

To prepare your water-soluble pencils, take two good-quality paint-brushes, one No. 6 and one No. 12, and a sheet of medium-textured watercolor paper of about 6 × 8 in. (16 × 20 cm).

You will also need clean water. Attach the paper to a base of wood or board with four strips of sticky tape and get ready to follow our steps. You can copy our example or choose another photograph.

The fact that we have used Caran d'Ache pencils does not mean that you cannot use another make.

If you do decide to use a different photograph, make sure that it offers a good balance between warm and cool tonal values. Remember that this is a first exercise and it would be counter-productive to launch into an orgy of color.

Choose the color range best suited to the subject. We have opted for a reduced palette: Emerald green, cinnabar green, yellow ochre, pink madder, burnt sienna—and that's it.

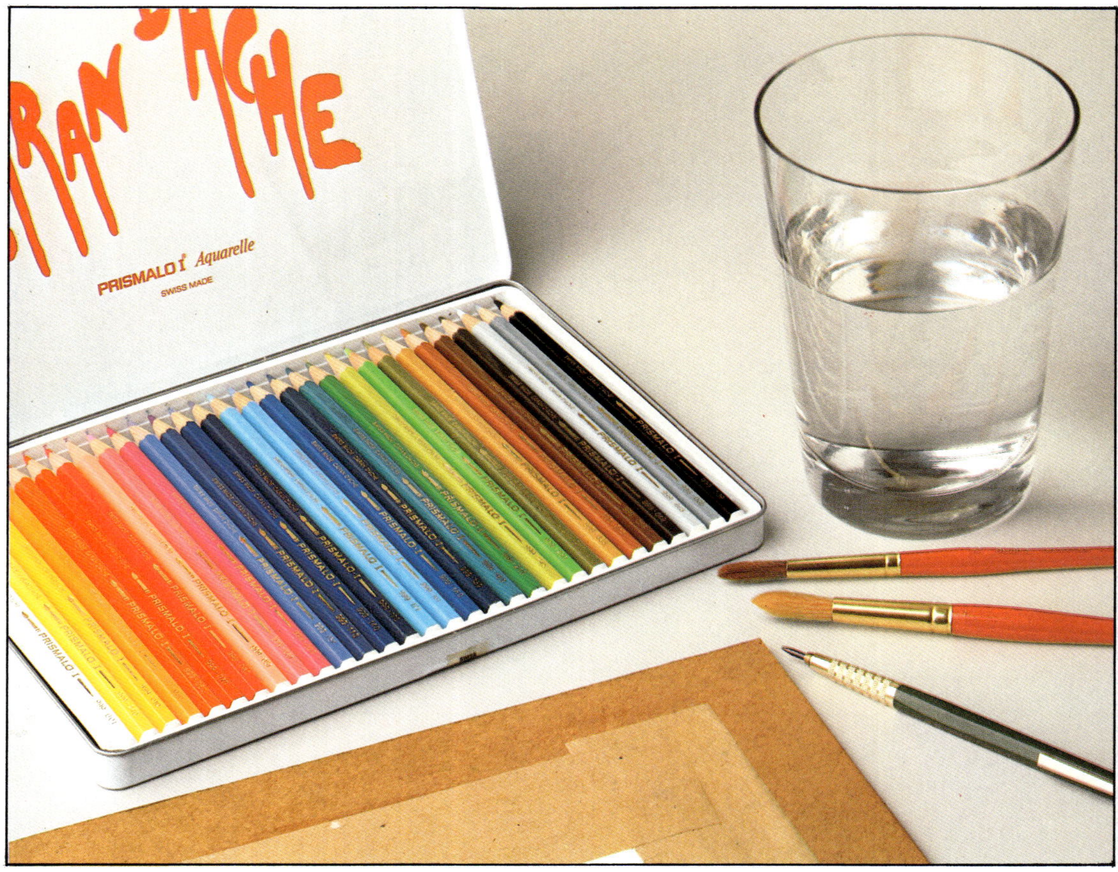

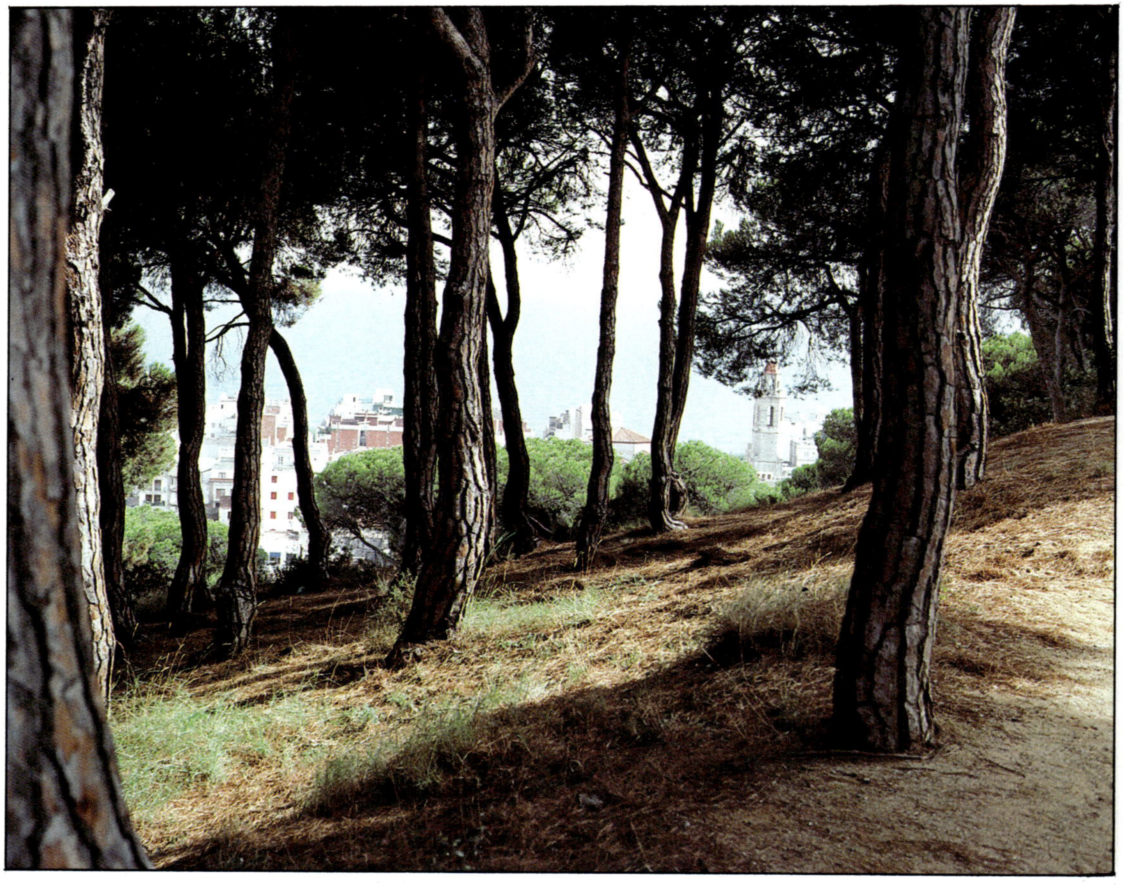

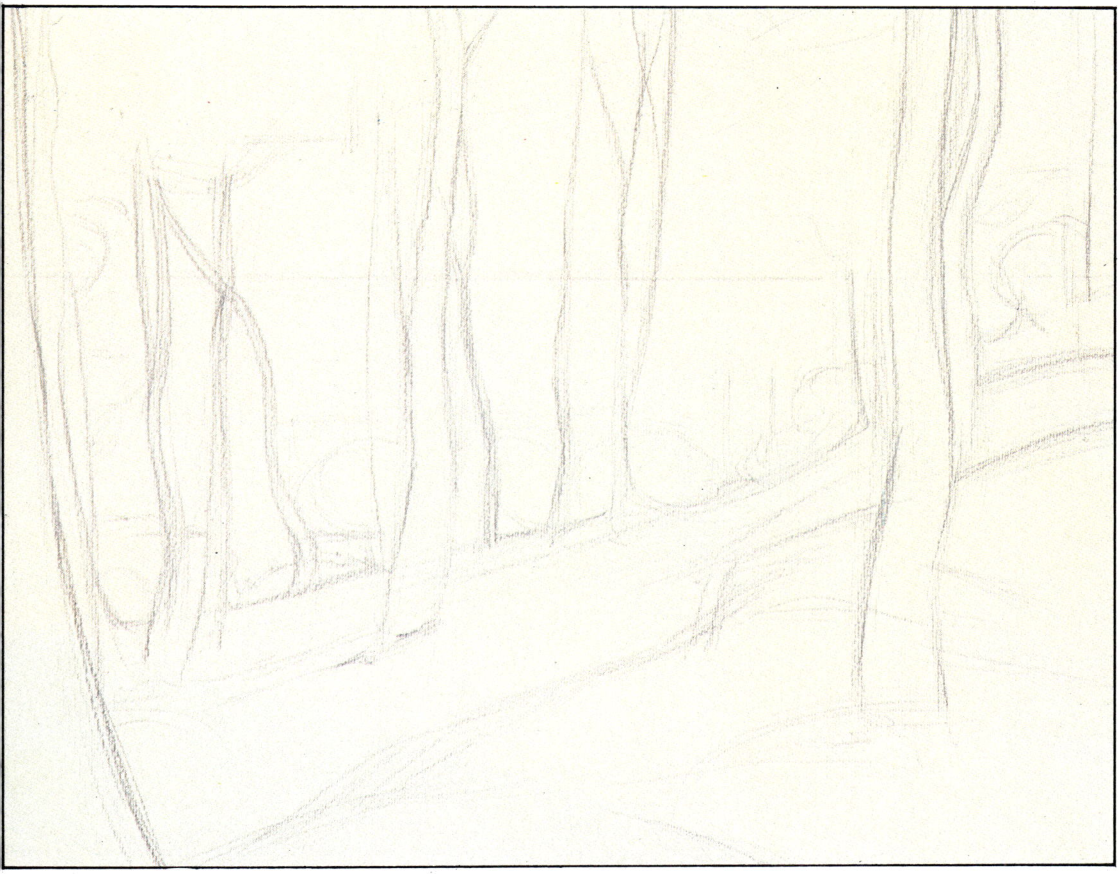

First step

Very lightly, with a dark-blue pencil, make a layout sketch of the subject. Bear in mind that a colored-pencil line is difficult to rub out. You should not make any pencil strokes in your outline sketch too decisive until you are totally sure that you do not want to modify them. If you analyze the dominant color quality of our subject, you will see why we have decided to use dark blue for the sketch: It is obviously the dominant tone in the dark areas of the picture.

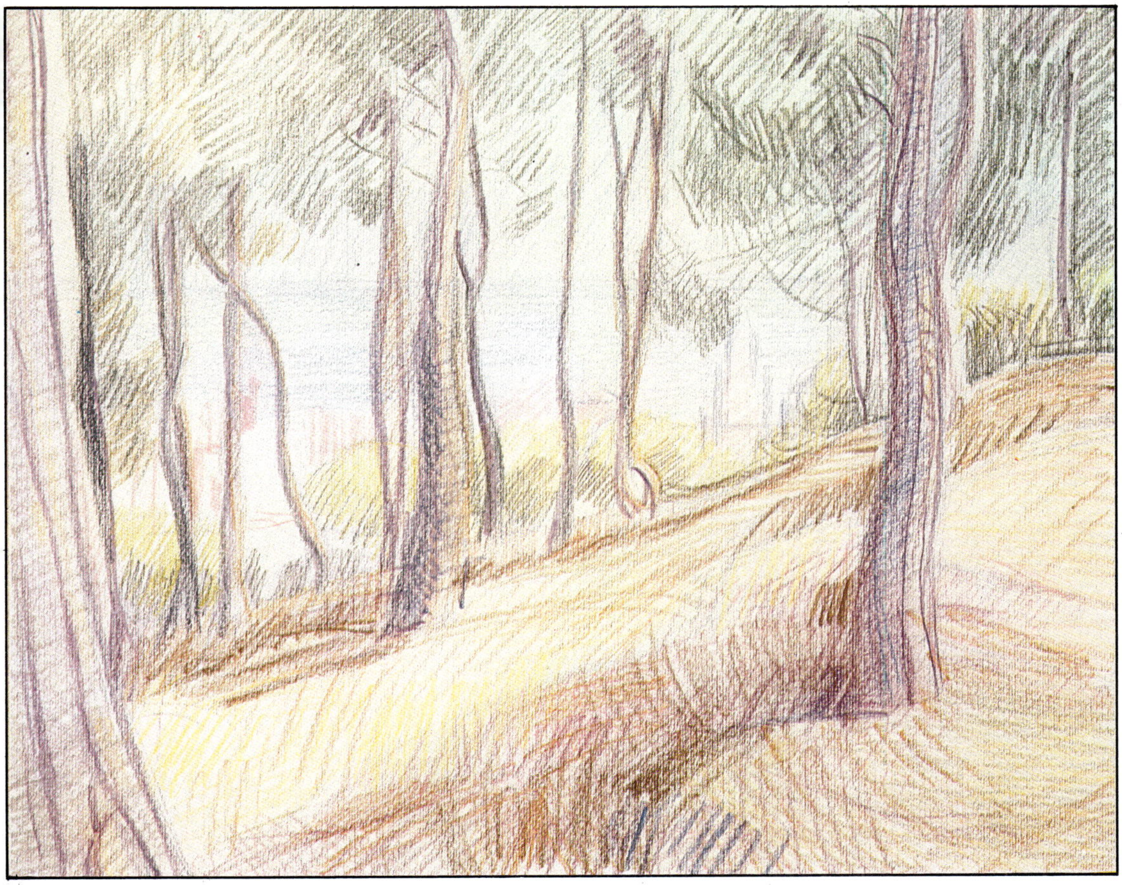

Second step

Our second step has been to establish the overall tonal values of the subject and to hint at the local color in each part of the picture. As you can see, all this has been carried out using very subtle strokes that suggest the color rather than define it. Using the vocabulary traditional to painting, we might say that in this second phase we have "*blocked in*" the picture, establishing a base for its chromatic development.

Third step

We continue with the same colors, gradually intensifying them by means of cross hatching and by adding coordinated layers of tone. At this stage, the idea is to leave the picture as a completed pencil drawing but without much color contrast. We must remember that when we carry out the watercolor wash and touch up the final version of the picture, a unity, depth, and general darkening of color will become apparent.

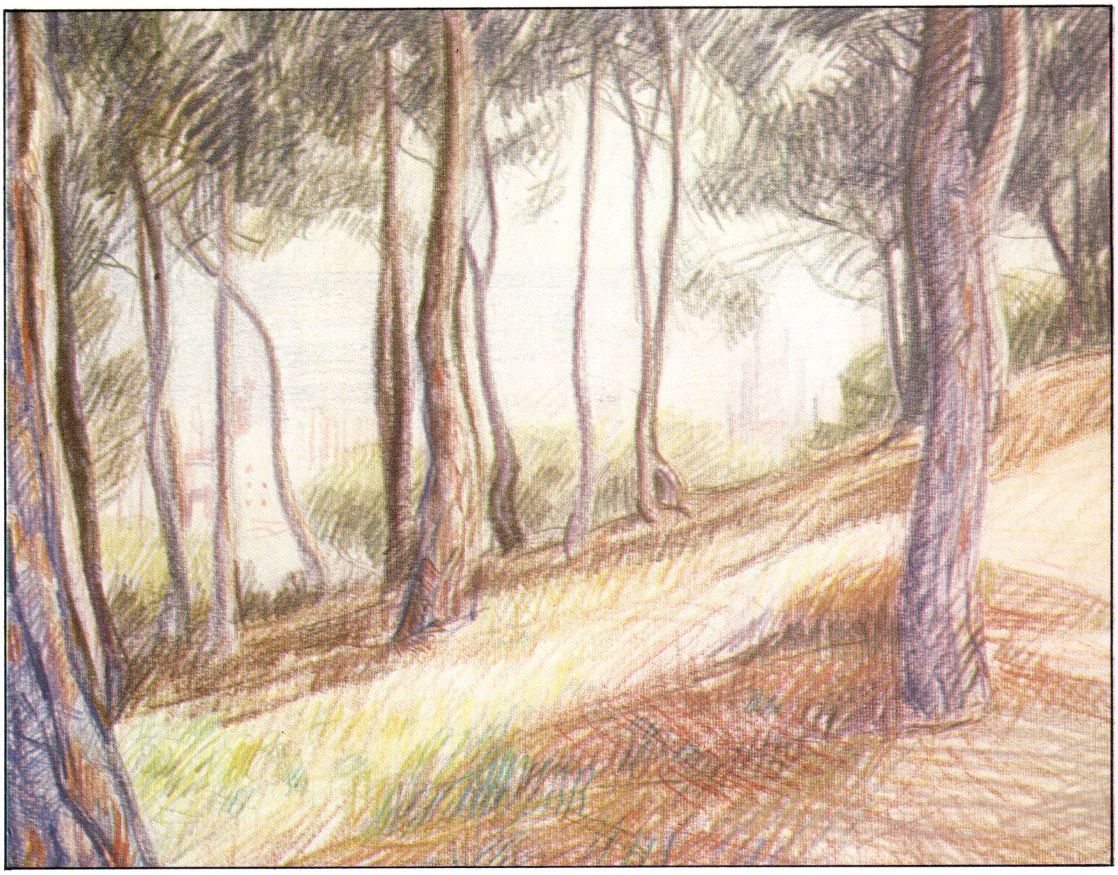

Fourth step: The watercolor wash

Following the method shown in these four close-ups, work on one area at a time. Allow the brush to distribute the water evenly to avoid the colors binding too closely together and to prevent the outlines from becoming blurred. Running a wash over a pencil drawing is not the same as producing a wash in the traditional way with watercolors. Neither the method nor the intention is the same. You do want to blend color—that is certainly the objective—but without sacrificing the characteristic strokes of a colored-pencil drawing.

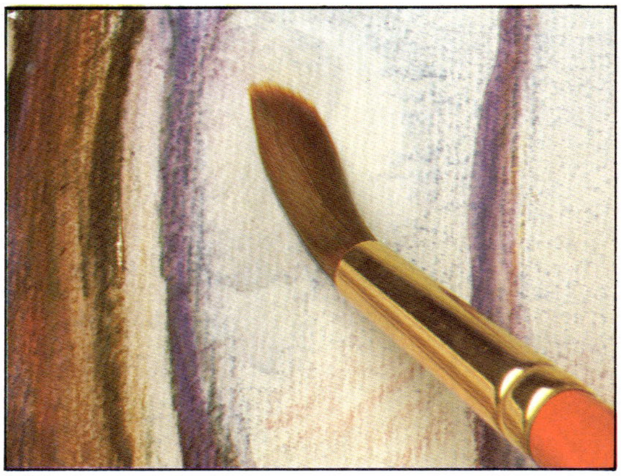

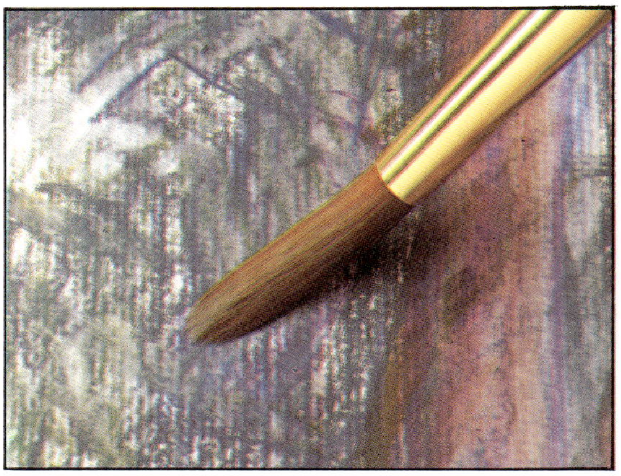

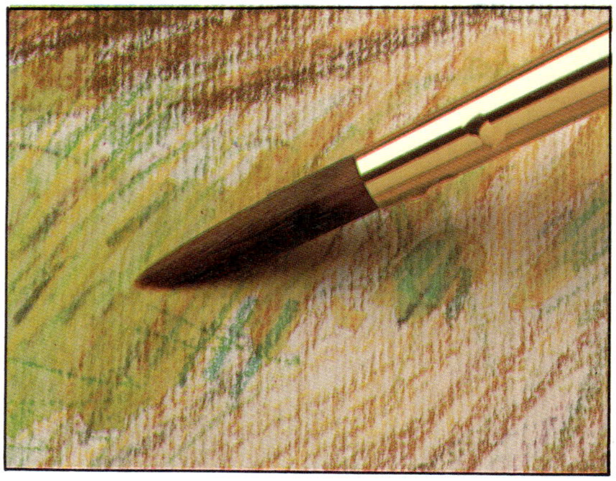

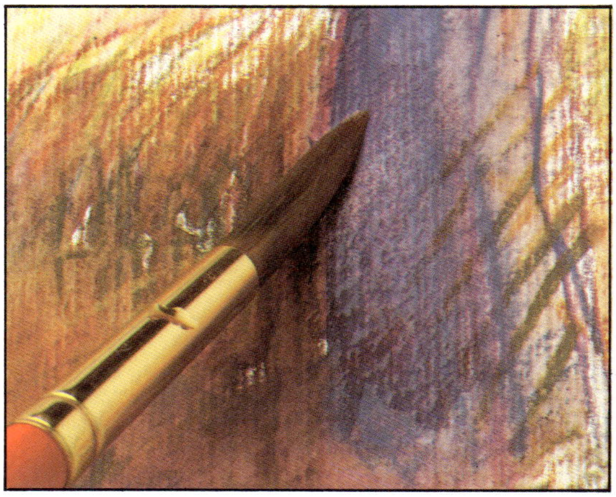

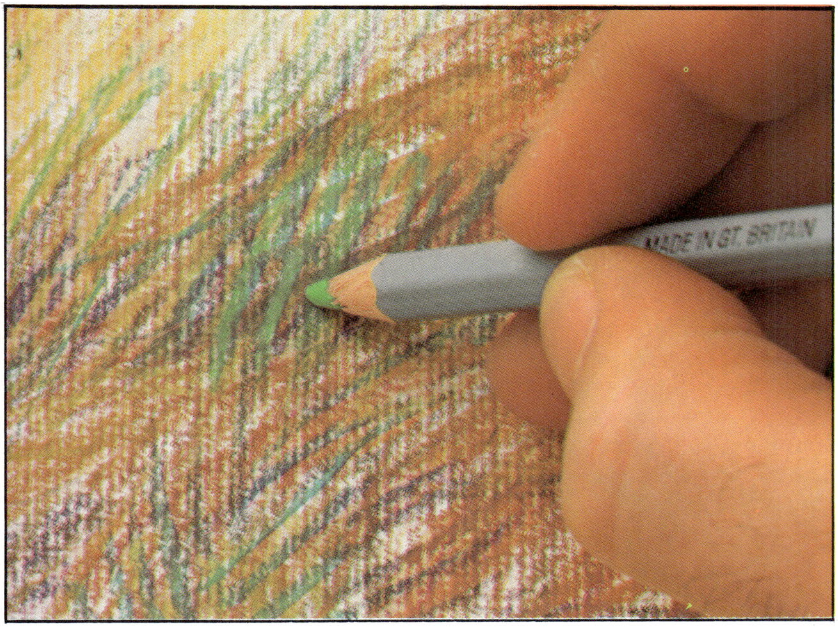

Fifth step: Final touches

When your watercolor wash is practically dry, but not totally, use the tip of the pencil to highlight certain colors and contrasts, redefining shapes that might have become blurred if the wash caused the colors to blend.

The finished picture

Notice the almost "doughy" texture of the last few touches made by the pencil on areas that still retained some moisture. These strokes, drawn on top of the watercolor wash, give the painting a really appealing character. Try it for yourself: On washes with a greater or lesser amount of color, use the point of the pencil at different stages of dampness and compare the results of each experiment.

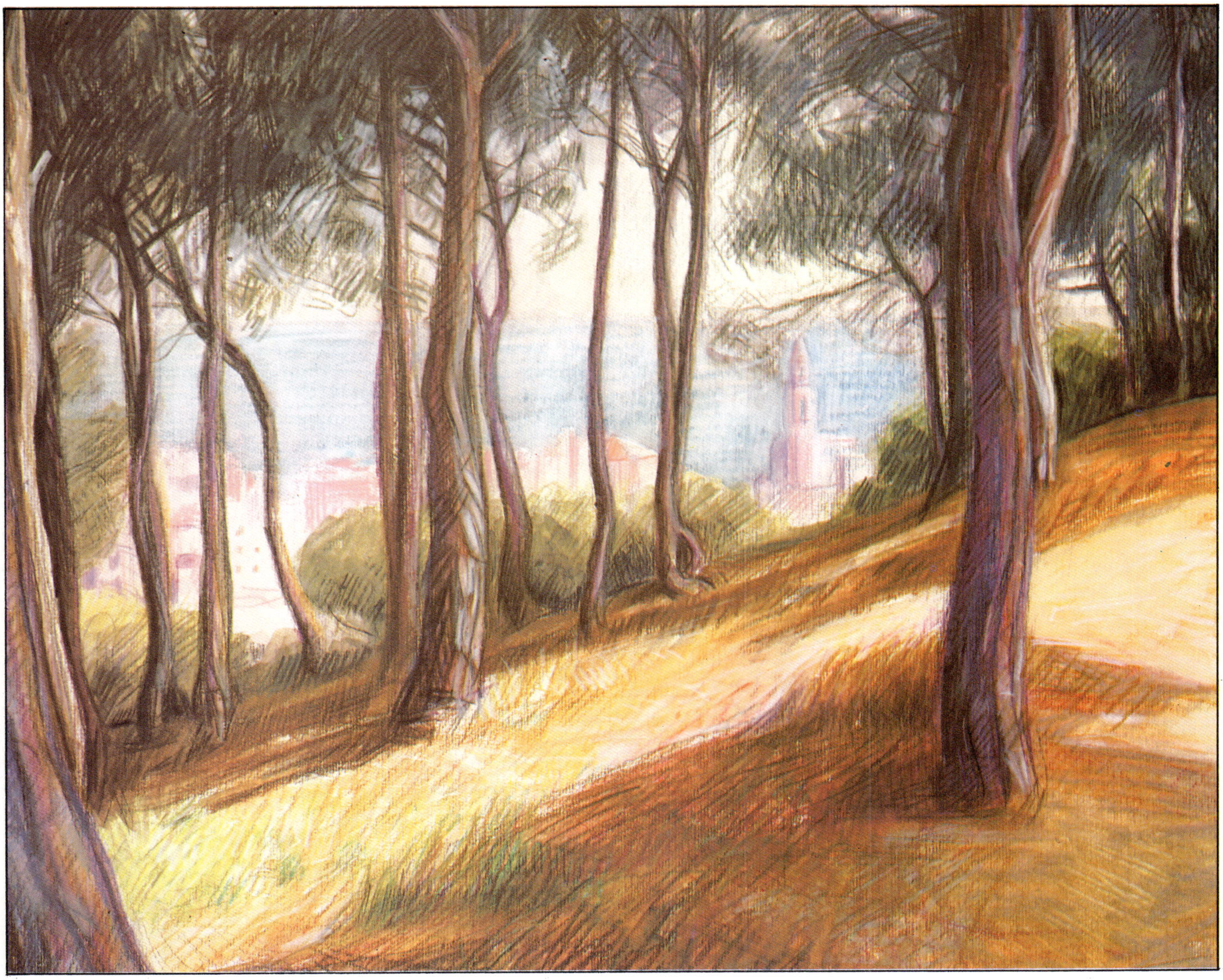

Sanguine, chalks, and charcoal

We are not going to discuss the still life as an artistic theme. Neither are we going to refer to the valuable lessons it can offer us in the art of composition. We will have to go in to all of this later and there is no point in repeating ourselves. Here we are looking at the still life strictly as a means of studying the practical possibilities of media that are infrequently used, especially in a single picture.

We are talking about sanguine, chalks, and charcoal used in conjunction with one another. In other words, we are not going to examine the creative potential of our subject, but purely and simply how to use the materials themselves.

It is very important, when switching from one medium to experiment with another, to accept as a truth the following:

The choice of medium determines the style.

This means that you must adjust your style of painting or drawing to the means you have chosen to express yourself. You will have to adapt your usual way of doing things to the distinctive characteristics of the new medium.

For example, you have your own particular way of using a pencil, don't you? But if you have to make a drawing with a soft pencil, such as a 6B, on a rough watercolor paper, you will have to forget about fine lines and minute detail.

In the same way, you cannot try to apply the identical stylistic criteria to a still life produced with sanguine, chalk, and charcoal as you would to one painted in oils.

So this is what you have to do: Compose a still life similar to the one in our example, and draw it in sanguine, chalk, and charcoal, working out how to adapt your normal style to these materials. This will undoubtedly demand a different style and treatment.

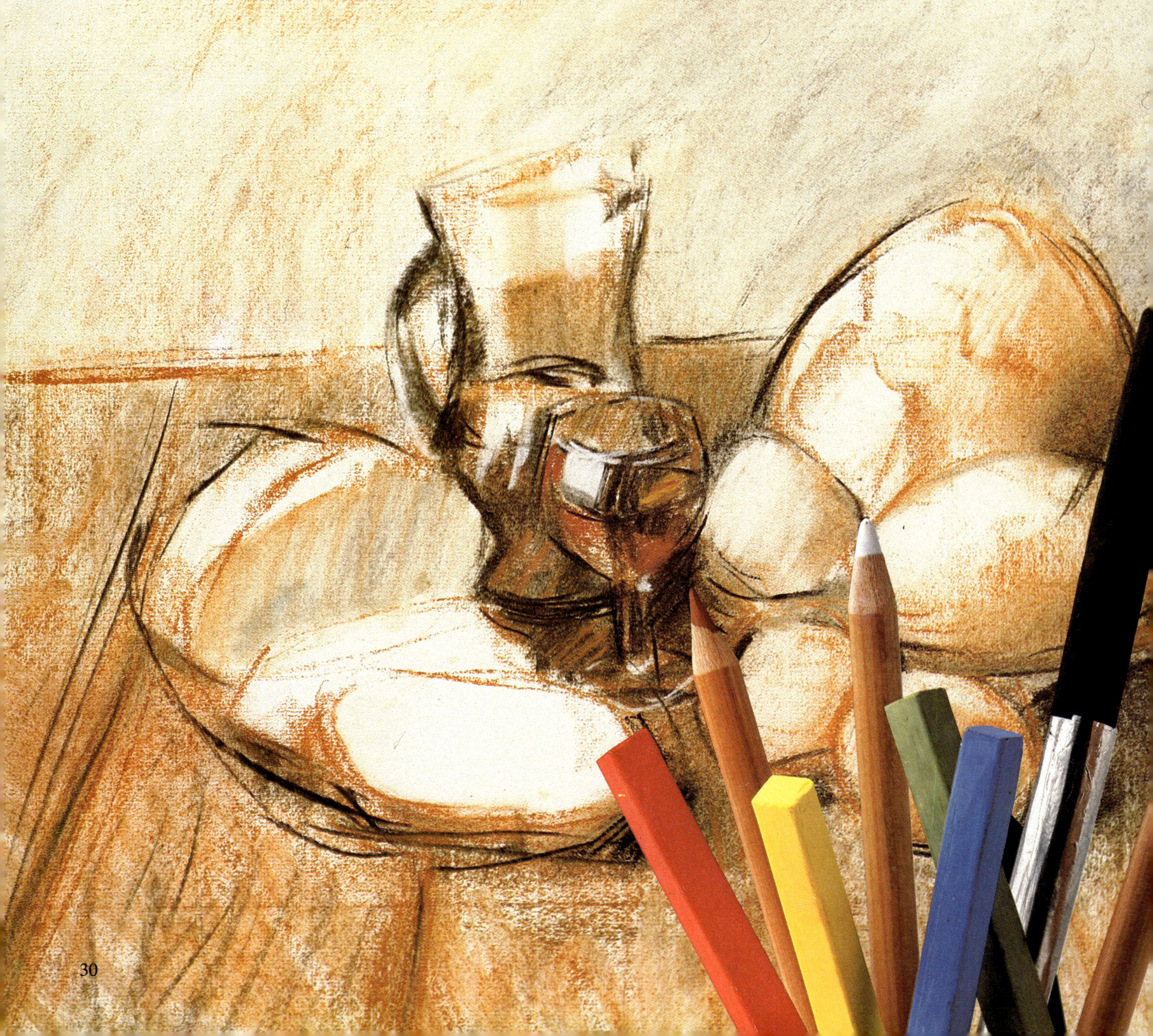

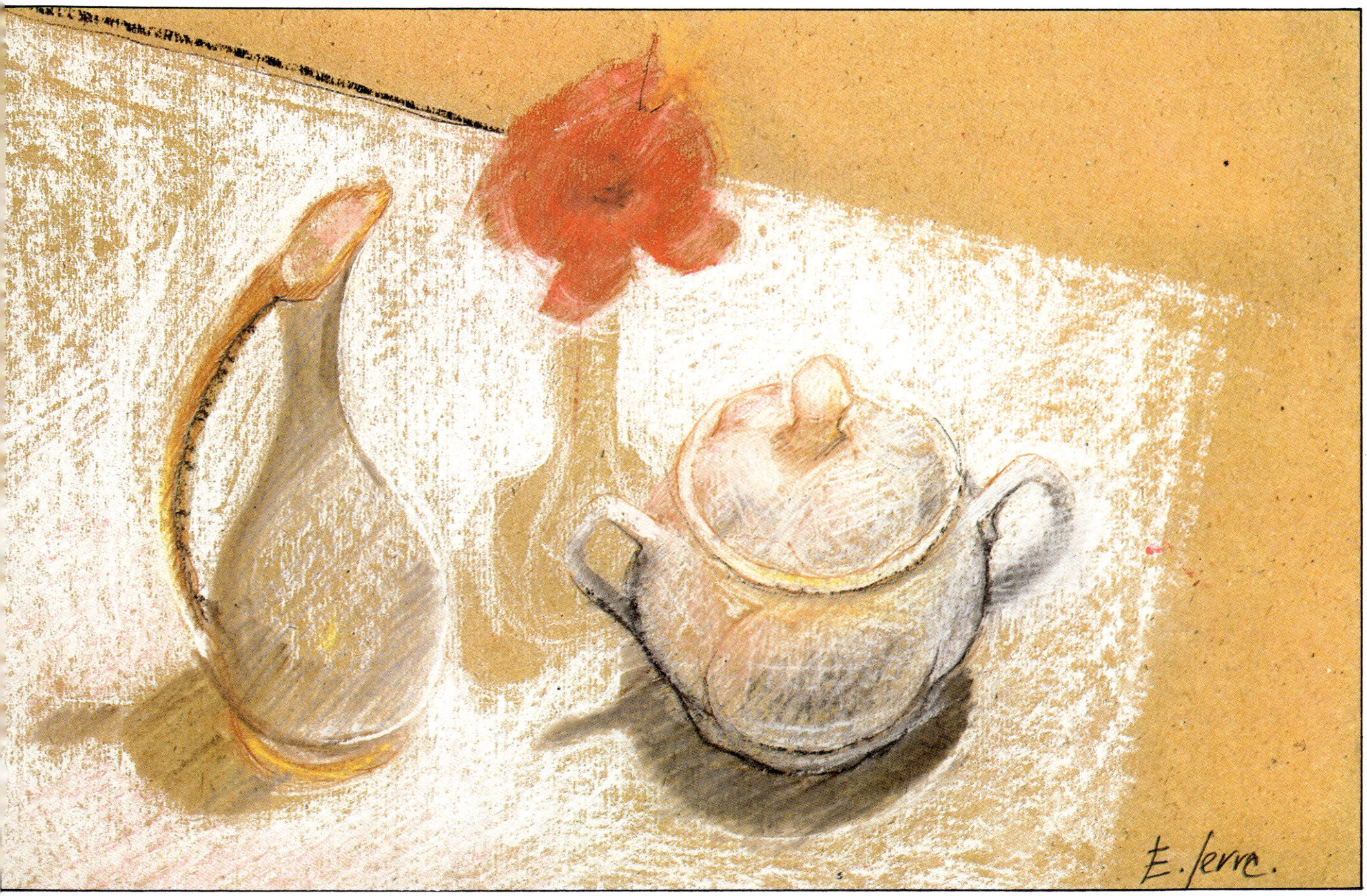

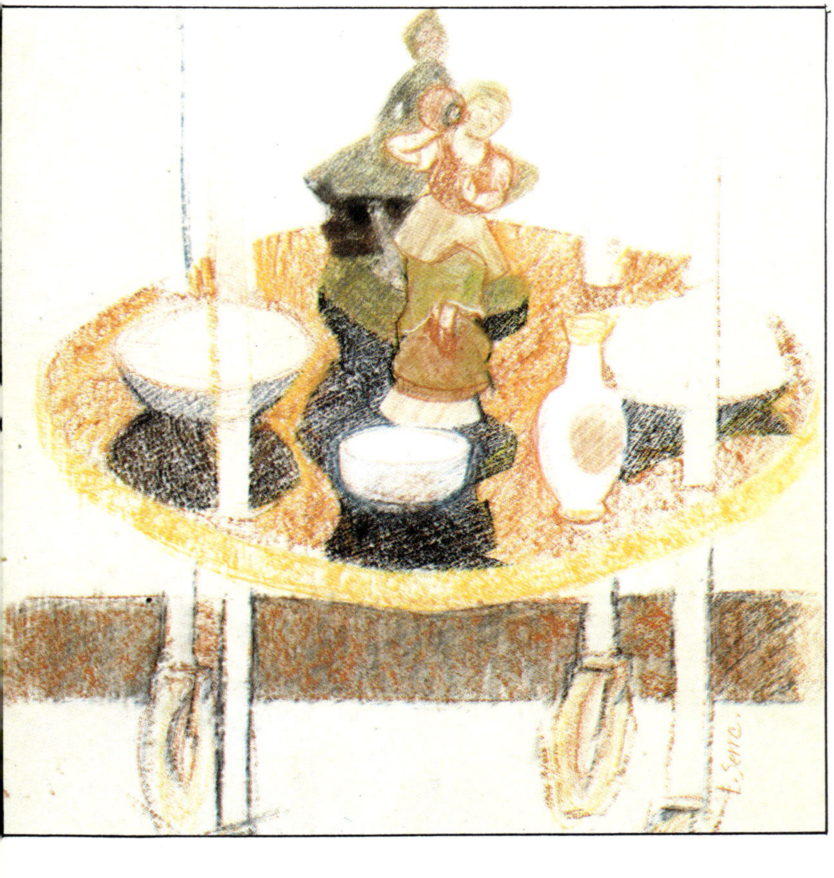

Two still life drawings by Ester Serra, in which she demonstrates that chalks and sanguine can create a more pictorial than draftsmanlike image of a subject. In these two examples the pictorial qualities can be seen through an extremely synthetic treatment of form and color, in which the color of the paper (cream in the top picture and white in the one on the left) plays as much of a part in the rich color scheme as in the compositional values.

The materials and the subject

On the right is a photograph of the materials you might need to carry out this exercise: A box of chalks (depending on the subject of your picture you may only need a few colors), a stick of charcoal for the black areas, some torchons or stumps, an eraser, a sanguine drawing pencil, a white chalk pencil, and paper. Juan Sabater, who has completed this exercise for us, used tinted watercolor paper of a warm, pale gray color. As for the subject matter, you are free to copy Sabater or to go for originality. If you do the latter, we recommend that, as he has done, you look for objects and backgrounds with a predominantly uniform color range, warm or cool, that do not require an extensive use of color. In this still life composed by Sabater, all the elements fall into a warm color scale, except for the glass jug which has a green-blue tone. But even this exception is influenced by the reflections of the other objects and by the transparency of the glass.

The abundance of bread, the "naturalness" of the wine as a complement to the most symbolic of all foods, and the rustic table on which everything is set, lend this still life a distinctively rural quality.

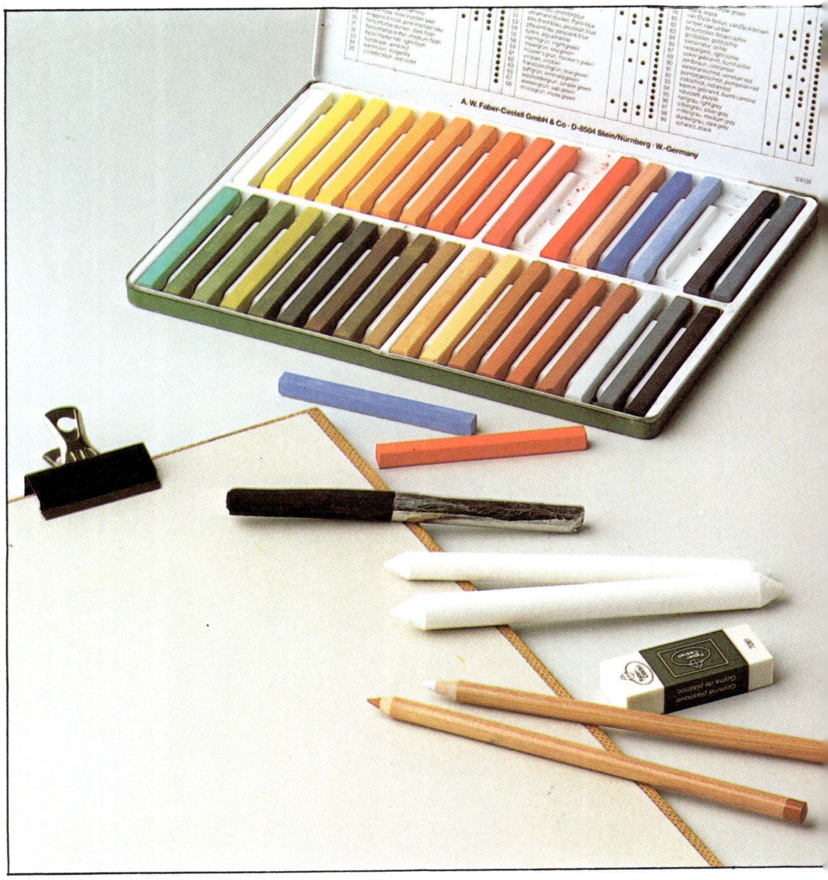

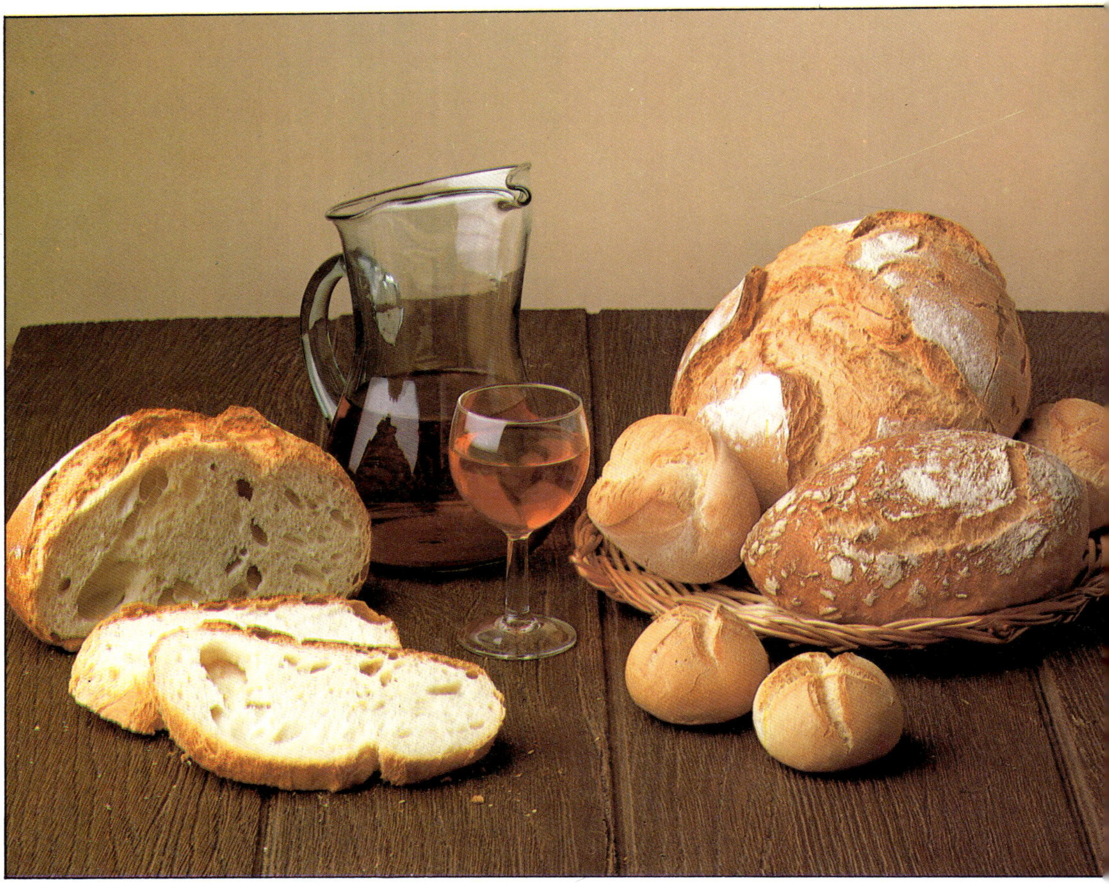

Right.
Photograph of the composition created by Juan Sabater to which one might apply a symbolic significance. For instance, we might like to give it the title, "panem nostrum quotidianum," or "our daily bread."

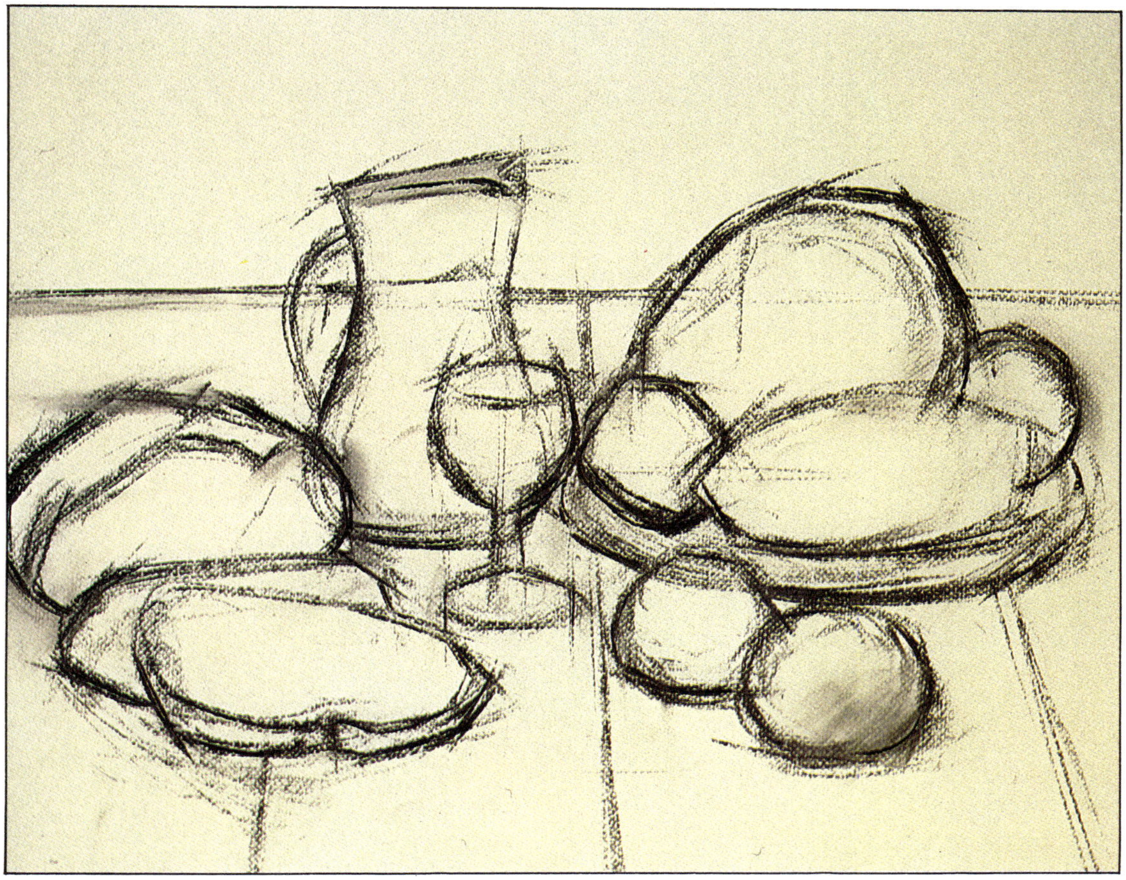

The initial sketch

Sketch the basic layout of your picture in charcoal. Take your time with this, trying to be accurate about the size and shape of each element of the composition and its place on the plane of the paper. Be careful about perspective, especially when it comes to objects with circular planes (the glass, the jug, and the bread basket); this is where most people make mistakes. If, as with the table in this still life, you can see clear parallel lines, don't forget that they must run to the same vanishing point on the horizon. Get rid of excess charcoal dust using a cloth or by blowing it away.

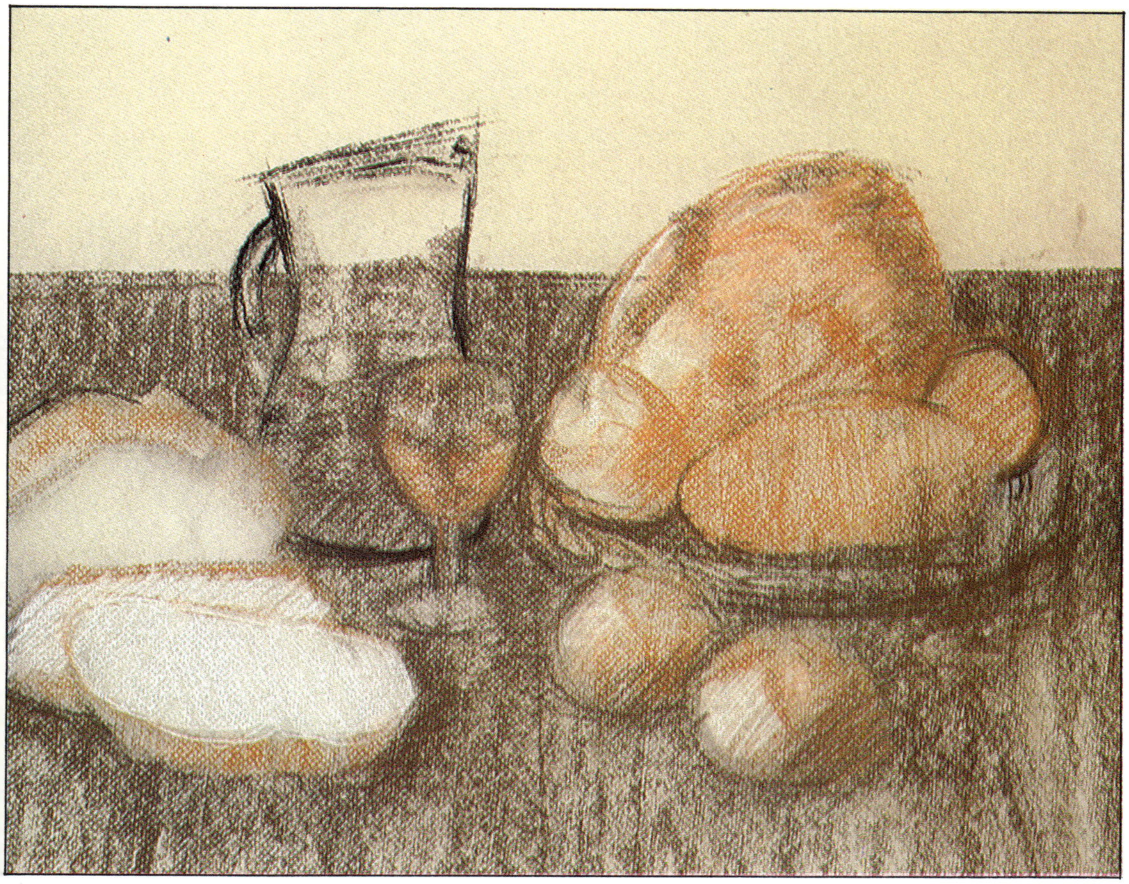

Setting the tone

At this stage, the objective is to establish the general color range of the picture, based on that of the majority of its elements. Sabater, faced with predominantly earth colors, has covered the paper with just two colors: Sanguine, using the crayon, and sepia using a chalk stick. Both colors define, throughout the picture, the objects themselves or the areas of shadow. To this color base the artist has added a few touches of white chalk where the natural color is vaguely white.

The basic colors

Sabater's next step, which you should also follow, is to define the basic colors of each element of the composition.

For instance, he has described the bread in distinct areas of deep cadmium yellow, sanguine red, and whitish shades. With a minimum of color, each object has been more clearly defined. Notice also the addition of some complementary tones (blues) on the table, in the background, and in the handle of the jug; these bring out the yellow tones to much greater effect.

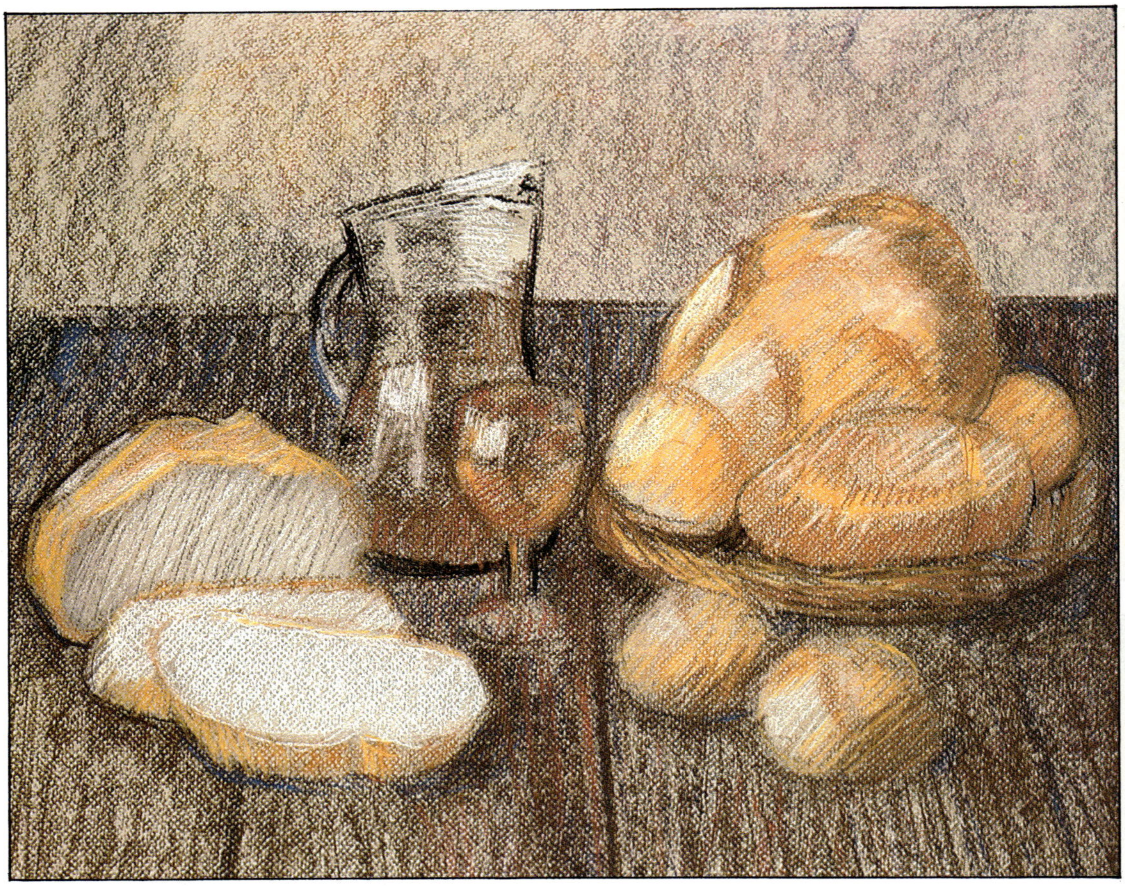

Blending colors

Here the intention is to blend the colors by working on the whole surface of the picture, as Sabater has done, with a good size stump or torchon. Compare the two photographs on this page and notice how much softer the second one is. From here we move on to the final phase of the picture in which we add and blend in more color, as shown on the next page.

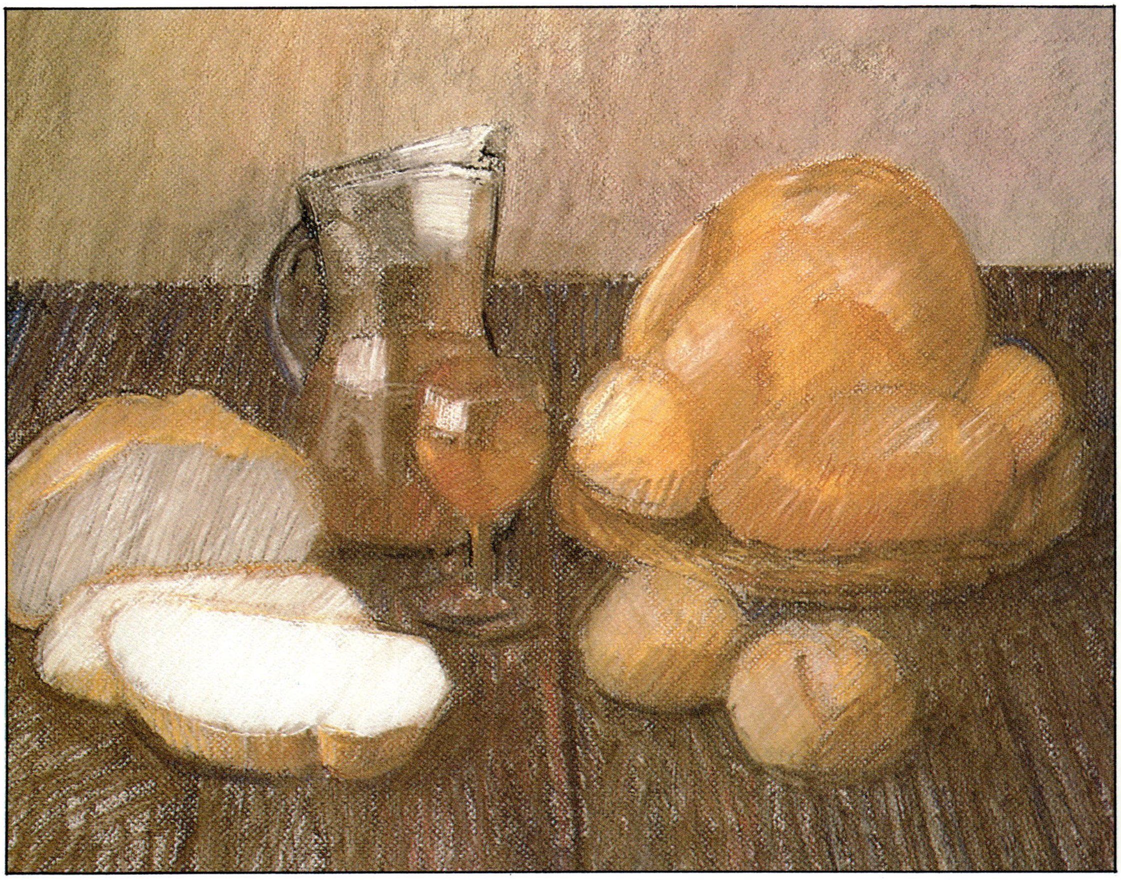

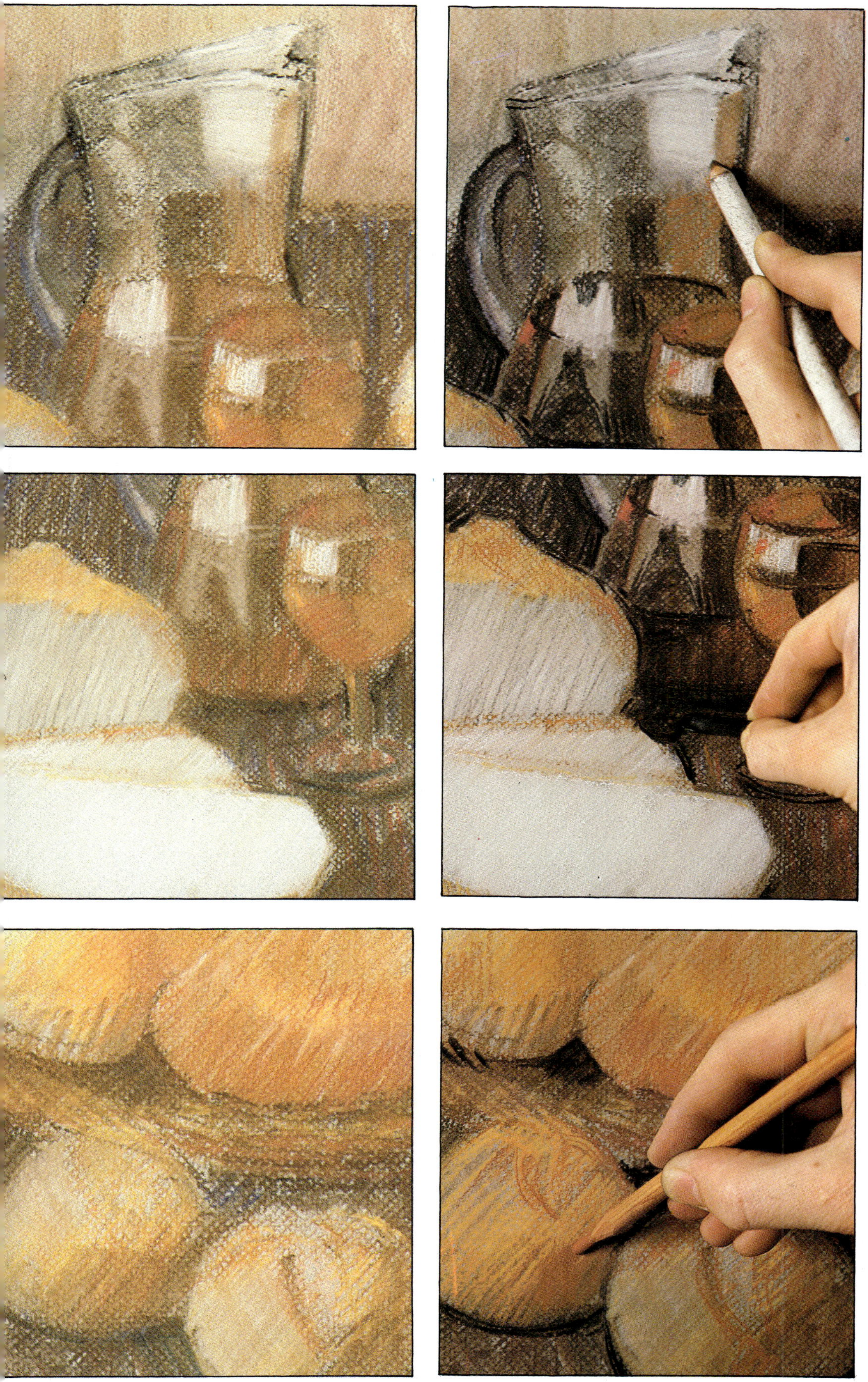

Completing the picture. First stage

Here are six close-up photographs of three small sections of Sabater's still life, showing first how they appeared after the colors had been spread using the torchon (left-hand photograph) and then after having new color added (right-hand photograph) to reinforce, but not to change, the existing tonal values. Note how, through the process shown in these close-ups, a greater degree of contrast has been achieved by deepening all the colors already present in the picture. As seen on the previous page, the chalk, pencil and charcoal work has been blended with the fingers or the torchon. You will notice, especially in the first and second pair of close-ups, that the pigment has been ingrained in the texture of the paper and that, in those areas where no blending has taken place, the pencil or charcoal stick has been generously applied to build up layers of color.

Completing the picture. The final touches

On the right you can see Sabater's work after the process we have just described. We don't know what your own still life looks like, but in any case it should be at the stage where only minor details have to be added, such as highlights or tiny details that complete the picture. If you compare this photograph with that of the finished work, you will see that the main difference is the detail drawn in with the white pencil.

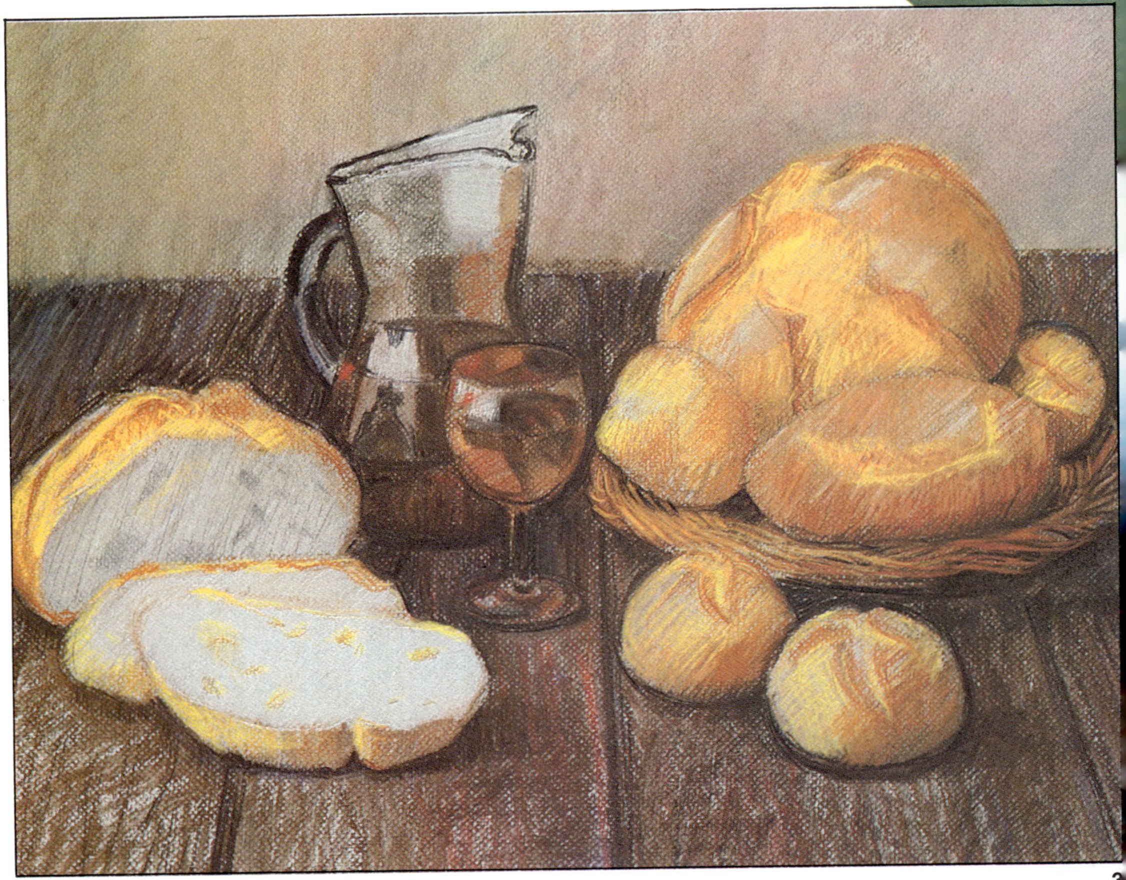

Close-ups.
1. *Effect of the white pencil on the rim of the glass and its reflections.*
2. *Detail of the top of the glass in the completed drawing. Notice the greater tonal variation in the reddish areas.*
3. *Effect of the white pencil on one of the rolls.*
4. *The same section of the roll after the white chalk had been used. Note, also, the addition of yellows and sanguines within the overall reddish color scheme.*

1

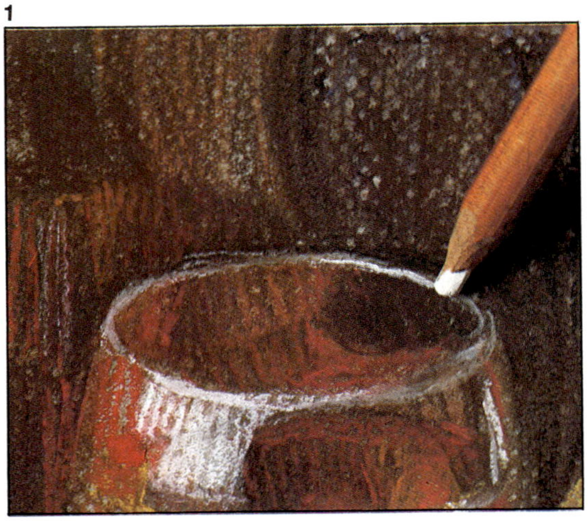

2

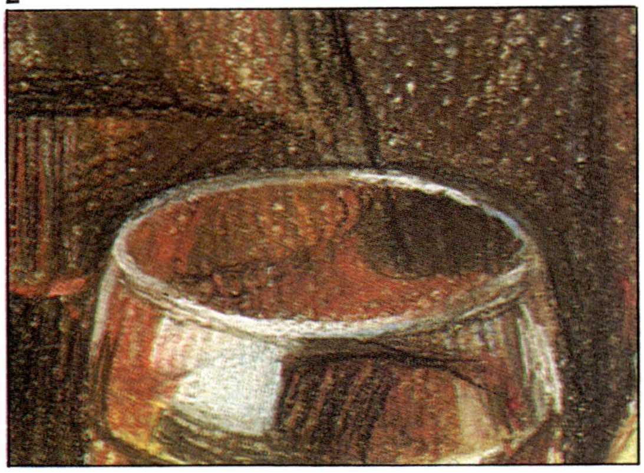

3

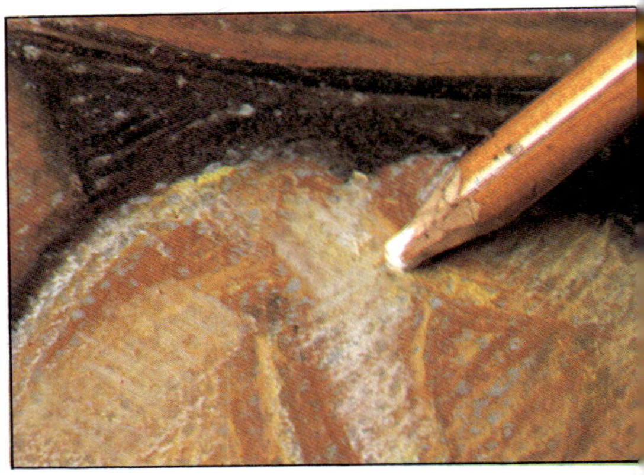

4

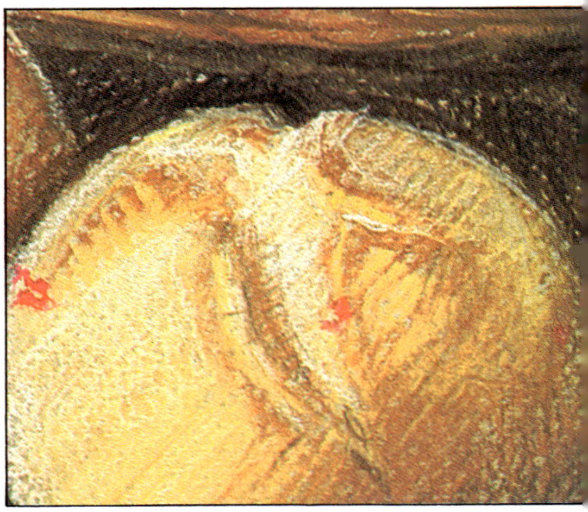

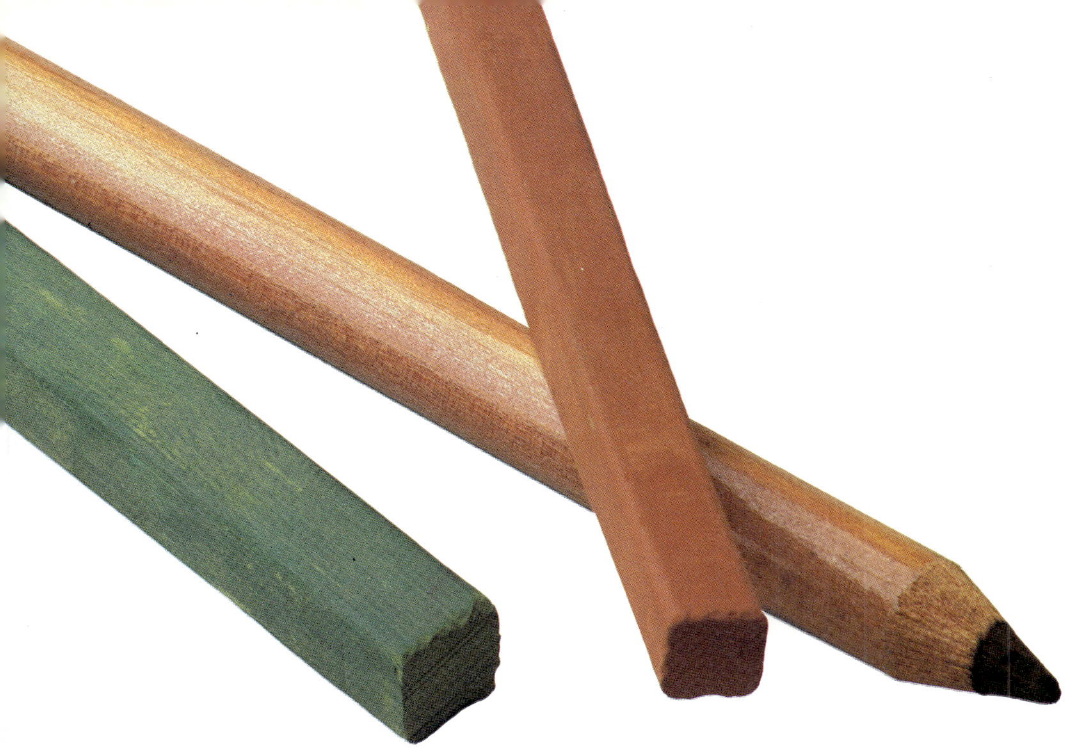

Below.
"Panem nostrum..." Still life drawn by Juan Sabater using sanguine crayons, chalks, and a little charcoal. The warm harmony of earth colors, reds and yellows, contrasts with the reflections and the whiteness of the slices of fresh bread.

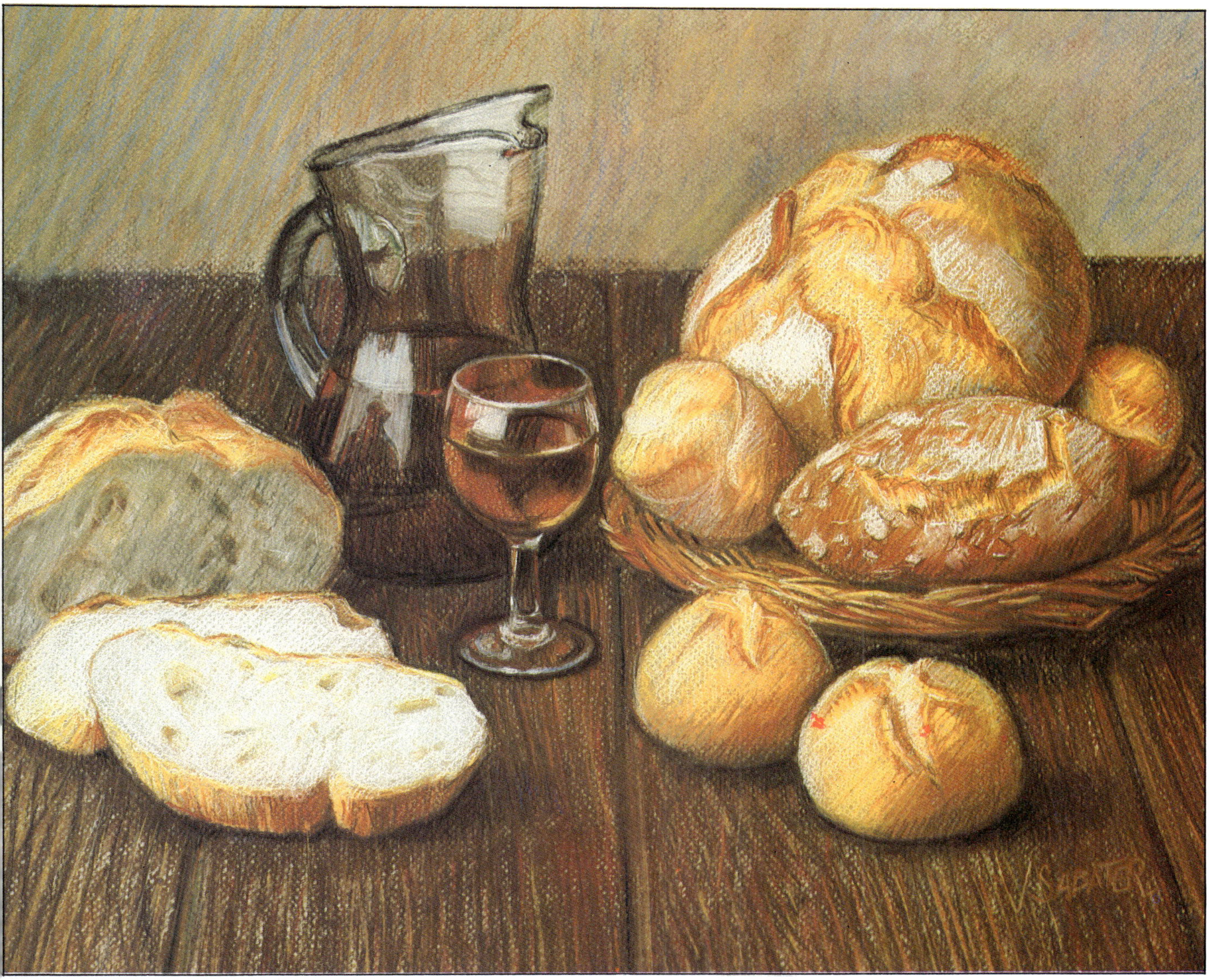

The wash

What is a wash? Is it a technique used in drawing? A pictorial technique? Some people even compare the wash with painting in tempera. The one thing everyone is agreed on is that the wash is the preliminary step to watercolor painting. Certainly, the techniques of the craft are identical to both. For those of us who consider the wash to be a form of painting, the following is its correct definition:

The wash is a pictorial process that basically consists of drawing and painting in a single color, diluted with varying amounts of water, and conveying the tonal values of a subject by using the white of the paper and transparent layers of color.

A layer of color is applied directly onto the paper, or on top of another existing layer of color, to vary, mix with, or intensify the original tone. Washes are carried out using one color, diluted in water. They have a transparent finish and cannot be touched up or overpainted with white paint. Therefore:

With a wash, whites are created using the color of the paper itself, in previously determined areas.

In other words, it is water that dilutes and lightens the tone of the color in order to create degrees of shading and gradations. You can lay a wash with watercolor and drawing inks; with watercolor you can use tap water, but you will need distilled or boiled water if you intend to use inks. As far as equipment goes for painting washes—and watercolors—we will introduce it in the sections dealing more specifically with watercolor painting. On the following page some of the basic equipment is illustrated.

To achieve the entire range of grays from black to the white of the paper, the color will have to be diluted, bearing in mind that the more water used, the greater the degree of transparency; the more water in the mixture, the more you will see the white of the paper and the lighter the tone will be.

From an artist's point of view, the expressive possibilities of the wash could be summed up by saying that it is a technique especially suited to figure studies and landscapes, for tonal sketches, and for certain projects in the field of advertising.

This introductory section can be rounded off with a truism: Knowing how to paint a wash does not automatically mean you have mastered the technique of watercolor painting. You have to paint many washes and to acquire the appropriate skills and techniques needed to succeed with that particular craft—to which we will, of course, turn our undivided attention later on.

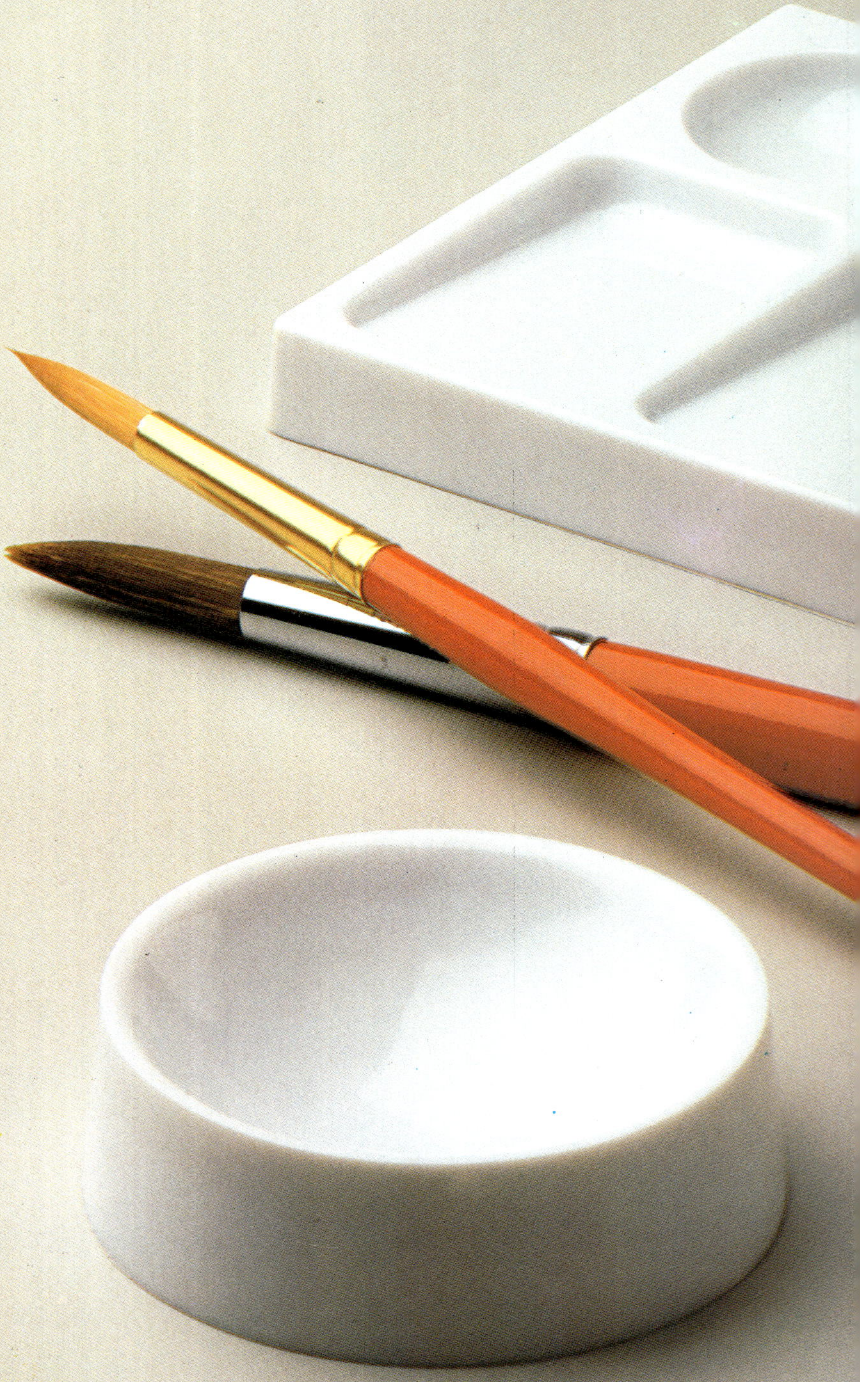

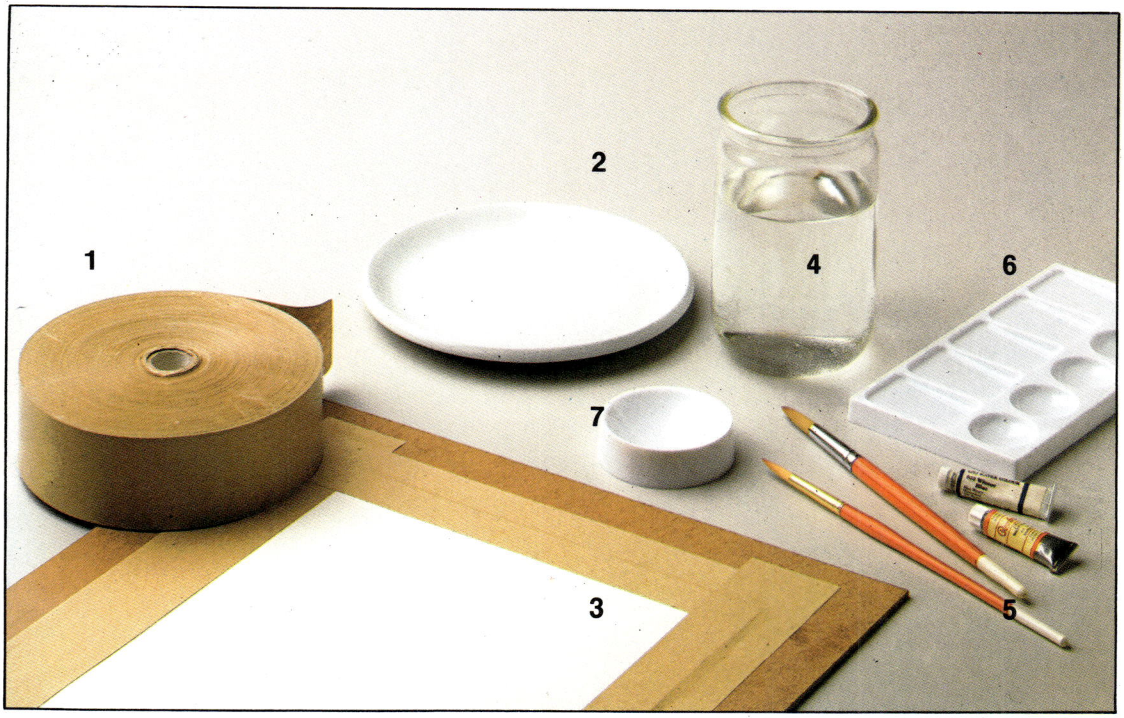

Basic equipment
1. Roll of sticky tape for the mounting and stretching of paper;
2. Ceramic plate for mixing paint;
3. Painting surface with stretched paper;
4. Container for water;
5. Sable brushes;
6. Palette;
7. Small mixing well.

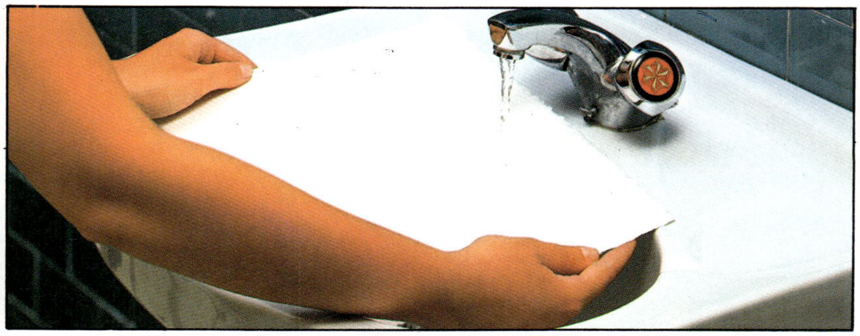

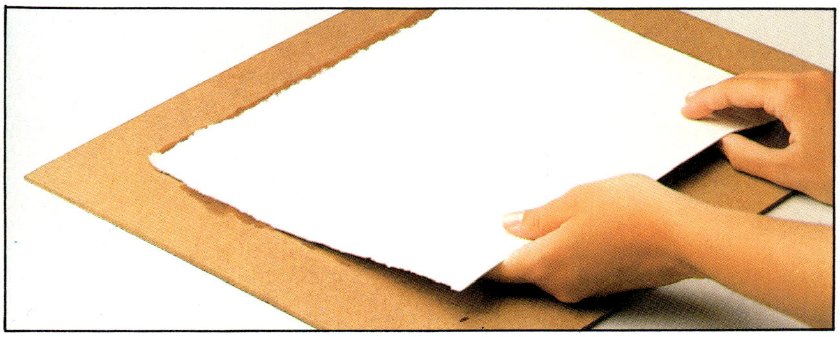

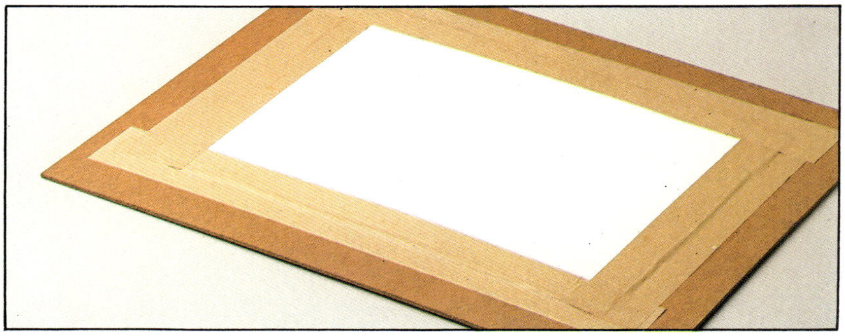

Mounting and stretching the paper

To prevent the paper from buckling and warping when wet, it should be mounted and stretched before being used. To do this, follow these steps:

- Hold the sheet of paper under running water for a couple of minutes.
- After letting any excess water run off, place it on a wooden board, gently pulling it taut to help it stretch.
- Fasten the edges with sticky tape, keeping the sheet of paper smooth and flat.
- Let it dry naturally. After four or five hours, keeping the board horizontal, peel off the sticky tape.

The paper is now ready to be used, with a smooth, taut, and wrinkle-resistant surface, no matter how much water we apply to it.

If you paint on paper lighter than 7 oz, you will notice that, owing to the dampness of the watercolor, the paper will buckle badly. To prevent this happening, you should stretch it following the procedure outlined, or alternatively, use a heavier paper that you can just fasten down with some clips.

Basic techniques

Half-tone wash, on dry paper

On the following two pages some of the basic wash techniques are introduced. To begin, try this simple exercise.

1. Draw a square of about 8 × 8 in. (20 × 20 cm), on a piece of paper and prepare a cobalt blue wash similar to the one in the picture. Use a No. 12 brush. Load the brush with enough color and paint from left to right, starting at the top, using strokes of about 1 in. (3 cm) in width.

1

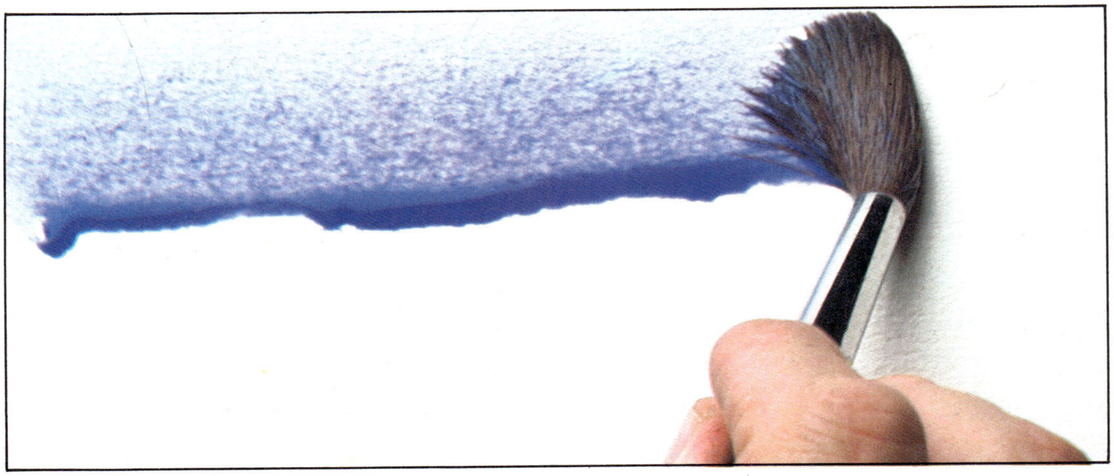

2. Don't stop! Keeping it wet, drag the wash down the page, retaining color at the bottom of the area in which you are working. The random progress of the paint can be regulated by the angle of the drawing board.

2

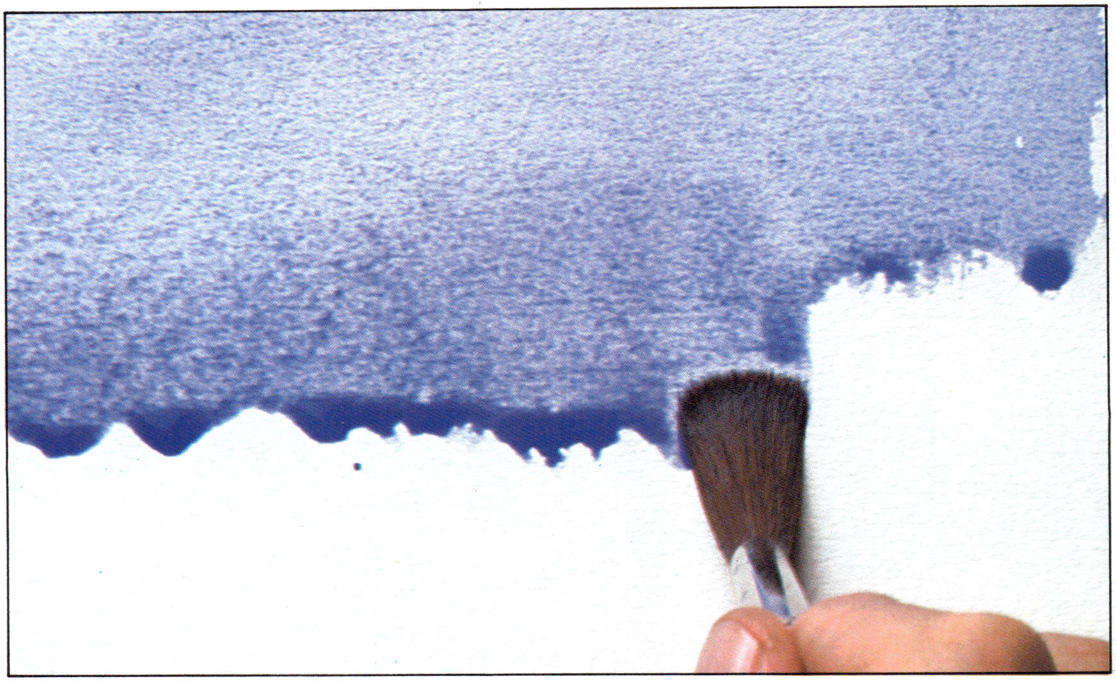

3. You will find that when you reach the bottom of the square you still have some paint left. Rinse and gently squeeze your brush and when it is dry, run it along the line of excess color, repeating the process until the wash has a uniform tone. And don't forget that with a wash—as with watercolors—you can't touch it up later.

3

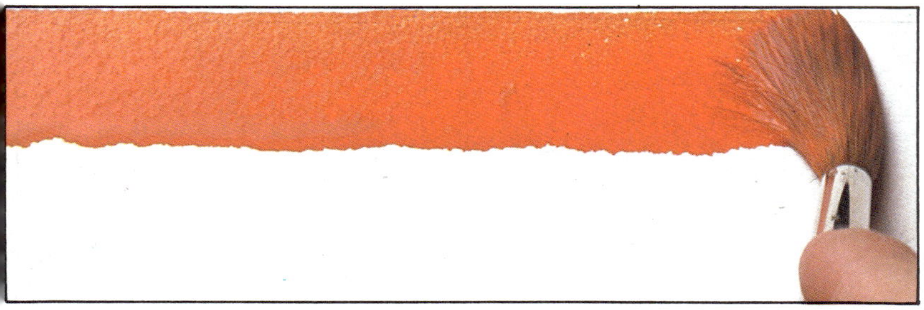

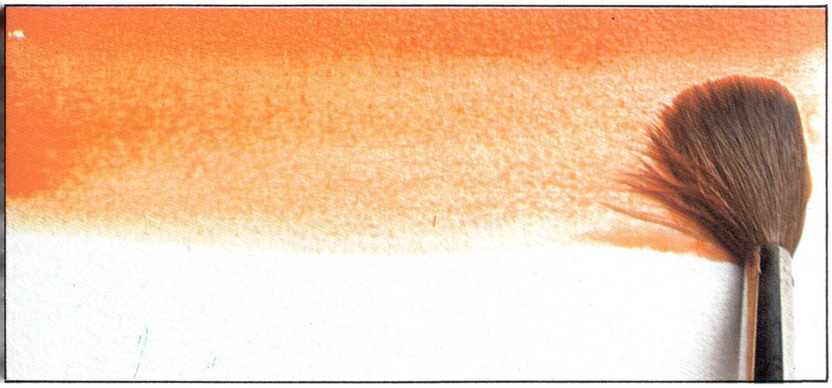

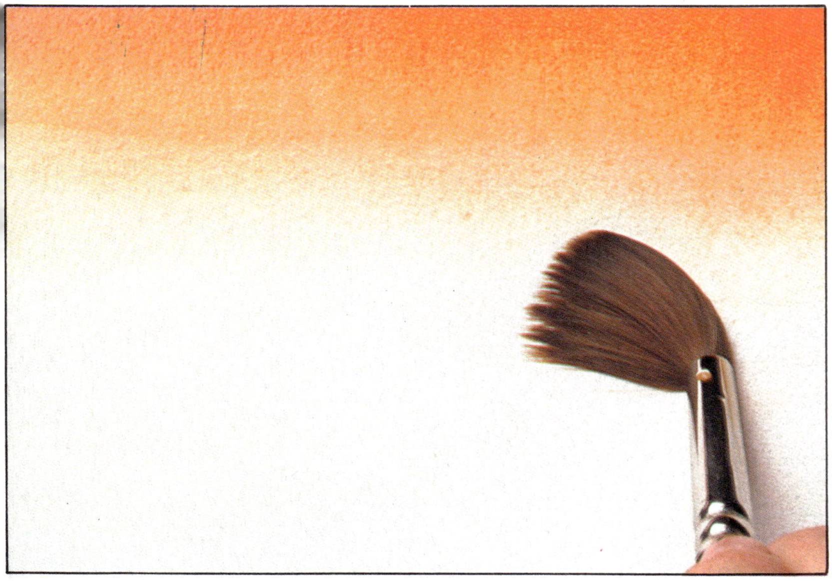

Gradated wash on dry paper

As in the previous exercise, draw a square about 8 × 8 in. (20 × 20 cm) and prepare a wash of cadmium red or vermilion for your attempt to create a gradated wash on dry paper. The first step is to load the brush with plenty of color to apply to the upper section of your square. Use a stroke of about ¾ in. (2 cm) wide, not of dry color, but a wash. It must contain a fair amount of pigment, but should still be a wash.

Now, on with the job! Clean the brush, press it against the rim of the water container ensuring that it retains a good supply of water, and then apply it to the bottom half of the painted strip, dissolving and gradating as you work your way down the paper, moving from side to side, exerting pressure to release more water, and trying not to let the paint accumulate at the point where you remove the brush from the paper. Remember that the quantity of color you are able to dilute and pull down from the initial stroke of color will depend on the amount of water held in the brush. So, the larger the area you want to cover with your wash, the more water your brush must hold. Just keep washing your brush, draining it a little, and gradating the wash downwards until you reach the bottom of the square.

It is possible that during this final stage you may have to do a little retouching, loading and unloading the brush, but do it with extreme caution to avoid making a mess of the wash.

You can pass from the deepest saturation of color to white, depending on the amount of water left in the brush after each rinsing and draining.

How to "open up" white areas by absorbing color

Although there are many ways of creating areas of white in a wash that is still damp, here we show you the simplest: Wash your brush and drain it on absorbent paper. Apply the brush to the damp area you wish to leave white and the brush will soak up the color.

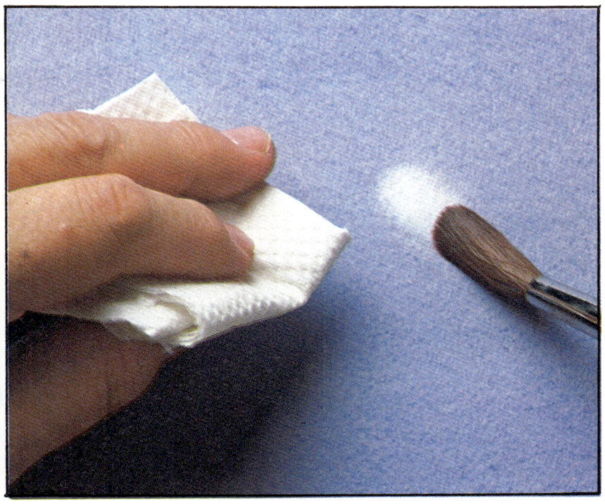

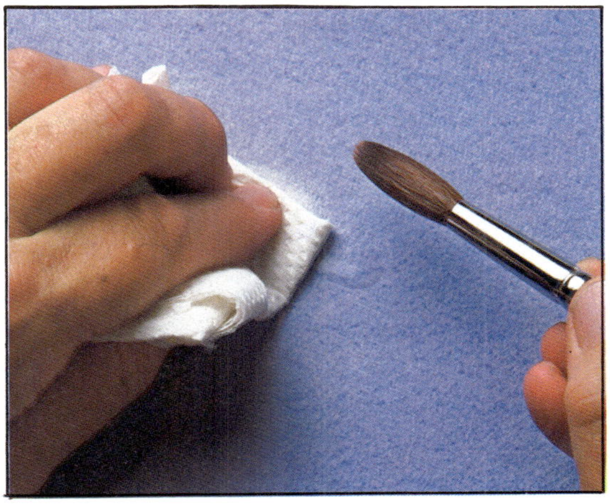

"Opening up" whites with the paintbrush is a two-stage operation:
1. Apply the damp brush.
2. Dry the white patch with absorbent paper.

Preliminary exercises

Superimposition of tones or layers of color

When using washes or watercolors, layers of color are laid over one another to intensify the tonal value, to define shape and volume, and to create contrast. The layers are built up gradually, bearing in mind that it is always preferable to err on the side of paleness than to apply too much color. A tone that is too pale can be darkened with new washes. However, there is no way of lightening a tone that is too dark.

In this practical example, the objective is to give the cube form and volume.

1. Paint in all shaded areas of the cube, using a fairly diluted blue wash.
2. Wait until the first layer is dry and then apply a wash over the darkest plane of the cube.
3. Paint a narrow strip of color on the far corner of the upper plane of the cube.
4. Deepen the shadow along the upper edge of the darkest plane and try to gradate the wash, avoiding sudden changes of tone.

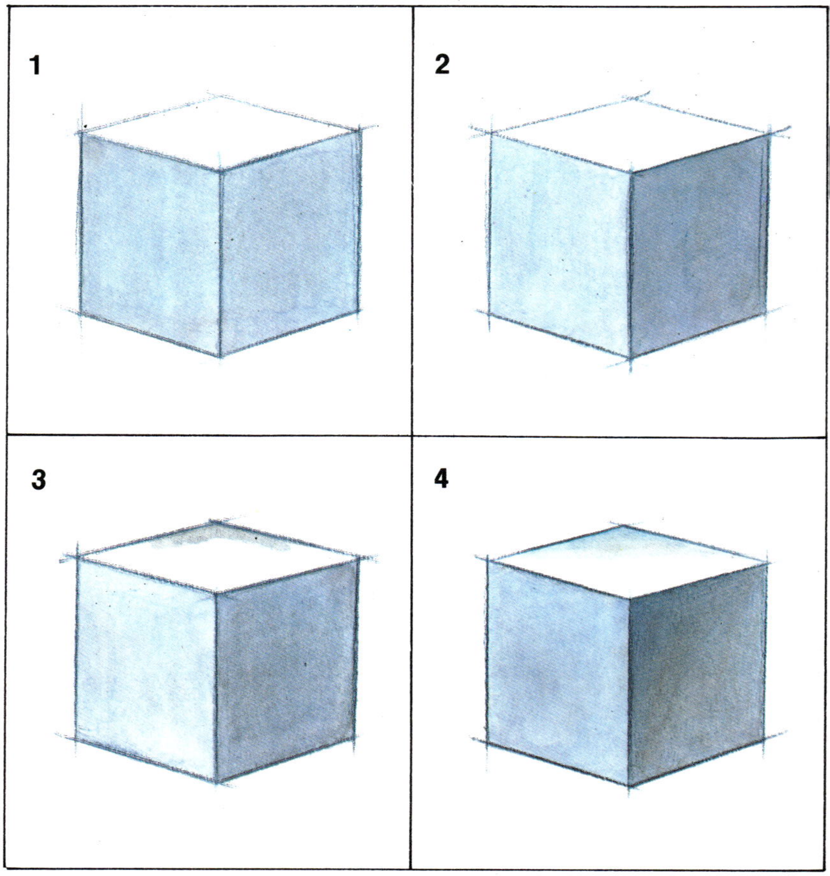

Shading and gradation in the wash

This exercise is a little more complicated. We have done it with a sepia color wash, following this method step-by-step:

1. Draw a book in perspective, like the one in our example.
2. Then apply an ordinary wash on the lower planes (on the spine and the pages), watching the edges and without going beyond the depth of tone we have achieved. Look at the subtle gradation along the upper edge of the spine, executed with a dry brush that absorbed the color.
3. Paint the cover. The part farthest away needs a deeper tone, and the nearest part (next to the pages of the book) is subtly gradated—something you should also try to achieve.
4. Strengthen the tone on the book's edges and spine. Note the fading away at the outer edges of the shadow. Keep on building up a gradated wash until you achieve the same result as in the example.

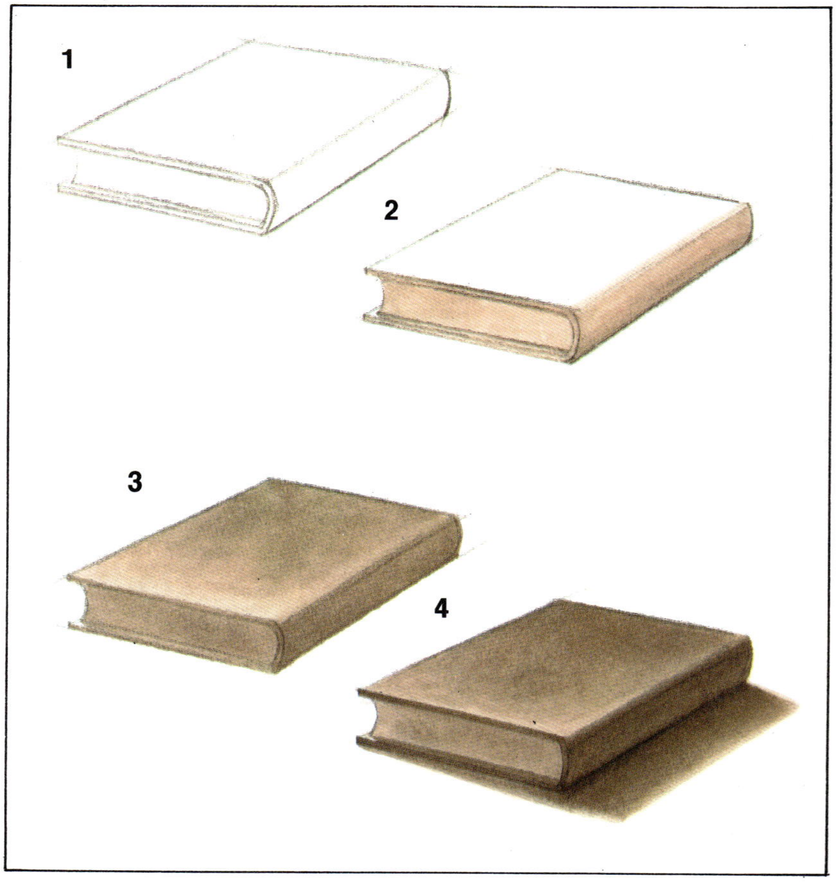

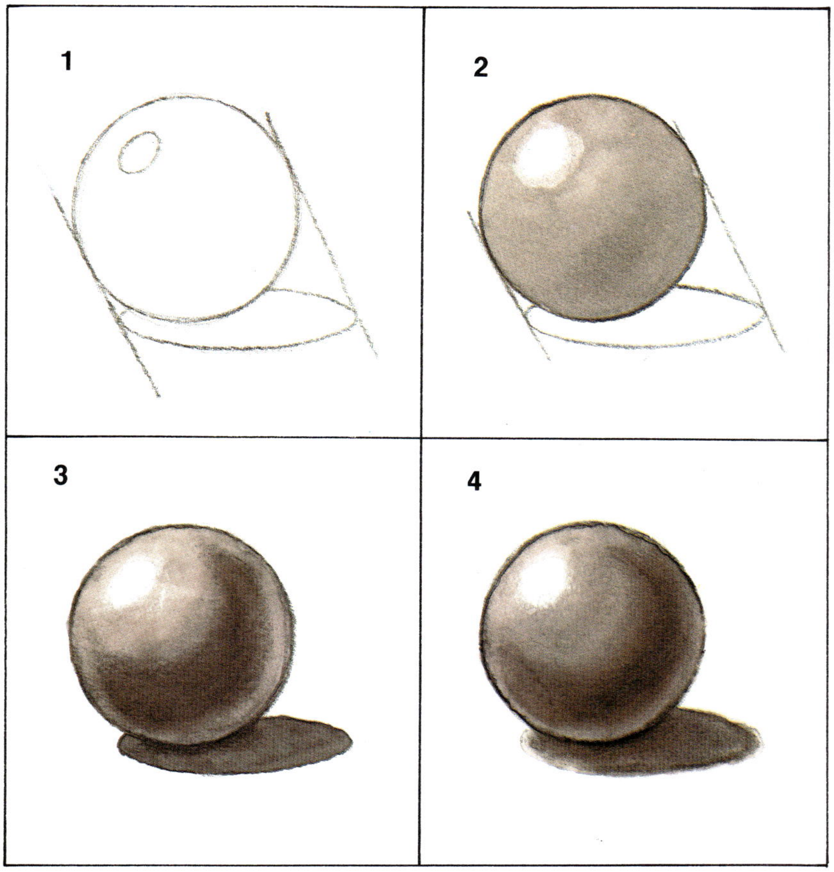

Painting a sphere using the wash

1. Draw a sphere, indicating with a small circle the point where the main light falls. This spot will be left white.
2. Apply a first wash to determine the tone of the sphere, gradating a little from bottom to top, and remembering to avoid the white area.
3. Fill in the shadow made by the sphere and, using the same tone of wash, color in the area of shade on the sphere itself. Without waiting for it to dry completely, keep adding new layers until you think that the tone of both shade and shadow have reached the right depth. Immediately gradate the deepest tones (using the dry paintbrush technique) so that they blend with the surrounding areas.
4. Apply some more solid color to the lower edge of the shading on the sphere itself and gradate it as before. Give the final touches to the shadow, strengthening the part closest to the sphere and blurring the edges a little (using a clean, damp brush) until you have a result similar to the picture.

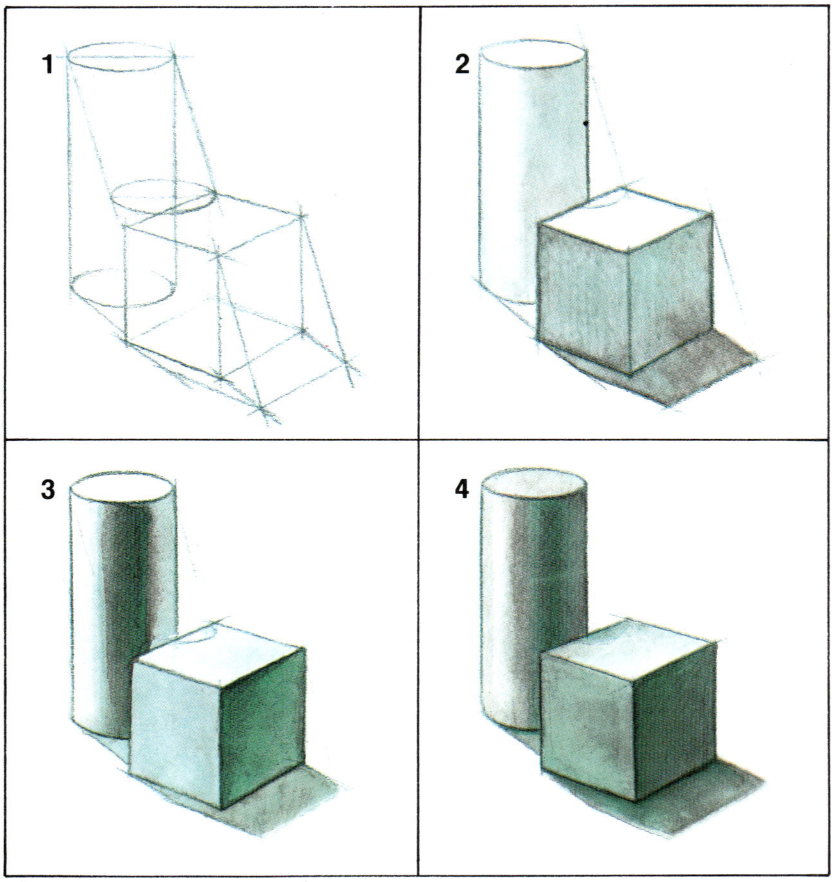

Painting a cylinder and a cube using the wash

1. Draw the subject with meticulous attention to the perspective of both geometric forms and their corresponding shadows.
2. Lay a first wash, very transparent, over the cube and cylinder, except on their upper surfaces. Wait until this dries and then go over the two faces of the cube. Also apply more tone to the cylinder to indicate the shaded area. Color in the shadow projected by the cube.
3. With a very diluted mix of color, lay a light wash over the upper surface of the cube. Turn to the cylinder and with a deeper tone go over the central part of the shaded area. Using the same loaded brush, go over the right hand face of the cube again.
4. Gradate the shading on the cylinder, making the bright area stand out by adding a little line of color down the left hand side of its body. Add the final touches: The shadow and the upper surface of the cylinder, gradation of the upper plane of the cube, and a few last subtleties in its projected shadow.

Interpretation of a photographic subject using wash

Laying a wash is not easy, but with the preliminary exercises you have just completed, and following the step-by-step method we have devised for you, you will begin to get the hang of it. The next project consists of painting an urban scene from a photograph using the wash technique. So, without further ado, let's get on with the first stage of the exercise.

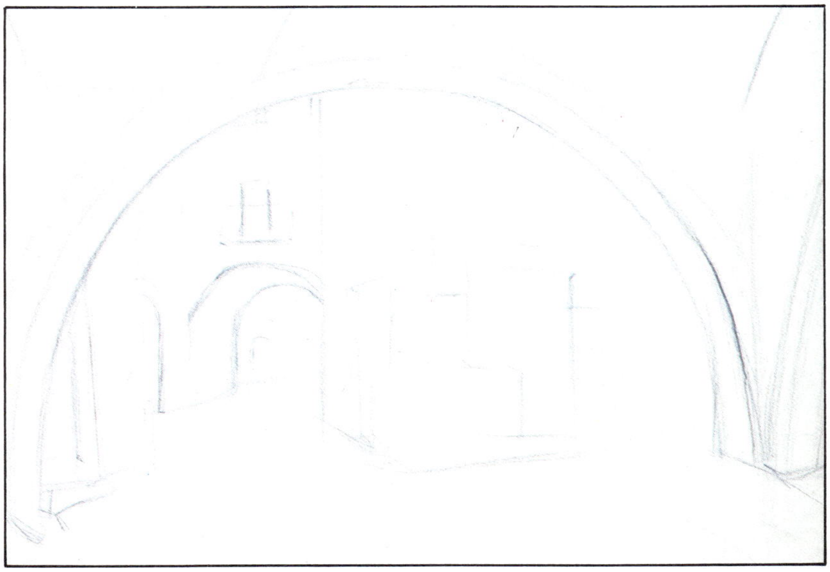

First stage: Preliminary sketch

If you think it might be useful, use the grid system to sketch out the subject on the paper you intend to use, which should be a good quality, smooth watercolor paper of about 9 × 12 in. (25 × 30 cm). It might be easier to make your initial sketch on a separate piece of paper and then trace it on to the good quality paper, to avoid too many erasure marks. The cleaner the paper you are going to work on, the better.

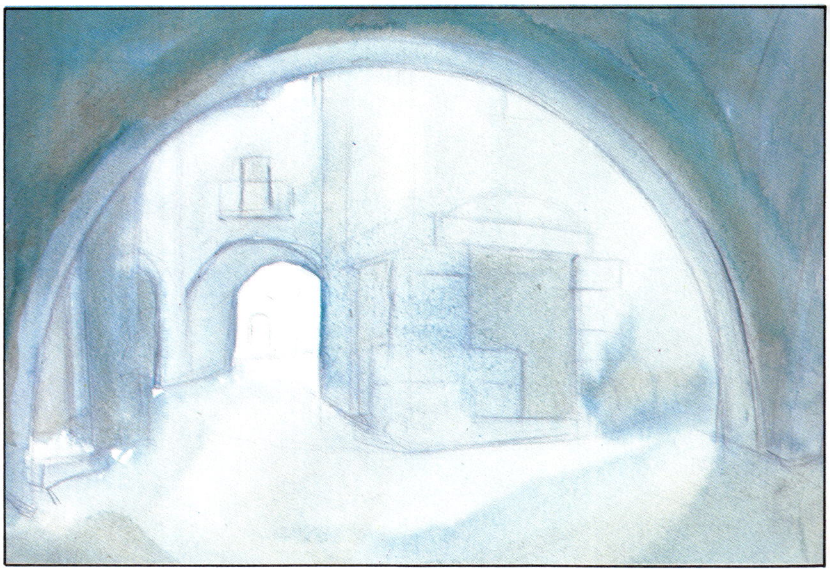

Second stage: Setting the tone

Using your paintbrush and clean water, wet the surface on which you are going to paint. Then cover this area with a general layer of pale background color, deciding as you go which are going to be the lightest areas of the picture.

Without waiting for this layer to dry, working "wet into wet," apply a new wash, this time strengthening the tone of the darkest areas of your subject.

On the right, you can see what your picture should look like at the end of this second stage.

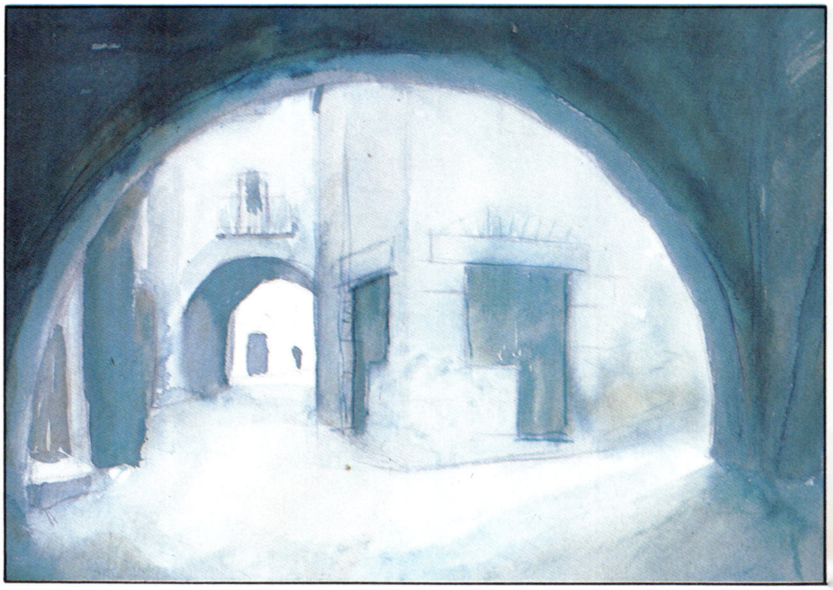

Third stage: Adjusting the tone

Keep sight of the overall picture. Don't get carried away in one small area and forget the rest of your subject. You should be moving all over your work, always having a clear vision of the general tones and contrasts.

Work on wet or dry areas according to whether your intention is to shade, to gradate, to emphasize or intensify tonal values. Remember the previous exercises—the cube, the book, the cylinder—and apply brushstrokes quickly, without lingering too long on one section, really working against the clock, as is the way with this method of painting.

You should end up with a result similar to the one on the right.

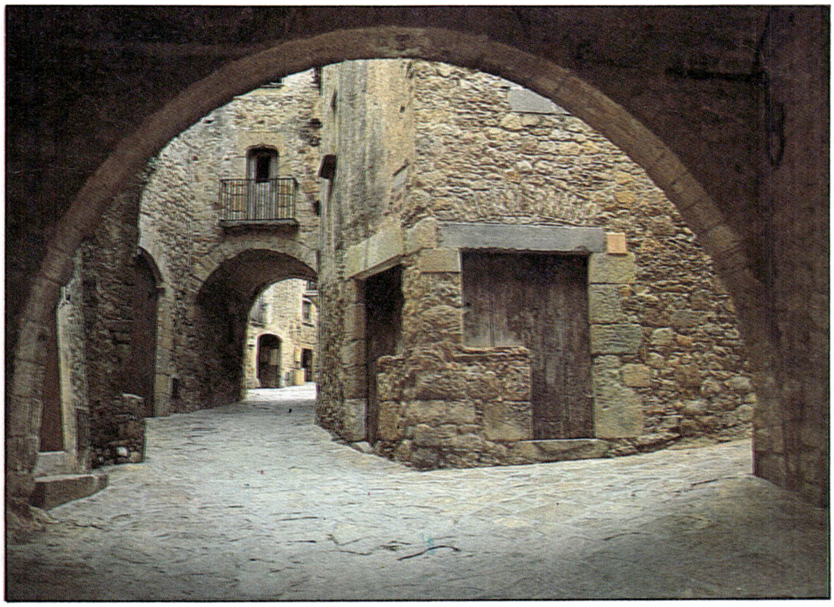

Fourth stage: Completing the picture

Refer often to the photograph. It is possible that you may have accidentally allowed some blue paint to run over what should be a white or pale-toned area. If this happens, try using a razor blade, scraping very gently to reveal the whiteness underneath. Make sure that the paint is dry before you do this and don't overindulge in last-minute emergency measures.

On the left is the photograph that inspired this exercise. A final word of advice: However good a photograph might be, there is nothing like working from nature if you can. But at the beginning, when the important thing is to become familiar with a technique, a good photograph is a perfectly acceptable alternative.

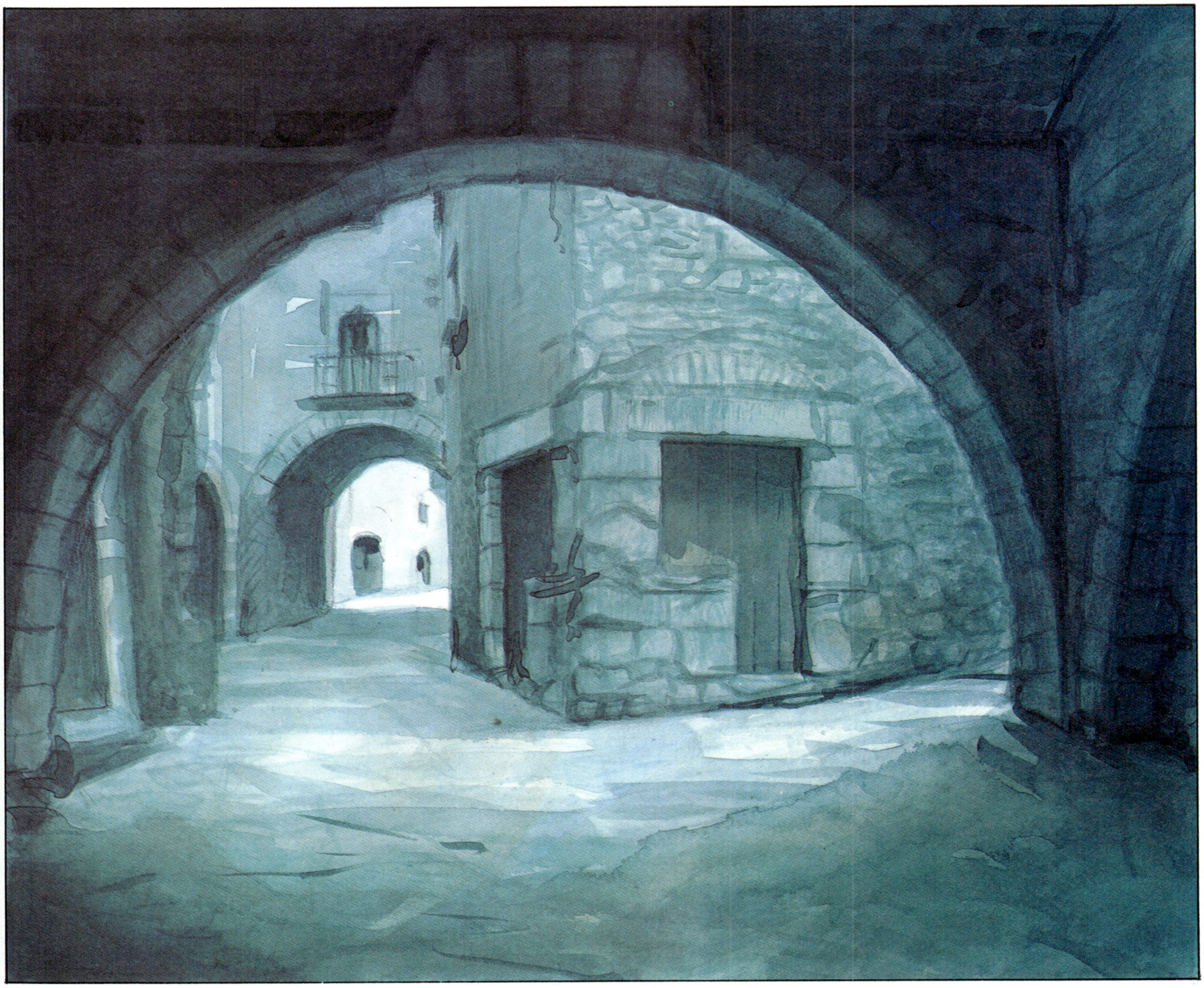

The ink wash

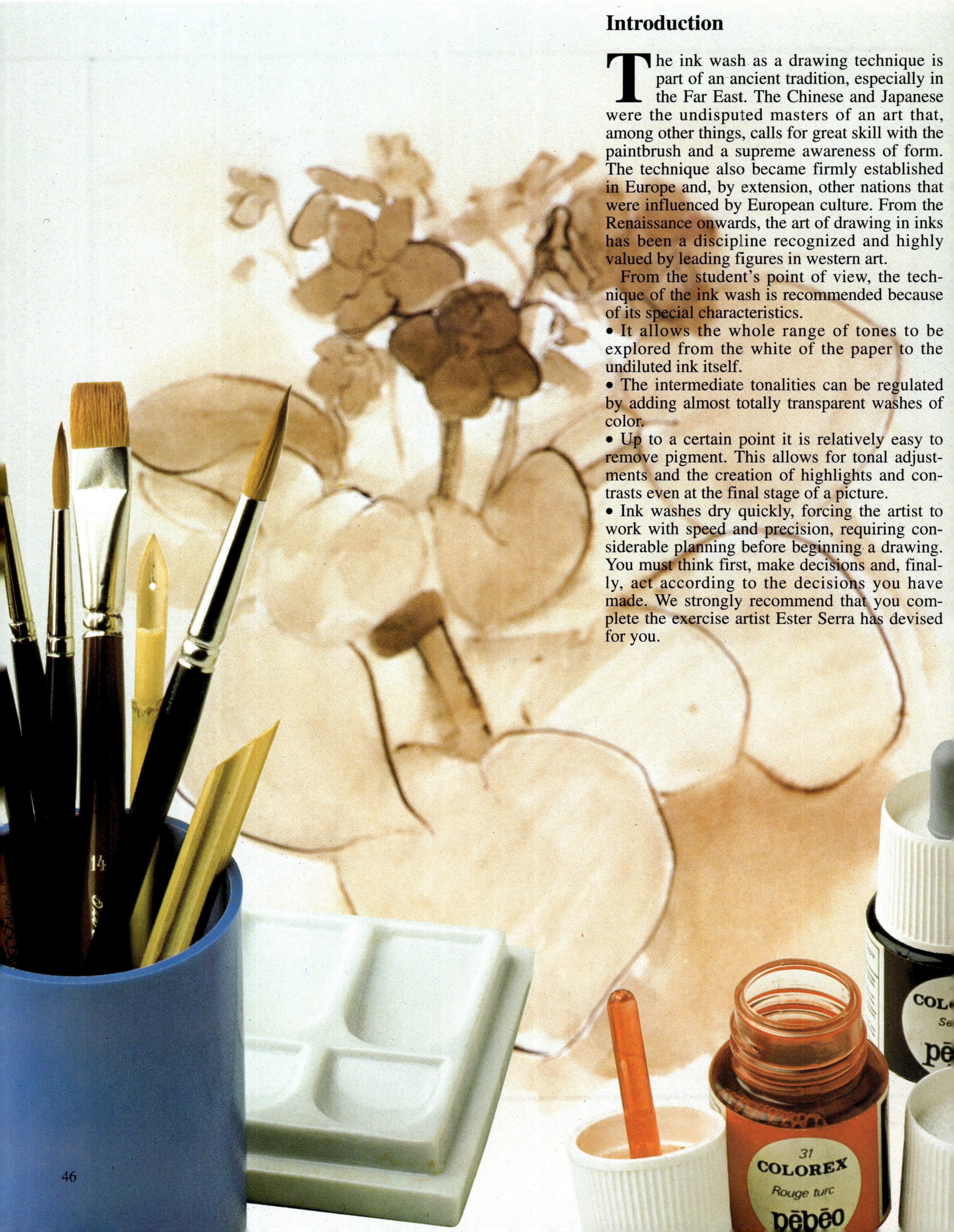

Introduction

The ink wash as a drawing technique is part of an ancient tradition, especially in the Far East. The Chinese and Japanese were the undisputed masters of an art that, among other things, calls for great skill with the paintbrush and a supreme awareness of form. The technique also became firmly established in Europe and, by extension, other nations that were influenced by European culture. From the Renaissance onwards, the art of drawing in inks has been a discipline recognized and highly valued by leading figures in western art.

From the student's point of view, the technique of the ink wash is recommended because of its special characteristics.

- It allows the whole range of tones to be explored from the white of the paper to the undiluted ink itself.
- The intermediate tonalities can be regulated by adding almost totally transparent washes of color.
- Up to a certain point it is relatively easy to remove pigment. This allows for tonal adjustments and the creation of highlights and contrasts even at the final stage of a picture.
- Ink washes dry quickly, forcing the artist to work with speed and precision, requiring considerable planning before beginning a drawing. You must think first, make decisions and, finally, act according to the decisions you have made. We strongly recommend that you complete the exercise artist Ester Serra has devised for you.

Three examples from masters of the medium

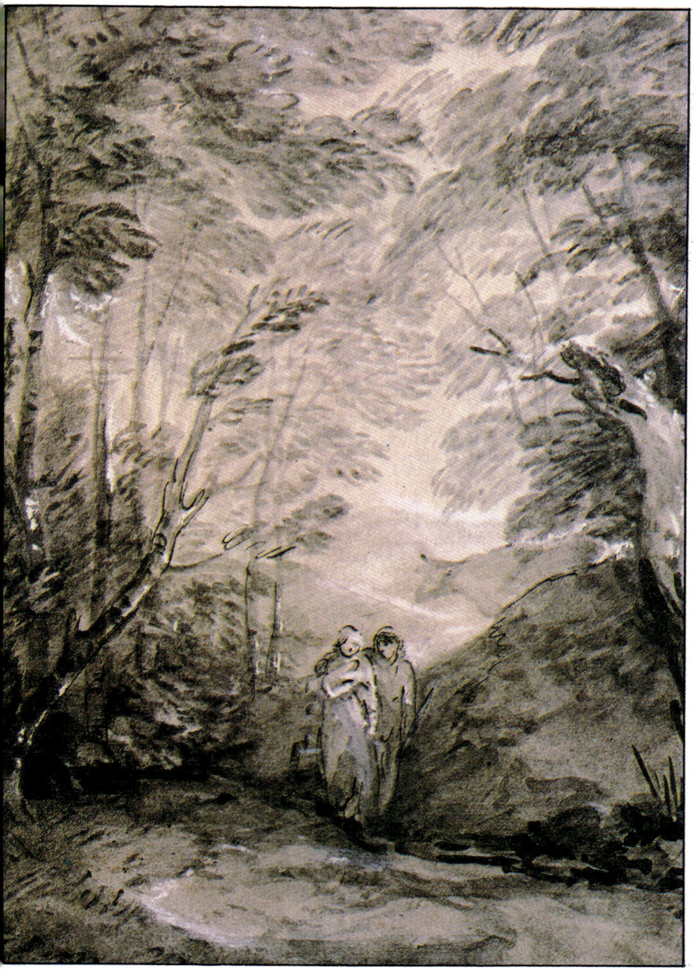

1

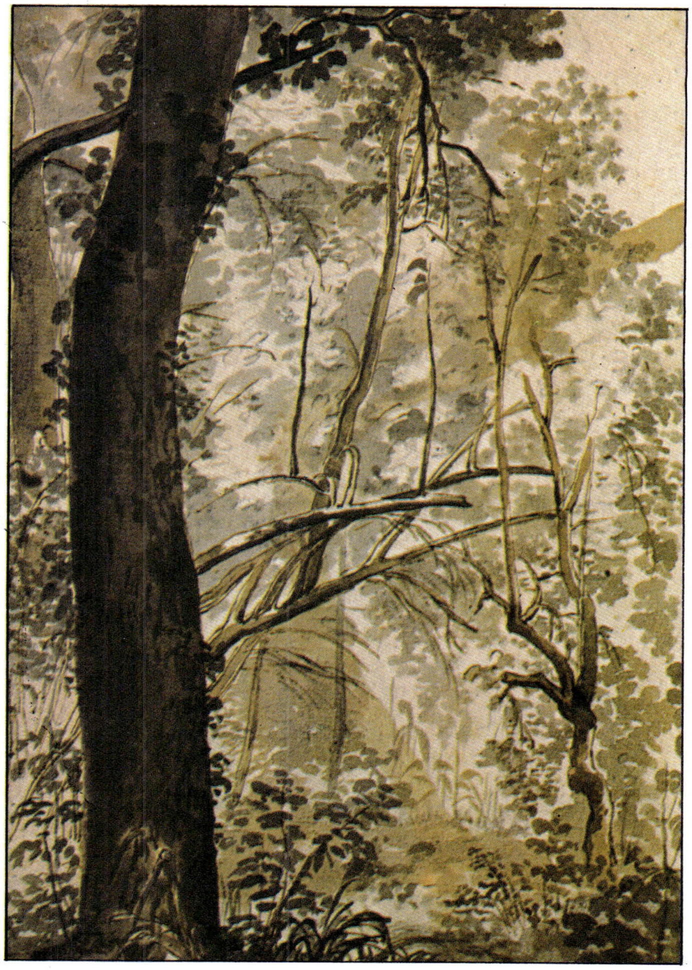

2

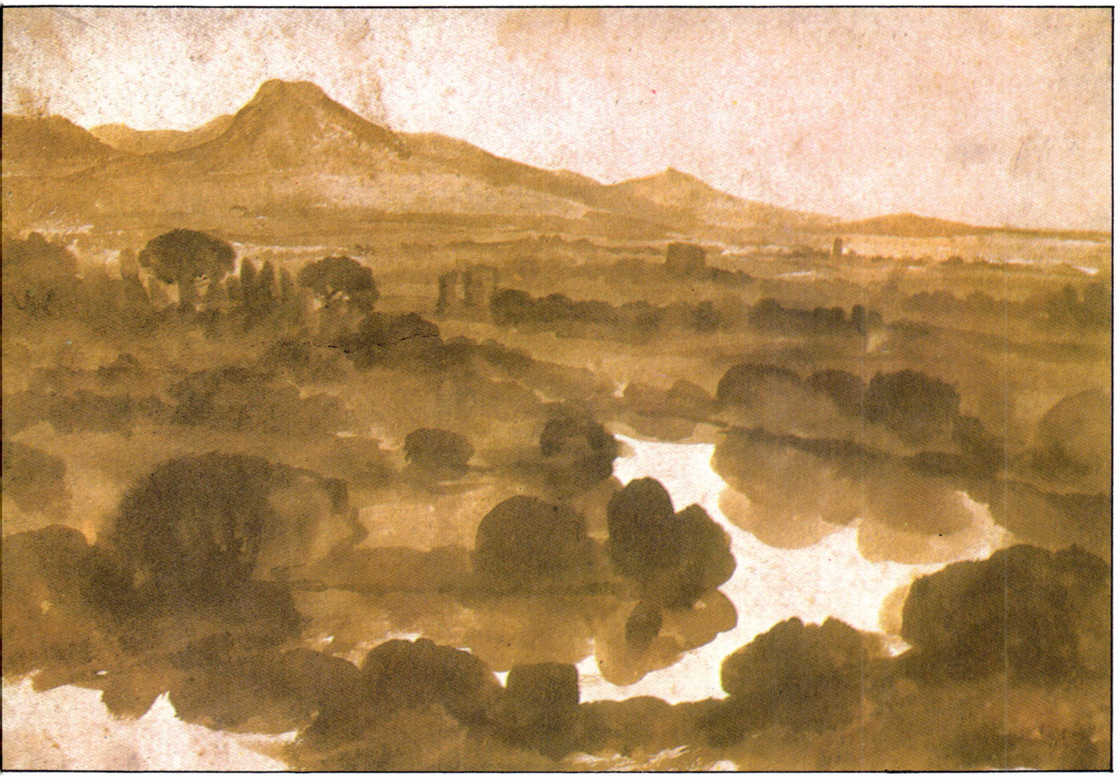

3

1. "Pair of lovers of a country road," by Thomas Gainsborough (1727–1788). A drawing in gray ink with white highlights and final touches using a pen with black ink. (Louvre Museum, Paris.)

2. "Woodland scene," by Nicolas Poussin (1594–1665). An ink drawing in two colors of extraordinary transparency. (Albertina Museum, Vienna.)

3. "View of the Tiber from Monte Mario, Rome," by Claude Lorrain (1600–1680). A sketch with ink wash in which all the essential characteristics of the medium have been put to use. (British Museum, London.)

A wash with sepia ink

Introducing the subject

Ester Serra, seated in front of her easel, is about to demonstrate for you her method of creating an ink wash drawing. She is going to use as her subject the humble potted plant to her right, from which she will derive the shape of the leaves and flowers, although she is not going to copy the object in its entirety. Ester will work exclusively with sepia-colored ink, which is less intense than black ink, and which, in the artist's opinion, is better suited to a floral theme where there are no great contrasts.

Any make of ink is fine, as long as it is water-soluble; there is a vast range on the market. As for paper, a robust, smooth cartridge or glossy surface is best suited to this medium.

Other necessary equipment: A good round, soft-haired paintbrush (preferably sable), No. 10 or 12, a metal nib, and a suitable holder to go with it, and a few drops of bleach.

You will also need a snippet of the same type of paper you will use for your drawing to keep permanently alongside the original. You can try out the tonal intensity of the paint in your brush on this before applying it to the drawing you are working on. The idea is to establish the tone of paint you are about to apply while you still have time to correct it. On this bit of paper you can also make little experiments as Ester Serra has done in the two details illustrated below.

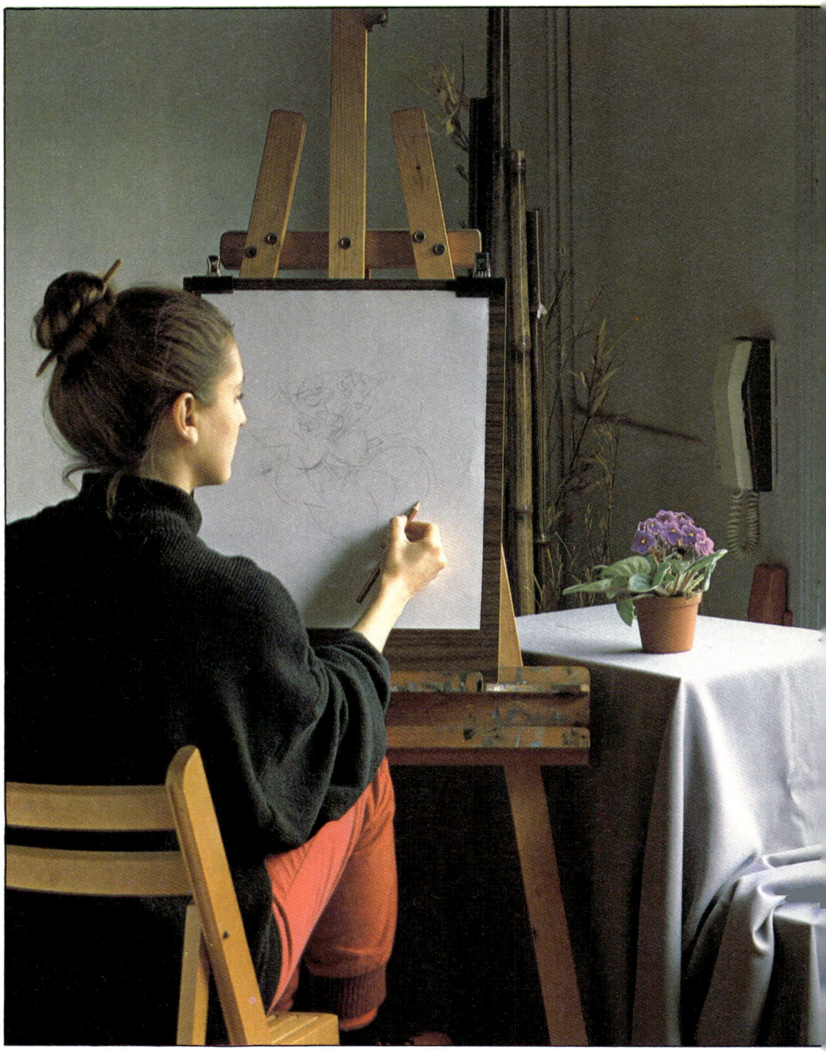

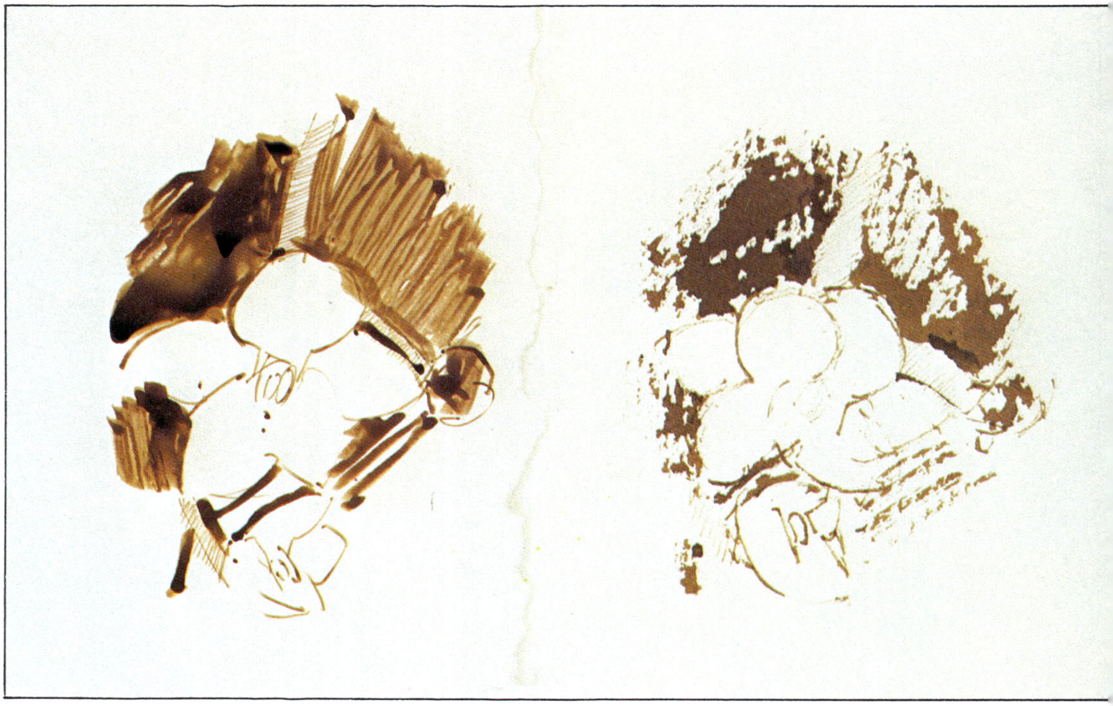

Right.
"Trial runs" that our guest artist carried out before beginning her drawing. In these experimental sketches she tried effects she could achieve by scraping still damp blots of ink with the end of her brush, or by applying the paint with a piece of very rough watercolor paper. Remember that an ink wash does not have to be applied with a brush. Depending on the result desired, diluted ink may be applied in many different ways: using shreds of paper, sponges, rags, fingers, and so on.

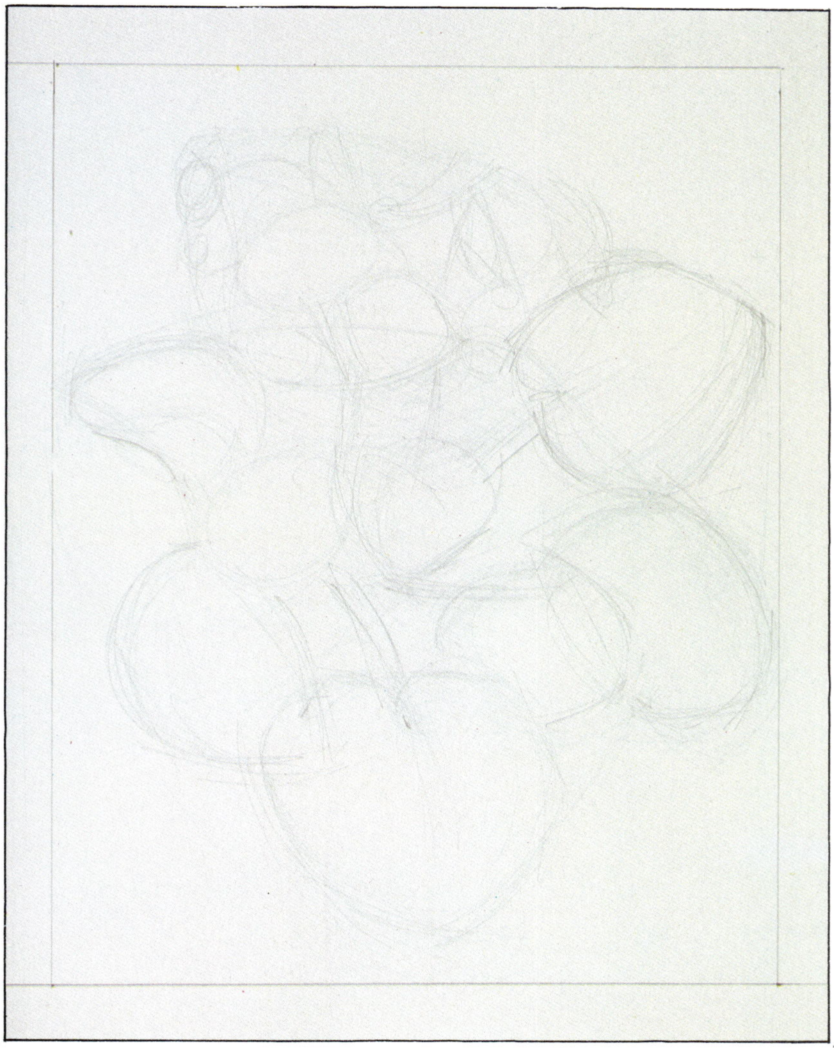

Step 1: Outline drawing and first decisions

In spite of her earlier experiments, Ester Serra decided to adopt traditional methods; that is, to apply the ink with a paintbrush, over a basic layout drawn with very faint pencil strokes.

Notice that, as mentioned before, the subject was used exclusively as a reference for the shape of the elements to be included in the composition. Actually, the composition devised by the artist has very little to do with the real appearance of the flowers and leaves.

Begin to make an outline sketch of your flowers and leaves (with an extremely light touch, using an HB pencil), trying to create a predominantly symmetrical composition that leaves a minimum of gaps on your paper.

Now, prepare four or five washes of varying depths of tone: Very pale, pale, medium, and dark, but none as dark as the undiluted ink. You can do this in the wells of a watercolor palette or on individual little plates, such as white china saucers, for instance. Start trying out, on a small piece of paper, the tonal values you can create with your four wash mixtures. If a tone looks too dark, dab the brush on the corner of the test paper so that it loses some of its paint. Try again after this operation and you might have the tone you want. You can also dab the brush on some absorbent paper and then dip it in clean water. However you do it, the objective in each case is to reach the tone of sepia you need.

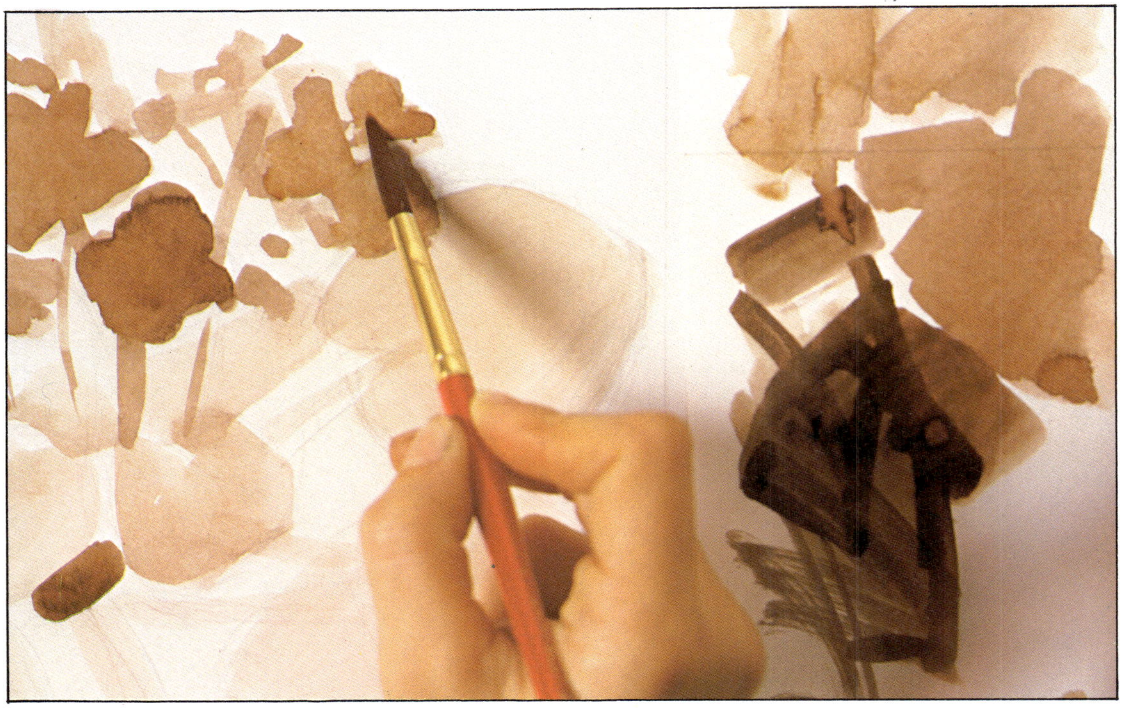

Left.
A fragment of the piece of paper that Ester Serra used for testing before beginning her work. Notice (toward the right) a series of random brush-strokes, made simply to test the tone of the wash. More toward the left is a preparatory study, made on top of an outline sketch, to try out the different washes and to see how superimposition of two or three of them would appear. This process of becoming familiar with the medium, before getting into the drawing itself, is essential. With ink washes it is very difficult to work backwards.

Step 2: The first strokes

Once you have established the strength of the washes, the moment has arrived to start work on the drawing itself. As with any transparent medium, the correct procedure is to start with the palest tones.

The artist began by going over her layout sketch with a general base tone, using the palest wash of all those she had prepared. Notice that the heavily laden paintbrush has been used quickly to try and achieve uniformity of tone. It is worth remembering, though, that total uniformity of tone is hard to achieve (and the larger the surface area to be covered, the harder it becomes). This is not something you really need to worry about; the number of occasions when tonal uniformity will be of any importance will probably be very limited.

With a halftone wash, Ester has covered the surfaces relating to the flowers at the center of the composition. She has done this on top of the first, dry (or nearly dry) wash, so no excessive dampness will dilute the edges of brushstrokes intended not only to create a tonal value, but also to define form. In the two close-up photographs at the bottom of this page, you can see that tonal irregularity is often caused by the number of times the brush has passed over the paper: Once in the lightest parts, twice in the areas of medium tone, and three times in the darkest places.

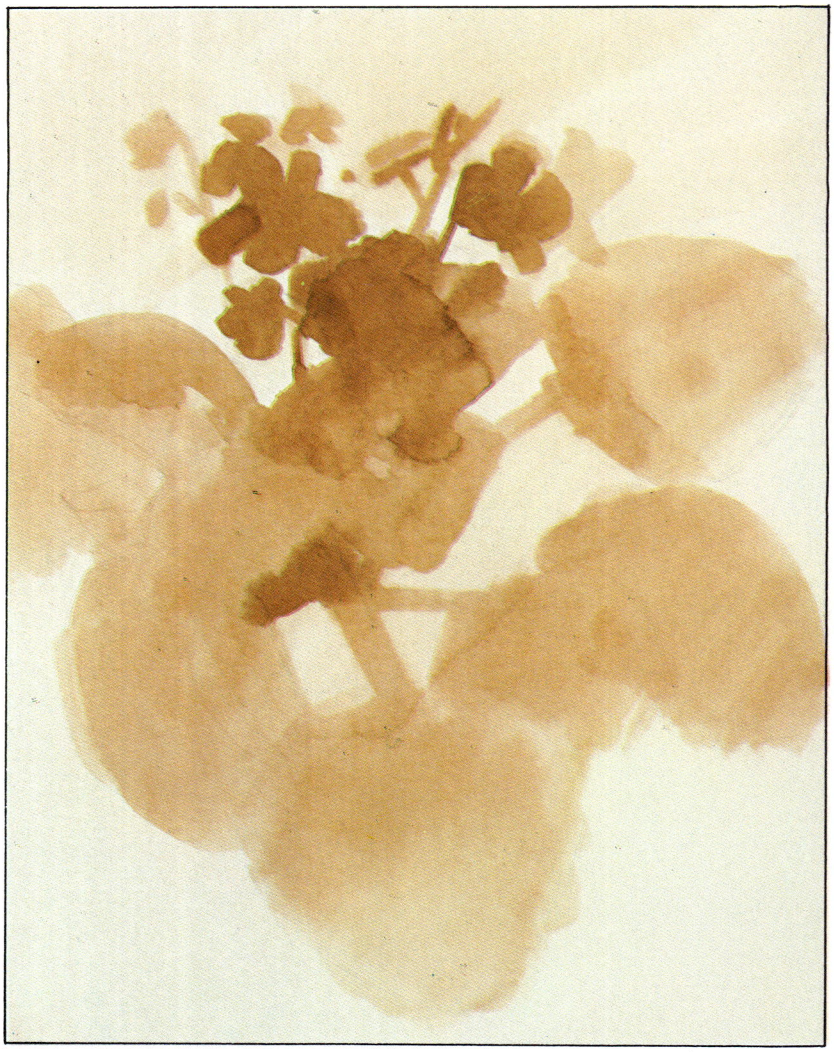

Right.
Close-ups in which the role of the brushstroke, loaded with halftone wash, can be appreciated. Rather than by using a different wash, it is by means of several successive layers of brushstrokes that the nuances of tone have been created in this part of the drawing.

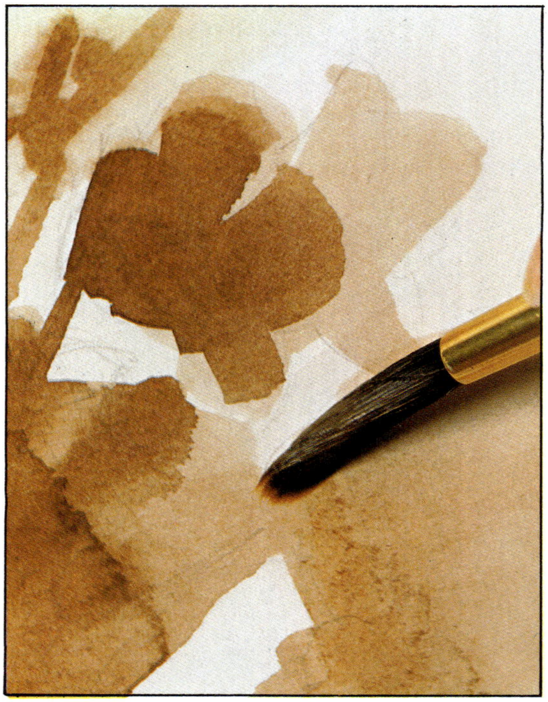

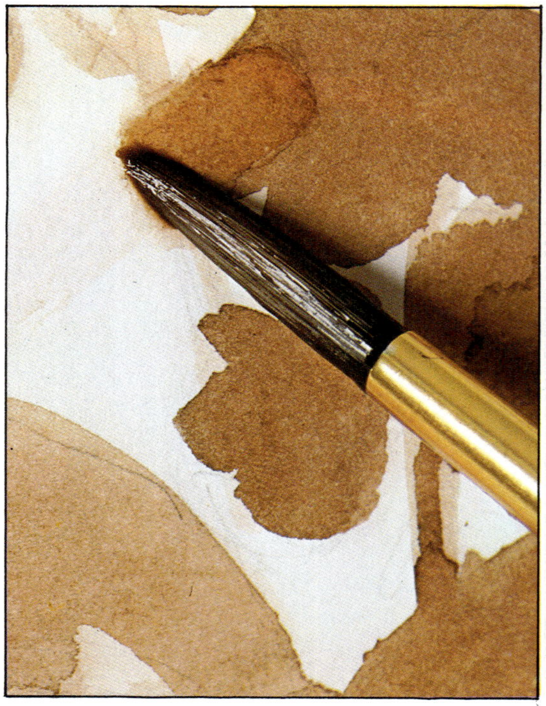

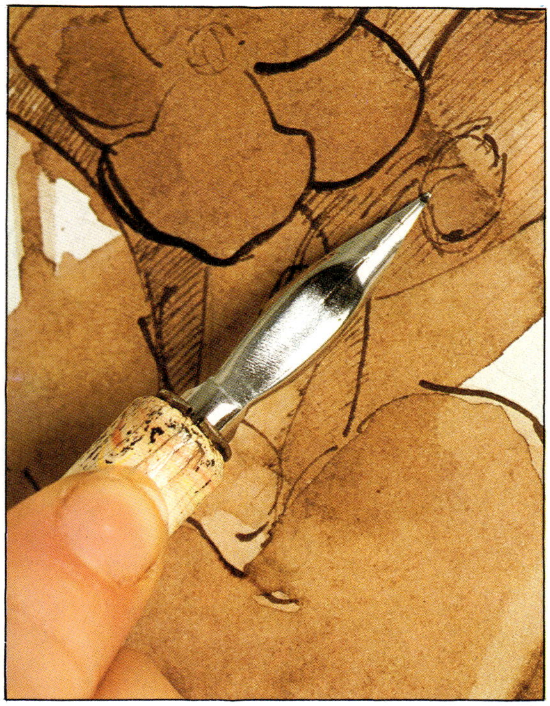
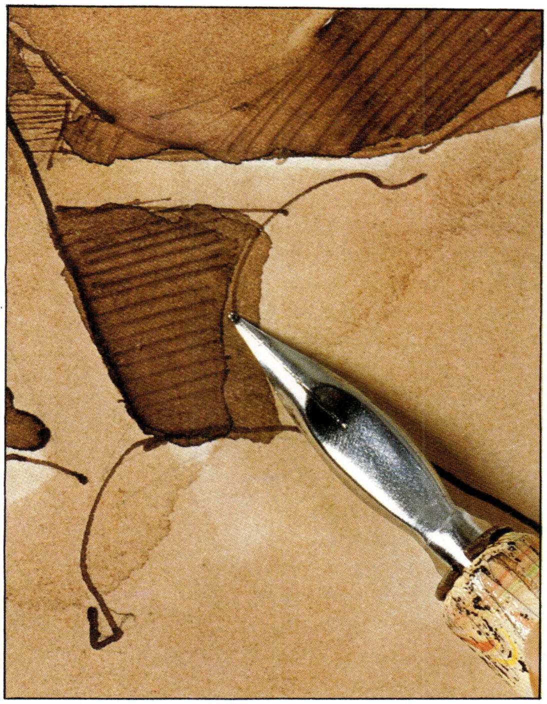

Left.
Close-ups in which you can see how the pen has been used in two different areas of the drawing. In Ester Serra's hand, the loose pen lines make a striking impact in a way not expected of a tool normally used to convey small details.

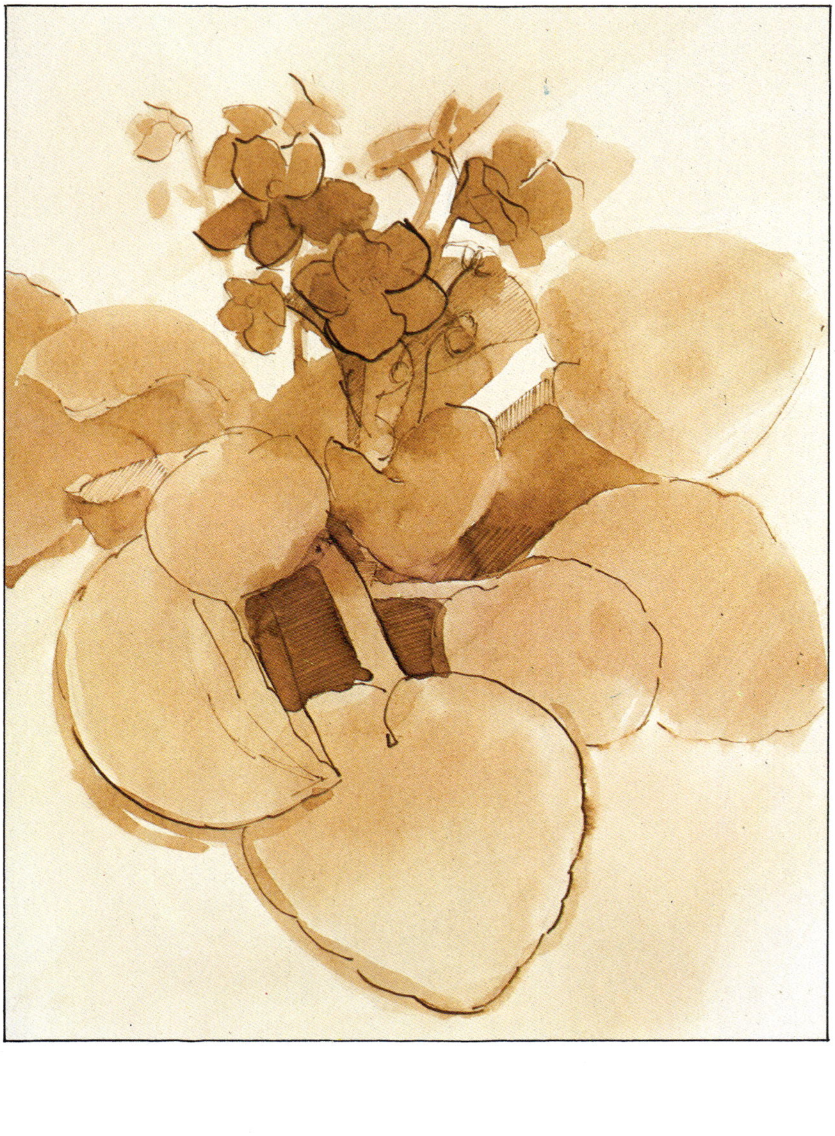

Step 3: An important decision. Introducing the pen

Ester Serra began to wonder whether an ink drawing carried out using just a paintbrush could bring enough interest to a theme as simple as the one she had chosen for her demonstration. Her fear was justified by the rather bland softness beginning to emanate from her drawing.

So the artist, to ensure that she was not about to produce something rather insipid, made an important decision: Her composition would be completed with pen lines and hatching.

With a fairly thick-nibbed pen she started to define the outlines of the subject, so that the tonal variations took on new meaning. Notice that from this moment we know where each tonal element belongs, where it starts, and where it ends.

In addition, at this point the lack of depth of the composition begins to disappear, thanks to the dark hatched areas that fill the central spaces. These make the larger areas of the drawing stand out and project forward. It is important to realize that Ester Serra is not making the slightest attempt to use the pen as an instrument of detail. Her lines are not neat and tidy and carefully considered; they are "linear vibrations" (if you will pardon this rather imprecise expression) that bring spontaneity and vigor to a subject that, without these marks of genius, would be lacking in interest.

Step 4: Tonal evaluation

After completing step three, the drawing is ready for the tonal evaluation and the additional penstrokes that will turn it into a completed work of art. The three close-ups illustrated on this page represent the work this involves. The first picture shows, more or less, the upper right-hand corner of the composition with part of the much darker and more clearly defined central group of flowers (dark washes have been applied as have penstrokes around the edges). The pen has been used to draw lines across the leaf on the far right and a pair of uneven washes have lent it a certain depth. One of the flowers in the group on the top right is being outlined with the pen, but not using ink, to obtain a "negative" line. Take note!

The second close-up shows the central area of the drawing that seems, if compared with the previous stage, much more labored. By means of successive washes, each leaf has taken on a tonal value. But that's not all! Washes of ink, irregularly applied, have brought out the contrasts, so these leaves are no longer just flat areas but undulating surfaces. Look at the leaf on the far right: The pen lines have indicated its depth and made it interesting as a drawing in a way it was not before. In this photograph you can spot other little details: In the top left-hand corner is a series of negative strokes produced with the dry pen when the paper was still damp. Between the two little stems, the brush is opening up an area of white. Because we have already said that it is hard to take color away, you might be wondering how Ester achieves such a successful result.

Take a small coffee cup or similar-sized receptacle, and mix in it a solution of one part water to one part bleach. This solution, when applied with a clean paintbrush, will quite efficiently take color away from washes that have turned out too dark. For proof of this, look at the third photo on this page and, for that matter, the finished work on the next page as well. You can see the different effects created using bleach: The discoloration of many areas of the drawing and the mottled effect that appears around the outline at the bottom of the picture and in the dark, central area between the leaves. If you apply little drops of diluted bleach with the brush on a wash that is still damp, you will produce the irregular spread of color seen in the areas we have mentioned.

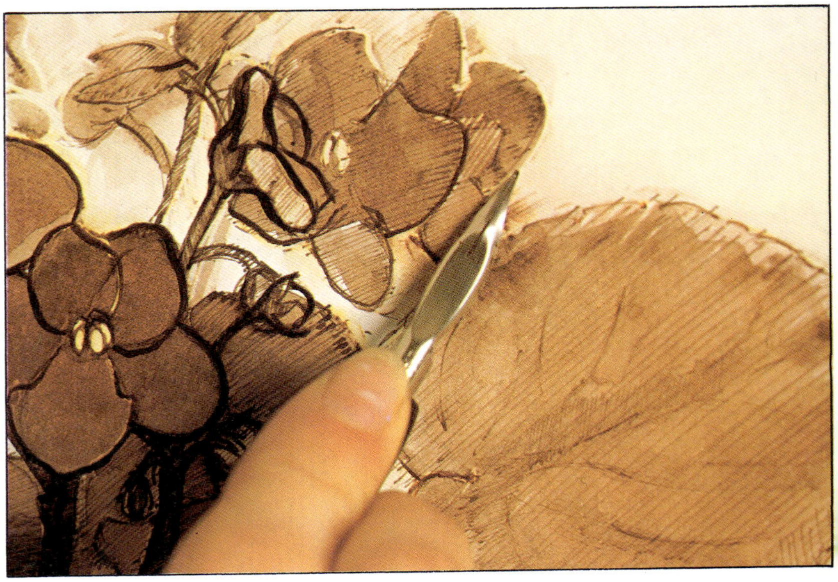

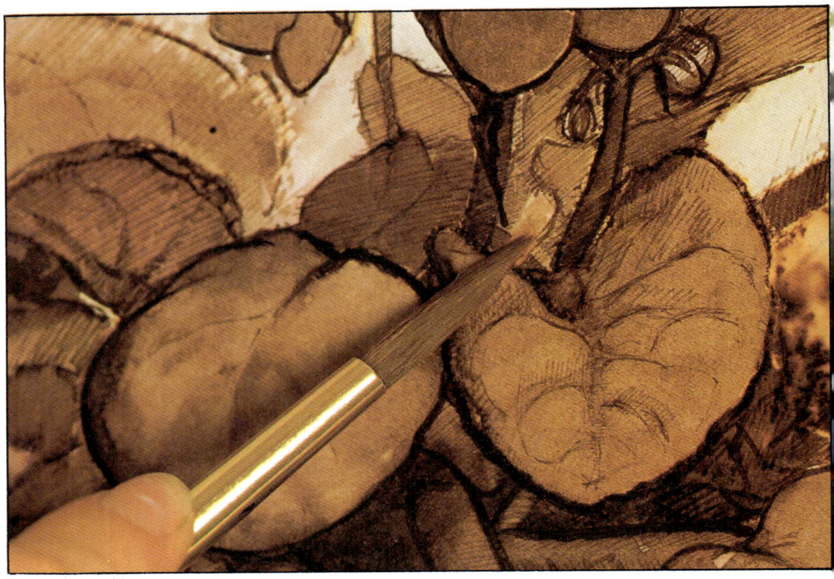

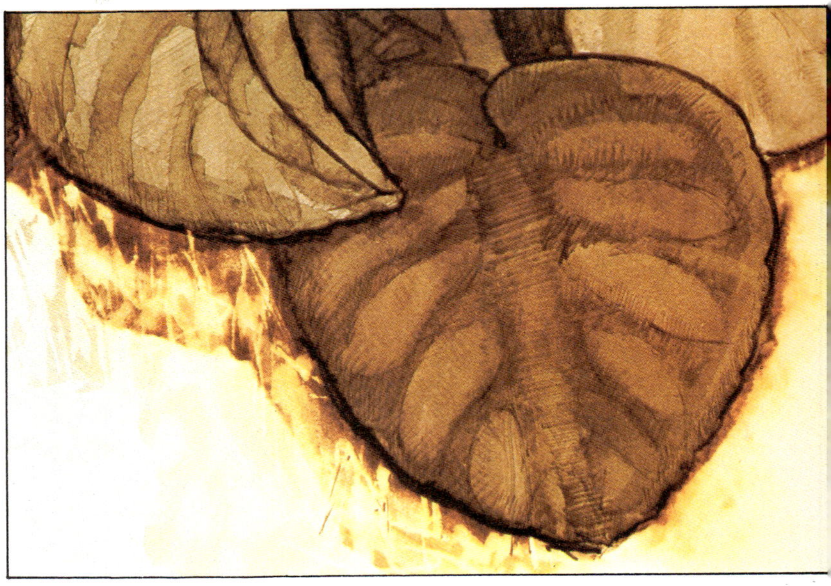

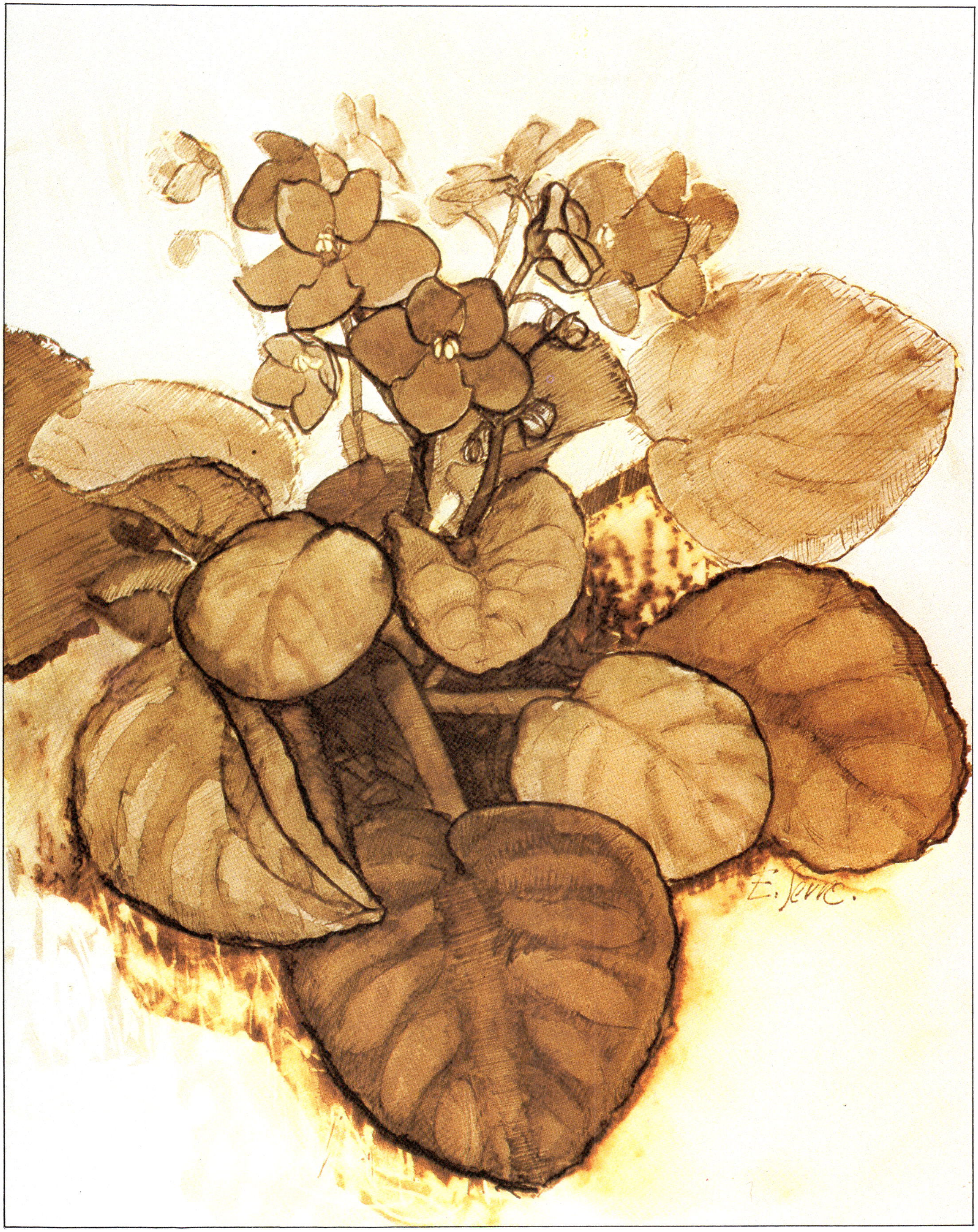

The watercolor wash

In the last year of his life alone, Van Gogh painted about 850 pictures and made more than 1,000 sketches and pencil studies. Van Gogh, like many great painters, was a tireless worker. Like Van Gogh, you or anyone else who decides to enter the world of painting pictures will have to accept this simple fact: Hard work, and the constant search for progress and professionalism are unavoidable. With watercolors, the effort is even greater. Beginning to paint, as with any intellectual activity, always represents an effort we try to postpone with excuses of every kind. Knowing how to use watercolors is not something that can be learned in half a dozen lessons. It takes technique, skill, a great deal of patience, and an infinite number of sketches and preliminary studies—many to be discarded because they were not successful. With any type of wash, if the goal is not achieved first time around, there is no possibility of going back and redoing what has already been done. But we mustn't give up when we've barely started! We took the first step a little while ago, with the preliminary monochrome exercises in wash technique. Now we are going to look at the two-tone watercolor wash, as a threshold to the unrestricted glories of watercolor. And before long, when you discover for yourself through a watercolor painted by your own hand, all the spontaneity, freshness, delicacy, and character of this almost magical medium, you will see that this initial effort was more than justified.

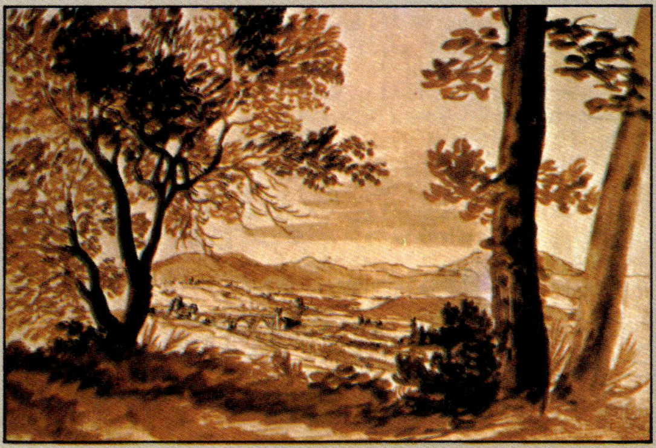

Left.
"The Moller Bridge near Rome" by Nicolas Poussin. (Albertina Museum, Vienna.)

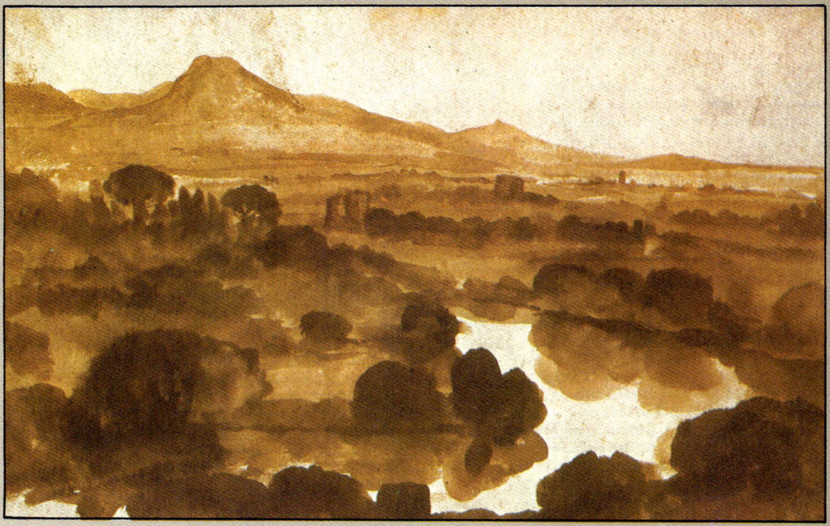

Below.
"Landscape with a river; view of the Tiber from Monte Mario, Rome," by Claude Lorrain. (British Museum, London.) Two classic examples of painting with wash.

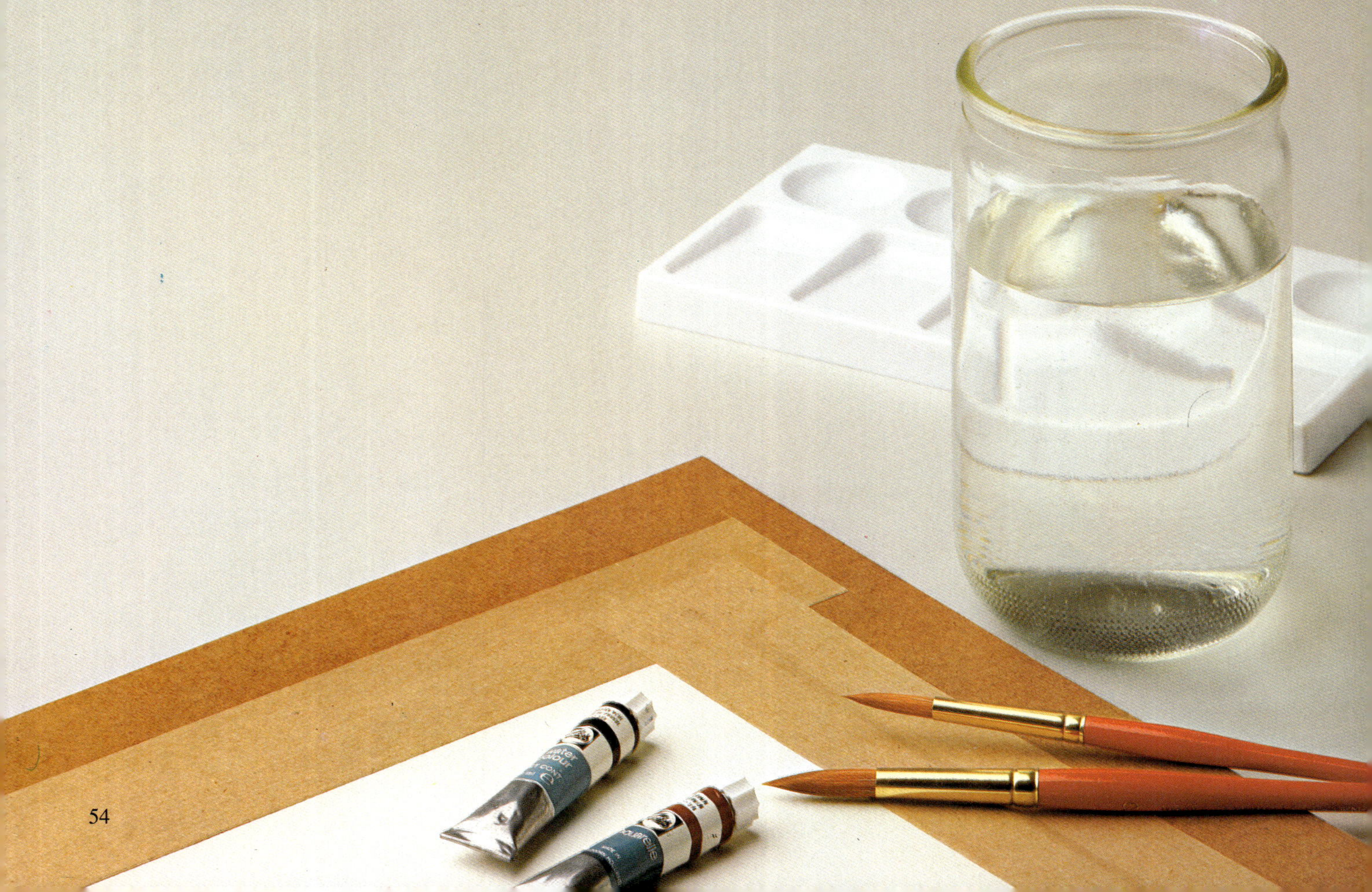

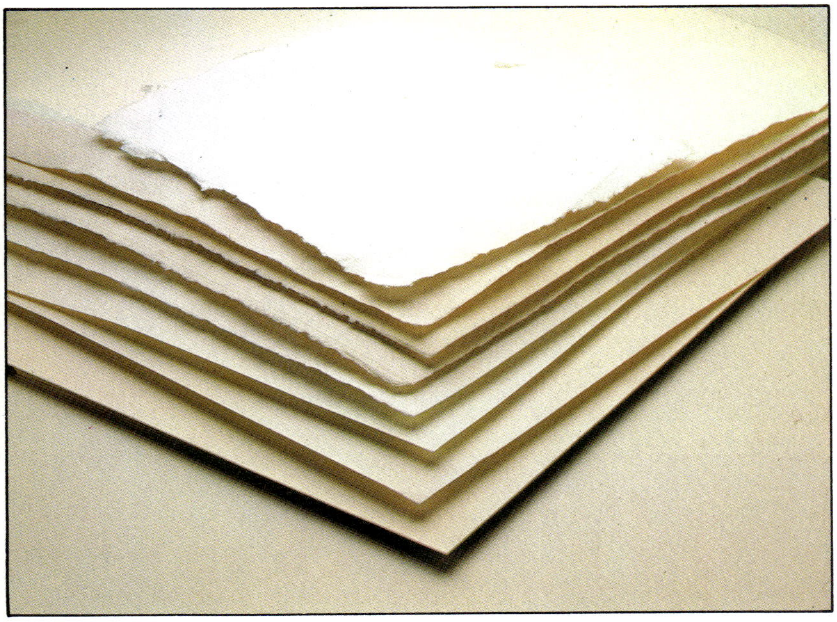

Paper

One of the elements that most influences the quality of a watercolor is the paper. There are various qualities of paper available on the market, ranging from student quality to high quality, handmade papers. Within the superior or professional quality range, there are three main types of paper:

- **Hot-pressed (fairly smooth) paper**
- **Cold-pressed (semi-rough) paper**
- **Rough (heavily grained or "toothed") paper**

These papers are easily recognized by their watermarks, which will be visible if you hold them up to the light. They come as loose sheets in a variety of different sizes.

All good-quality papers have a front and back. The front generally has a better finish and has been sized. For sketches and preparatory studies, a medium-quality paper with a medium "tooth" will do fine.

Watercolors

Watercolors of professional quality come in small pastilles of dry pigment, in pans of semi-moist paint, or in tubes or bottles of liquid watercolor.

Above, left.
When you go to buy watercolor paper, remember that you will find loose sheets, sheets on backing board, and pads of paper. The highest-quality papers often have characteristic uneven edges to show that they have been made by hand. The pads are very practical for sketches and quick color notes.

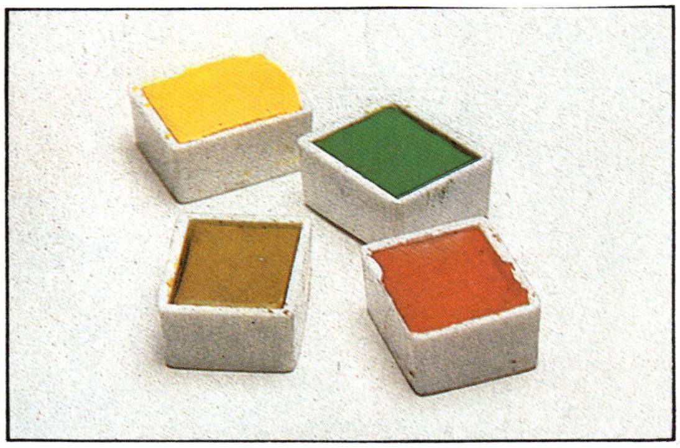

Pans of semi-moist watercolors, professional quality. The colors dissolve easily and give excellent results. They are sold singly and in little boxes (which double as palettes) containing 6, 12, 14, or 24 colors.

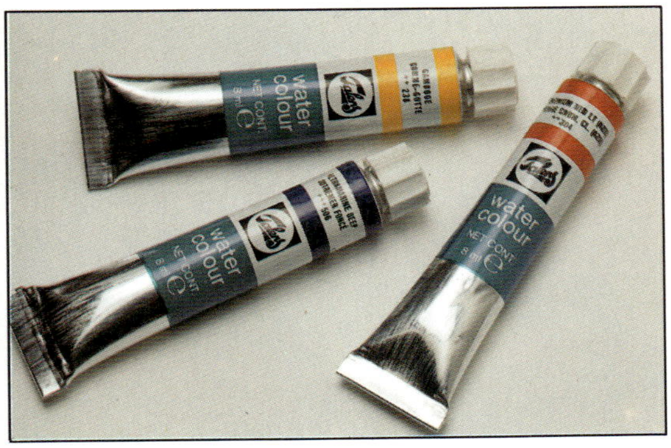

Professional quality watercolors in tube form; this paint has a similar consistency to that of oil paint, with the advantage that it dissolves immediately in water. These tubes may be bought in sizes of 2 to 5½ oz. (8, 21 ml).

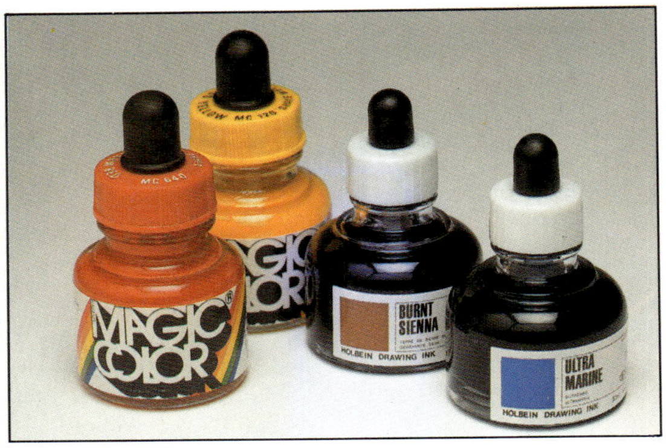

Bottles of professional quality liquid watercolor. These are widely used in the field of illustration. Similar to dyes, very concentrated, they are sold singly and in sets of 12 or 16 bottles.

PRINCIPAL MANUFACTURERS OF WATERCOLOR PAPERS

Arches	France
Canson	France
Fabriano	Italy
Grumbacher	United States
Guarro	Spain
RWS	United States
Schoeller	Germany
Whatman	United Kingdom
Winsor & Newton	United Kingdom

Two-tone study

A two-tone watercolor study is the subject of our next practical exercise. Our subject will be a cylinder, a cube, and a sphere, arranged as a still life on an attractive piece of drapery. And, we repeat, we are only going to use two colors. These two colors will actually become four: The Prussian blue and the carmine we intend to use, when mixed, become black (see the illustration on the right) and, if you add to the equation the white of the paper, you can see that we have four colors with which to work.

In fact, as shown in the illustration at the bottom of this page, the variety of tones obtained by mixing these two basic colors—Prussian blue and carmine—is extensive, so it would be fair to say that we are not going to be hampered by color limitations.

These are the materials we have used in carrying out this exercise:

- The colors Prussian blue and carmine.
- 10 oz. hot-pressed paper.
- Lead pencil No. 2.
- A soft eraser.
- Sable brushes, Nos. 8 and 12.
- Two water holders.

But before starting on the practical side of the exercise, let's study a few of the unavoidable preliminaries.

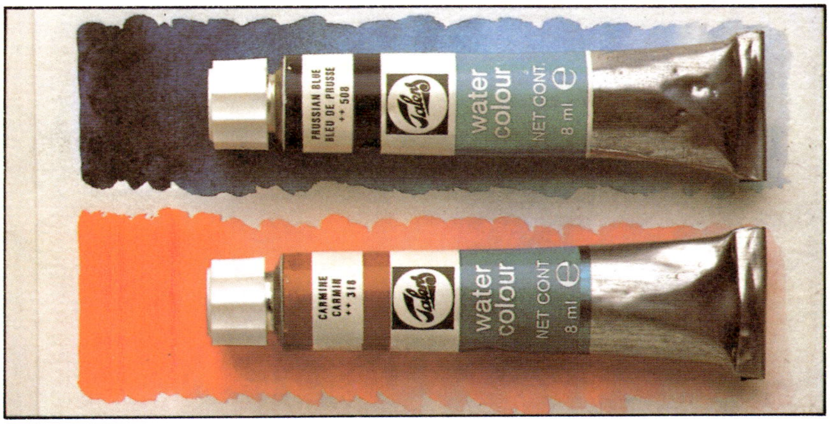

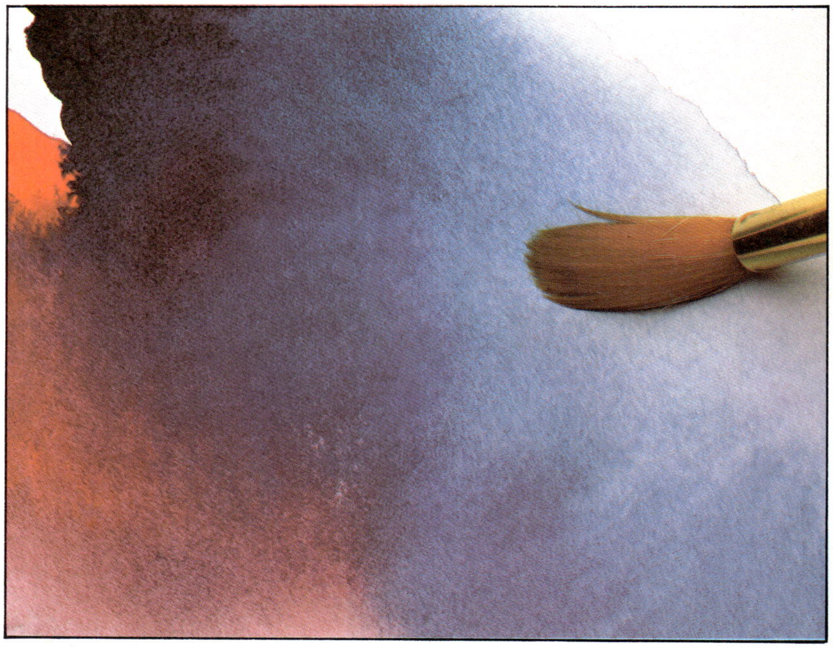

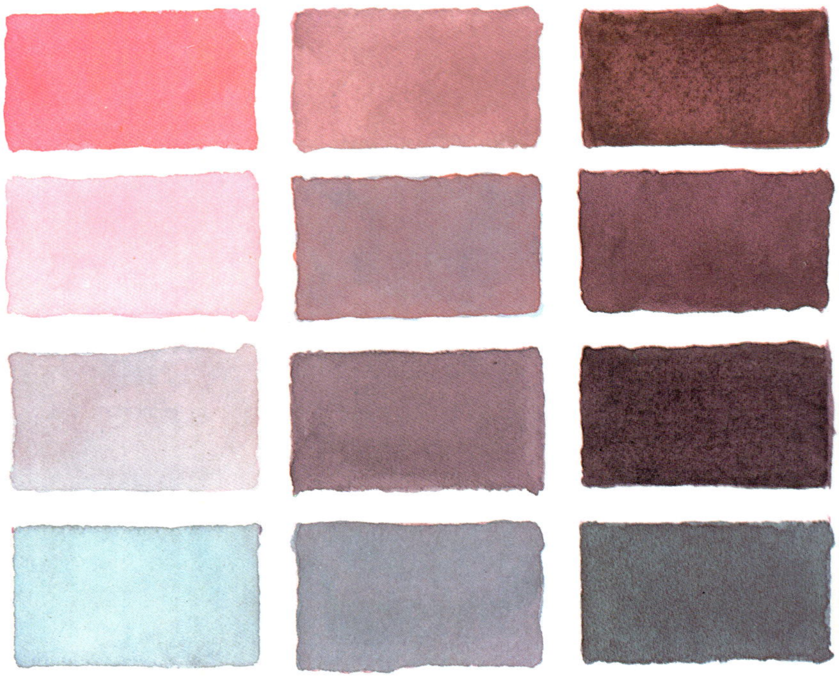

***Above,** the two colors we are going to use: Prussian blue and carmine. In the middle picture you can see that by mixing the two colors you make black. **Below,** the range of possible colors if you mix the two in question.*

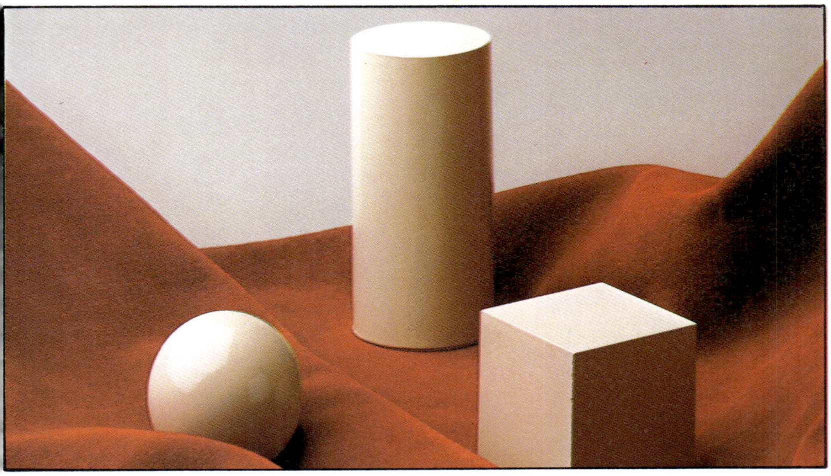

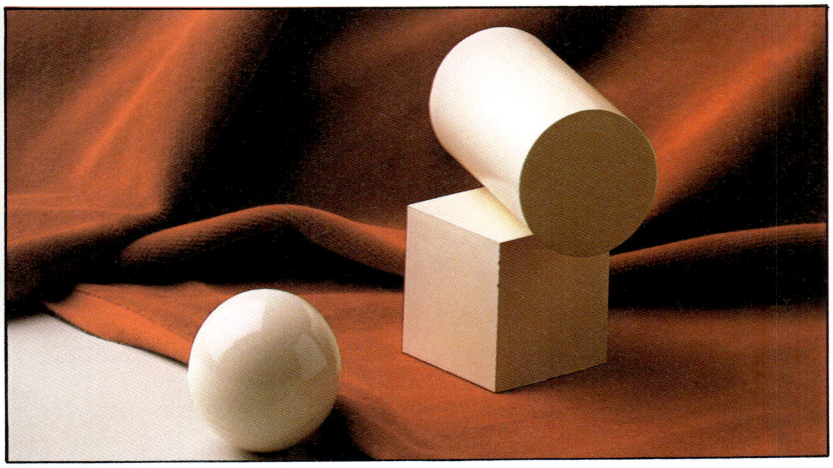

Besides the arrangement we have chosen, and that you can see at the bottom of this page, the variety of possible compositions is as unlimited as the imagination of the painter. On the left we have shown you two possible alternatives, as valid as the one you are going to begin shortly.

It is worth repeating that it is best to work from nature, studying directly the idiosyncracies of the subject. With this in mind, we are offering you the opportunity to construct these geometric shapes for yourself (the following page) and, therefore, to adapt the arrangement of these elements to suit your own preferred composition.

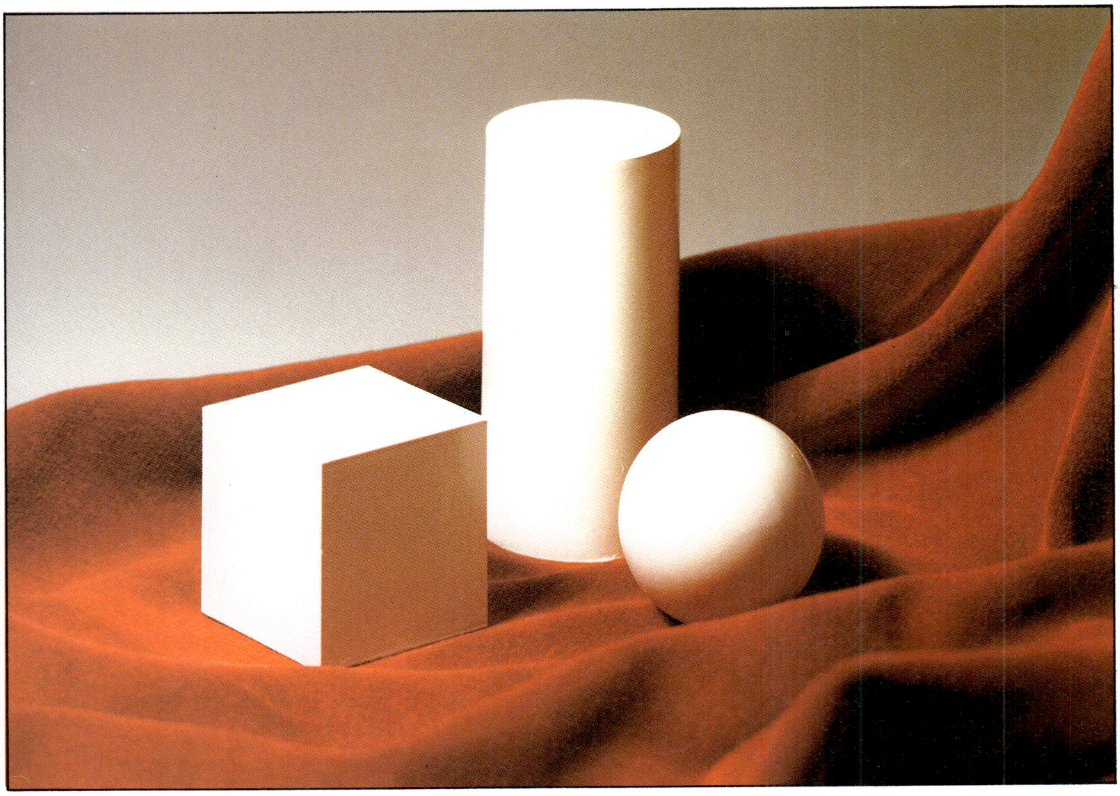

Here is the subject we are going to work on. Assess the balance of volume and the number of objects that make up the subject, the direction of the light, and the composition, trying to avoid excessive space between the objects as well as a feeling of ordinariness.

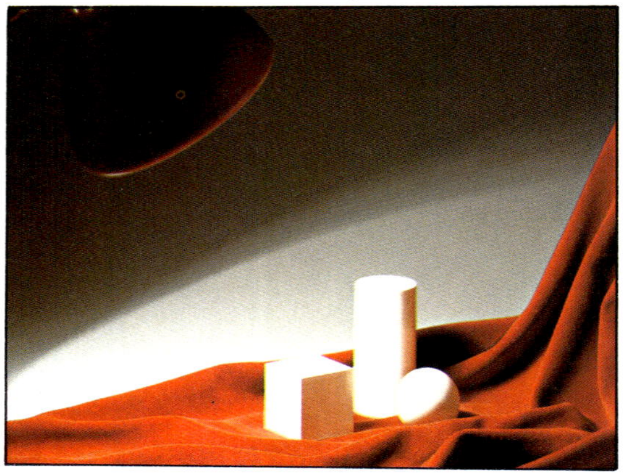

Above. *Essential to a good composition are the direction of the light (from the side in this case) and the position of the subject. As you can see, for the purpose of the exercise on the following pages, the light was provided by a table lamp.*

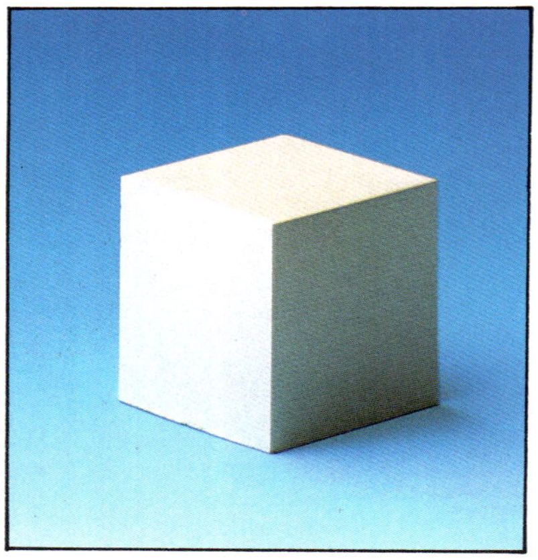

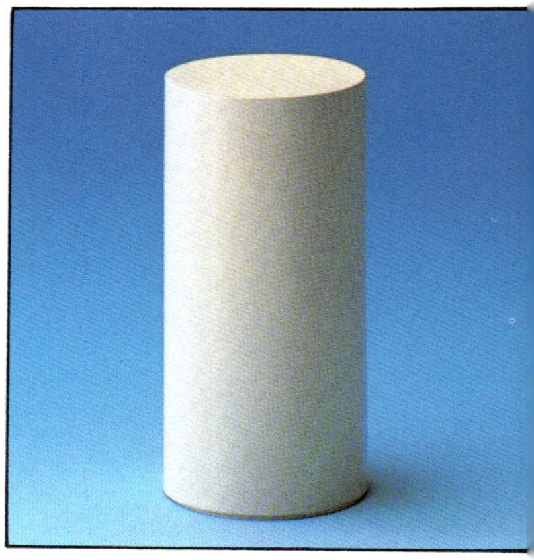

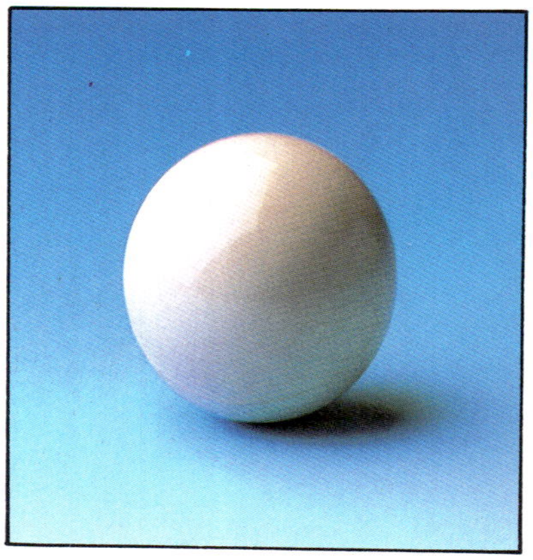

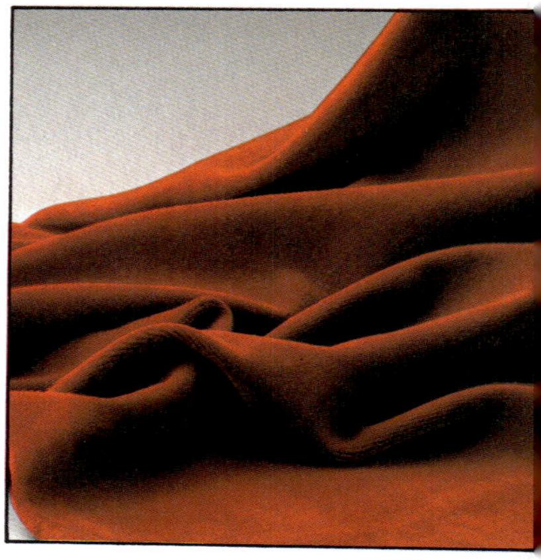

Right. *A cube, a cylinder, a sphere, and the necessary background drapery, form the basic elements of the subject. The sphere could be replaced by a tennis or ping-pong ball.*

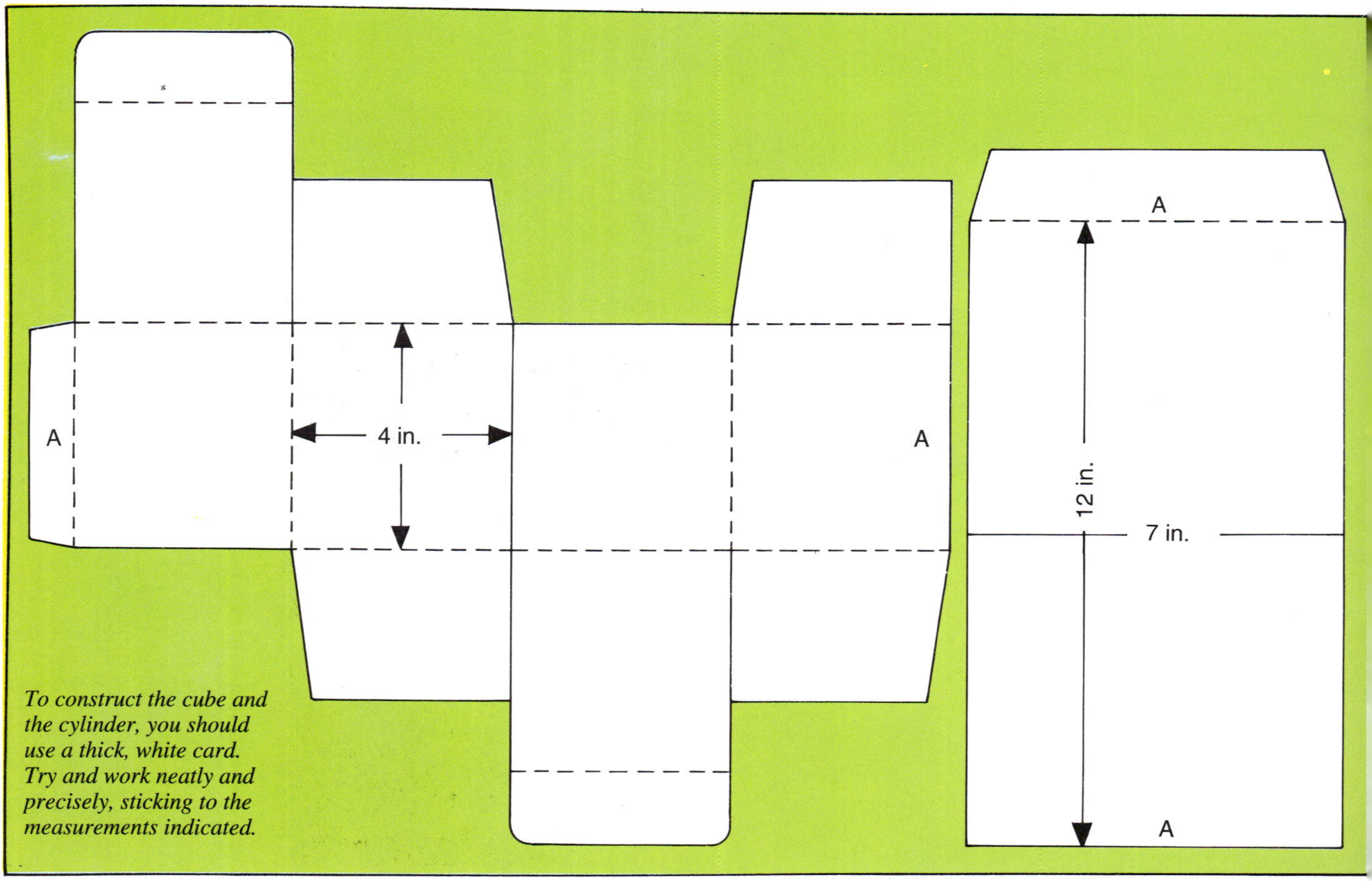

To construct the cube and the cylinder, you should use a thick, white card. Try and work neatly and precisely, sticking to the measurements indicated.

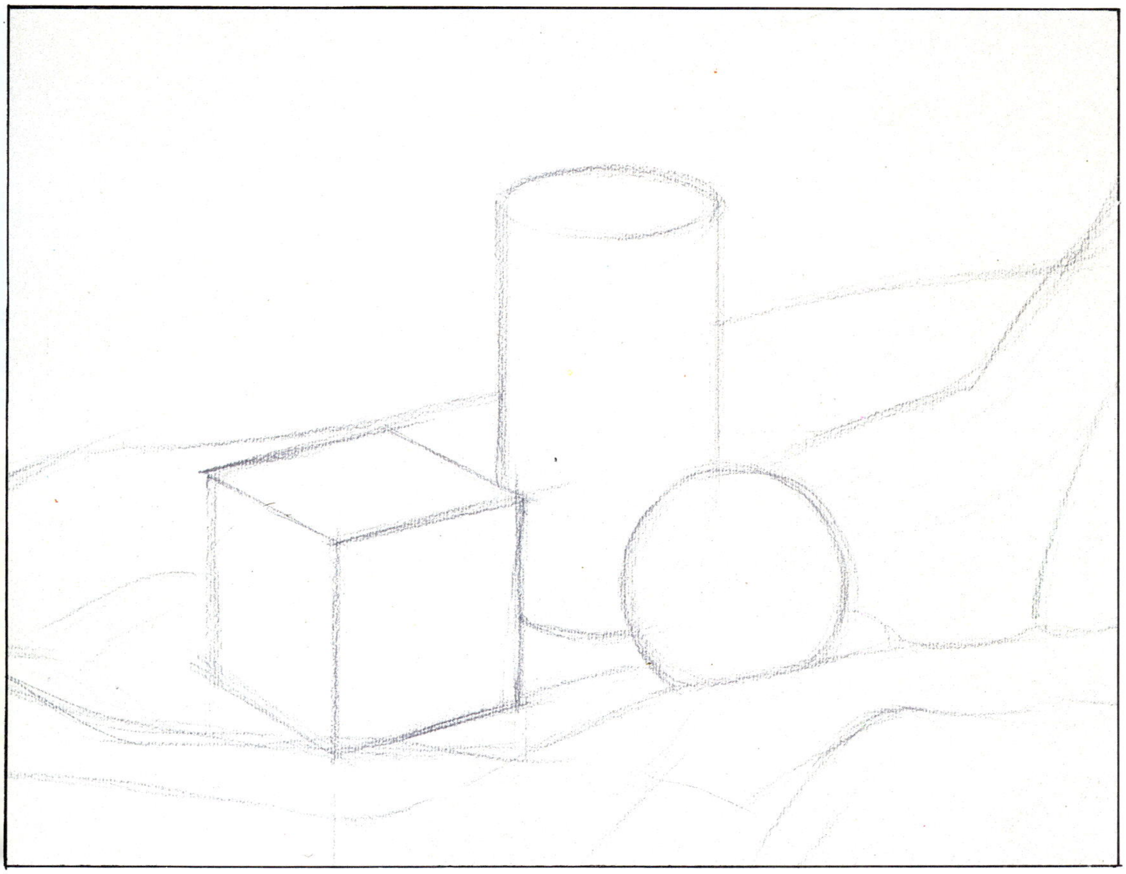

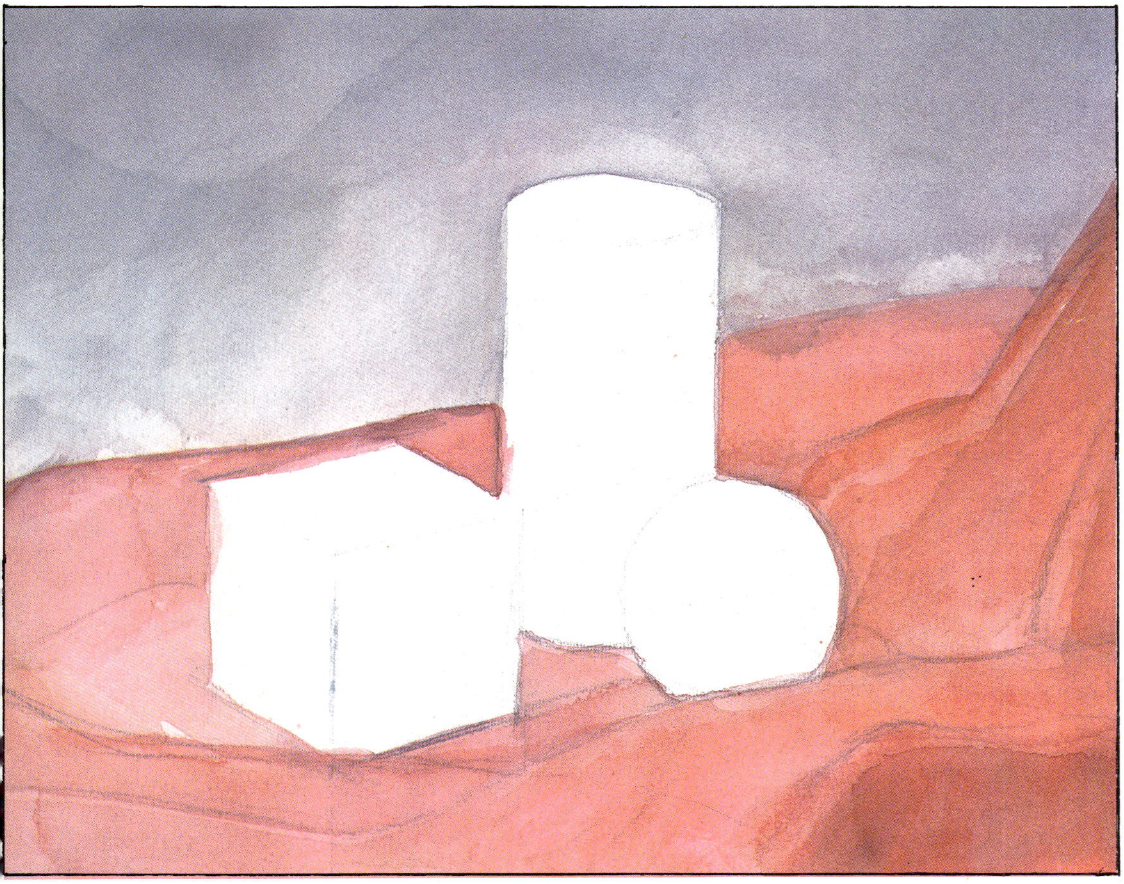

Construction of figures for the exercise

Using a fairly thick, white card, draw the plans illustrated on the previous page and, with a knife, cut out the shapes, following the measurements as accurately as possible. It is not a difficult job and it will allow you to create your own subject and to work from it directly.

First stage: Initial layout

Draw the subject without any shadow, as a simple line drawing, so that later there will not be any problems with proportion and perspective. Pay particular attention to the cylinder, the dimensions of which will serve as a guide for the other elements.

Second stage: General background

Dampen the surface of the paper and, when it has dried, dampen it again with the brush, avoiding the cube, the cylinder, and the sphere. Try not to go inside the outline of the geometric shapes, because otherwise the background color might filter in later on, making subsequent stages of the work more difficult. Without waiting for this layer to dry, paint in the general background with a wash of carmine and blue, using a little more carmine so that the color is warmer.

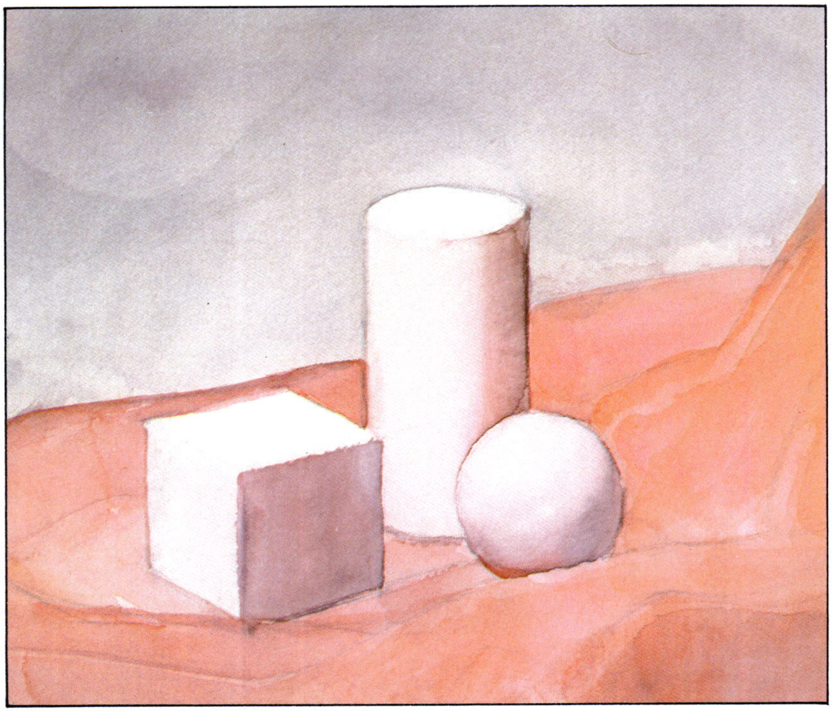

We have already mentioned one way of opening up white areas in a watercolor. However, it is more useful to determine these areas in advance, especially with small highlights. There are many ways of whiting out areas ranging from the application of masking fluid, which is removed when the picture is finished, to using sandpaper, synthetic brushes, a scalpel, bleach, the handle of the brush, or even a fingernail. We will go into some of these later on.

Third stage: Adding tone to the figures

Lay a light wash over the shape of the cylinder and then the cube and the sphere, leaving out the areas to be shaded. Then apply a darker wash to the areas in shade. If you tilt your drawing board, the excess color will accumulate at the bottom of the paper; take some of it up with your brush and then use it to gradate the shaded areas. We will turn later to the shadows cast by the objects across the folds of the drapery.

Fourth stage: Completing the picture

Concentrate now on the drapery, laying deep shadow in the folds of the cloth, generally darkening its color, opening up whites on the figures where you want to show highlights. Enrich the overall color of the painting, making subtle alterations of tone, adding a little more blue to the shade on the figures and the drapery. Sometimes it helps to apply just a few lines with a ballpoint pen to emphasize some of the sharper outlines. You will become familiar with little tricks, like protecting the white areas with masking fluid during the sketching stage.

So that's all there is to the two-tone technique. Practice whenever you can because in the next exercise we are moving on to painting with no color limitations whatsoever.

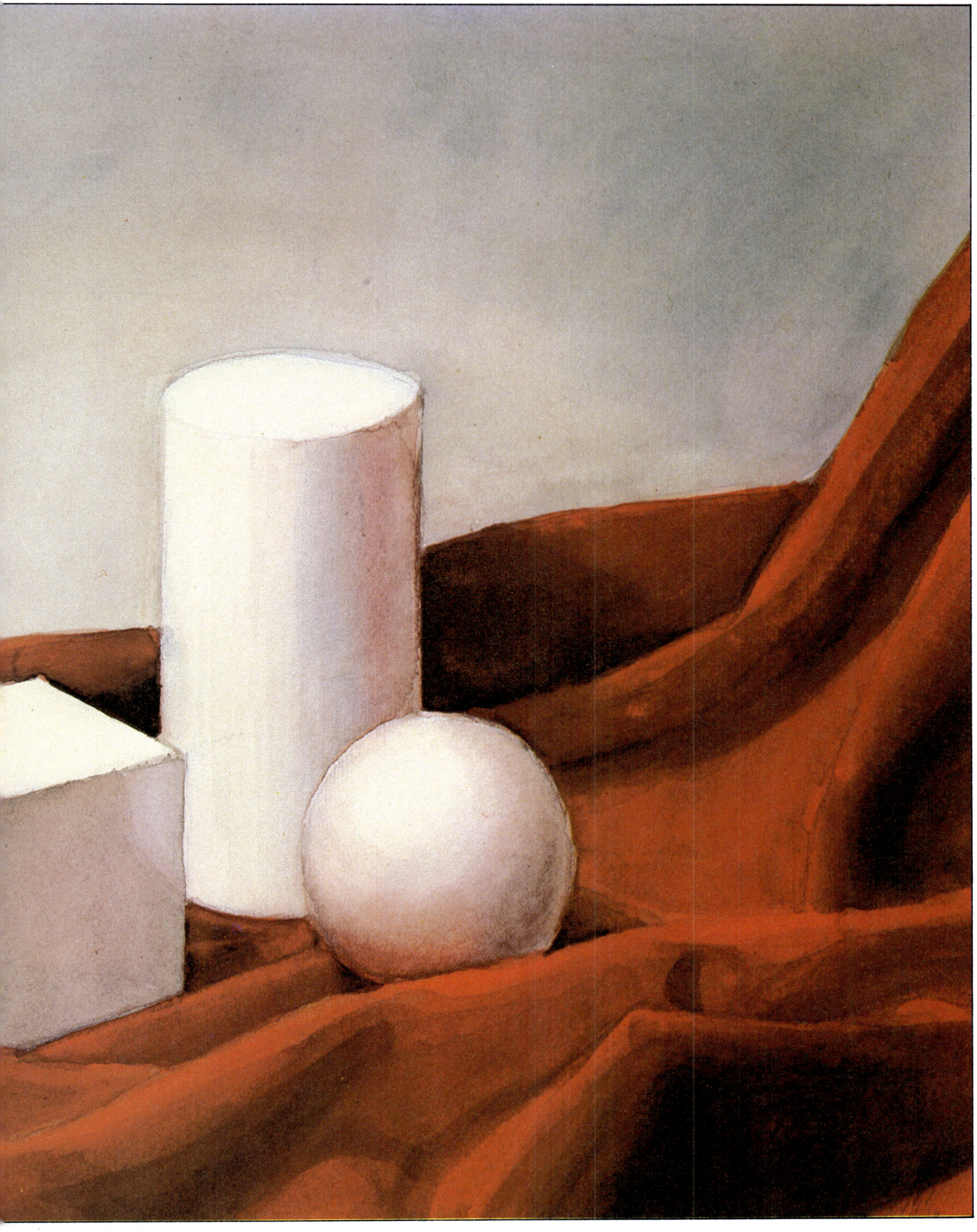

Watercolor painting

It was more than 3,500 years ago that man started to write and illustrate books, never imagining that he was building the foundations of the art of watercolor painting.

The Egyptians took the first step when they discovered a plant called *cyperus papirus*—the famous papyrus—the bark of which became paper used for illustrating and writing about history, science, religion, and magic. These elementary volumes were buried with their authors, so these eminent people could show what they had achieved in this world when they reached judgment day in the next.

The colors used to paint these books were transparent, made with earth pigments for the ochres and siennas, minerals such as cinnabar for red, burnt willow for black, and gypsum for white. These pigments were bound together using gum arabic and egg white, and were used diluted in water. In other words, they were watercolors. Another thousand years passed before, in AD 170, the properties of parchment were discovered—goat or sheepskin treated with lime and rubbed down with pumice stone—as a suitable material for preparing "codices," the individual sections of manuscripts. The man responsible for this development was Eumenes II, King of Pergamon.

The illustrations, which we call *miniatures*, that accompanied the text of these manuscripts were painted with watercolor mixed with white lead, resembling the *gouache*, or opaque watercolor, we use today. In the 9th Century, during the reign of Charlemagne, Emperor of the Carolingians, these illustrations began to take on a greater importance and painters were commissioned who alternated the use of transparent watercolor with the opaque mixture already mentioned.

This was the most widely used medium from the Early Middle Ages until the Renaissance; by the height of the Renaissance, the use of watercolor was widespread. More than ten centuries of constant development and discovery separate this time from the sophisticated techniques available today. The spread of literature was really the significant force and ally in the development of this important painting medium.

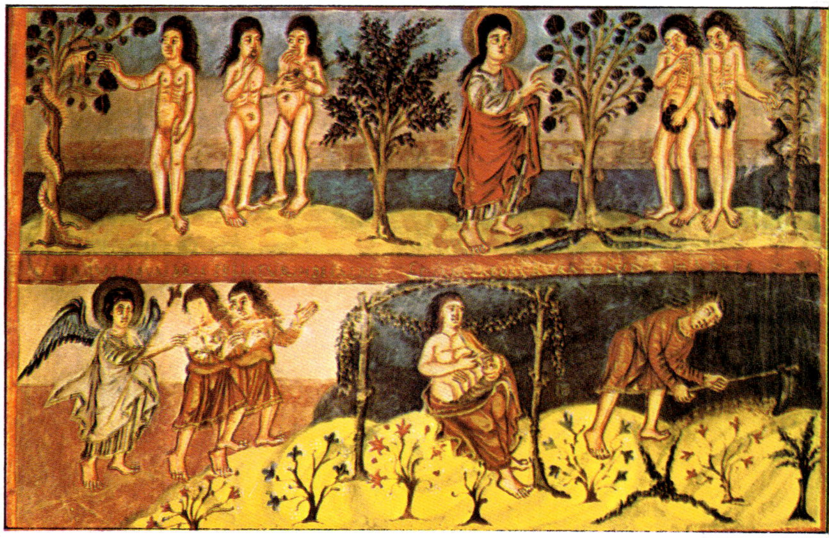

Above.
"The story of Adam and Eve," from a manuscript of the Gospel-book by Alcuin or Moutier Grandval, produced between 834 and 843 (at the height of the Carolingian period), watercolor on parchment. (British Museum, London.)

Below.
"Hare" by Albrecht Dürer, watercolor on paper (Albertina Museum, Vienna). Durer (1471–1528), the greatest German painter and engraver of the 16th Century, painted many watercolors of animals.

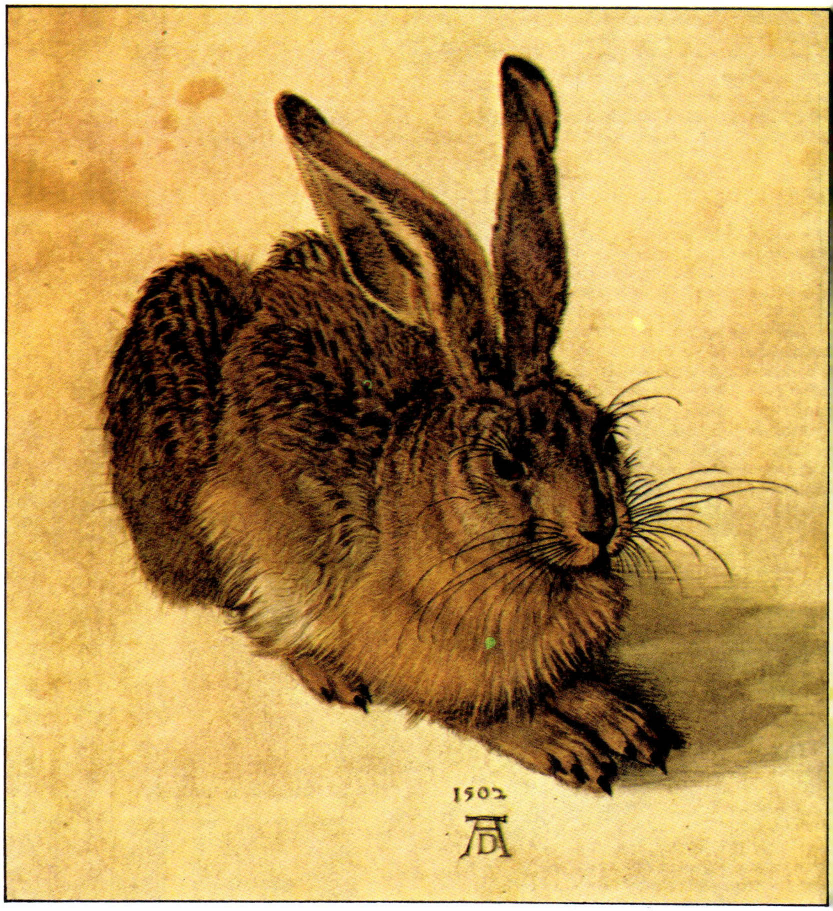

The origins of watercolor

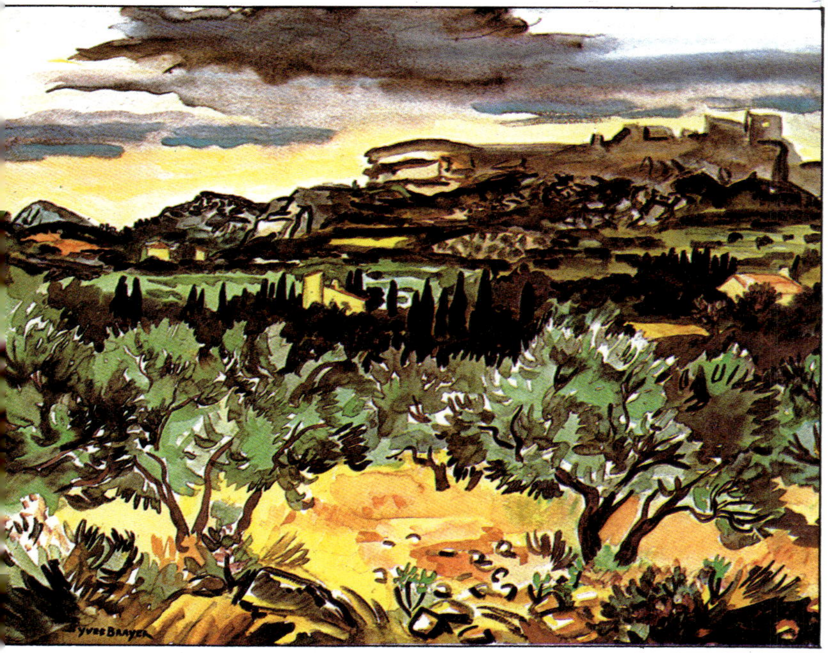

Between the earliest watercolor painting described on the previous page, and the work of contemporary artists like that shown on this page, inevitable changes in the form, color and idiom of this type of painting have taken place, but the fundamental properties of watercolor have remained constant. The subject matter is the same: Landscapes, seascapes, portraits, figure studies, still life, and the artist's personal vision—impressionist or expressionist—of a subject, knowing that watercolor provides solutions to even the most technical demands of his work.

Left.
"Backlight in Baux-de-Provence," by Yves Brayer, private collection. Watercolor using a conventional color range.

Below.
"Landscape," by Julio Quesada, private collection. This Spanish watercolorist limits his palette to create a harmonious whole.

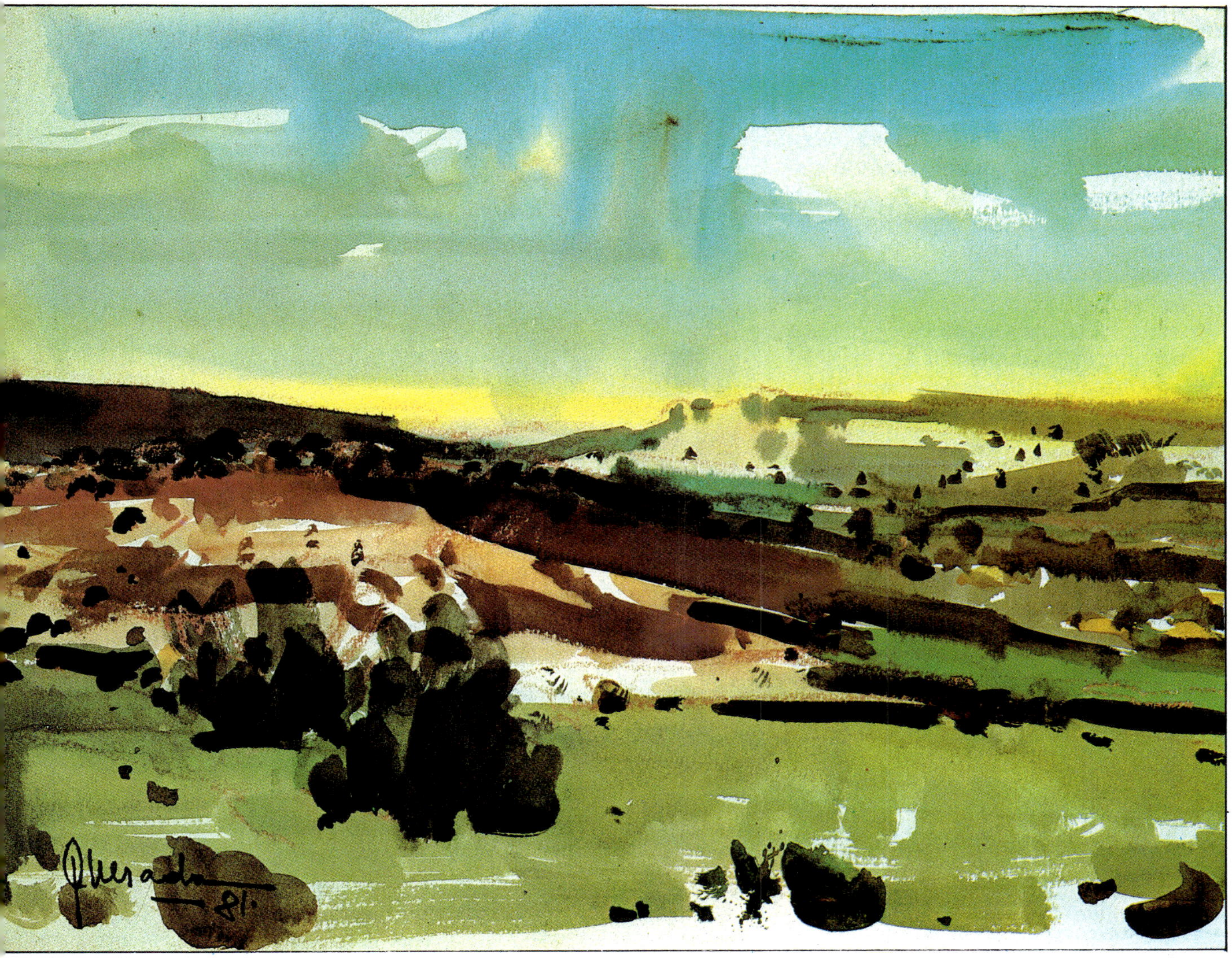

More about equipment

Color ranges and boxed sets

Sets of watercolor paints are available in lacquered metal boxes with various divisions painted white so that the box doubles as a palette. The number of color pans depends on the requirements of the purchaser; they come in ranges of 6, 12, or 24 colors.

A set like this is not essential: Many a professional mixes paints on a large white china plate or on a piece of thick, white watercolor paper, allowing him or her to see what a certain mix will look like before applying it to the painting.

Almost all the boxed sets have a little hole or ring on the case so you can hold it with the thumb of one hand while mixing color with the other.

Many watercolor sets contain white. You have probably heard a thousand times that it is a sin to use white in watercolor painting; you should use the white of the paper in predetermined areas of your picture. For some reason, manufacturers insist on including this color, which is similar in character to a white tempera or gouache. We would like to state as a basis for all future lessons, that there are dozens of ways to open up or protect white areas in a painting without resorting to white paint. So, from now on, its use is strictly forbidden!

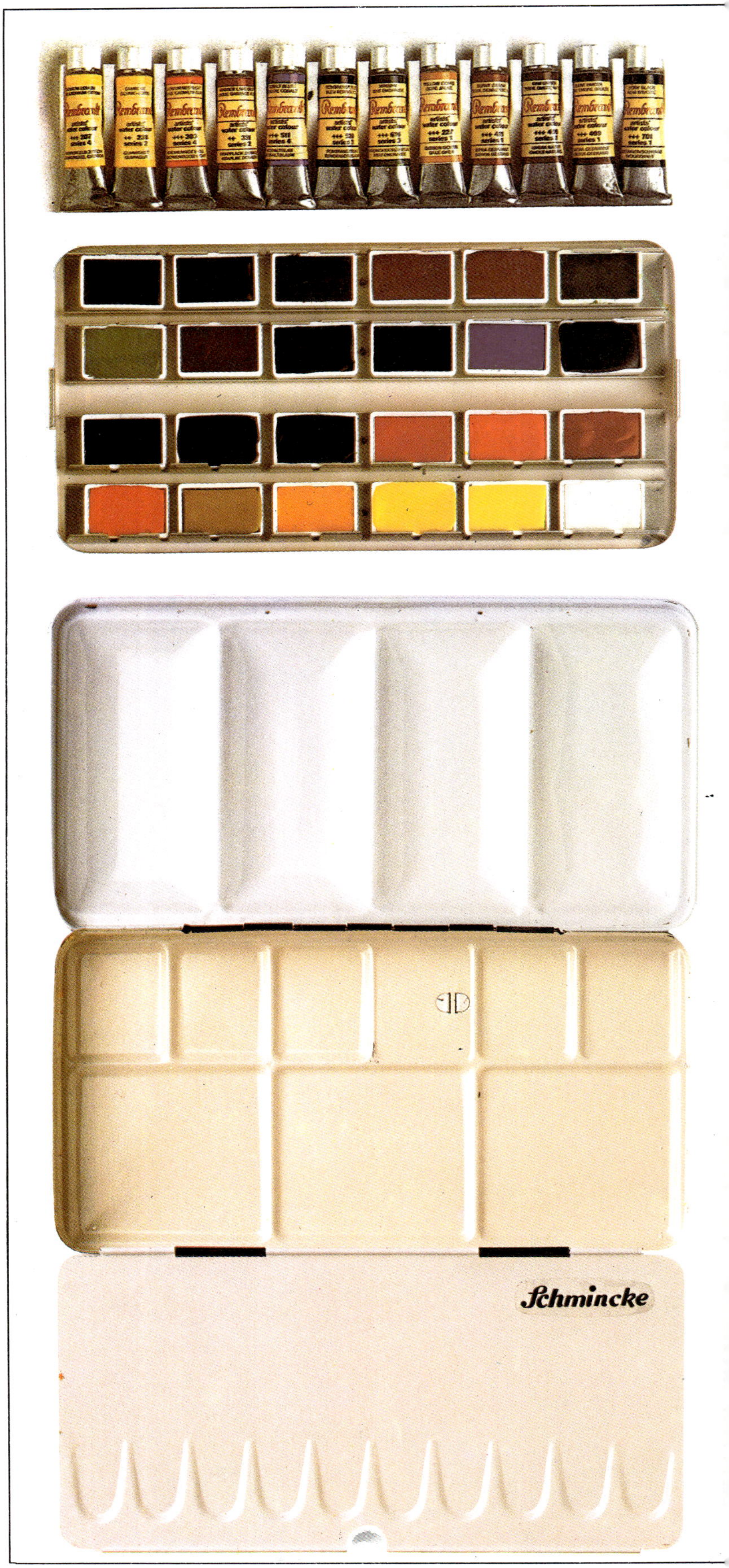

A big boxed set of twenty-four semi-moist watercolors. The tray of colors can be separated from the metal box, allowing more space to mix paint. The fastening of the box at the bottom attaches to the ring for holding the set while you work.

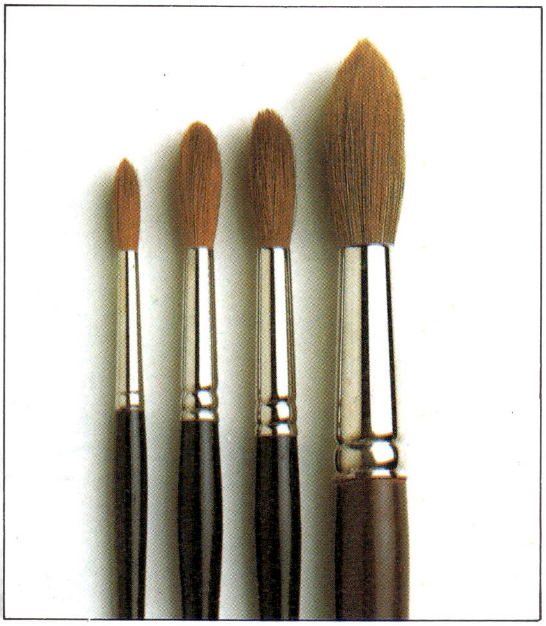

Left.
The minimum selection of brushes for the beginner: Three sable brushes, Nos. 8, 12, and 14 and a No. 24 ox-hair brush.

The watercolor chart below produced by the firm Talens shows thirty-five colors. Some manufacturers offer an even greater range of tones; Winsor & Newton, for instance, produce eighty-six different colors. Of course, you don't need this number of blues, reds and yellows, but every artist has his or her own preferences and usually chooses a basic range from which to work. When you are starting out, it is useful to have a range like this so you can experiment and decide on your preferences.

Bear in mind that all watercolors lose about 10 or 20% of their color intensity in the drying process. This color is restored if you glaze or varnish your painting.

Below.
A color chart from the Rembrandt range published by courtesy of the firm Talens. The chart does not include Chinese White.

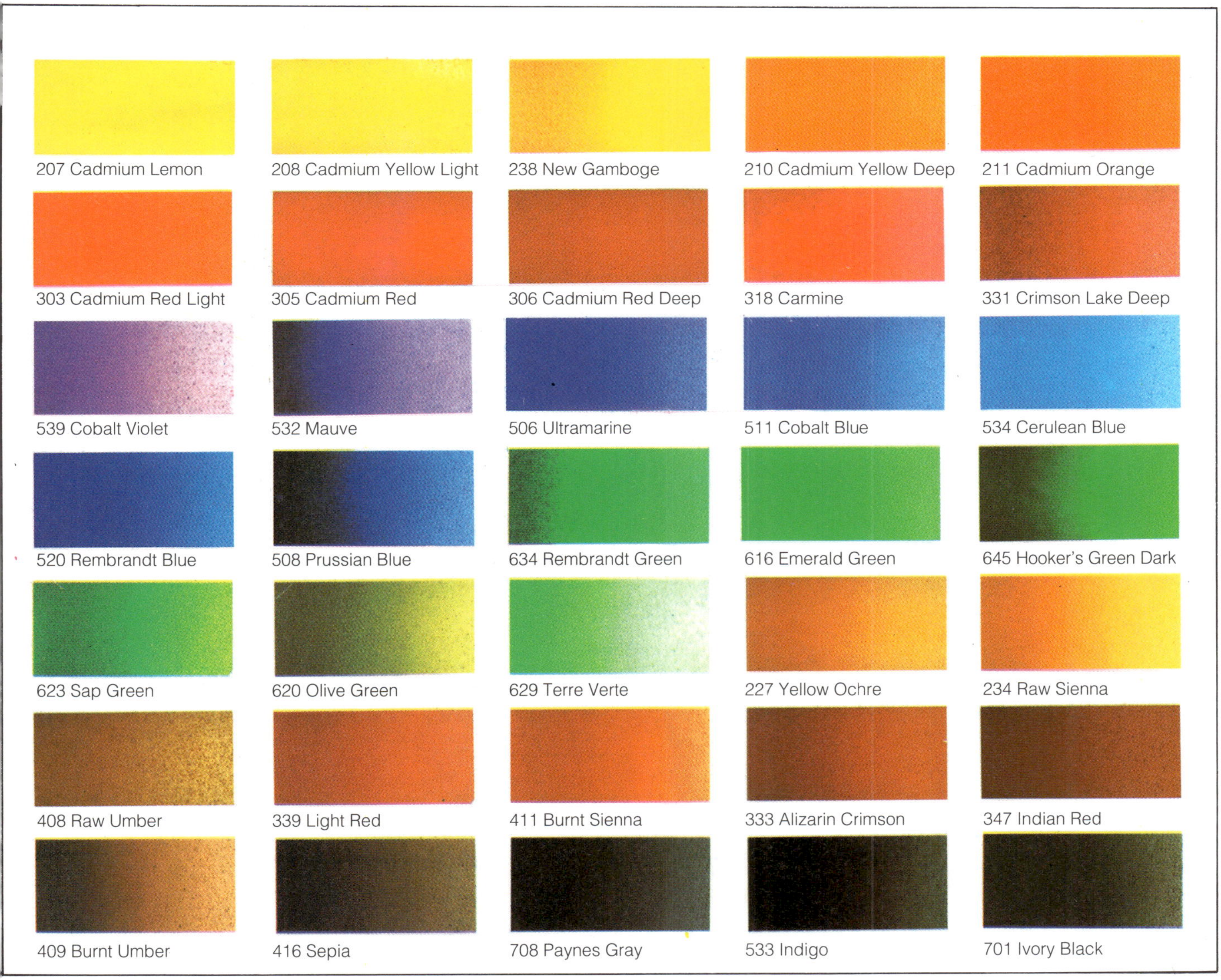

Watercolor painting in all its glory

Watercolor painting on dry and damp paper

Watercolor painting on a dry surface is simply a matter of painting with transparent color, defining the shapes of each part of the subject and using the white of the paper. Of course, this does not mean dispensing with gradation or softening of spherical shapes, or creating a strictly defined background area, which would rob a painting completely of any atmosphere.

Taking into account that watercolor applied to dry paper is easily absorbed, we have to work from light to dark, first of all filling in the pale areas—often more extensive—and going on to the darker ones. Really, describing this technique as painting on dry paper is just a way of distinguishing it from that of painting on a damp surface, which has some special characteristics. "Dry" watercolor painting is considered the traditional form.

To employ the "wet into wet" technique, we have to use damp paper, so outlines appear blurred or hazy. Naturally, all areas will be blurred using this method, even the background.

The damper the paper, the more the color will run and the greater the lack of definition. We are, therefore, obliged to control carefully the degree of dampness using the paintbrush or absorbent paper. Remember that when we talk about painting on *damp* paper, we are not referring to a surface covered with puddles of water.

The examples shown on this page represent the two styles. If you compare them, you will understand more clearly what we have been discussing.

Below.
"Marsh," by Aida Corina (First Prize at the 17th Autumn Salon in Madrid). Here is a good example of the wet-into-wet technique. The subject—marshes and mudflats—lends itself to this technique, in which the blurred outlines combine perfectly with the sharply defined lines in the foreground.

Above, right.
A wash on dry paper shows a "seam" where the painting was not carried out quickly enough; and a wash on damp paper that has been worked on from light to dark. Unwanted "seams" are a problem when working on dry paper. Water is an essential ingredient when using watercolors.

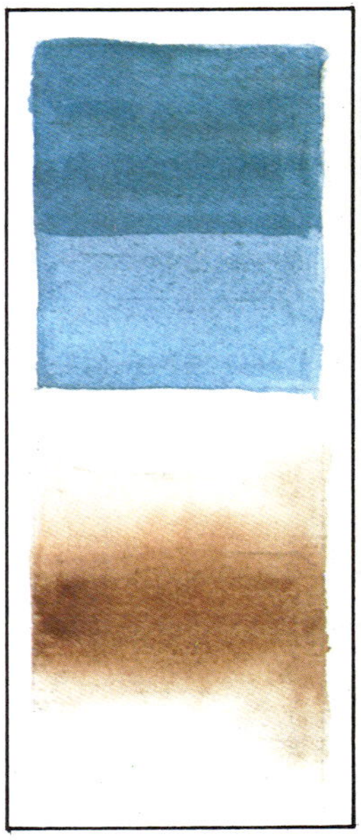

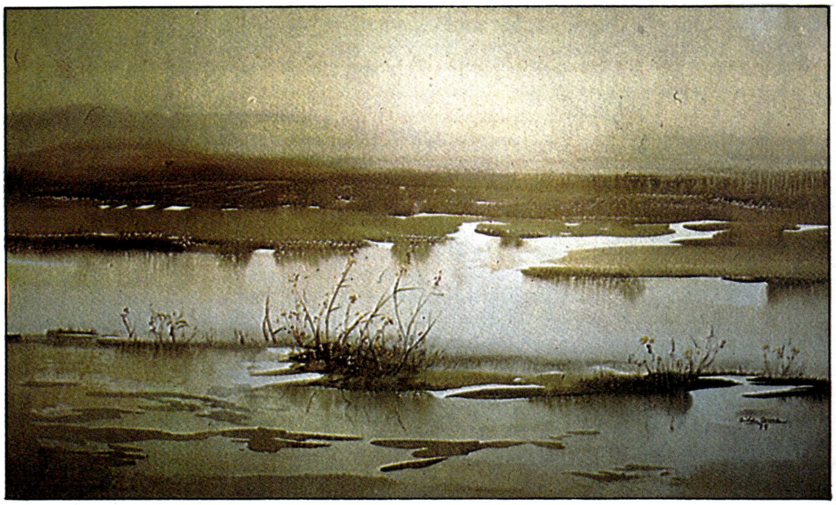

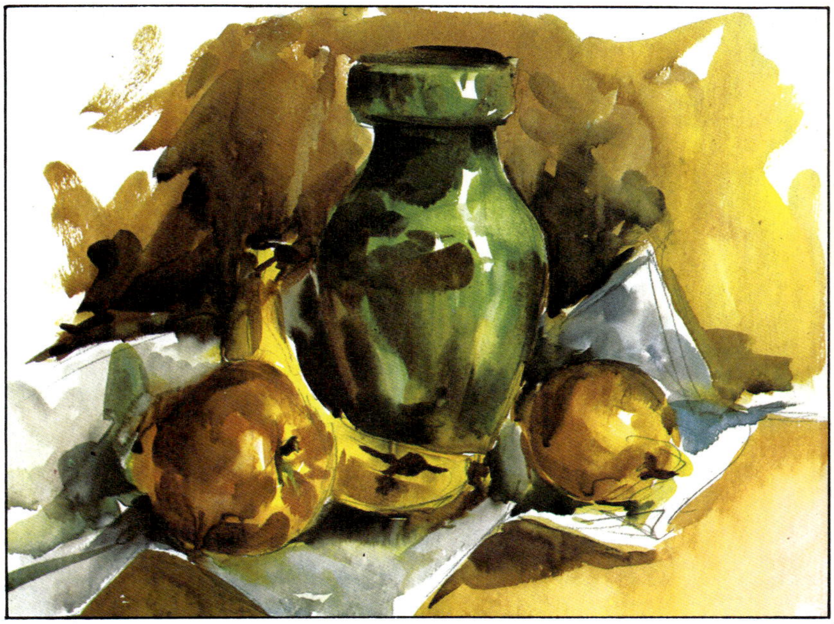

"Dead Nature," Guillermo Fresquet, private collection. Fresquet, one of the best Spanish watercolor painters, presents this superb example of classic dry watercolor in which all of the subjects are delineated.

A still life in watercolors

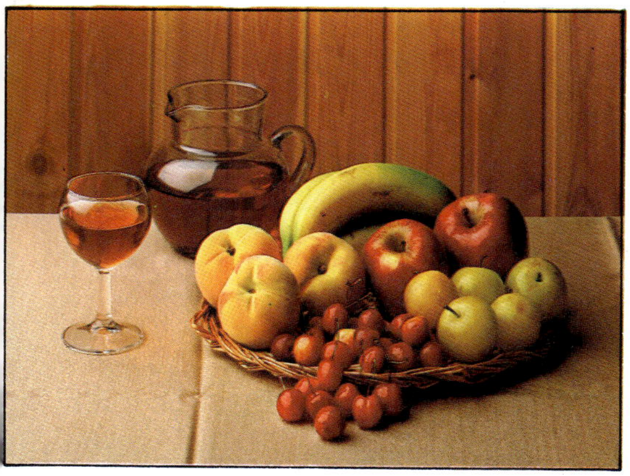

At last you are going to paint using any color you like; no more restrictions. You can use your complete palette without having to stick to two or three primary colors as on previous occasions.

We have chosen the still life you see on the left, but this subject should not put you off doing this exercise. As long as you follow the basic procedure you can choose any subject you like.

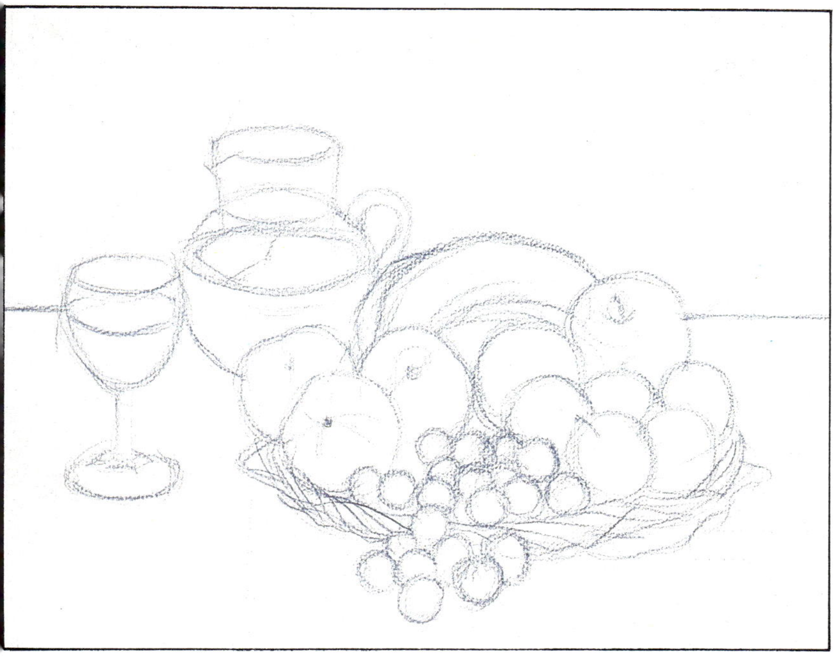

First stage: Layout drawing

We have arranged the elements of the still life in a triangular composition. We have used dry paper and a range of warm colors, as you can see from the finished painting.

Being able to use any color does not oblige you to use them all. On the contrary, it is best not to go overboard with color and to restrict yourself to the range within which you are going to work.

First, make a rough sketch, then draw in the outlines in pencil, without any shadows. At this initial stage, establish which areas are to remain white.

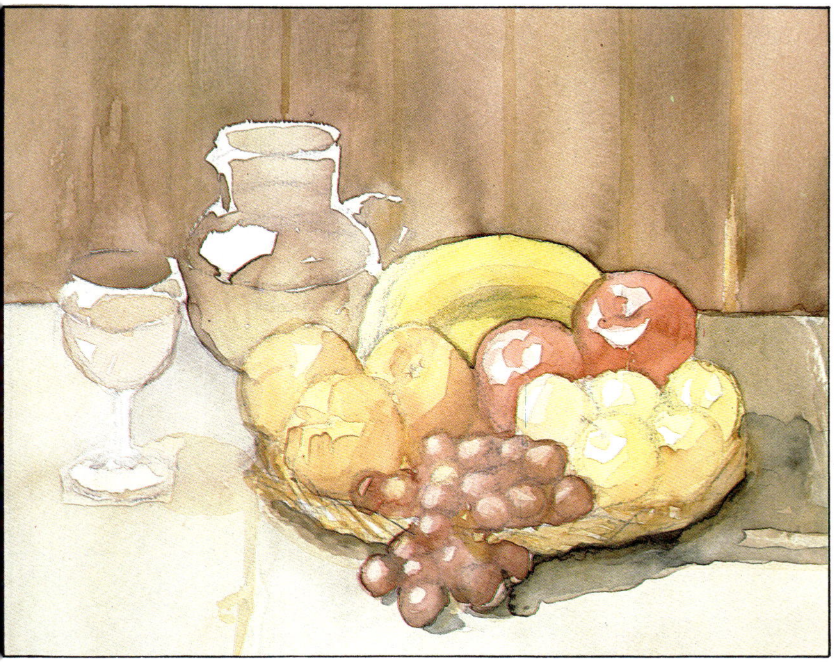

Second stage: Laying the tone in the main areas and the background

Using a No. 12 sable brush and with your working surface at 60 degrees (for those of you with an adjustable drawing board), fill in the background color and, varying the tone a little, the surface of the tablecloth and some of the larger areas of the fruit. It is worth deriving the tones of the other elements of the picture from the background color to produce a harmonious and uniform effect within a warm tonal range.

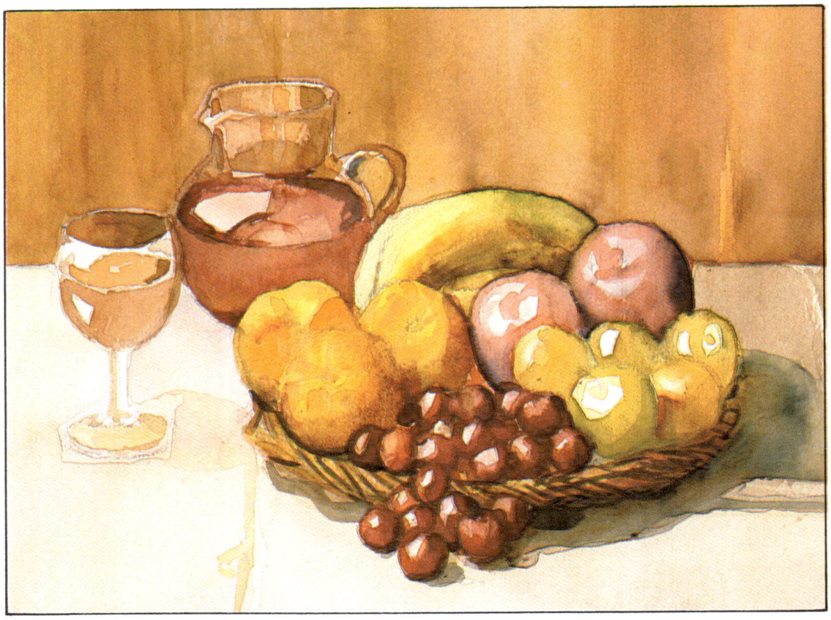

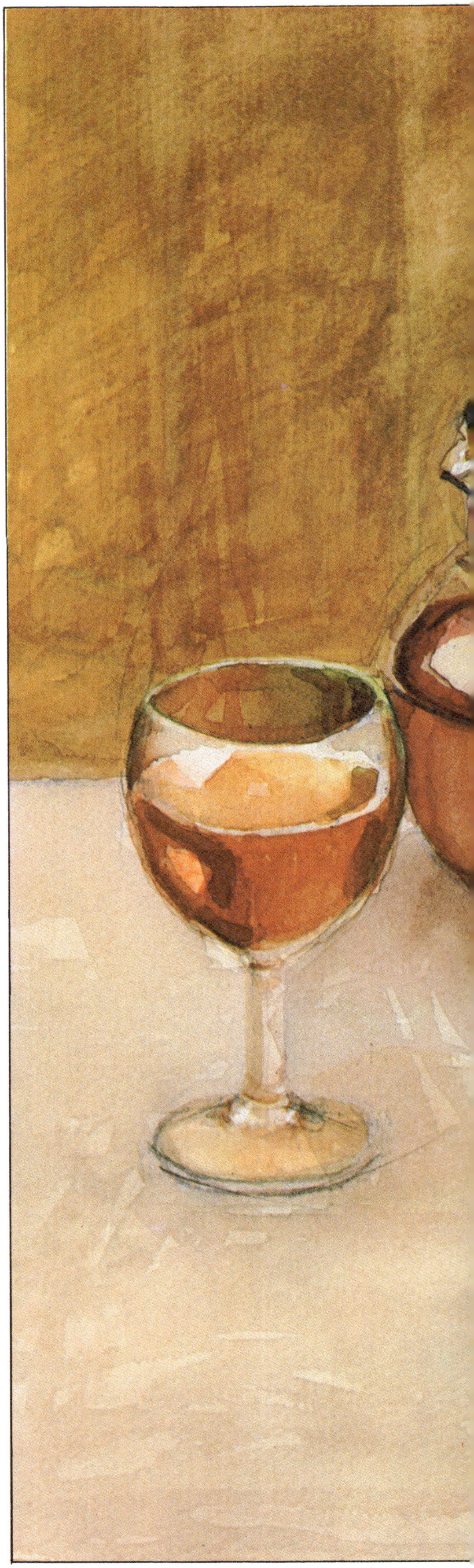

Third stage: Building up the picture

Paint in the rich colors of the fruit, flat and without shading, and the colors of the glass and the jug. Build up these areas, remembering to avoid the white areas. Soon the excessive contrast of the whites with the color around them will involve you in some touching up, softening of edges, and addition of further washes of color.

Fourth and final stage: Adjusting the tone and completing the picture

Tone in some of the whites by adding further washes. Strengthen the colors of the fruit and the basket and make any other necessary tonal adjustments. Sharpen the edges of the different elements, but not too severely, allowing some outlines to blend with the objects beneath them.

Before adding your signature, leave the painting for a day; you will always find some little detail that needs polishing up.

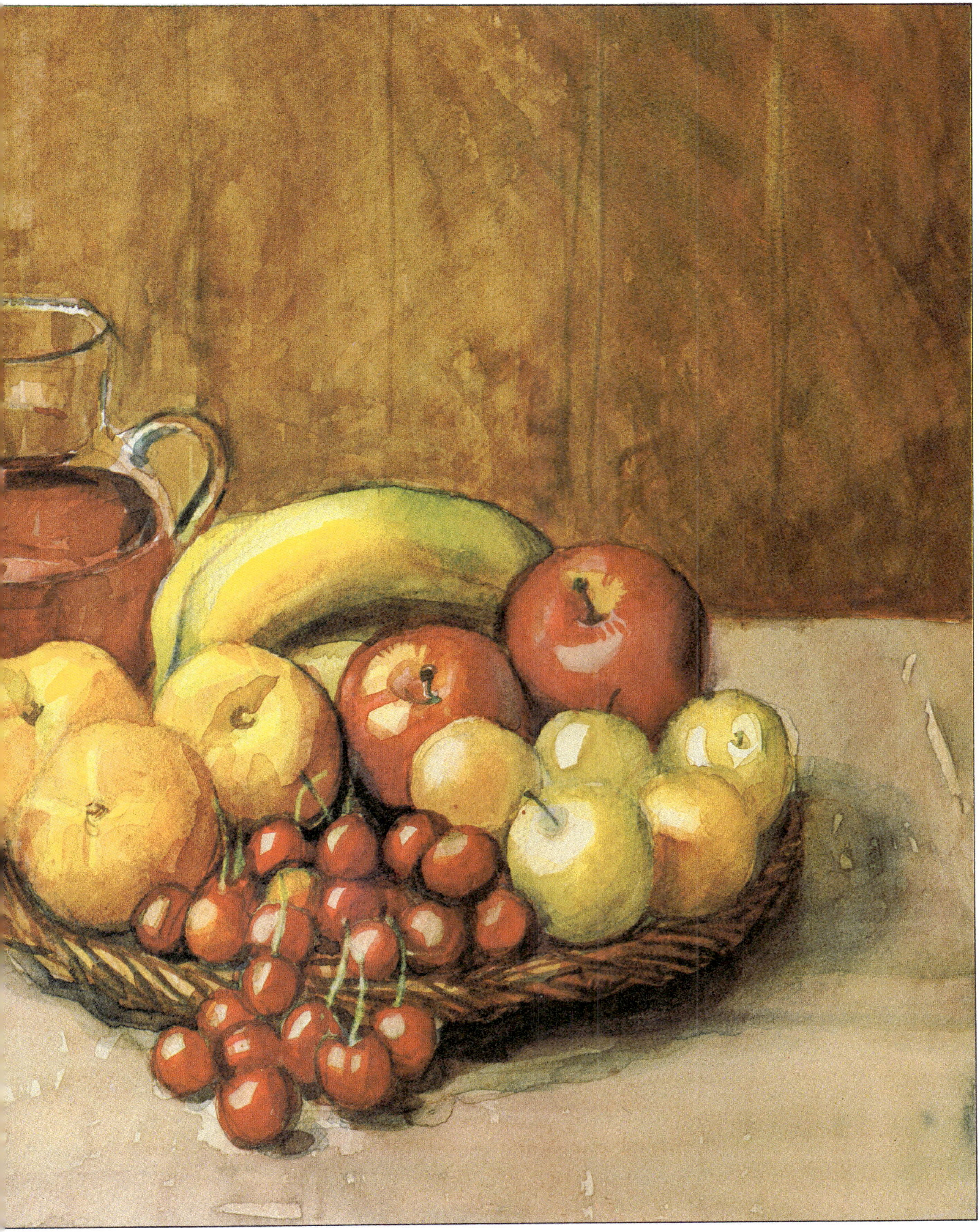

Pastels

The characteristics of pastels

Before beginning the exercises in this section, it should be said that, of all pictorial media, the pastel is the most fragile, the most sensitive, as well as the softest, the most flexible, and the noblest. Why is this? Perhaps because it does not contain oils, glazes, or resins, as do many other media. Pastels consist of ground earth pigments, held together with water and binding agents. This is why fixatives should never be used on pastel drawings. Let's emphasize this and two other basic conditions:

- **Never use fixative on a pastel drawing**
- **Colors are always applied directly in pastel drawing**
- **Color mixing is almost prohibited; it is only resorted to for tonal adjustments**

Being aware of these facts, manufacturers produce pastels in boxes of 12, 18, 24, 36, 48, 60, 72, 163, and 336 colors, to cater to the artist's every need.

What are these pastels like and what can they do? Pastels are opaque so light colors can be used on top of dark; they can be blended—but by using fingers, never a paper torchon, because this is a dry instrument whereas the fingertips give off a certain amount of grease and perspiration that help to fix the pigment to the paper.

Other technical points relating to pastels:

- Paper used for pastels must be semi-rough or rough drawing paper and is usually colored (although white may also be used).
- Pastels can be erased using a putty eraser, a clean cloth, or absorbent paper.
- Excellent complements to pastels are sticks and pencils of charcoal, sanguine crayons, and white chalk.

But let's return to the importance of not using fixative on pastels. If you fix a pastel drawing, the colors will lose their luminous quality and their opaqueness. Some theorists recommend using a little fixative and then touching up the affected colors, believing that the second layer of pigment adheres more effectively. Degas, a great master of pastels, soaked his drawing paper in essence of turpentine, convinced that this conserved the colors.

Neither of these processes is safe, hence the conclusion that fixing is not a good solution. You should protect your drawings with a sheet of coated paper, fastened at one end so it doesn't rub against the picture. Later on, the drawing should be framed, surrounded by a thick mount to stop it from touching the glass.

This is the method used by museums to protect the works of masters such as Chardin and Degas.

Below.
An extraordinary example of pastel painting by Francesc Serra, produced with a limited range of colors—three at the most—showing how perfectly suited pastels are as a drawing medium.

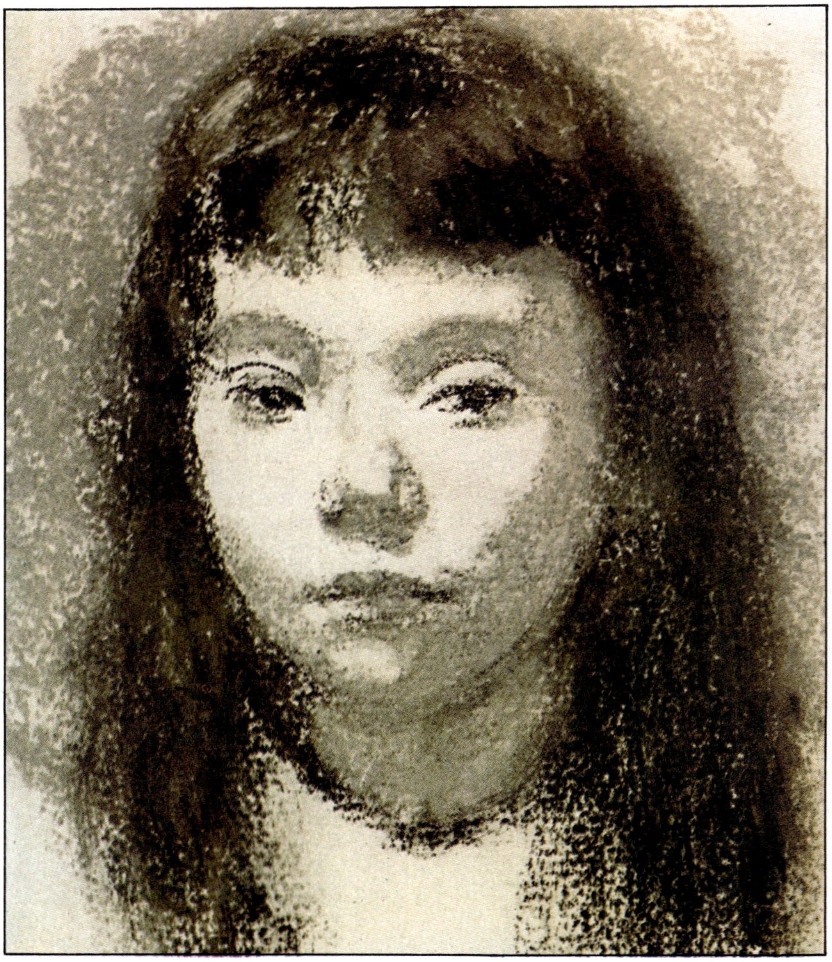

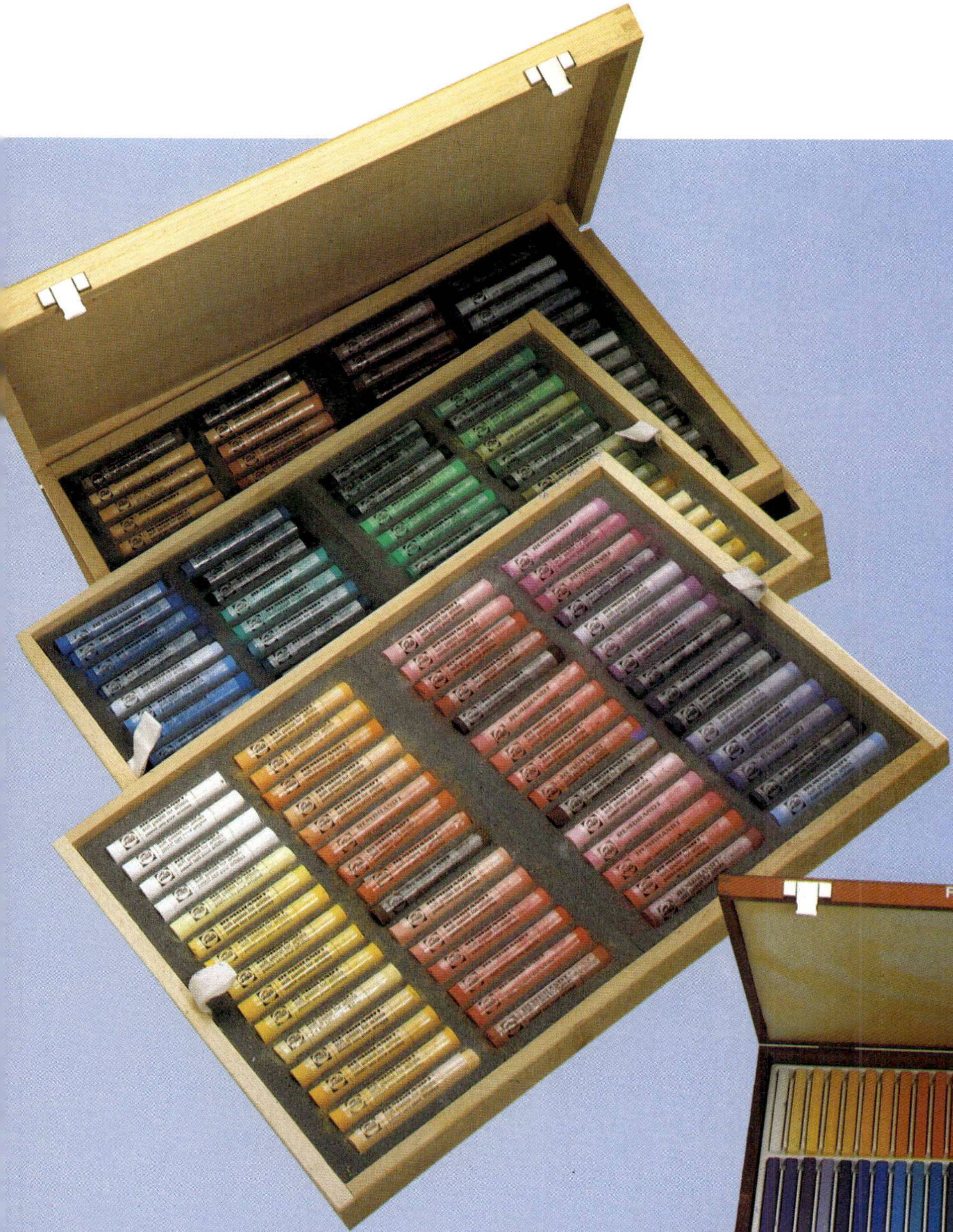

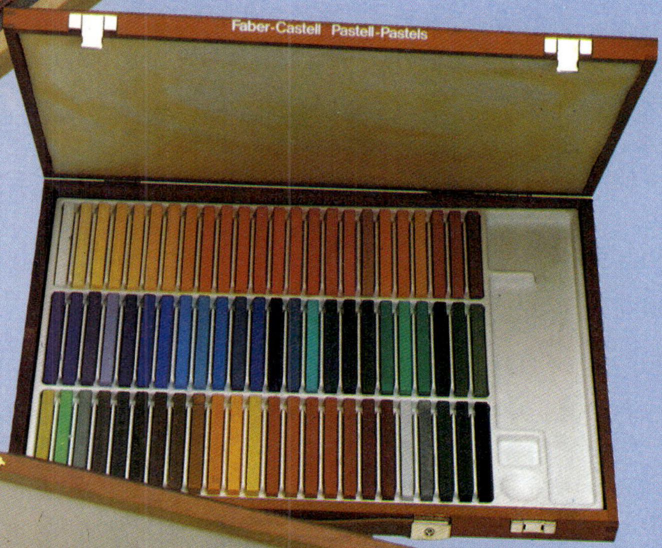

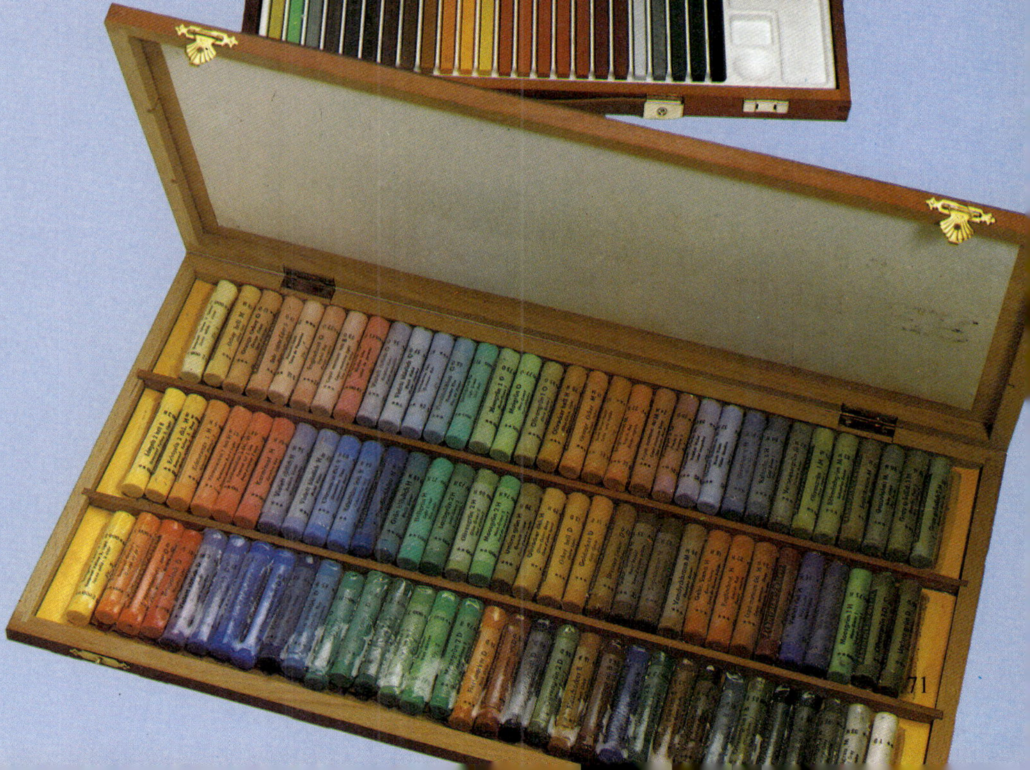

Above.
Boxed set with three trays containing 180 pastels in the Rembrandt range made by Talens. Talens also makes sets of 15, 30, 45, 60, and 90 colors in specially arranged color schemes, equally useful for portrait and landscape work.

Right.
Boxed sets from the manufacturers Faber Castell and Schmincke, containing 72 and 96 colors, respectively. Both firms also supply smaller sets, as well as individual sticks of color. These boxes are perfect for classifying colors in groups or color ranges.

Tools and techniques

1. Supports. *Although you can use single sheets of paper, it is better to work on paper mounted on board. The easel should be in a vertical position.*

2. Small pieces. *Don't throw small pieces of pastel away. They are ideal for drawing lines and shading, depending on how they are applied.*

3. Lines and thick strokes. *For lines, the pastel is used at a sharp angle, like a pencil. For thicker strokes, the stick is rubbed sideways across the paper, as illustrated.*

4. Pastels are opaque. *Pale colors can be applied on top of dark colors. This capacity is lost if it is used to excess in the same area of a picture.*

5. Mixing and blending. *The fingers should be used for blending and combining adjacent colors.*

6. Paper for pastels. *The best results are achieved on tinted paper, preferably Ingres paper, or Canson mi-teintes.*

7. Sides of the paper. *With the types of paper just mentioned, it is possible to use either side, as there is no appreciable difference between them.*

8. Rubbing out with a cloth. *If it is necessary to alter part of the picture, the professional uses an old, clean cloth to rub away and erase the pastel marks, making a fresh drawing on top.*

9. Using an eraser. *An absorbent putty or special pastel eraser, which can be molded into the right shape, may be used for small details.*

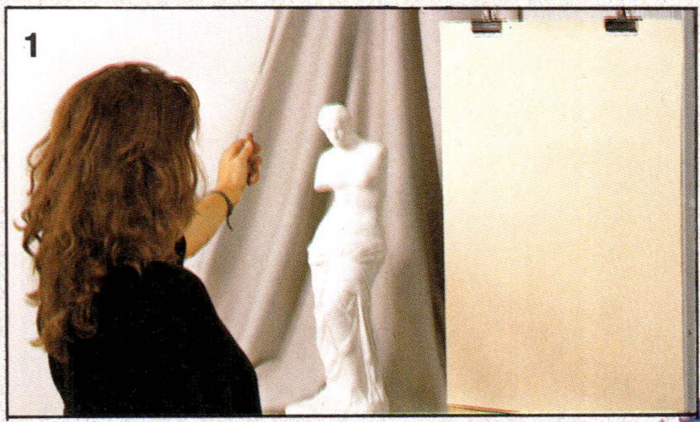

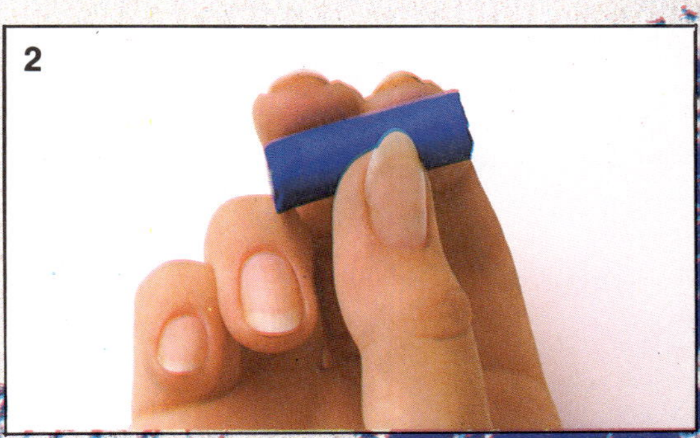

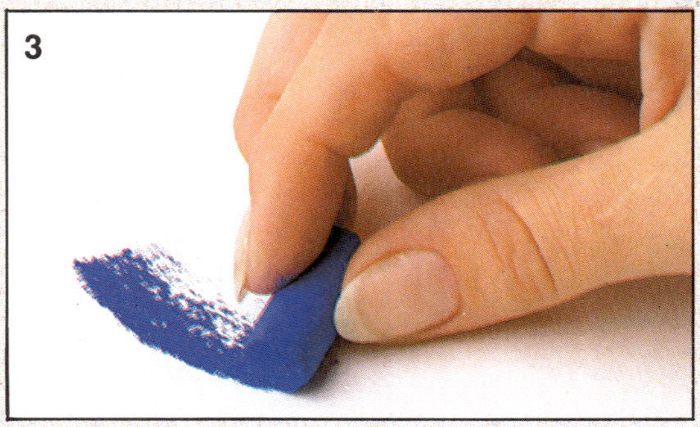

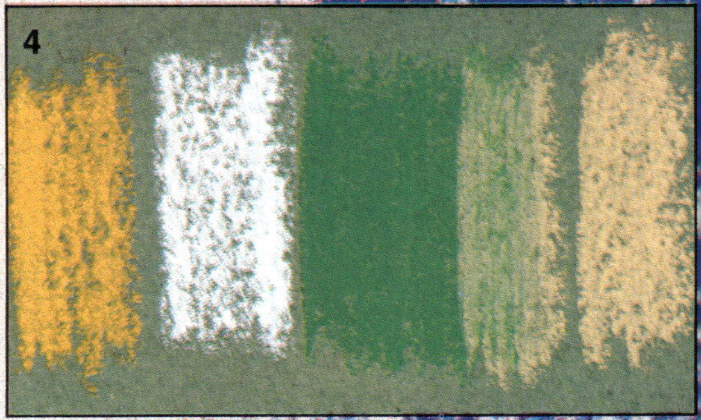

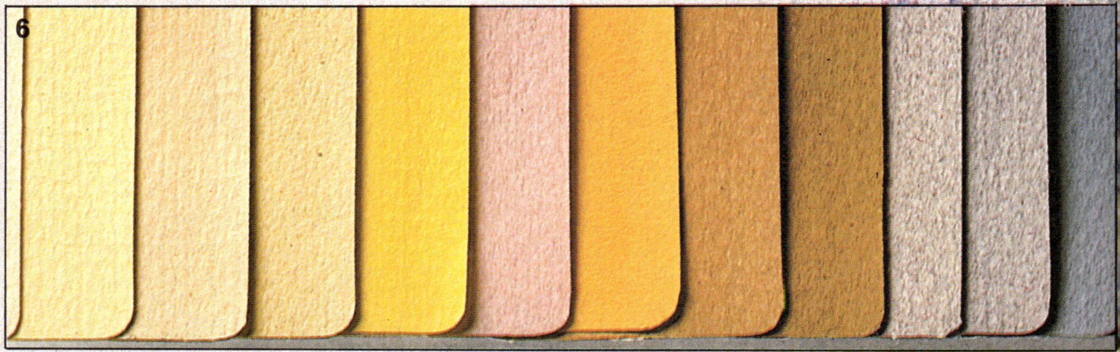

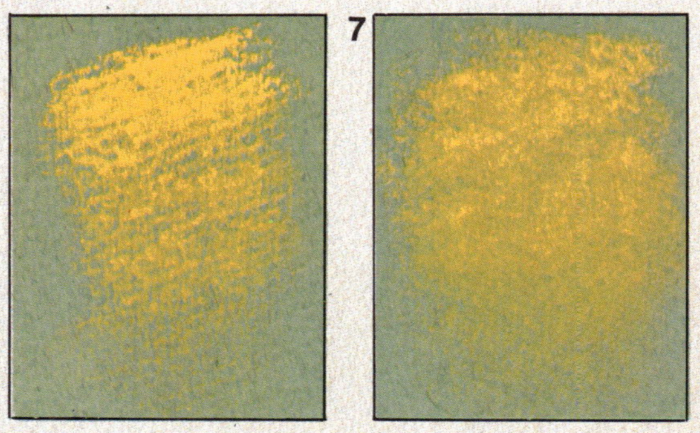

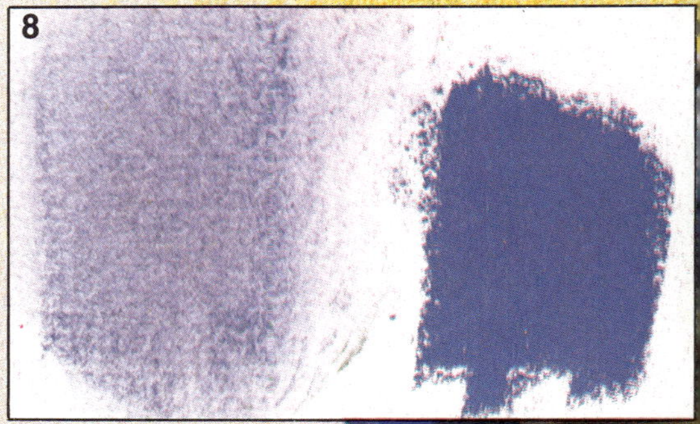

9

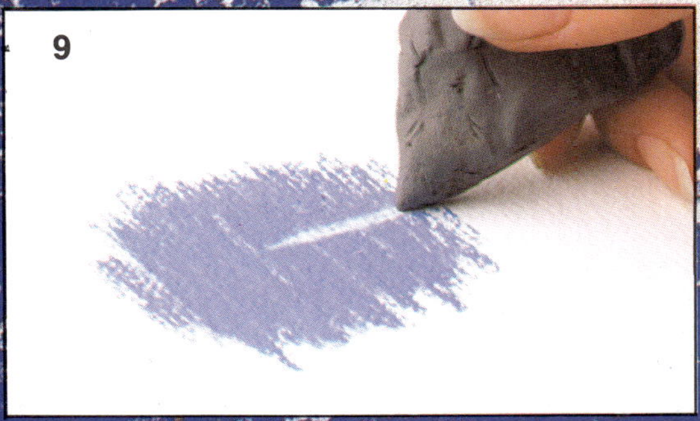

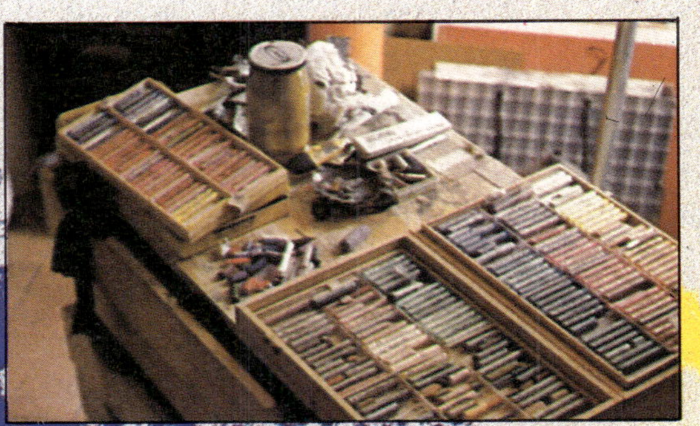

11

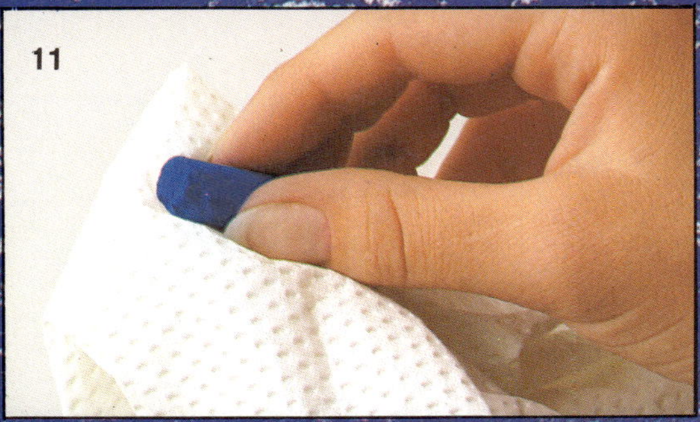

12

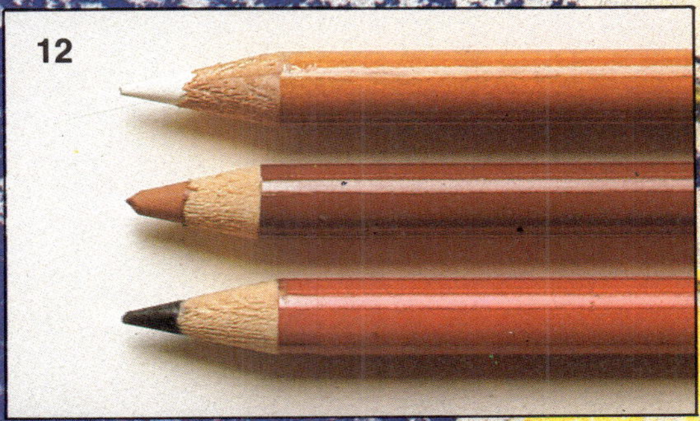

13

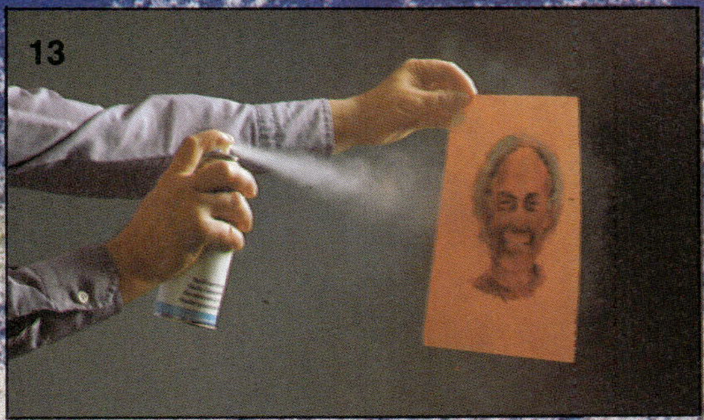

14

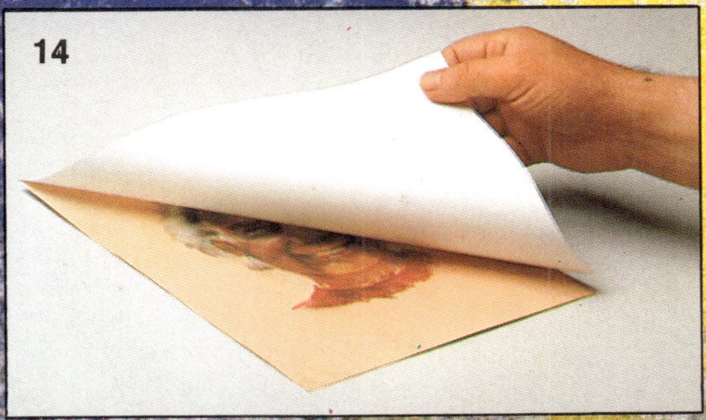

10. A boxed set. *If you need to work with more than 60 colors, it is wise to invest in a wooden box, with compartments for each color range: Greens, earth colors, and so on.*

11. Be clean and tidy! *Pastels make a mess; fingers get dirty. It is essential to keep both clean by using cloths and absorbent paper for the pastels and by washing your hands frequently.*

12. Complementary materials. *These are often soft charcoal pencils, sanguine crayons, and white chalk pencils. They are useful for fine lines, highlights, details, and so forth.*

13. No fixing! *Fixative darkens colors and lessens opaqueness.*

14. Protecting a pastel drawing. *Lay a sheet of "onion-skin" or coated paper on top of the drawing, attached at the back or side so that it does not slip and rub against the picture.*

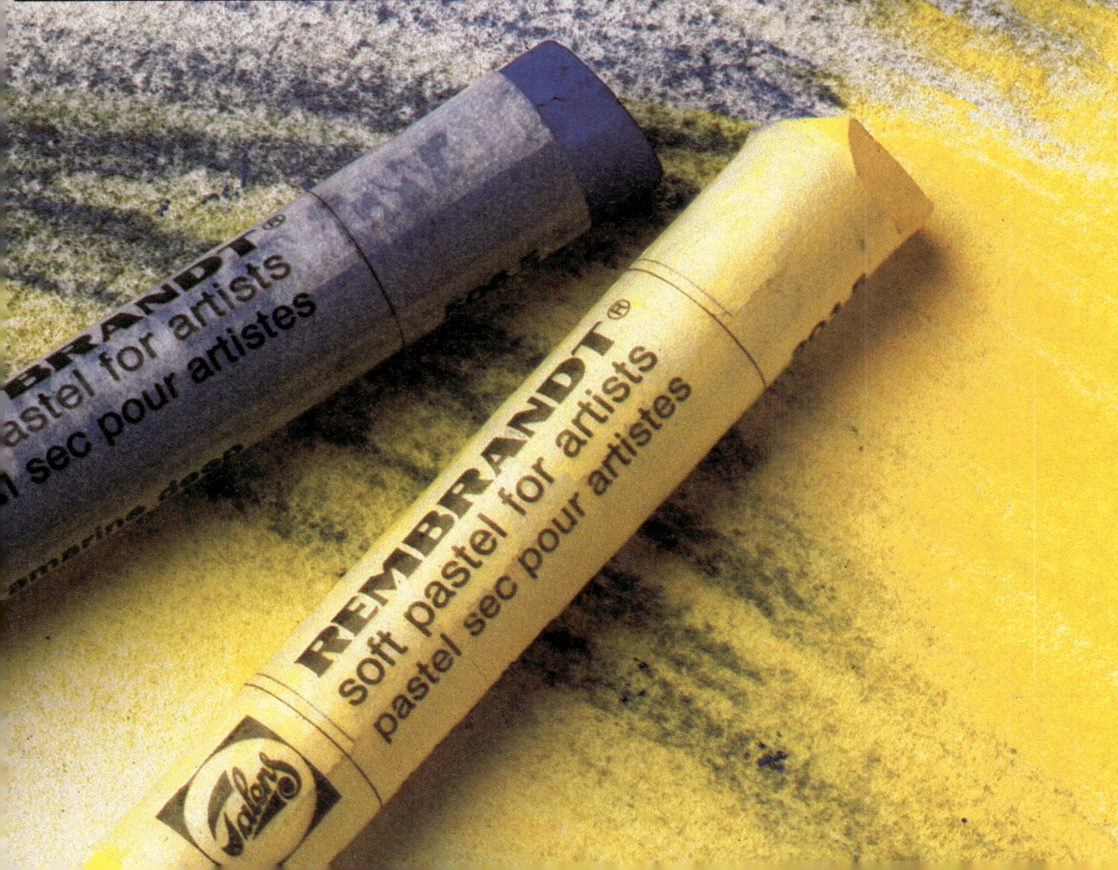

Masters of the medium

The old argument about whether pastel is a painting or drawing medium has raged ever since pastels were invented. The work of artists like Quentin de la Tour, Chardin, and Manet had more in common with painting than with drawing. They covered the surface of the paper with layers of color and produced impasto effects by blending and superimposing pigments, perhaps in an unconscious attempt to emulate oil painting. Then came Impressionism and, with it, Degas, who used this technique much more as a drawing medium, emphasizing line and form and working with colored paper. Nowadays, works like those of Francesc Serra (see the example on page 70) show that both points of view are valid: Pastel is a drawing and a painting medium. This dual role is perhaps the key to the greatest qualities of the medium we call "pastel."

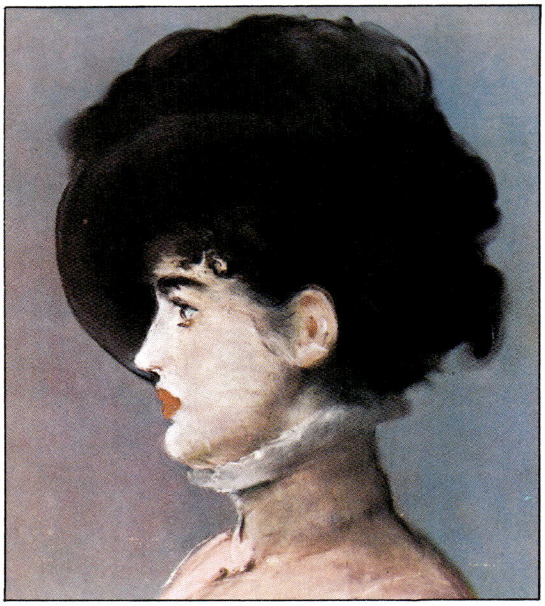

Left. *"Woman with Black Hat (the Viennese)," Edward Manet, 1882, pastel on paper, Jeu de Pome Museum, Paris. One of Manet's most famous pastels, it is the portrait of Irma Brunner.*

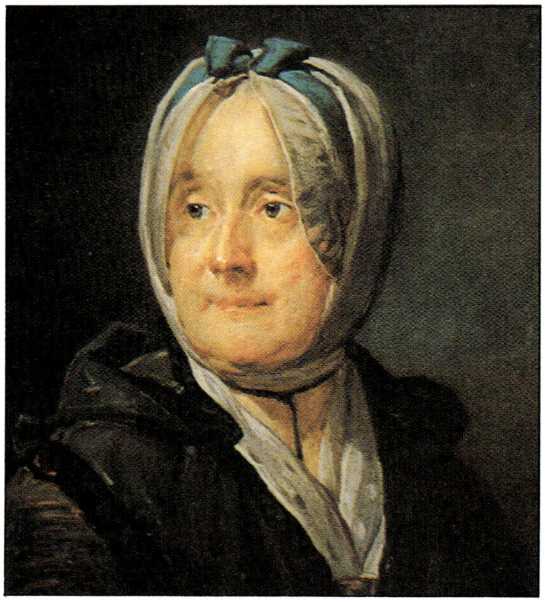

Above. *"Portrait of Mme. Chardin" by J.B.S. Chardin, 1775, pastel on paper. Presented to the Salon de Paris in that year, it is considered the best pastel painting of its time.*

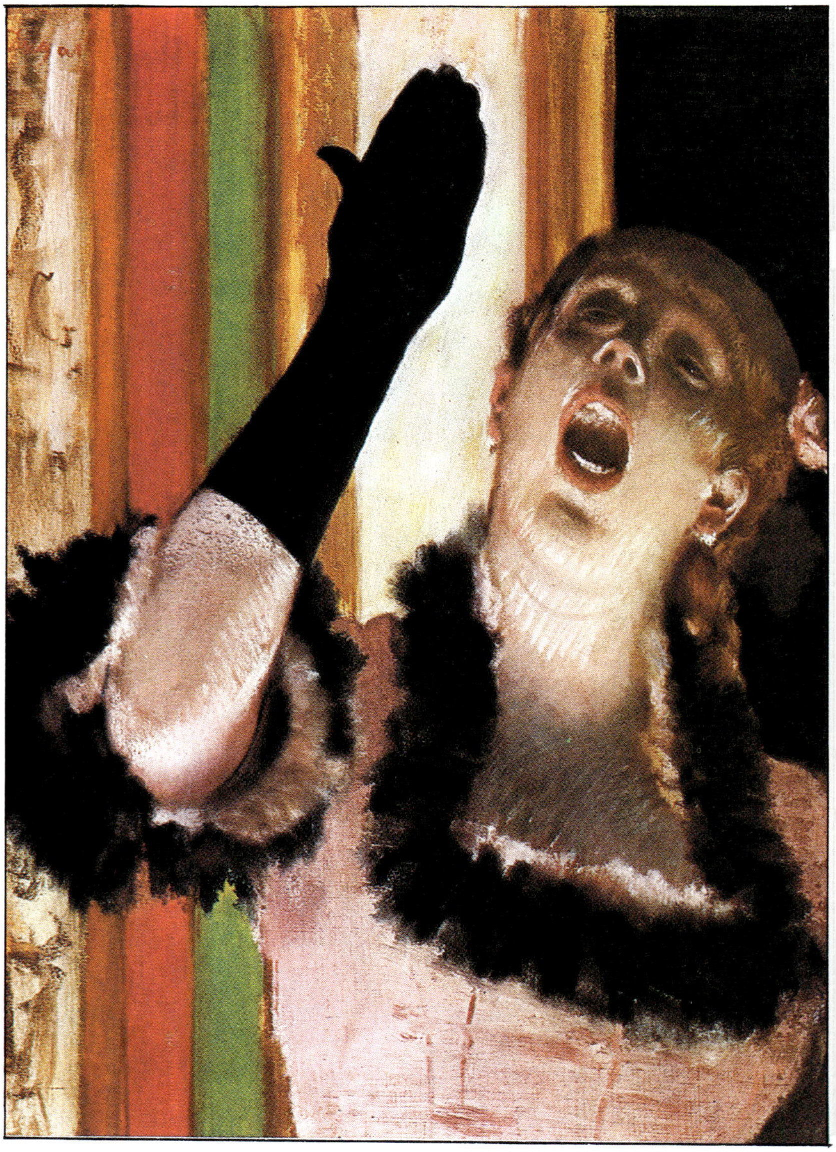

Right. *"Singer at the Cafe Concert" by Edgar Degas, 1878. Pastel and tempera on canvas, Fogg Art Museum, Cambridge. This picture was preceded by two similar ones. Degas' style with pastels has been described as bringing about the definitive advancement of this technique.*

A floral theme using pastels

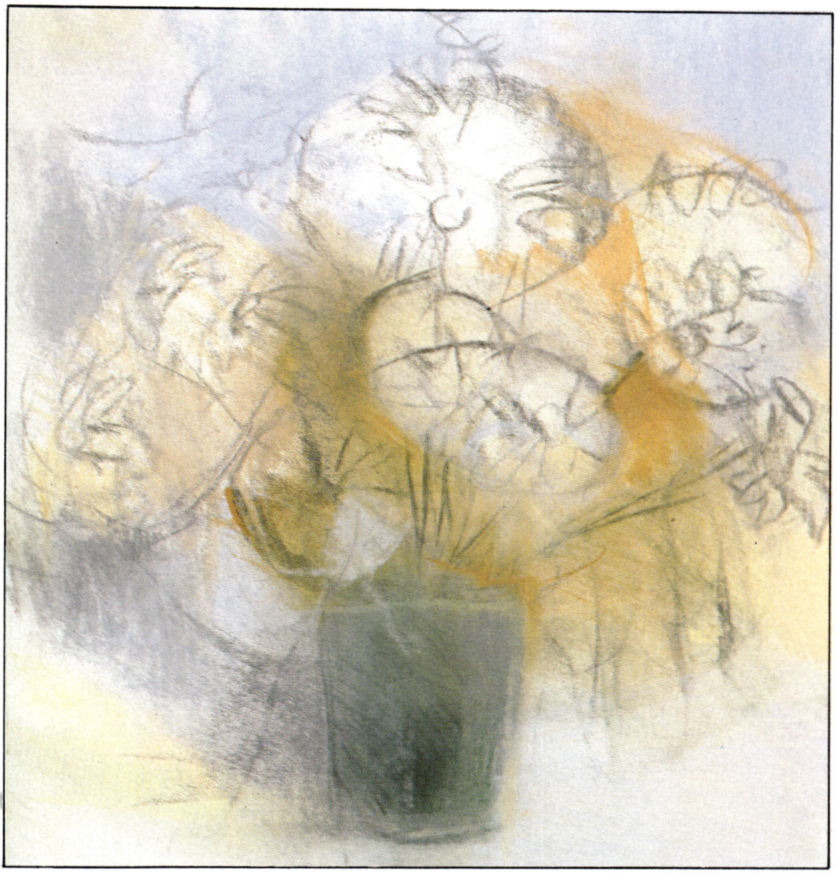

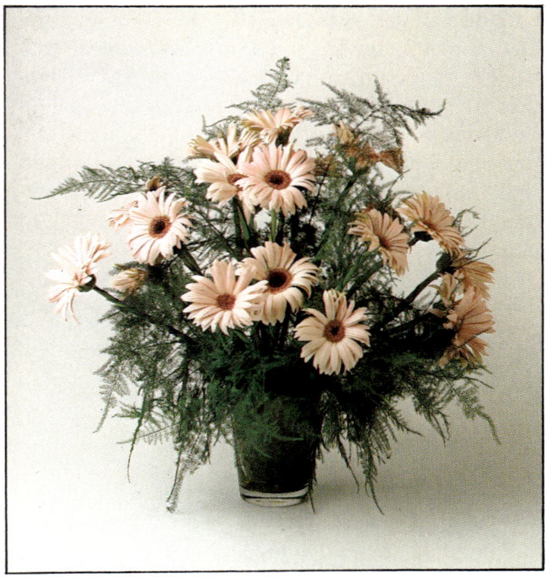

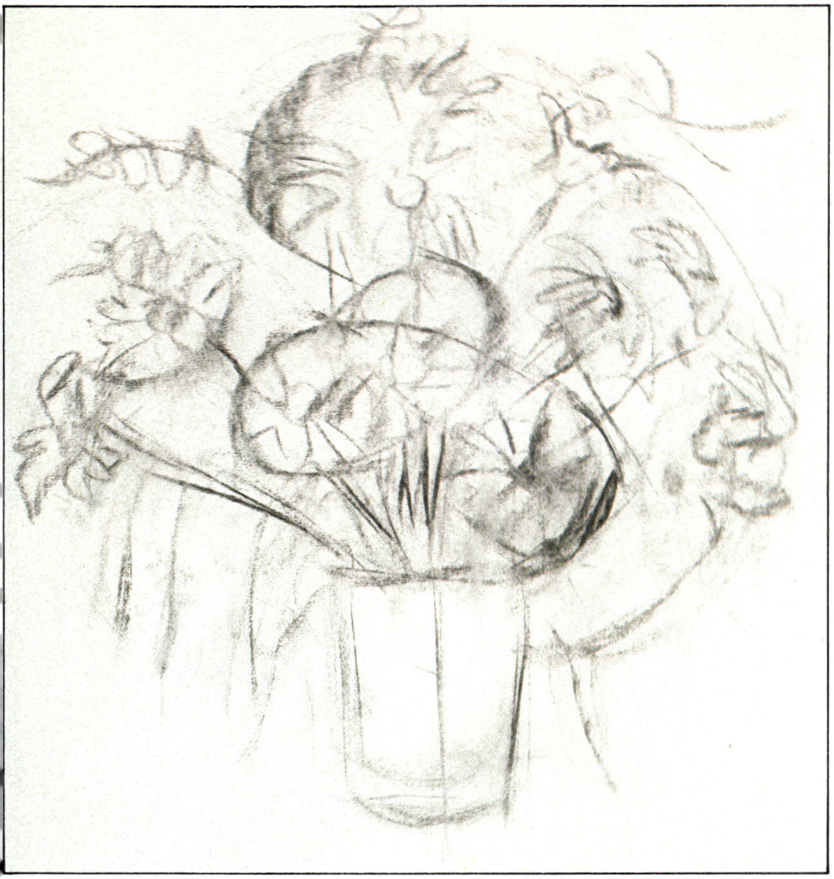

To test the theory that pastels are equally painting and drawing media, we suggest that you carry out this step-by-step exercise consisting of interpreting in pastel the vase of flowers in the photograph above. Our rendition has steered a middle course between painting and drawing the subject and we believe that it contains elements of both techniques. Try it for yourself following these four stages:

First stage: Layout sketch

Using rapid charcoal strokes, we have set down the shapes and proportions of the main elements of the picture. Charcoal allows for a loose, clean sketch; you can blow or wipe away with a cloth any surface dust. One can lightly fix the drawing so that the charcoal lines do not mix with the pastel colors later on.

Second stage: Background color

We have put in a light layer of color, using tones complementary to those we will use later. This stage brings out the subtle color contrasts that breathe life into the drawing. Notice, for instance, the ochres between the flowers, in the background, and the surface on which the vase sits.

Third stage: Applying color

At this point, rapid strokes are applied, covering the surface with color and yet allowing the tones from the previous stage to "breathe"—the green stems tinged with blue and yellow, the oranges and violets of the flowers, the warm and cold grays of the vase, the background grays. The whole picture takes on a pleasing quality of tone.

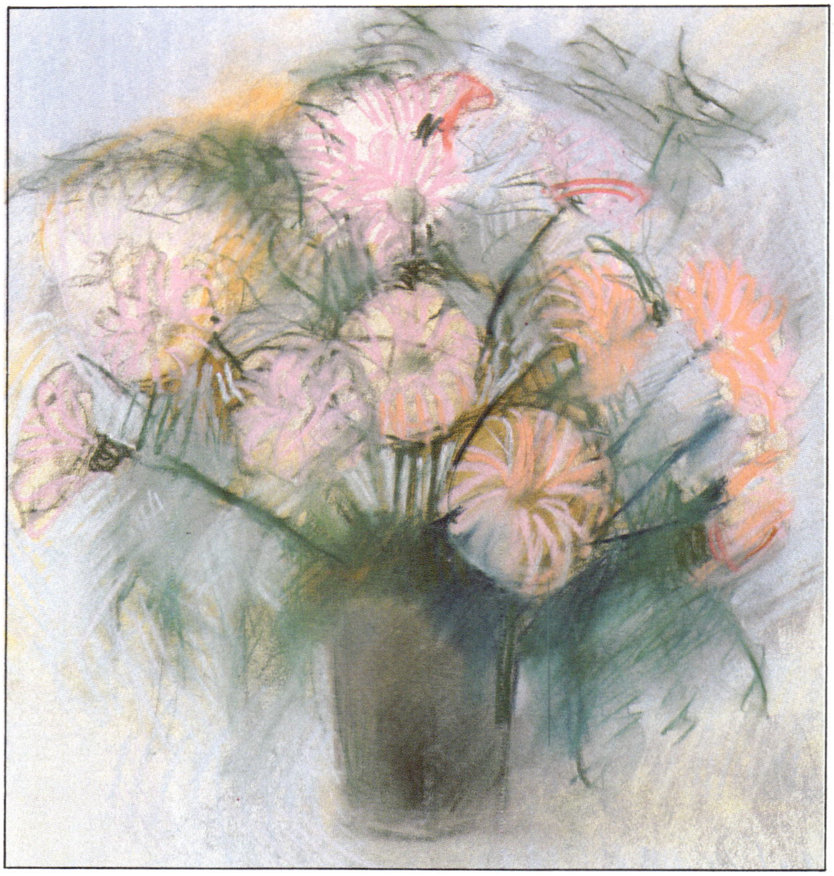

Fourth stage: Adjusting the tone and completing the picture

This subject is an ideal one for using color to bring out its luminous quality; we have subtly worked on the tone of the picture, here and there gently rubbing with the fingertips in areas where the colors melt into one another, then highlighting color contrasts by emphasizing certain important details. By this stage, the drawing is almost finished. The fragility of the pastel technique does not benefit from heavy layers of pigment that would tarnish the overall effect; it is better not to overwork the picture in its final stages.

In the close-up picture on the right, we can see that using the tip of the pastel to make bold, clearly defined strokes in some places heightens the contrast with the areas where the pigments are blended. These strokes suggest shapes and texture without needing to be worked in any way. Here we really have a picture that displays as many of the attractive qualities of a drawing as those we traditionally associate with a painting.

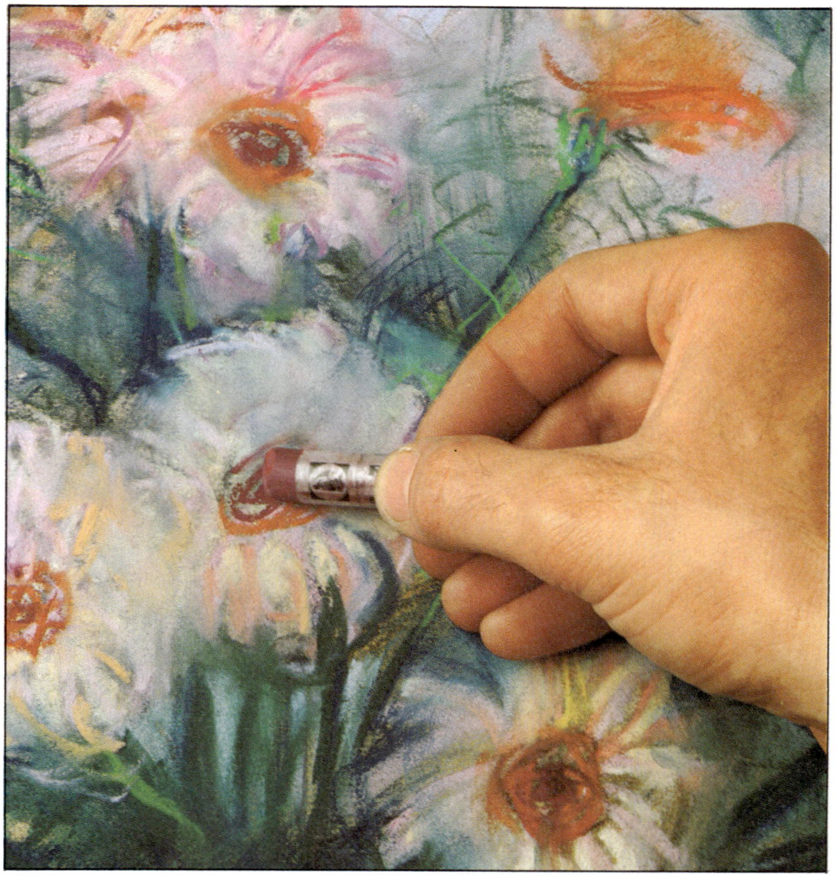

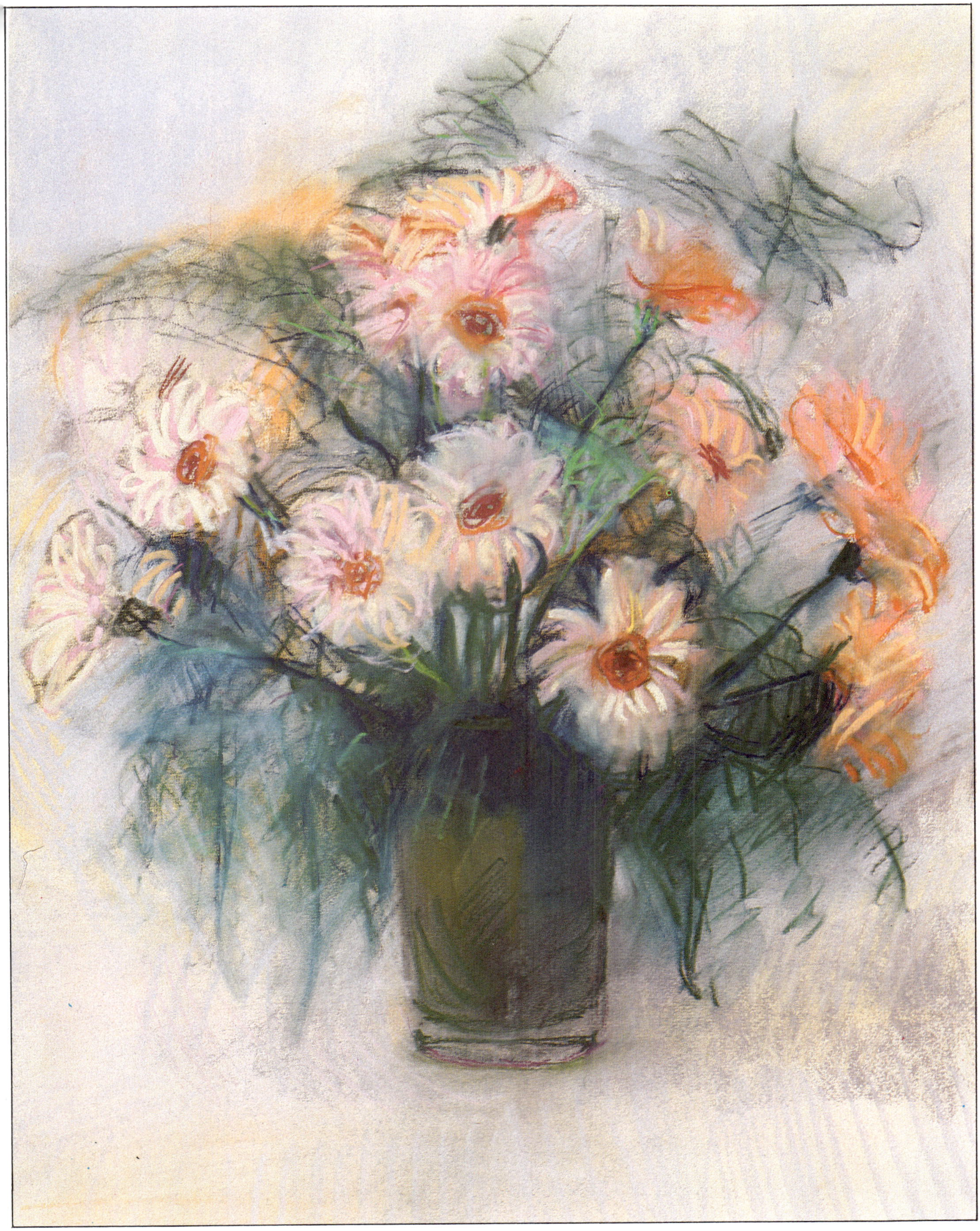

Wax crayons and oil pastels

Some 500 years before Christ, wax crayons were already in use. It was another 1500 years before the appearance of a medium with similar characteristics: Namely, the oil pastel. Oil pastels were invented in the 1960s but, in spite of their "age difference," both processes share various qualities and techniques.

Wax crayons are made of pigments and wax, while oil pastels contain pigments and oil.

The following list summarizes the points they have in common:

- Both are rubbed onto the paper surface and blended using the fingers.
- They are both opaque, and light colors may be used on top of dark ones.
- Both wax crayons and oil pastels are difficult to erase; you first have to scratch away the pigment with a razor blade or scalpel and then use a plastic eraser.
- When the pigment is scraped away, the texture of the paper reappears; you can draw on this with hardly a sign of the previous color showing through.
- Wax crayons and oil pastels are both soluble in oil of turpentine.
- If you apply a dark color on top of a light one and then draw with a scalpel, the light color will show through.
- Both materials may be protected using the same type of fixative.

The only difference between the two media is that the wax crayon is harder and therefore less flexible and more impermeable. If wax colors are mixed to any extent, the drawing surface becomes hard, shiny, and textureless. It is difficult to make pigment stick and you have to scrape away a layer of wax before adding highlights or sharp lines of light color. Oil pastels are softer and more pliant. As their name indicates, they are related to ordinary pastels and have the same ability to go over dark pigment with light. However, the color they produce is more intense and opaque.

Basic equipment for working with wax crayons or oil pastels: A dish for color-mixing, oil of turpentine, sable or hogs' bristle brushes, Ingres or similar quality paper, and sticks of color.

Opposite page.
Right, *Caran d'Ache wax crayons;* ***above, right,*** *oil pastels by the same manufacturer and,* ***below these****, pastels by the manufacturer Manley.* ***Below,*** *bottles of oil of turpentine.*

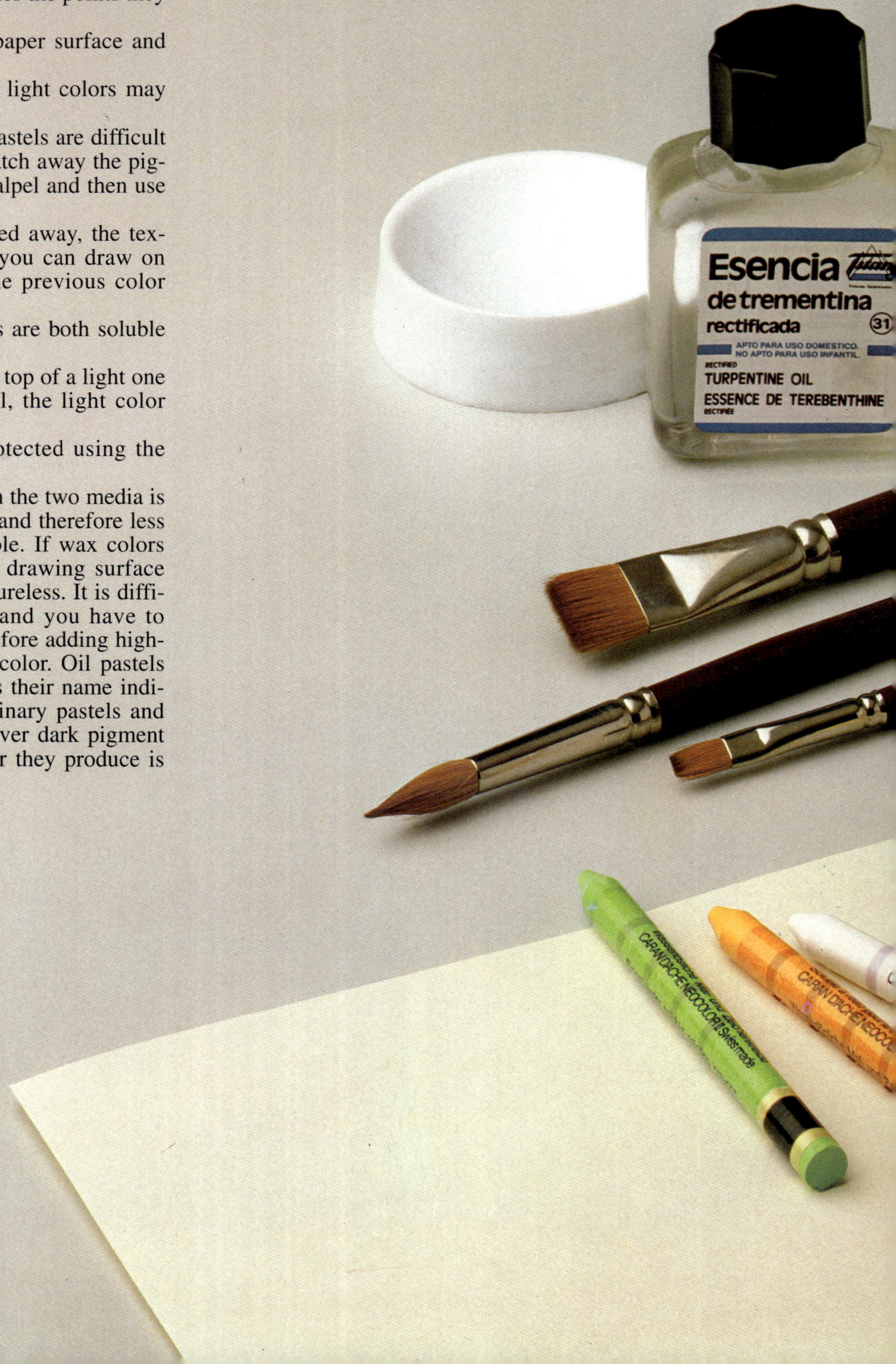

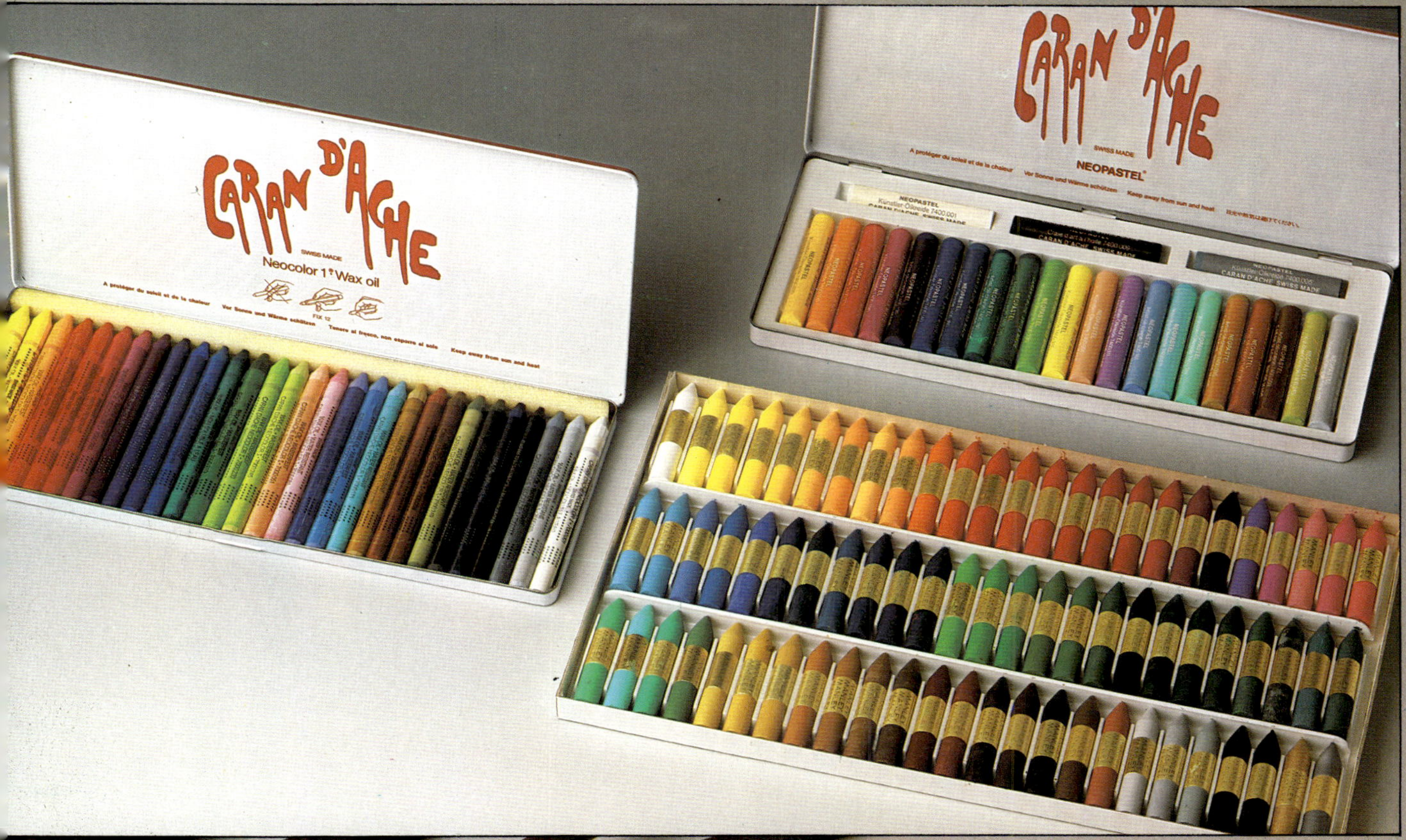
CARAN D'ACHE
SWISS MADE
Neocolor 1® Wax oil
CARAN D'ACHE
SWISS MADE
NEOPASTEL

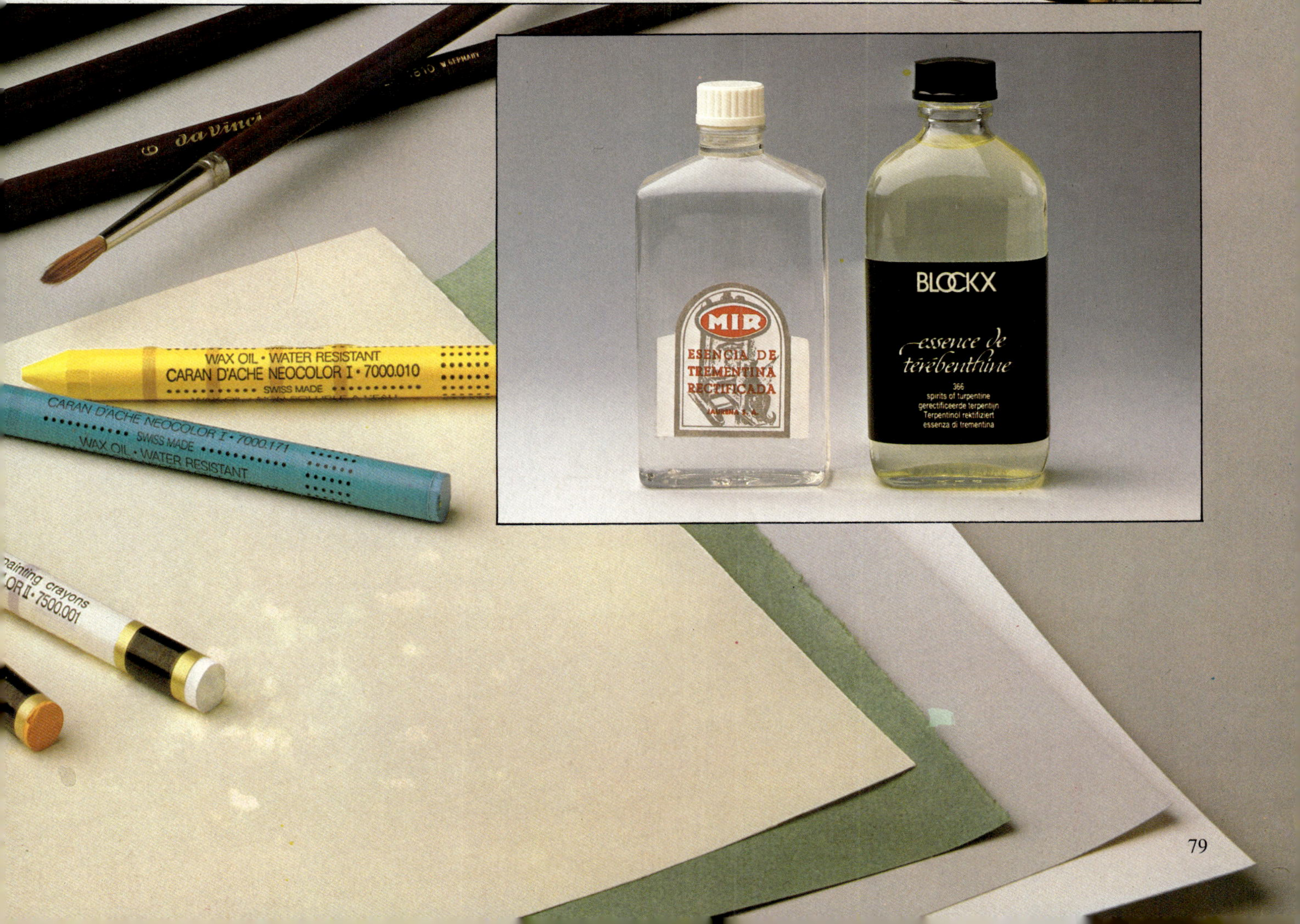
da Vinci
WAX OIL · WATER RESISTANT
CARAN D'ACHE NEOCOLOR I · 7000.010
SWISS MADE
CARAN D'ACHE NEOCOLOR I · 7000.171
SWISS MADE
WAX OIL · WATER RESISTANT
MIR
ESENCIA DE
TREMENTINA
RECTIFICADA
BLOCKX
essence de
térébenthine
366
spirits of turpentine
gerectificeerde terpentijn
Terpentinöl rektifiziert
essenza di trementina

Tools and techniques

The techniques described on this page are applicable to wax crayons and oil pastels. Before starting on the exercise in either medium, try to familiarize yourself with these techniques. It is always worth doing this with any new pictorial medium. In each case, before embarking upon any serious work, it is important to know what you can expect from the process with which you are going to experiment. Otherwise, you might waste a lot of time waiting for inspiration to strike.

1. Rubbing on the pigment. Take a wax or oil crayon or stick and rub it over different types of paper to learn how the texture and pressure exerted can affect the result.

2. Blending with the fingers. Draw an area of color and spread it with your fingers until you achieve something like the effect in the photograph. Experiment with different colors.

3. Coloring light on dark. We have applied a patch of green and another of white on top of some blue color. The colors do not cover the blue very well, but do provide some rich tonal effects.

4. Rubbing out. We scraped away this layer of carmine using a scalpel (A) and then used an eraser (B). As you can see, it is difficult to eliminate all the color.

5. Drawing in negative. We covered a light color with a dark one, carefully, so that the mix of pigments did not become muddy. Then the top color was scraped off to achieve this effect.

6. Turpentine washes. Areas of wax or oil pastel are diluted with turpentine, using a synthetic brush, as if they were water soluble.

7. Transparent layers. Color shavings are dissolved in a mixing dish with a little turpentine, using a brush to create a semi-liquid substance, perfect for transparent washes.

1

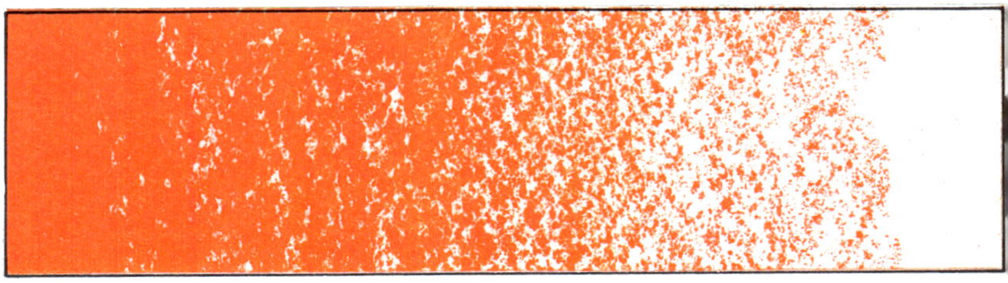

2

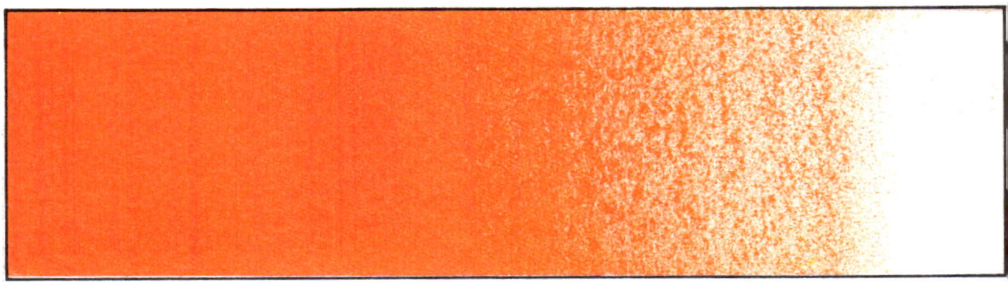

3

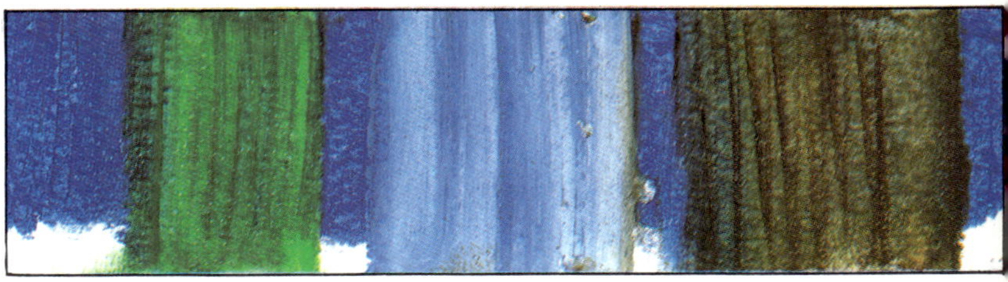

4

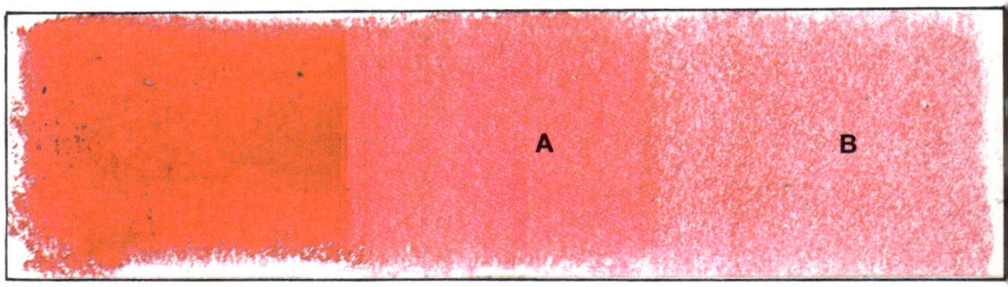

5

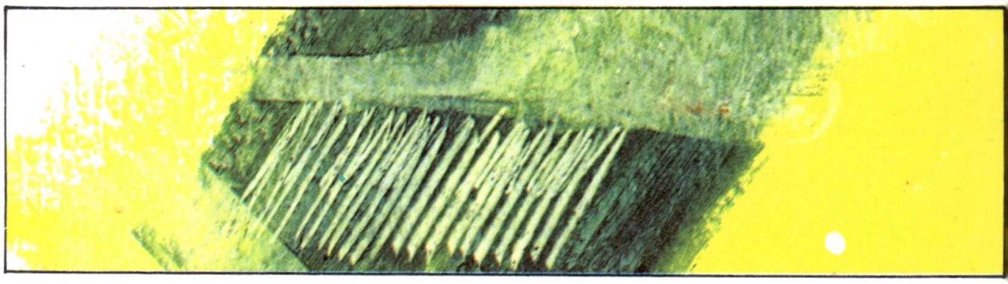

6

7

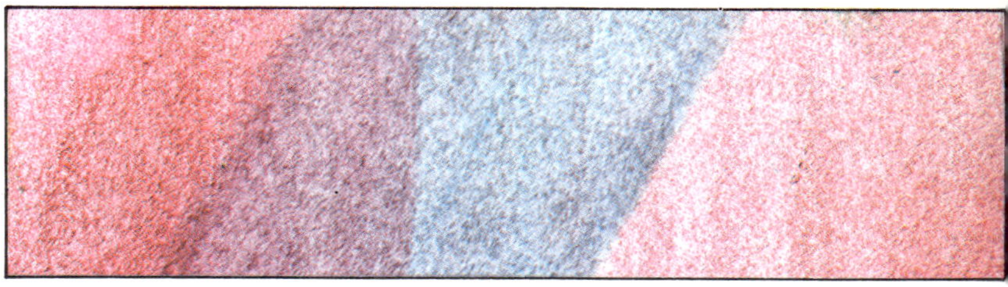

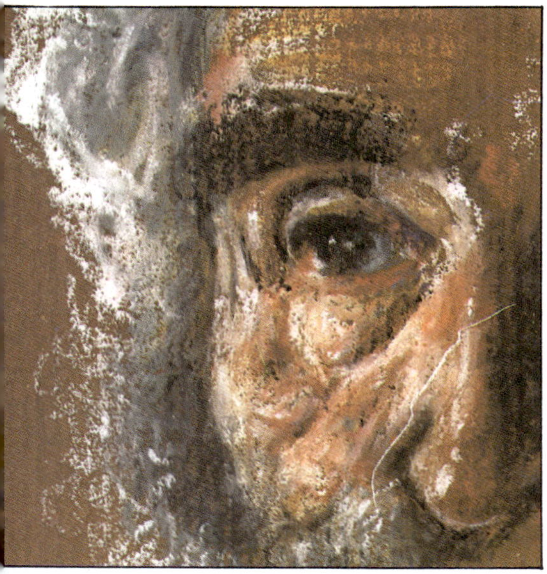

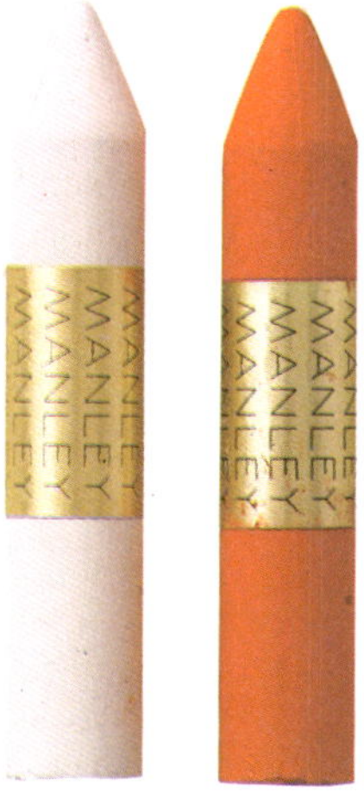

Characteristics of wax crayons

This drawing and the two below it are on dark brown Ingres paper. In this one we have used wax colors. Notice the greater definition achieved by these harder pigments—and the greater opacity and build-up of layers of color in the two oil pastel drawings.

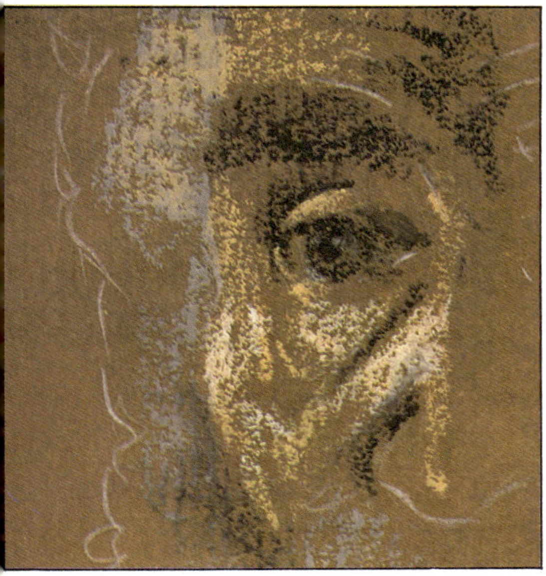

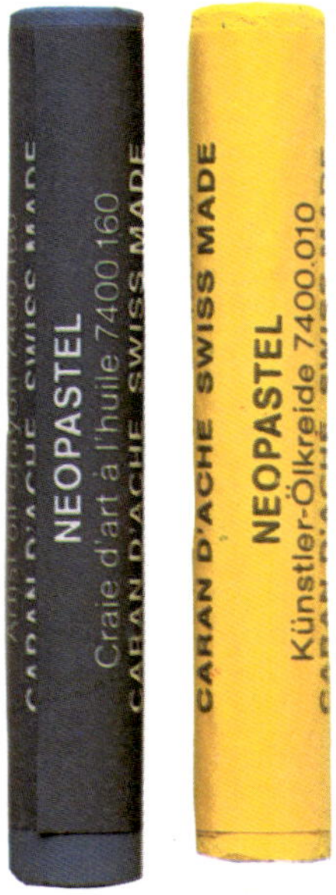

Characteristics of oil pastels

This is the outline sketch for the pastel drawing. The basic drawing was produced with a white crayon, with fine layers of color gradually being added, to create form and depth. In this drawing, the pale colors correspond to the bright or highlighted areas, while the color of the paper itself is used to suggest darker tones and shadow.

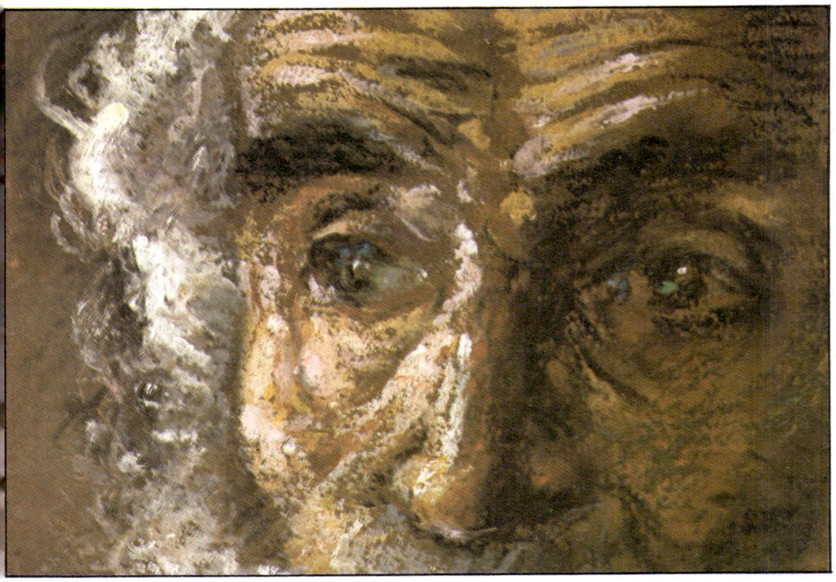

This example illustrates how much softer oil pastels are than wax crayons. See how well the pale colors are easily applied on top of one another, building up layers; they can be used to create an effect almost like that of oil painting. With practice, you will also be able to achieve results like these, which demonstrate the possibilities of this striking and expressive medium.

Two examples using turpentine on wax crayons

The turpentine on wax technique takes advantage of the fact that wax pigment dissolves in turpentine creating transparent color effects. The solvent is applied to a wax crayon drawing with a paintbrush, rather like the technique used for water soluble pencils.

We go into this technique in a companion volume in this series but, for the moment, let's take a look at these nudes, drawn with wax crayon by Miquel Ferrón. These show clearly the mobility of the medium which, when diluted with turpentine, creates some surprising results. The colors and tones in the middle range are so rich that the effects achieved invite comparison with water-based media such as watercolor, although the application is rather more vigorous.

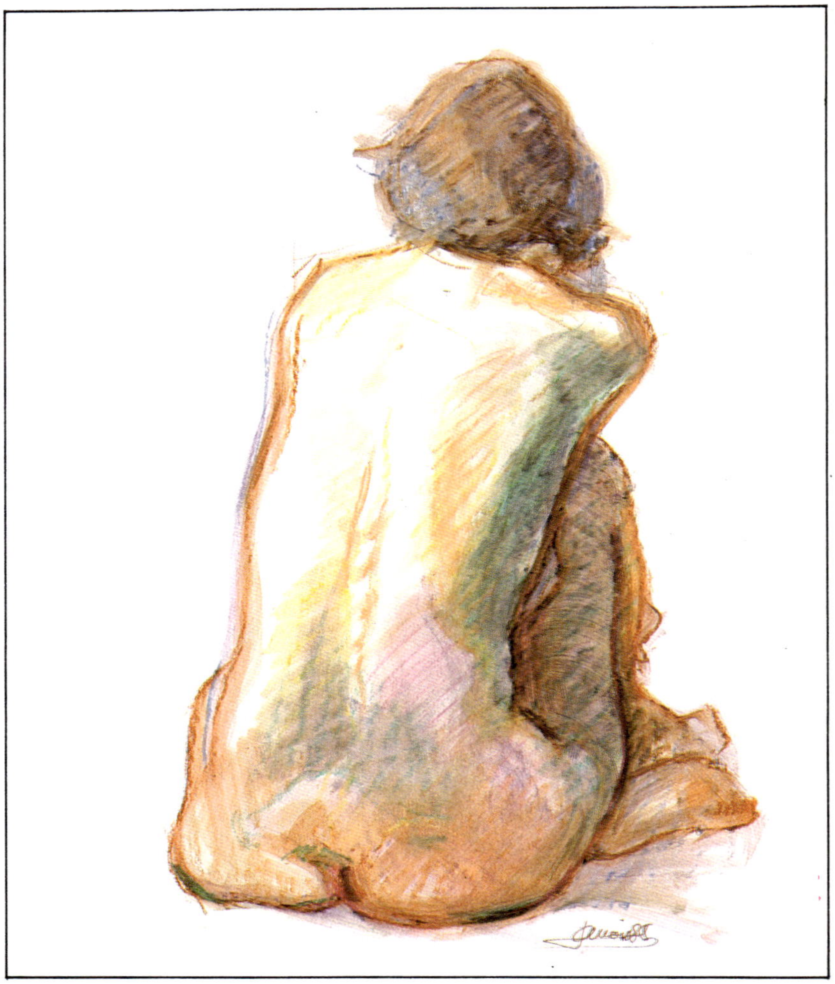

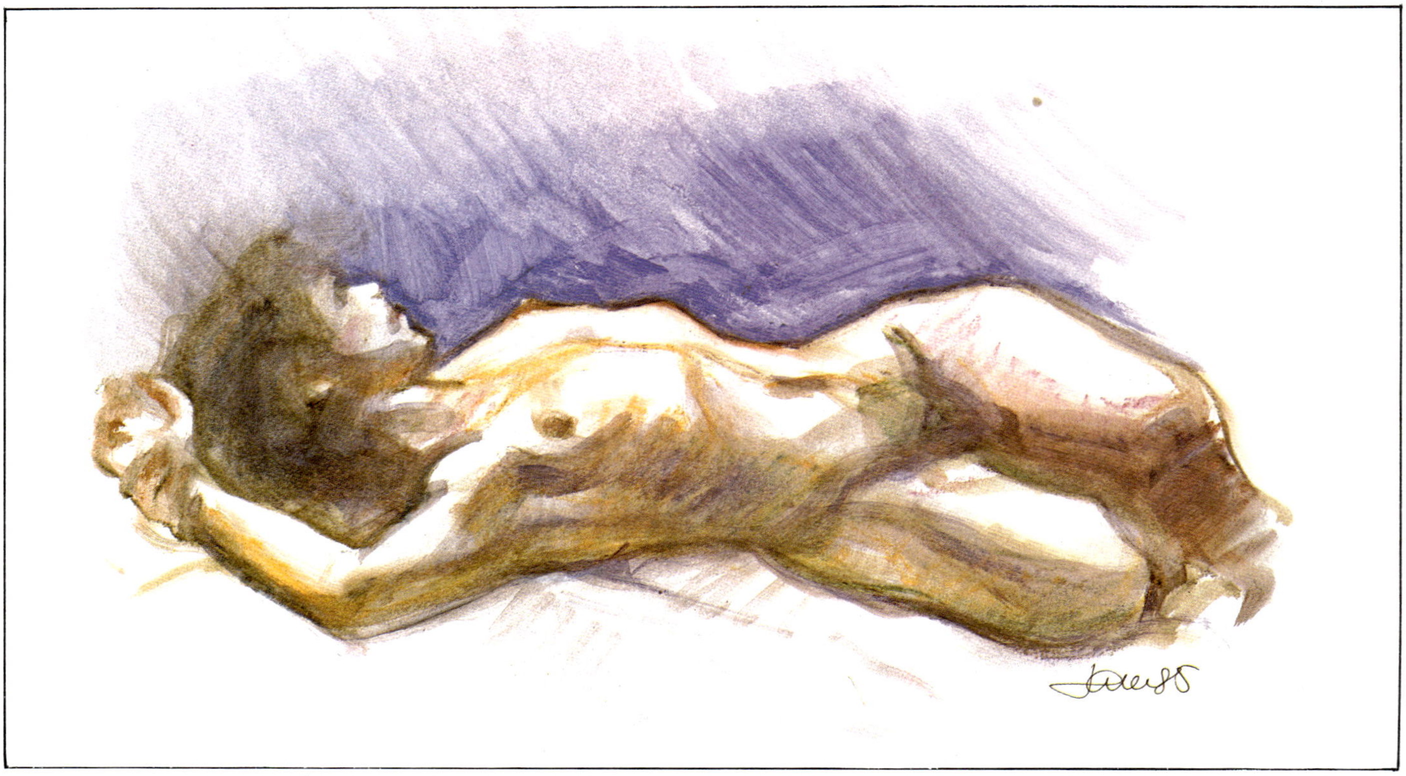

A seascape using wax crayons

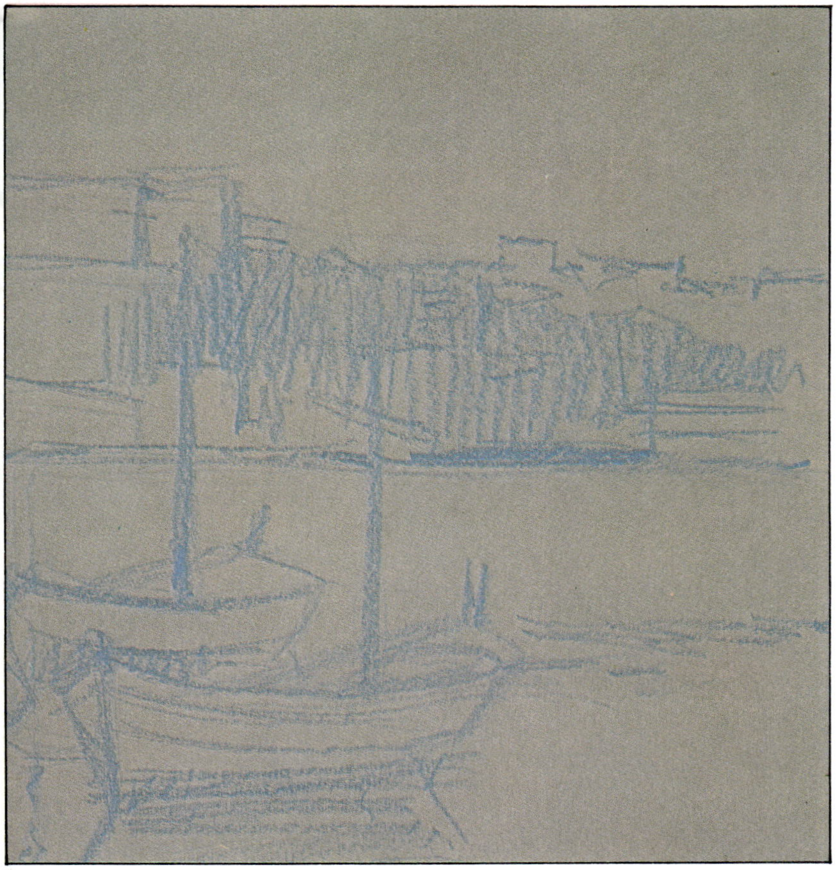

On this and the following pages we demonstrate the different stages of a seascape by Juan Sabater. He has used soft wax crayons on a mid-gray paper to create an atmosphere in which the white tones applied become the main source of the luminous quality of the picture.

We recommend that, in order to familiarize yourself with the use of wax crayons, you work on the same subject, sticking as closely as possible to the four stages into which we divided the process carried out by the artist. Use as your main guide the photographs showing the state of the picture at the end of each stage. Our words should be considered as a mere accompaniment to this exercise, there just to point things out from time to time.

First stage: Outline sketch

The initial layout sketch is carried out on the gray background using a blue crayon—always the best color for this task and particularly so in this case, given the dominantly blue tone of the picture.

Second stage: Setting the tone

The general areas of color are blocked in, the most luminous parts of the picture being drawn in white, which will gradually be varied as the picture progresses.

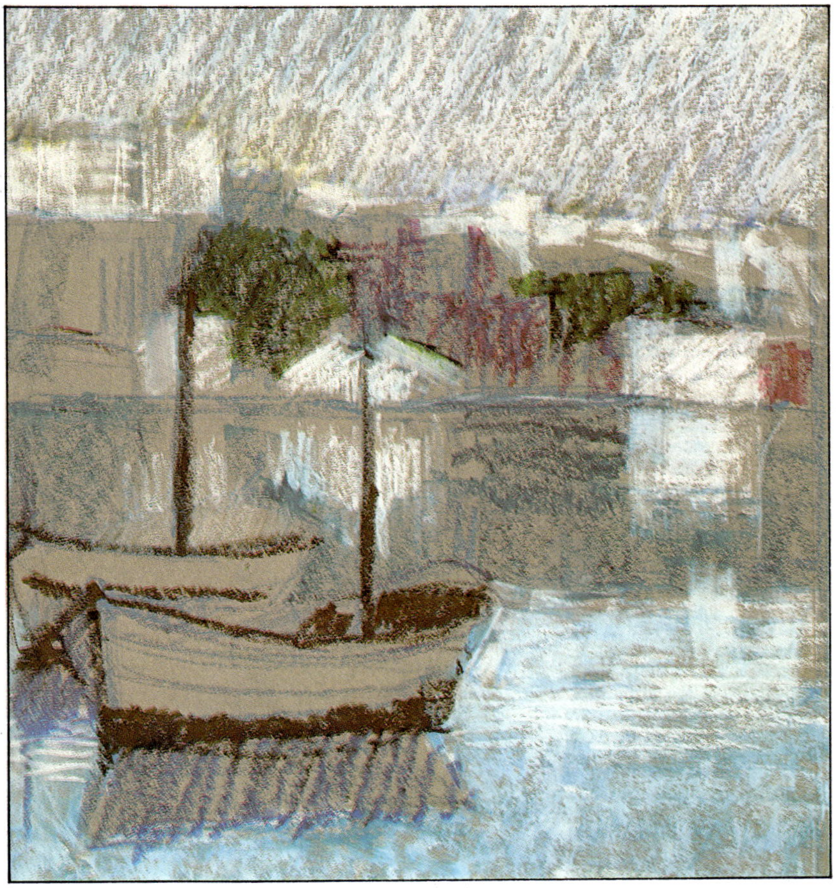

Below. *Chart of wax colors used in this exercise. Notice that some of the more luminous tones lose their brilliance when applied to a dark surface. The creamy texture of the wax pigment, when mixed with white, will bring out the quality of light we wish to achieve.*

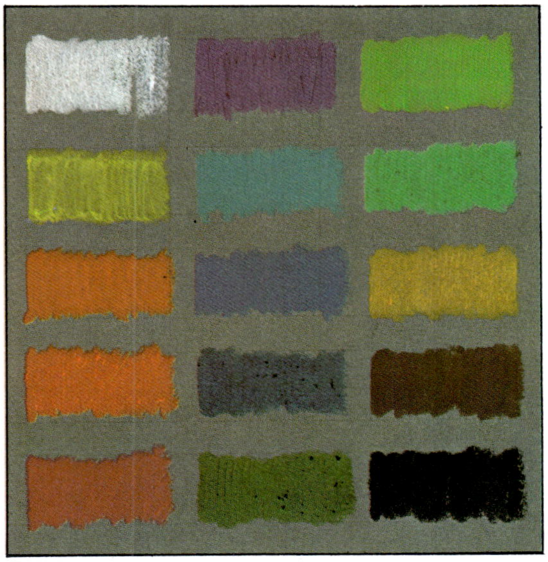

Third stage: Building up the color

By blending the colors and building up the general tonal values of the picture, we head towards the final stage of the exercise. It is important to stress that you should work on the whole picture simultaneously rather than spending too long on one area. This ensures that you keep an overall view of its pictorial qualities, until the moment you decide that your picture coincides with the aesthetic vision you started with.

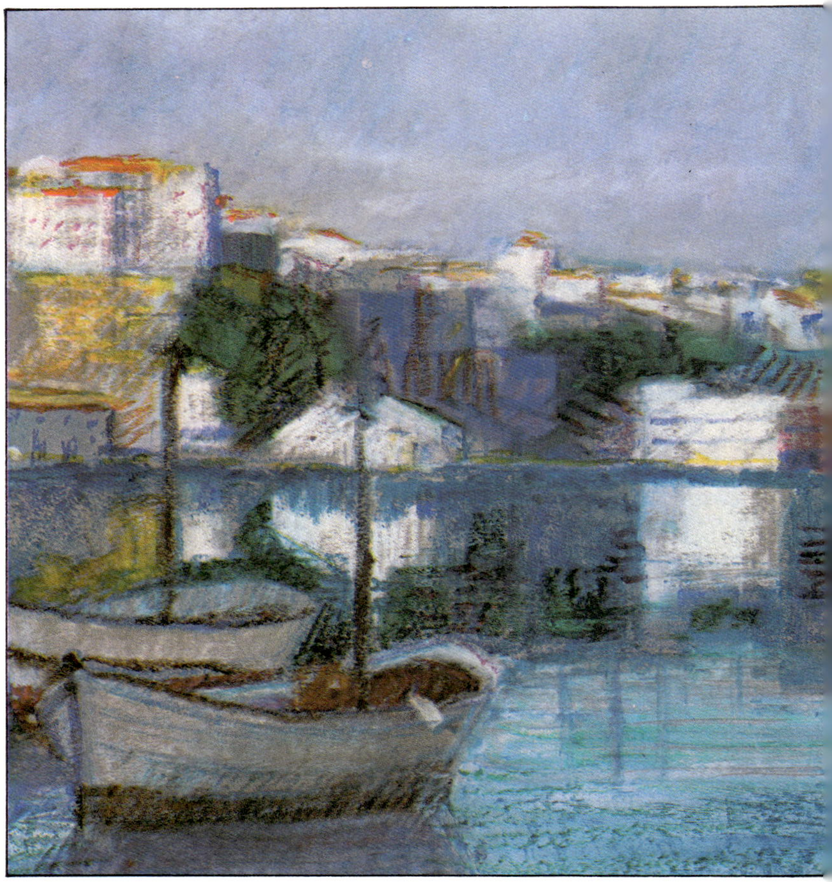

Fourth stage: Completion of the picture

Blending the colors of the sky and the greens and blues of the sea with the fingertips, opening up new or lost white areas and adding last-minute details such as the masts, we bring the picture to completion. To your right, on this page, you can see a fragment of the finished work, enlarged to show how the particular qualities of wax crayons were exploited in this exercise.

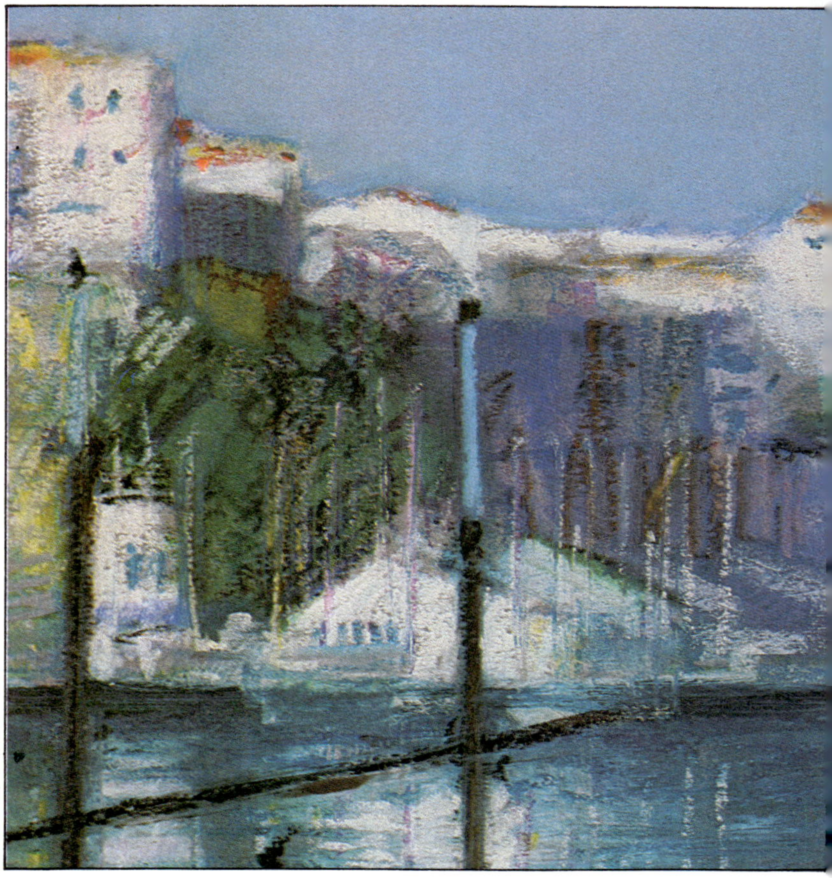

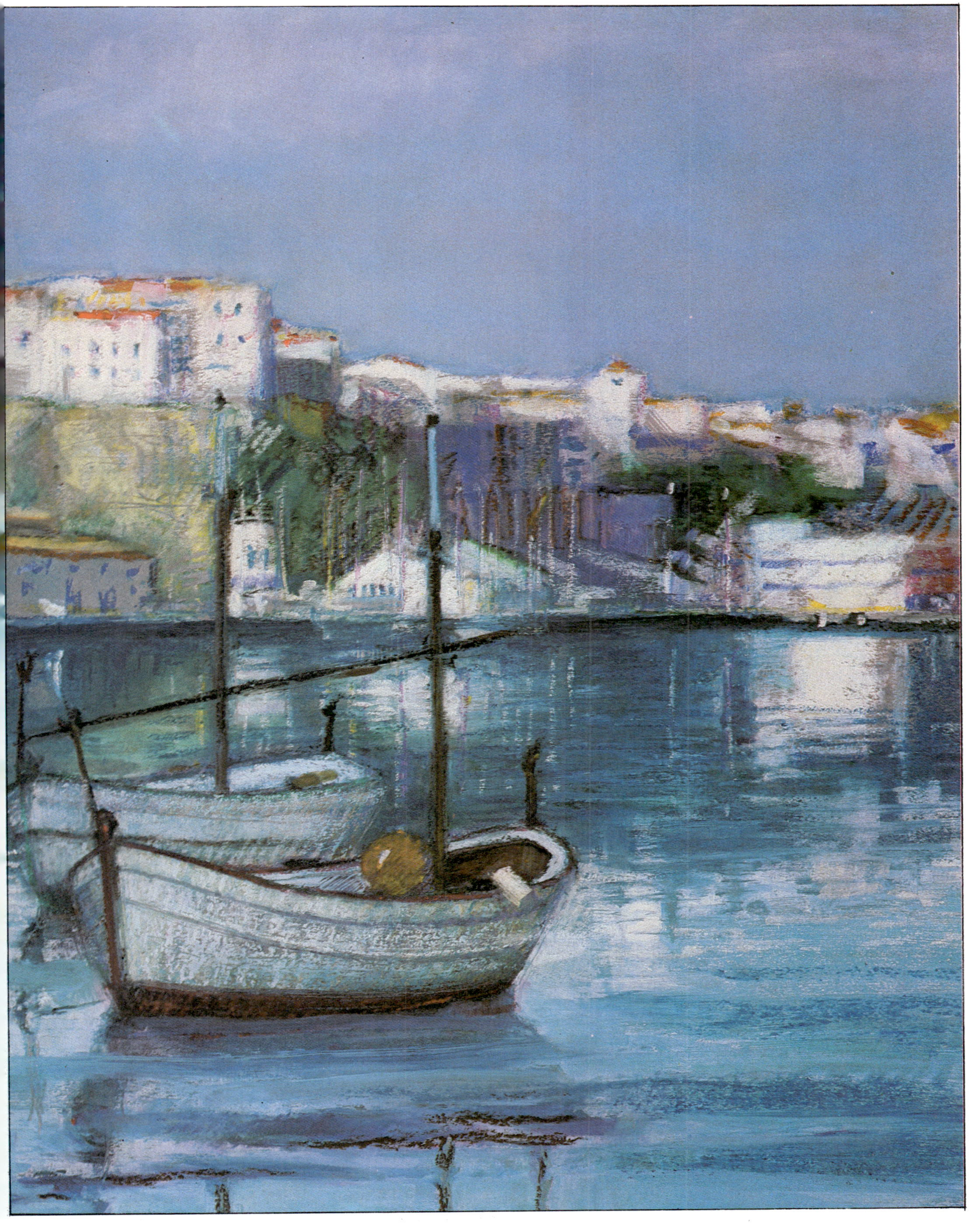

Gouache

Gouache is a French word to describe a pictorial technique that, certainly in its related forms of tempera and fresco, enjoyed a period of splendor in Persian, Chinese, Indian and, especially, Japanese painting. Its origins go back to the 4th and 5th Centuries and these days it is applied, not just on paper, but also on silk, ivory, parchment, satin, and other surfaces. We could describe it as being related in some ways to both watercolor and oils, because it has certain characteristics in common with both techniques. Like watercolor, it is diluted in water and applied with the same type of brushes on the same type of paper; like oils, it is an opaque medium with which the paint surface can be built up and overpainted.

Gouache colors are thick and opaque, a quality that allows light tones to be painted over dark ones. However, when diluted in a lot of water, they can produce an effect similar to that of watercolor. Gouache dries relatively quickly and the colors are less intense and almost matt once they dry.

They are used by many professional artists, especially for landscape painting, and are also popular for producing posters, publicity materials, and murals. Some theorists consider this technique to be the step that leads to oil painting.

Logically, as the paint to be applied is damp, one of the initial steps in gouache painting is stretching the paper, a process demonstrated on page 39. While we are on the subject of paper, it is worth mentioning that the most popular support for gouache painting is a good, lightly textured drawing paper.

Many artists have used gouache at one point in their career. On the next page are three examples, separated as much by time as technique.

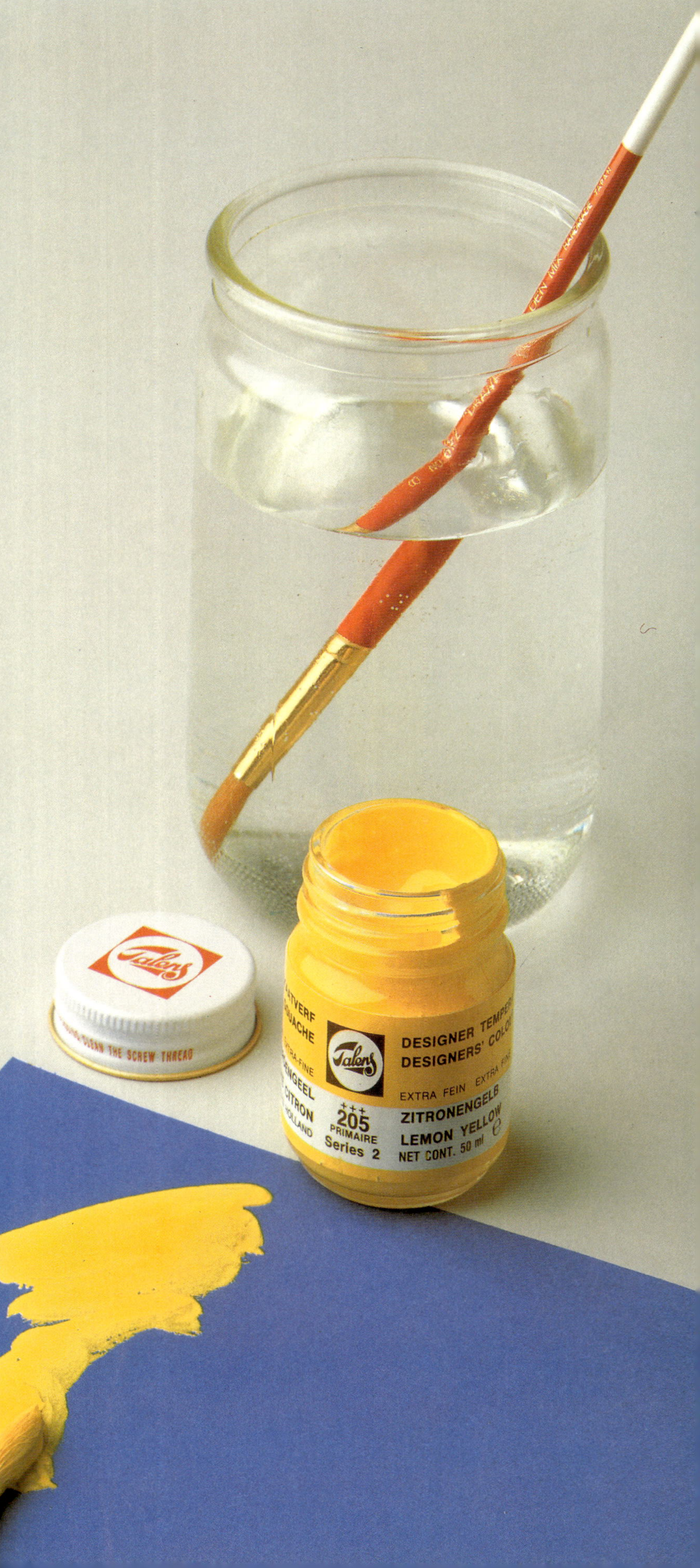

Three examples from masters of the medium

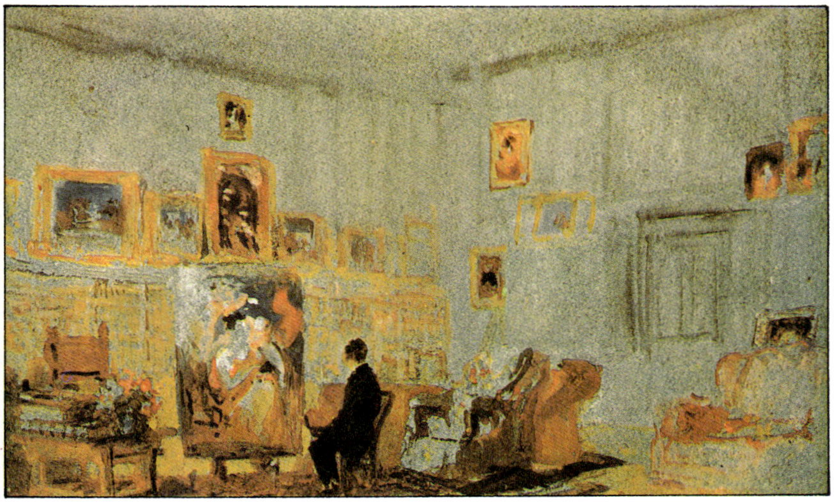

"Petworth: interior" by Joseph Mallord William Turner (British Museum, London). Gouache sketch, on gray paper. Turner, the great English painter, made various studies like this one in gouache on gray paper, a surface that allowed him to emphasize certain contrasts.

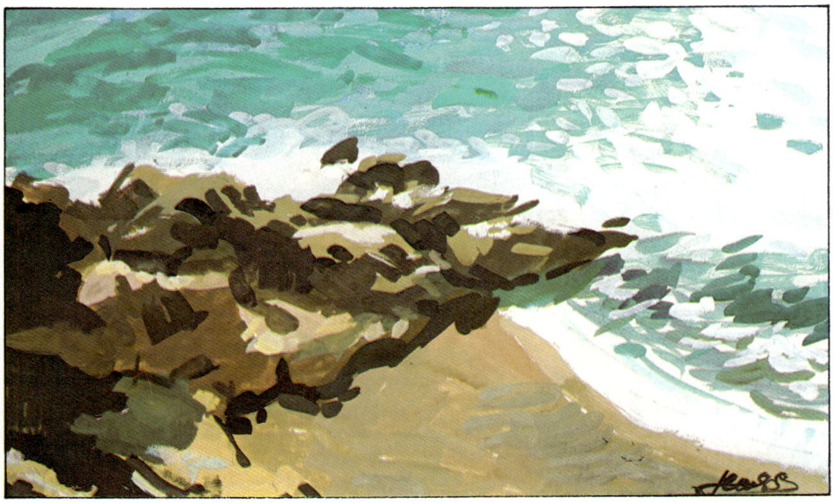

A gouache seascape painted by Miquel Ferrón to demonstrate the characteristics of this process. When you have developed a certain skill and freedom with the brush, the opaqueness of the color allows you to apply an almost white tone on top of black, without fear of color mixing, something that occurs frequently with water colors.

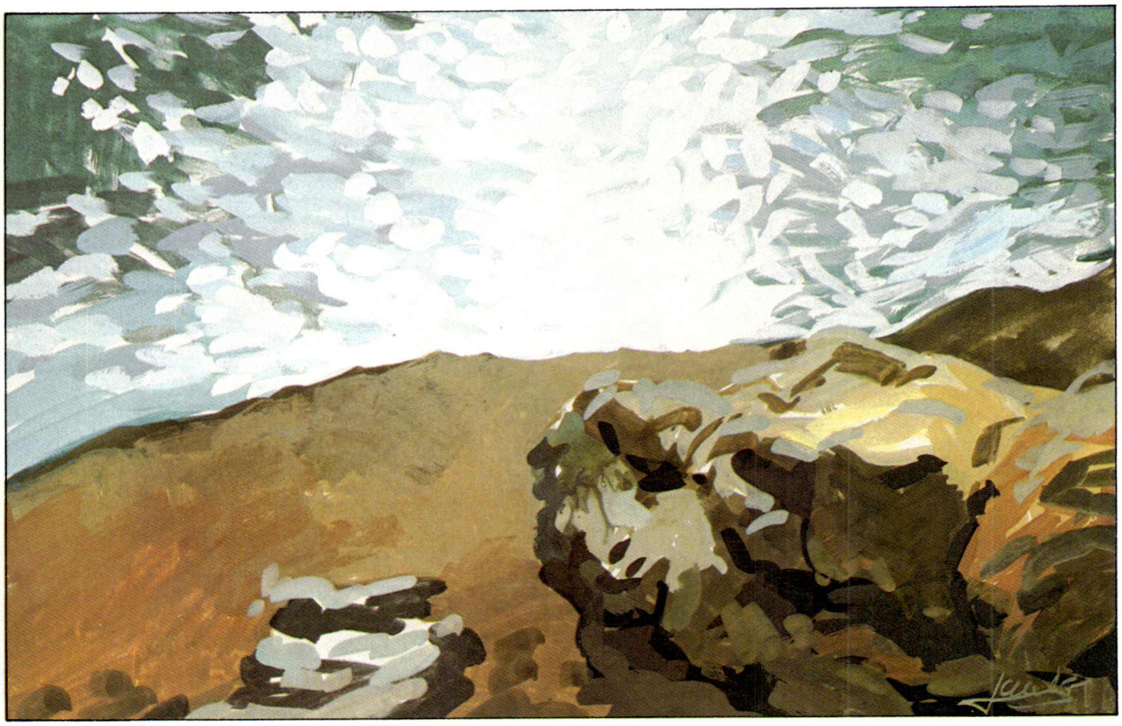

In this fragment of another seascape by Miquel Ferrón, the vigorous brushstrokes laid on top of some dark colors can be clearly seen—in the grays on the rocks, for example—and the almost pure white in the center of the water creating a blinding brightness.

Tools and techniques

Gouache paints are made up of the same ingredients as watercolors: Powdered vegetable, mineral or animal colorings, mixed up and bound with water-soluble gums, with certain gelling agents added so the painting doesn't crack when it's dry. Gouaches are available in tubes of 3½, 5½ and 10 oz. (14, 21, and 37 ml) and in 8 oz. (30 ml) jars. The paint sold in jars tends to dry out more quickly, because more of it is exposed to the air. The tube is much more suitable for artists.

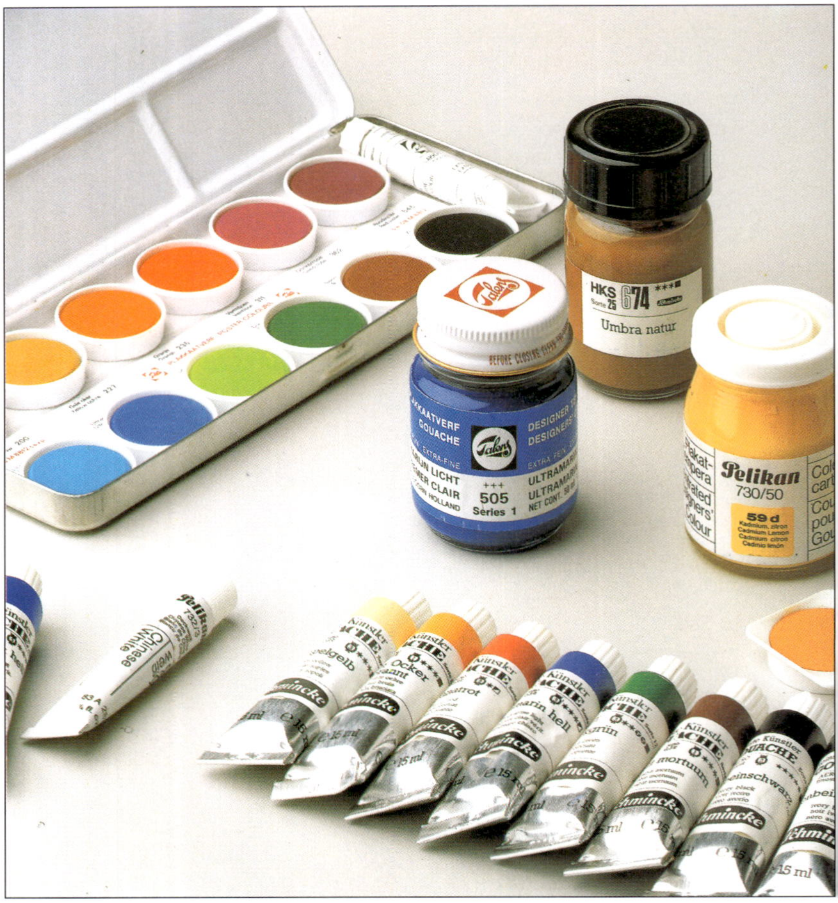

PRINCIPAL MANUFACTURERS OF GOUACHE PAINTS

Make	Country
Grumbacher	United States
Lefranc/Bourgeois	France
Pelikan	Germany
Rosal	Spain
Schmincke	Germany
Talens	Netherlands
Winsor & Newton	United Kingdom

Painting smooth background with gouache

When painting a background in gouache, various things can go wrong. The color might be too thick, or it might dry too quickly making it impossible to spread evenly. . .

. . . Or the color might be too liquid, leaving brush marks when it dries. In either event, the background will be uneven and some areas darker than others.

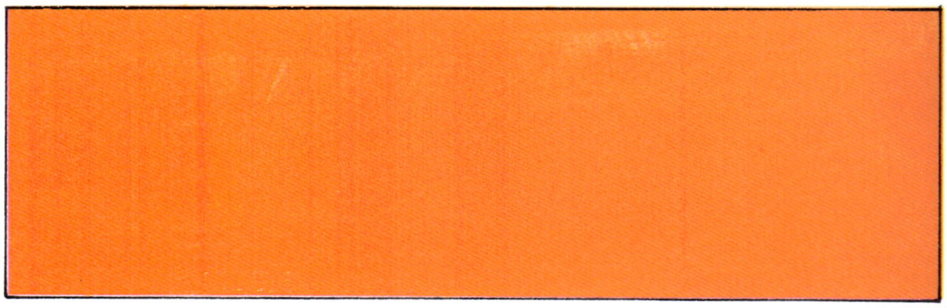

This is a well-painted background, with a good density of color, produced using a flat No. 16 or 20 brush to apply first a uniform, horizontal brushstroke, and then a second, vertical one—and so on.

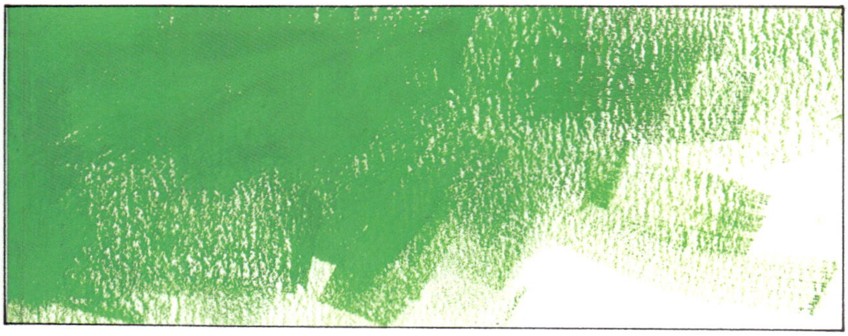

Background using a dry brush

To begin this demonstration of textures obtained using gouache paints, we offer a sample of color applied straight from the tube with a dry brush. The grainy paper provides the texture and finish characteristic of this technique.

Wash background, watercolor style

By mixing the gouache paint with a lot of water, an effect similar to watercolor can be achieved. Remember that the paper used for this kind of work must be heavy enough not to buckle when damp.

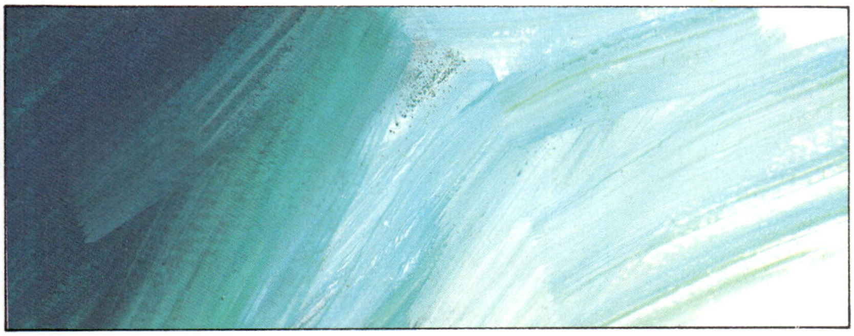

Background gradated with white paint

Here we can see that if we add white on top of gouache, it is difficult to mix the two colors completely and the brushstrokes leave streaks of both colors—in this case, blue and white.

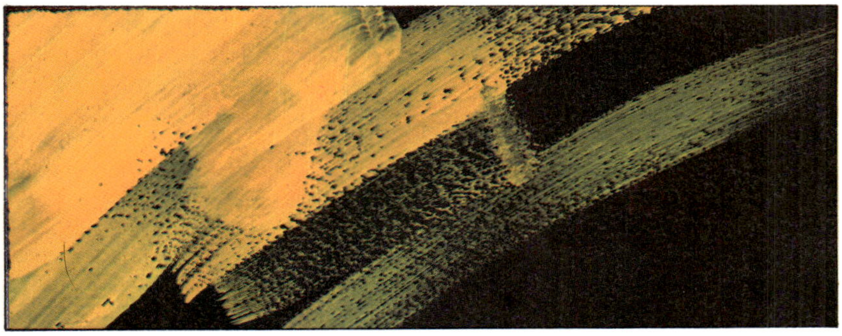

Pure color on a dark background

It takes a long time to produce a gradation on a dark background with pure color. This demonstrates the opacity of gouache, even with a black as intense as this one. The effect is similar to oil paint.

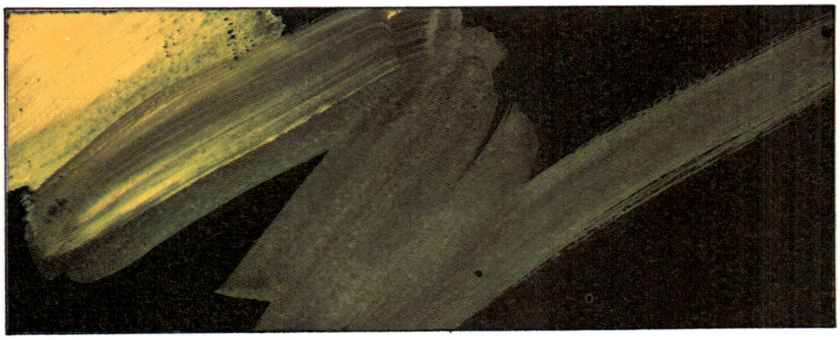

Color wash on a dark background

Using the same color as in the previous example—but this time diluted with water—the similarities to watercolor are obvious. It looks just like a typical gradated wash, practically from the moment the first strokes are applied. Finally, we should remind you that gouache loses its intense color once it dries.

A landscape using gouache

Landscapes, seascapes, nature—gouache lends itself to these subjects. Where intense, lively, and brilliant colors are called for, gouache produces some wonderful results. With good reason publicity professionals use these colors for their sales campaigns, their brochures, and their layouts.

Choose your subject and, using the exercise on the following pages as your guide, go ahead and paint your first gouache.

You can see from the photograph at the bottom of the page that a simple white plate makes a perfectly good palette when using gouache paints.

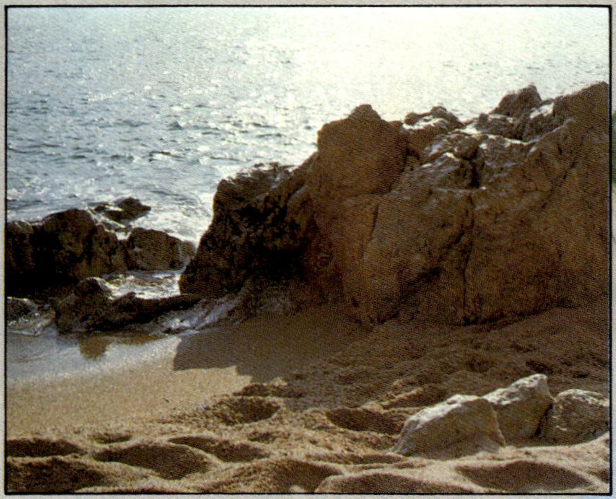

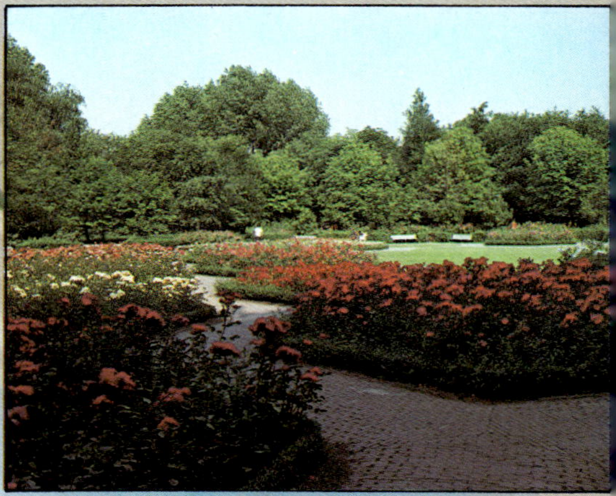

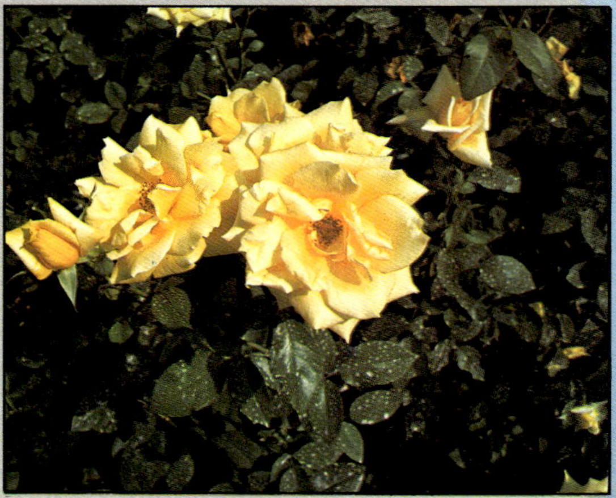

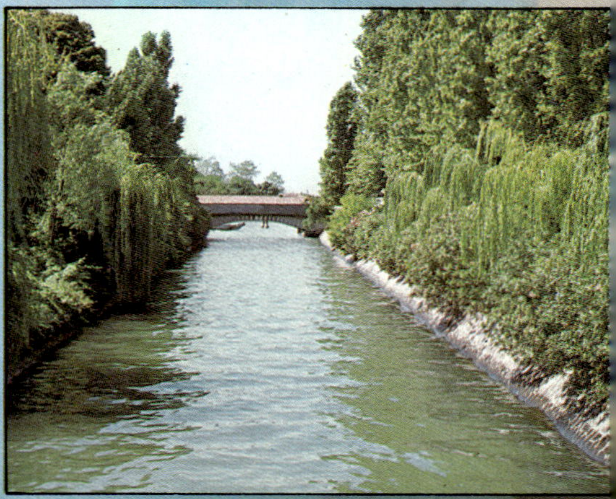

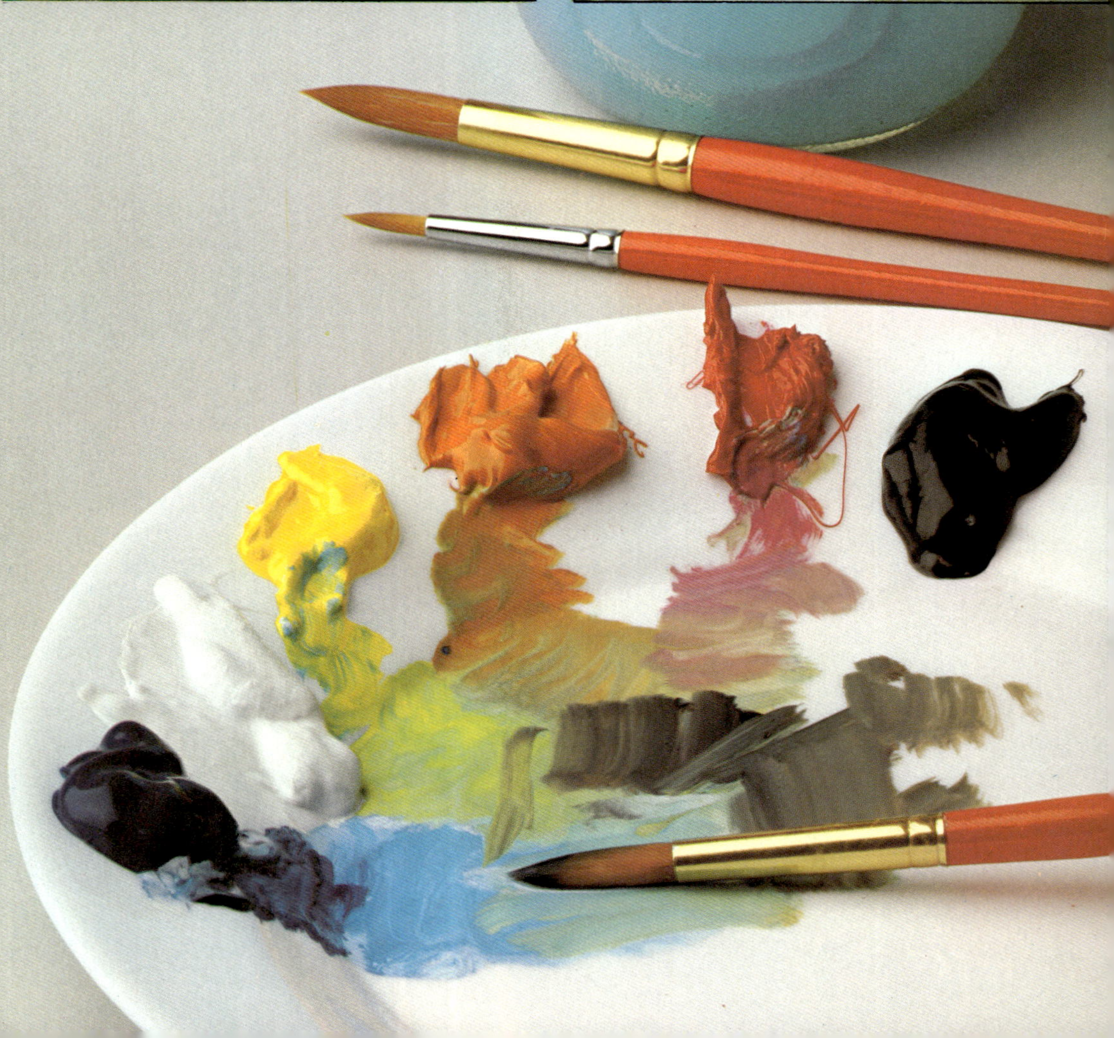

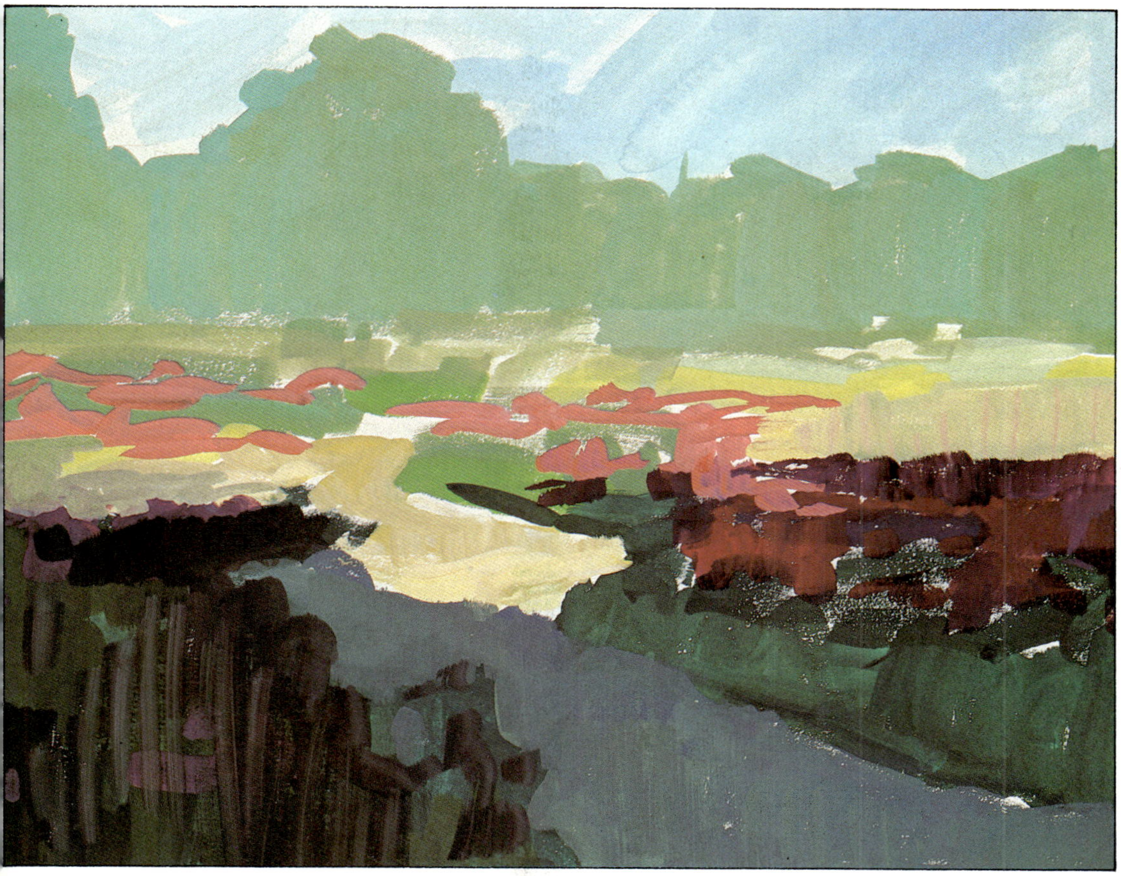

For this exercise we have chosen as our subject the garden on the previous page. We will show you in three stages how Miquel Ferrón rendered this scene, illustrating the use of nearly all the technical effects made possible by this medium.

First stage: Basic tone

Ferrón has blocked in the basic colors without an initial sketch, in order to achieve a greater degree of spontaneity in this picture, intended to be an uncomplicated representation of the subject.

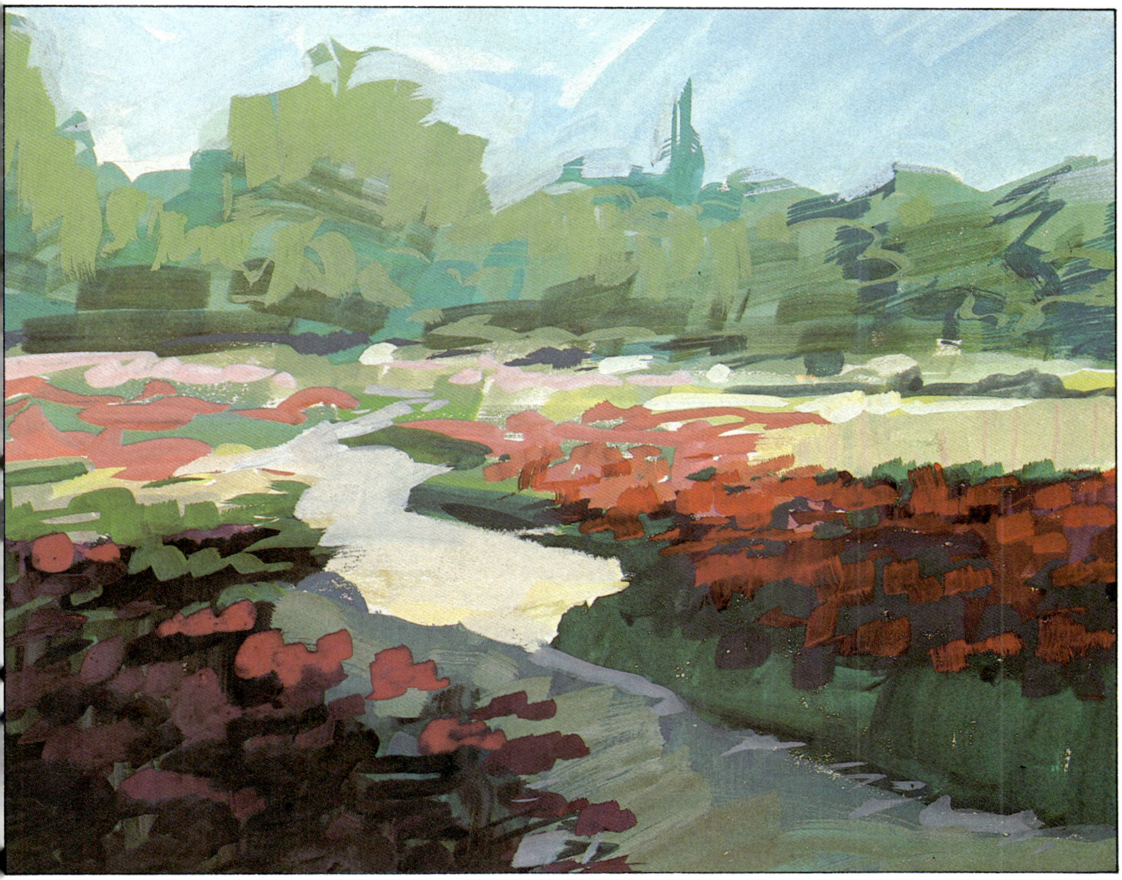

Second stage: Brighter tones

The opaqueness of gouache has allowed him to add these more luminous (and other darker) tones on top of the blocked-in color of the first stage. The colors have been superimposed without any problems.

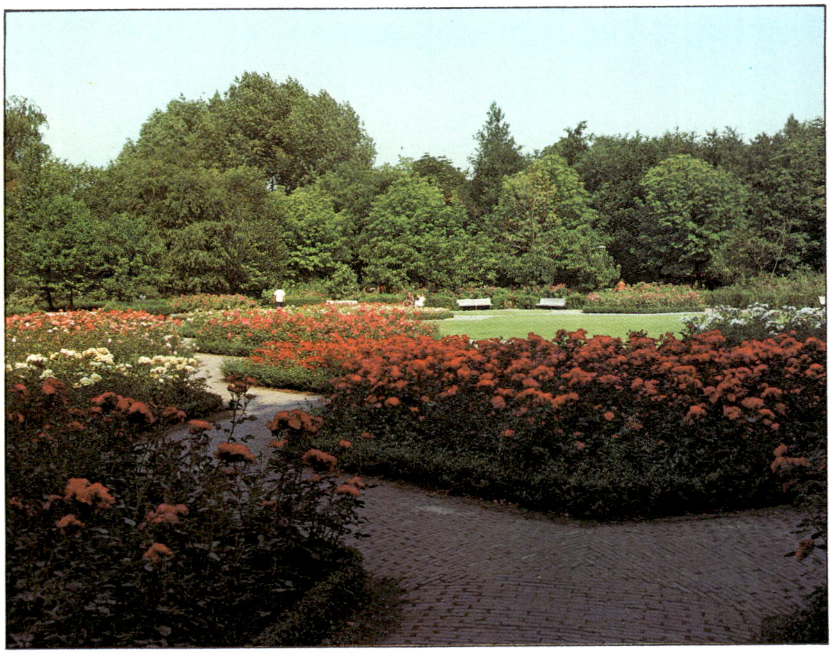

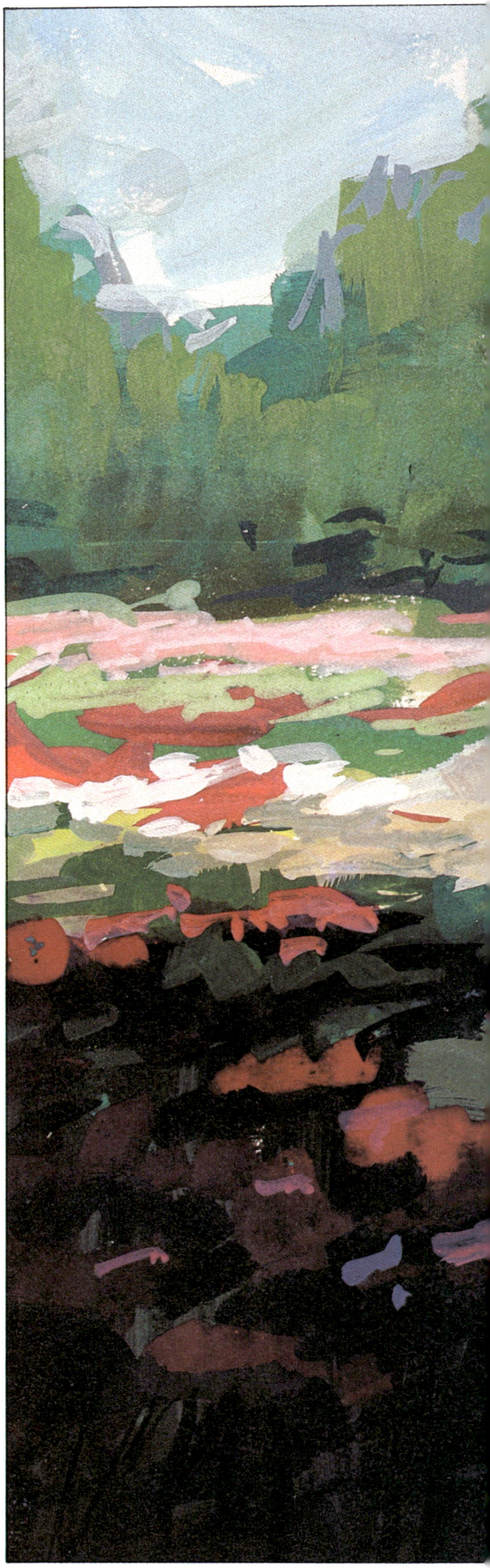

Third stage: Completion of the picture

The artist has finished the picture with more and more luminous layers, blending in some of the colors of the trees in the background. If you look at the finished work and compare it with the photo we used as a model (above), you might be tempted to think that we could have made a more careful study in the final stages. But bear in mind that gouache, like almost all pictorial techniques, allows us to express our personal feelings through our brushstrokes. This is undoubtedly what gives a work its individual character. Don't hesitate to follow this piece of advice to paint what you *feel*, instead of simply imitating the subject.

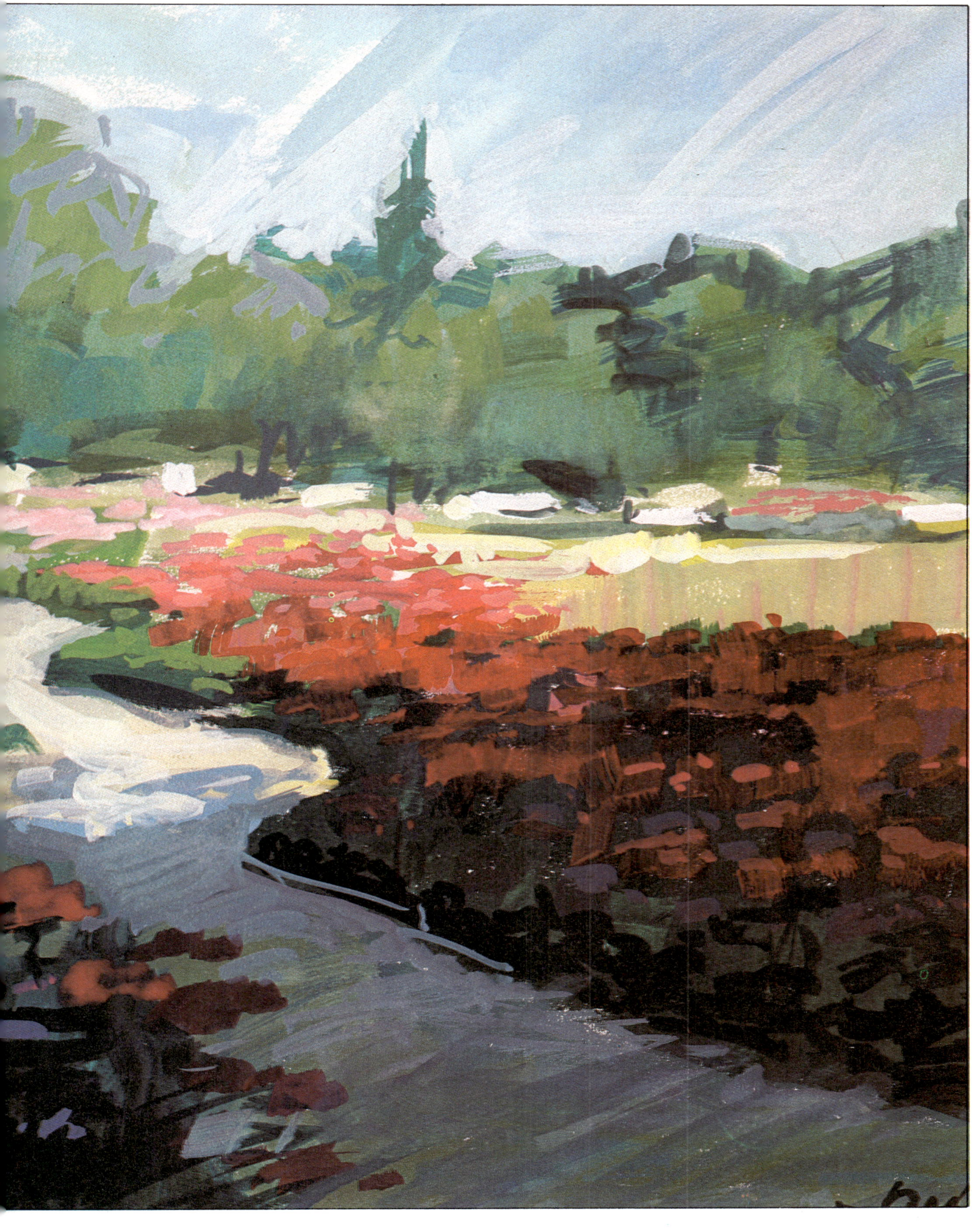

Painting in oils

The moment has arrived to turn our attention to oil painting. For the remainder of this book we will concentrate on introducing you to oils. You will find many more detailed analyses in other volumes dedicated exclusively to this pictorial medium. Why are oils often considered the highest form of painting? At least, artists who have mastered the medium tend to hold this view; they say that there is nothing as gratifying and complete as oil painting for expressing feeling and reflecting all aspects of nature. Of course, watercolorists put forward a few solid arguments contradicting this theory.

What is certain is that oil painting offers an almost infinite range of possibilities; the majority of the greatest painters since oils were first used have worked in this medium and many novices to the world of painting have started out in oils.

We are going to look especially at the practical aspects of oils, sharing some of the information gleaned from the experience of experts. For us, the practicalities include such things for example, as knowing that no other blue has the same luminous quality as cobalt blue; and that today you can buy synthetic brushes worthy of comparison with traditional hogs' hair ones, at considerably lower prices. But theories and tricks of the trade are meaningless if you do not follow the advice of the old saying:

Practice makes perfect

In other words, you have to get out there and work. Paint, set up your easel and canvas, and learn about the consistency of the colors and their combinations; discover which is the best frame for that seascape or this portrait; make mistakes and start again as many times as is necessary. It's the only way. We can promise you that the satisfaction you will gain from this fascinating medium, once you have come to grips with some of its techniques, will repay you with interest for the inevitable frustrations of the learning process.

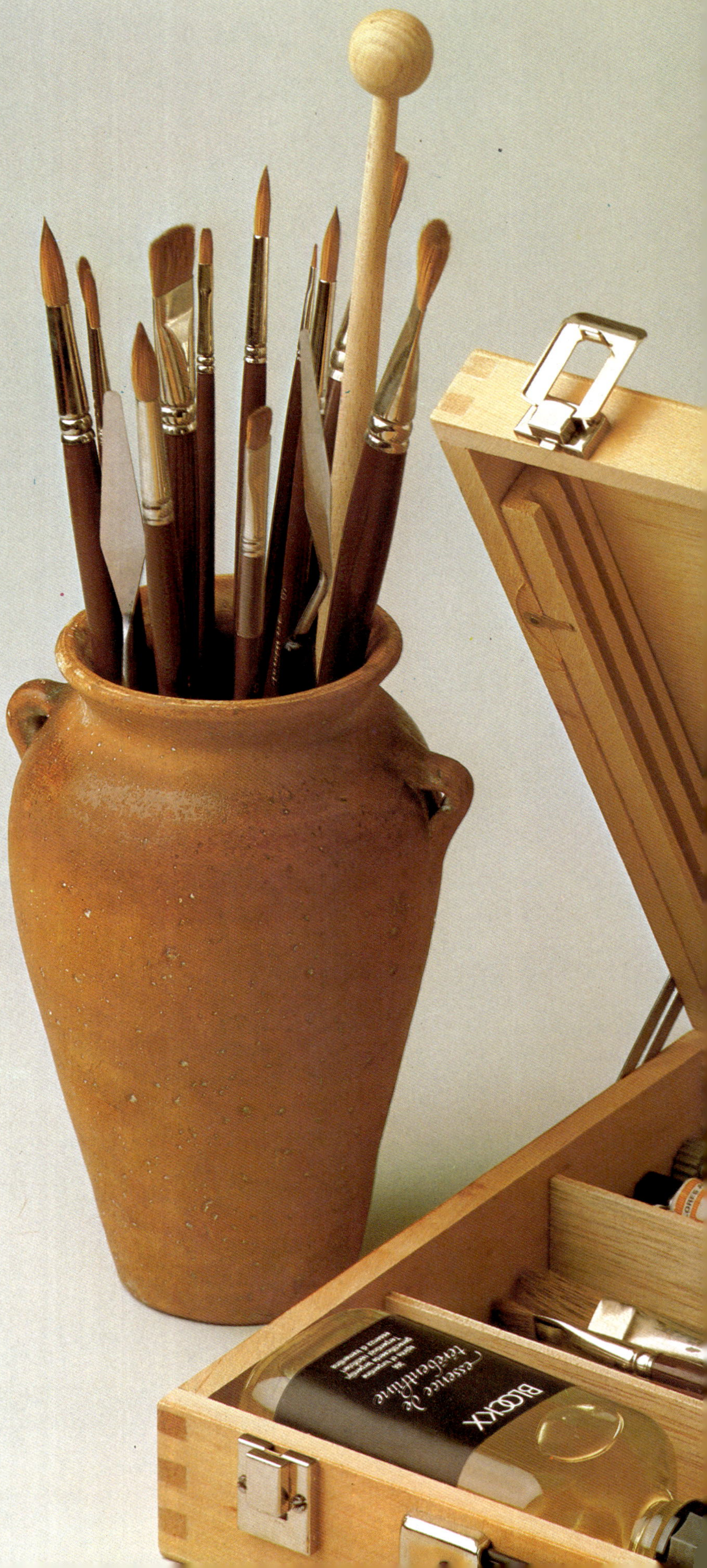

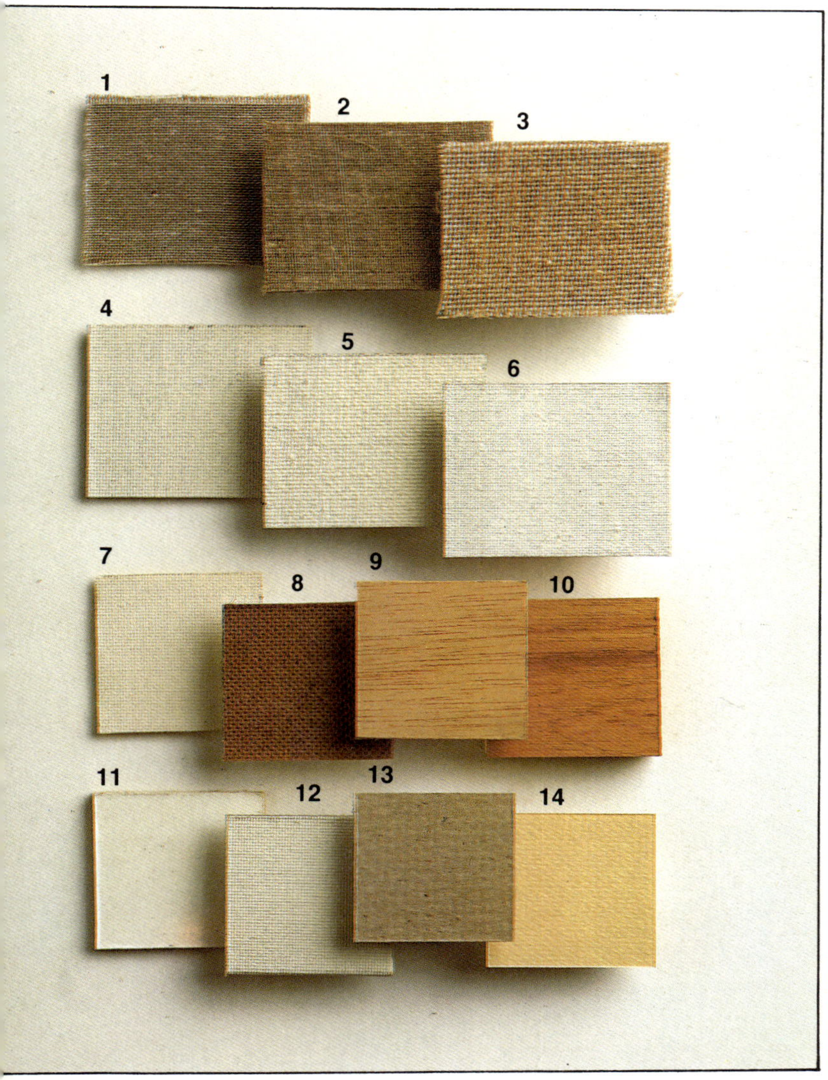

SURFACES FOR OIL PAINTING
1. *Cotton duck (notice the knots in the weave).*
2. *Linen, darker than cotton and with a more uneven weave. This is the best surface for oil painting.*
3. *Coarse hessian. Some painters still use this, in spite of its disadvantages.*
4. *Primed cotton duck.*
5. *Standard quality primed linen.*
6. *Fine artists' linen, an inspiring surface.*
7. *Cotton-duck mounted onto board.*
8. *Hardboard (rear).*
9. *Plywood.*
10. *Oak wood (other types of wood may be used).*
11. *Primed board or card.*
12. *Cotton-duck mounted onto board with acrylic primer.*
13. *Thick cardboard (prepared with a single coat of glue size or by rubbing with a garlic clove).*
14. *Colored drawing paper.*

STANDARD INTERNATIONAL MEASUREMENTS OF CANVAS STRETCHERS (IN CM.)

No.	Portrait	Landscape	Seascape
1	22 × 16	22 × 14	22 × 12
2	11 × 19	24 × 16	24 × 14
3	27 × 19	27 × 16	27 × 16
4	33 × 24	33 × 22	33 × 19
5	35 × 27	35 × 24	35 × 22
6	41 × 33	41 × 27	41 × 24
8	46 × 38	46 × 33	46 × 27
10	55 × 46	55 × 38	55 × 33
12	61 × 50	61 × 46	61 × 38
15	65 × 54	65 × 50	65 × 46
20	73 × 60	73 × 54	73 × 50
25	81 × 65	81 × 60	81 × 54
30	92 × 73	92 × 65	92 × 60
40	100 × 81	100 × 73	100 × 65
50	116 × 89	116 × 81	116 × 73
60	130 × 97	130 × 89	130 × 81
80	146 × 114	146 × 97	146 × 90
100	162 × 130	162 × 114	162 × 97
120	195 × 130	195 × 114	195 × 97

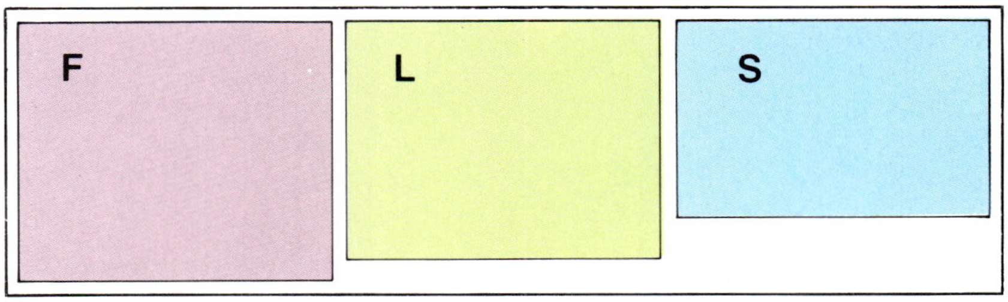

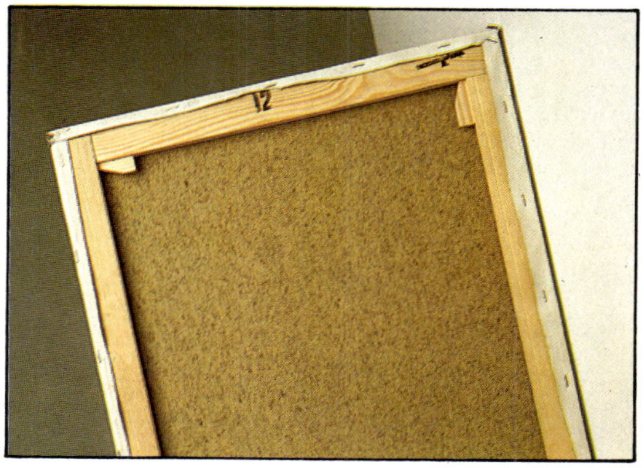

Above. *The horizontal and vertical proportions of stretchers of the standard formats, Figure (F), Landscape (L), and Seascape (S).*
Left. *Canvas mounted on a number 12, figure-format wooden stretcher.*

Below. *Complete range of hogs' hair brushes, from numbers 0 to 24. The real size of the brushes has been reduced in this illustration, so a No. 16 brush would, in reality, be approximately the size of a No. 24 shown here.*

Right. *Palette knives have wooden handles and steel blades. The blade is flexible, round-ended, and has no cutting edge. These tools are used for erasing (scraping paint off the canvas), for cleaning the palette, and also for painting, in the place of brushes. The mahl stick (top of picture) is a length of wood with a little ball at one end that is placed gently on the picture and used as a rest for the hand when painting small details.*

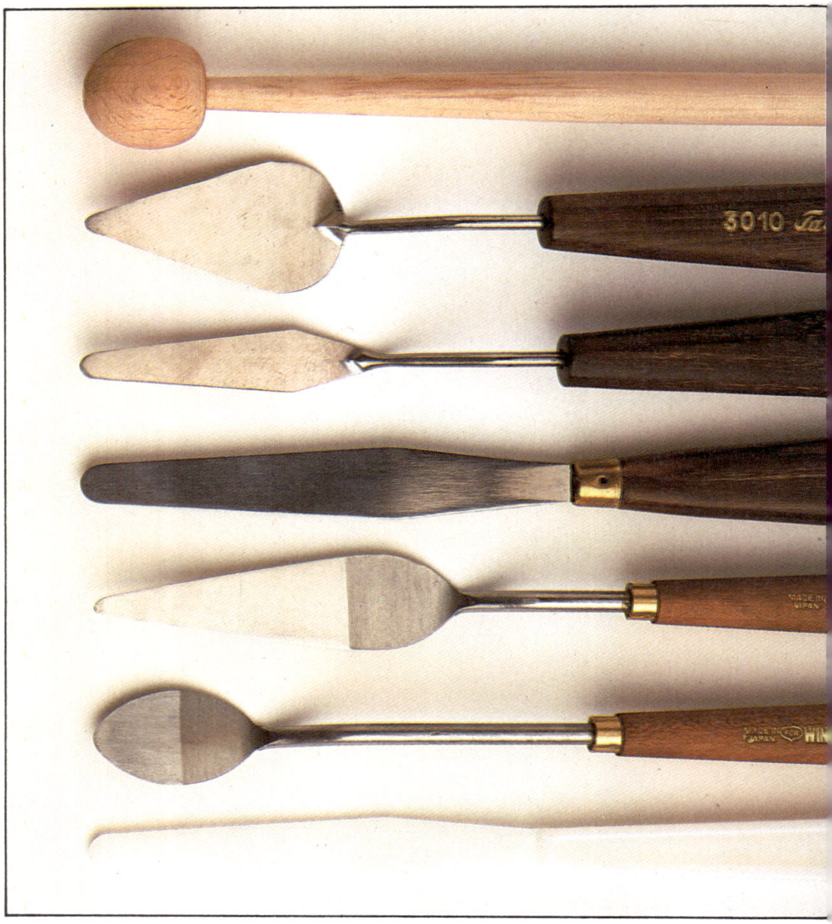

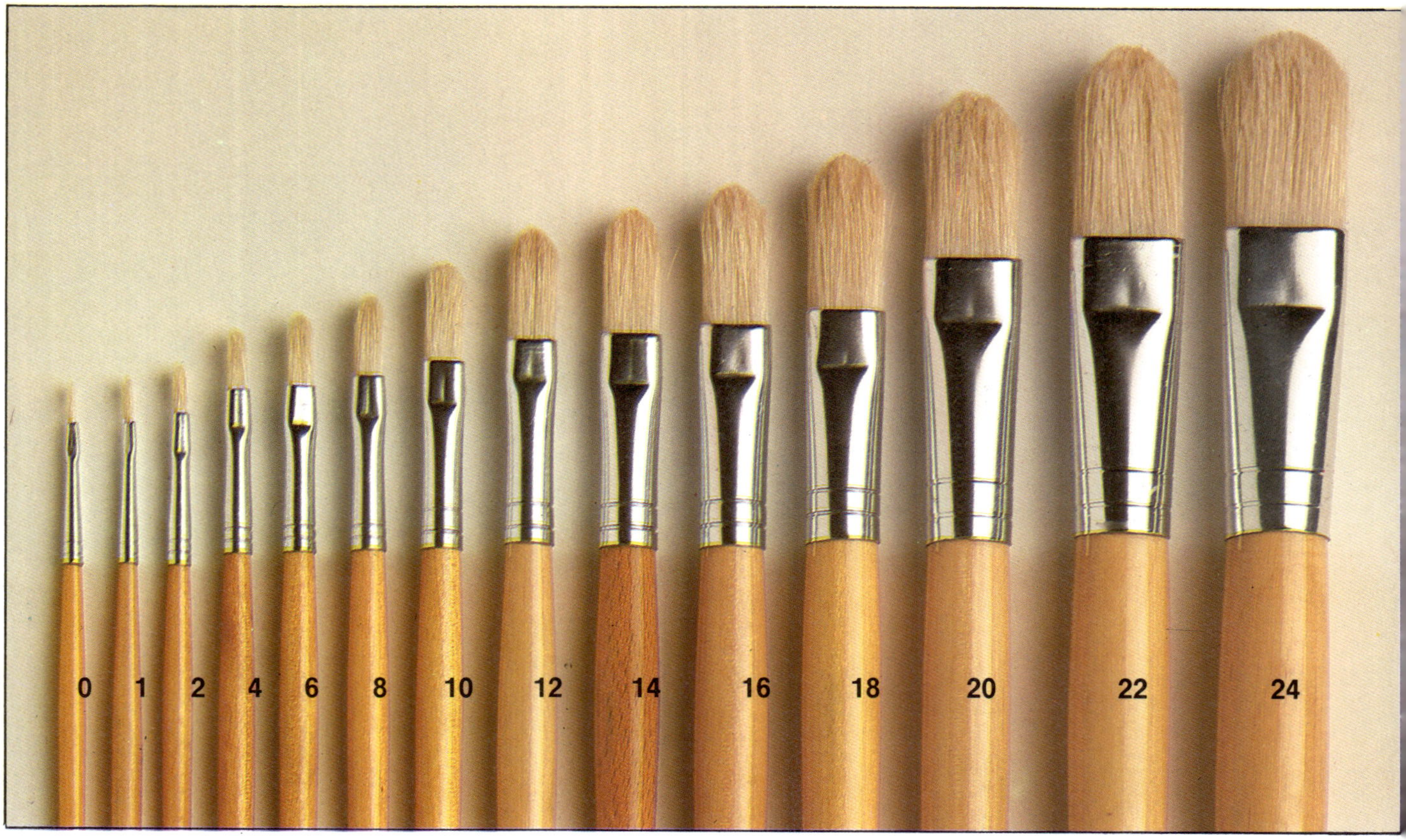

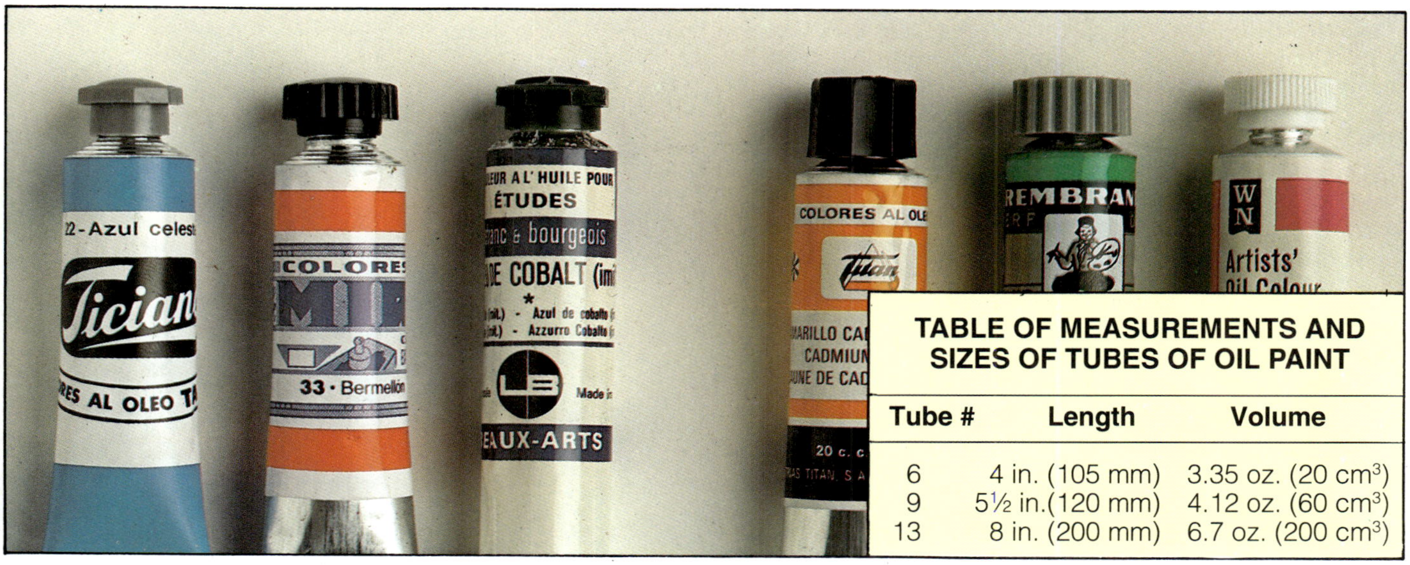

TABLE OF MEASUREMENTS AND SIZES OF TUBES OF OIL PAINT

Tube #	Length	Volume
6	4 in. (105 mm)	3.35 oz. (20 cm^3)
9	5½ in.(120 mm)	4.12 oz. (60 cm^3)
13	8 in. (200 mm)	6.7 oz. (200 cm^3)

Lemon yellow

Burnt umber

Emerald green

Cadmium yellow medium

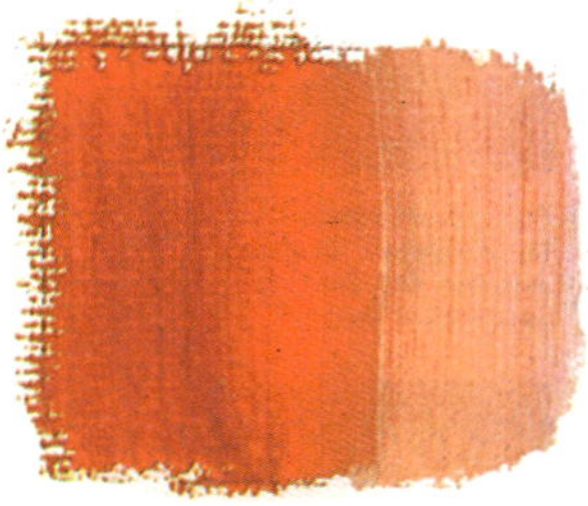
Vermilion

Ultramarine

Yellow ochre

Alizarin crimson

Cobalt blue

Burnt sienna

Permanent green

Prussian blue

Most frequently used oil colors

You will probably have seen some of the extensive color charts offered by manufacturers. You will have seen them and been confused by the number of colors and tones to choose from.

Each artist has his or her preferred range of colors—there will always be someone who will not use any but Naples yellow—but the fact is that most professionals since painting began have worked with no more than ten or twelve basic colors, as well as black and white. On the left is a fairly typical selection.

From this range, if we had to leave out four, we would opt for cadmium yellow, burnt sienna, permanent green, and black. Black can easily be made from Prussian blue, alizarin crimson, and burnt umber.

Depending on the dominant tone of his subject, the artist can put together his palette using one of these ranges: Cool colors, warm colors, or subdued colors. We will look at these in more detail in the following pages.

Above. *Tubes of oil paint from different manufacturers. The three on the right are professional quality and those on the left are from the students' range.*

Color scales

Warm color scale

This consists of yellow, ochre, red, burnt umber, alizarin crimson, permanent green, emerald green, and ultramarine blue.

We have left cobalt blue and Prussian blue out of this range, although these, or any other color, may be introduced into a warm color scale. By warm colors we mean all those with a chromatic tendency towards red, yellow, orange, ochre, and sienna. But these colors may be mixed with blues, greens, and violets to darken tones or to paint shadows and half-light—to "dirty" the picture, as Titian put it.

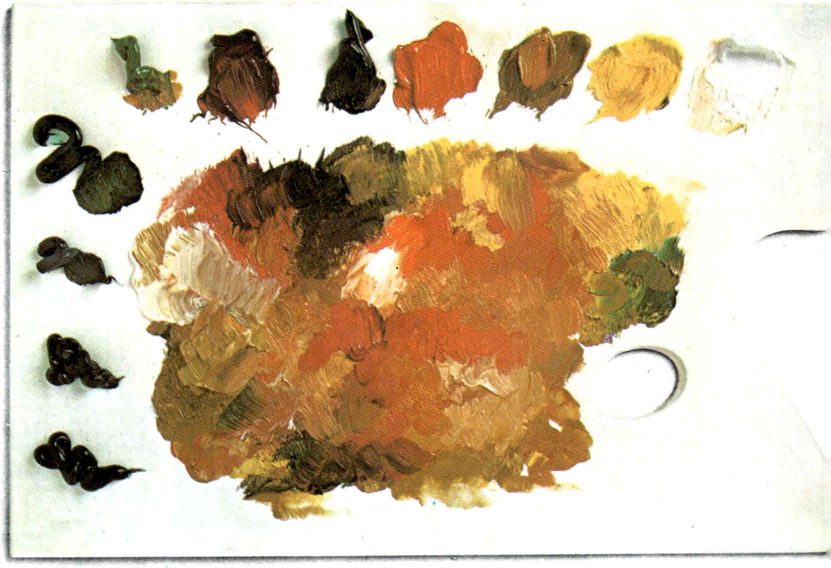

Cool color scale

Basically, this consists of Prussian blue, ultramarine, cobalt blue, emerald green, permanent green, alizarin crimson, raw umber, and yellow ochre.

A cool scale need not necessarily be blue, as Degas and other great artists have demonstrated in their works. However, the overall tendency in the painting must be bluish, even in flesh tints.

On the next page you can see some examples of famous paintings in which the chromatic tendency is quite obvious.

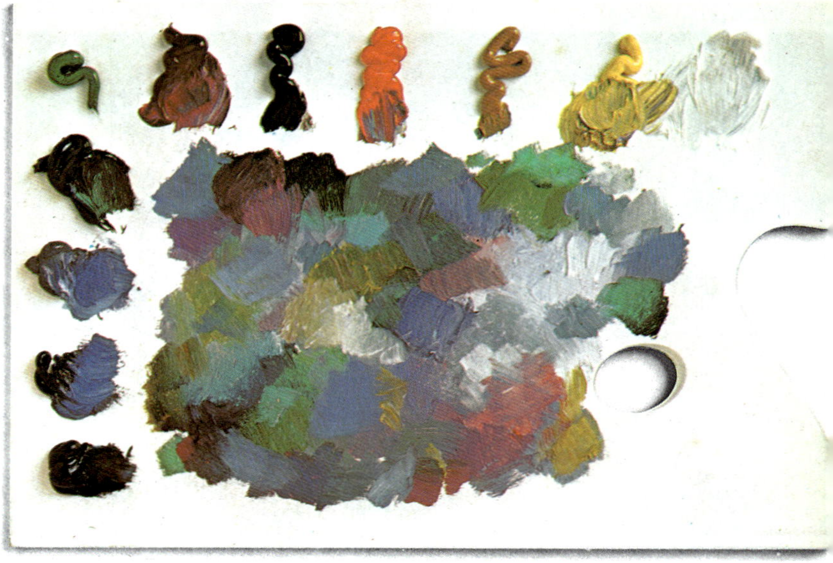

Subdued color scale

Subdued colors are the result of mixing complementary colors with white. For example, a green and an intense red. The result can be a brown, a khaki, an ochre, a green all toned down, or "dirty" colors.

The more equal the proportions of each complementary color, the darker the mixture will be, and the more white added, the grayer the result. Subdued colors may be predominantly cool or warm. No shade is excluded from this palette.

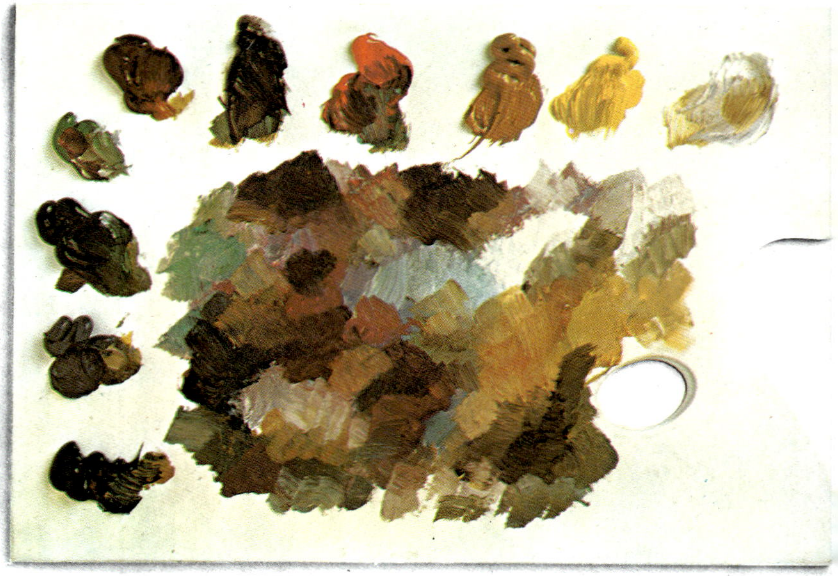

Three examples from masters of the medium

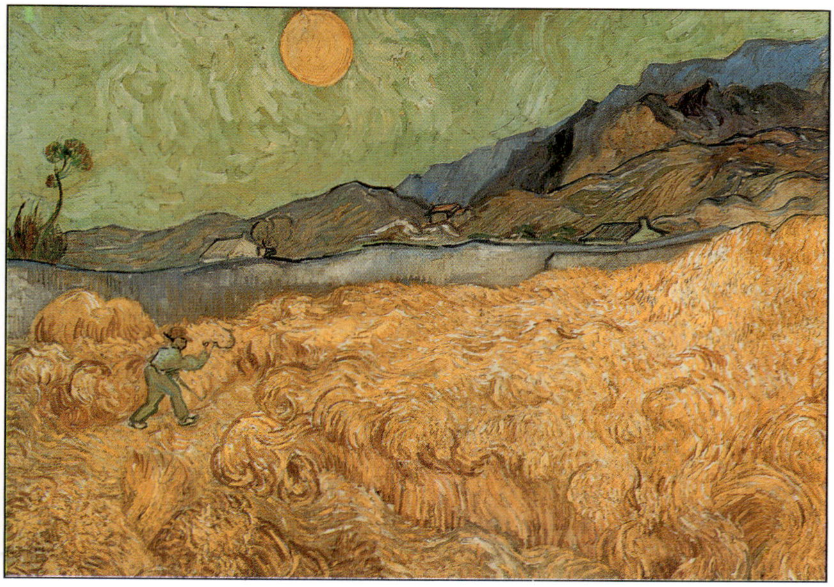

"Field with reaper" by Van Gogh (1889), oil on canvas. This superb painting uses a warm range of colors; it paints more than a thousand words.

THE WARM COLOR SCALE
Greenish-yellow, yellow, orange, red, carmine, purple, and violet.

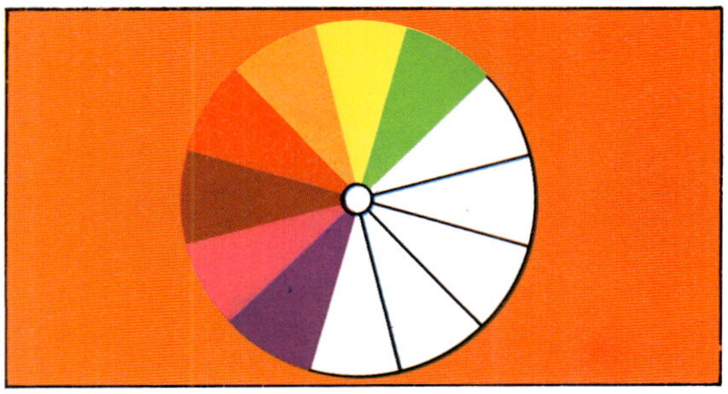

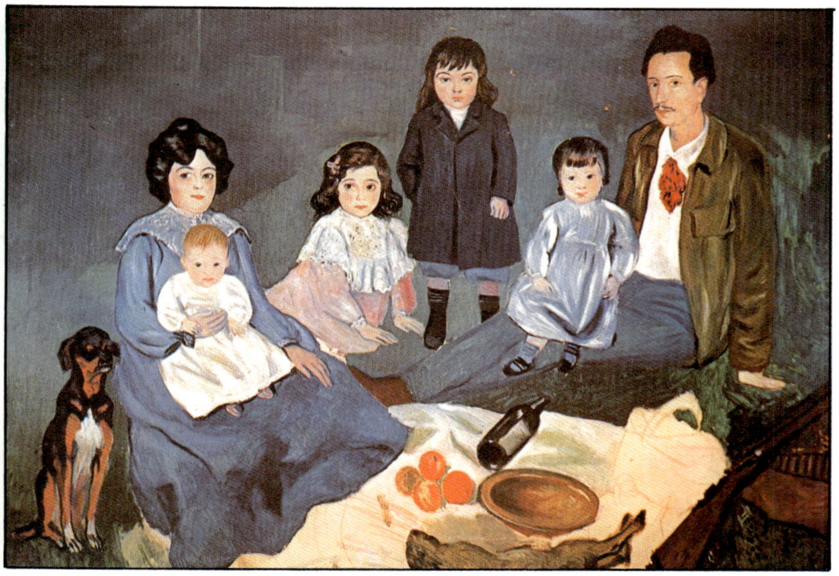

"The Soler family" by Pablo Picasso (1903), oil on canvas. It would be hard to find a more masterly use of the cool color scale than in this work by Picasso.

THE COOL COLOR SCALE
Greenish-yellow, green, emerald green, cyan blue, blue, ultramarine blue, violet.

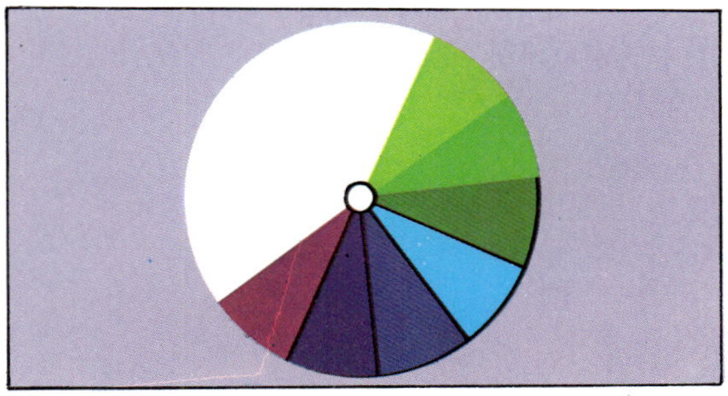

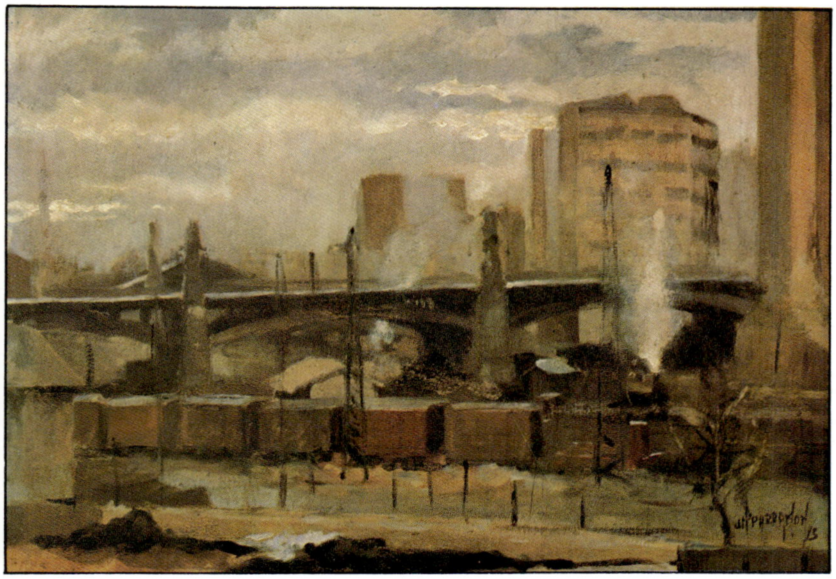

"The bridge over Calle Marina" by José María Parramón (1973), oil on canvas. A gray day and a gray subject, captured with exceptional skill by Parramón; this provides an excellent lesson in the use of subdued colors.

THE SUBDUED COLOR SCALE
This consists of a mixture of complementary colors in varying proportions in combination with white.

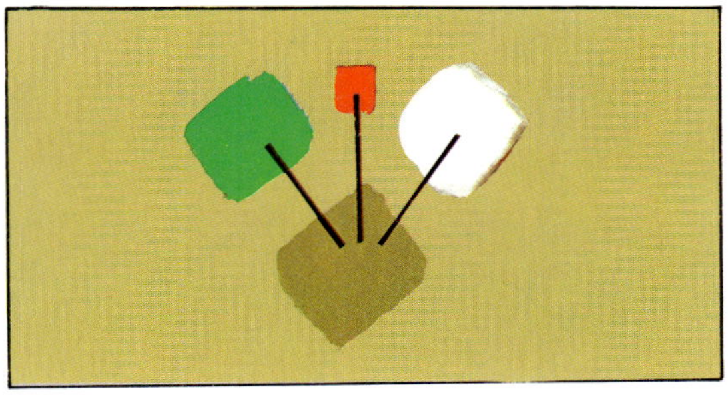

The method to follow

It is logical that, before starting on a painting, the artist will spend some time (though this is never wasted) contemplating the subject at some length, discovering the nature of it, deciding which details to explore and which to ignore, which contrasts to emphasize, how to interpret forms and colors; in short, seeing in his mind's eye the finished painting.

Normally, this stage is complemented by a preparatory sketch, although the controversy surrounding this point is as old as painting itself. Is it better to start with a sketch, or to go straight into the painting itself? The "colorist" school (painters who use very little shadow, differentiating between objects purely by color) tend to work directly, while the "tonalists" (those who work with light and shade) begin with a sketch.

If we may offer some advice, we suggest an intermediate course between the two extremes—make a very quick sketch, just as a pointer. Of course, a lot will depend on how confident you are in your own ability. Perhaps Van Gogh, Cézanne, or Manet would not have restricted themselves in this way, but as beginners they undoubtedly took similar precautions before beginning a painting.

First stage: Layout sketch

Start with a charcoal sketch, keeping the lines simple because if the sketch is too detailed, you will need to use fixative. Charcoal will dirty the color and it is worth fixing if you have been liberal with it in your initial sketch.

Second stage: Setting the tone

The color is blocked in, without any detail. The objective, at this stage, is to cover the surface to obtain an overall picture.

Third stage: Building up color and form

Once the general tone has been blocked in, the third and longest phase begins. Gradually, and working on all parts of the picture simultaneously, the color is adjusted and the contrasts of light and shade are clearly established. This stage is really about the artist creating the "atmosphere" he wants in his painting (illustration at top of next page).

Cleaning is basic in oil painting. Get accustomed to cleaning your brushes and palette frequently with the help of a solvent, old newspapers, and rags. Wipe the brush various times over the newspapers, soak it in a solvent, and clean it with a dry rag. Repeat this process until the brush is paint-free.

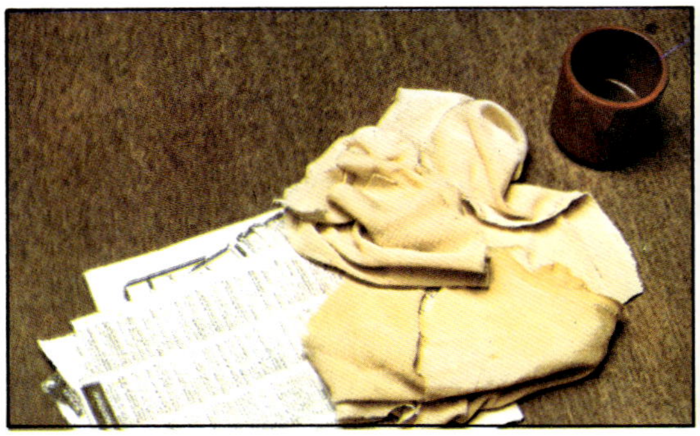

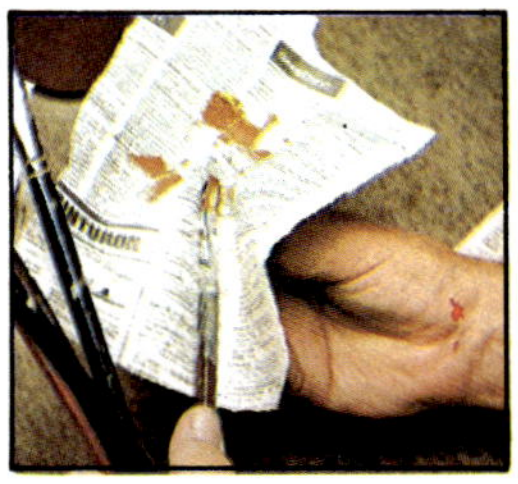

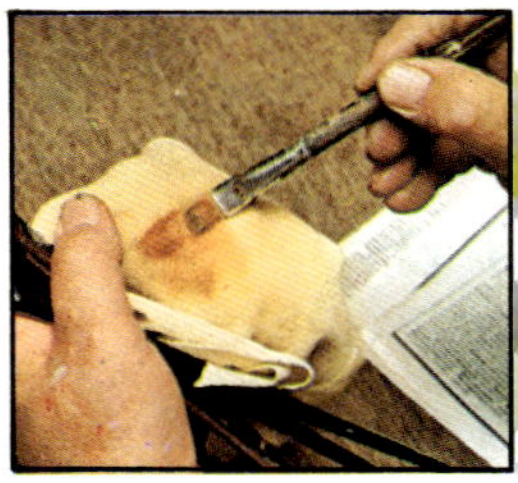

1

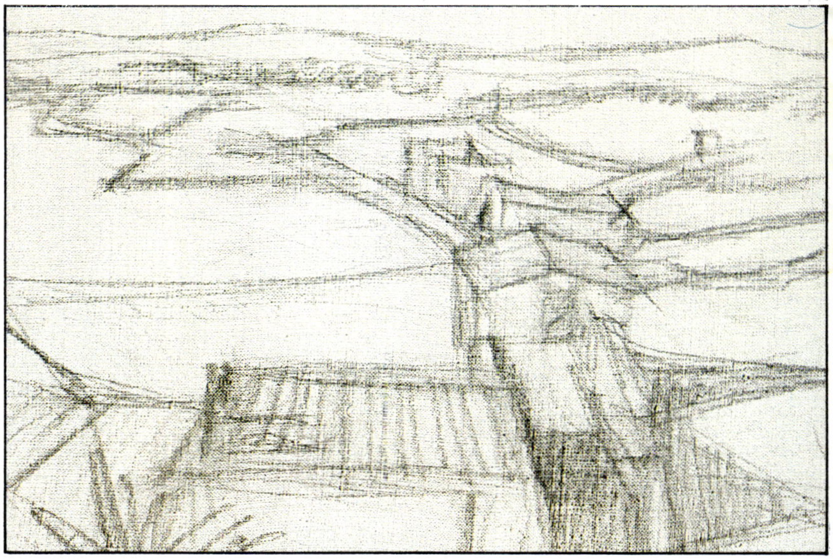

2

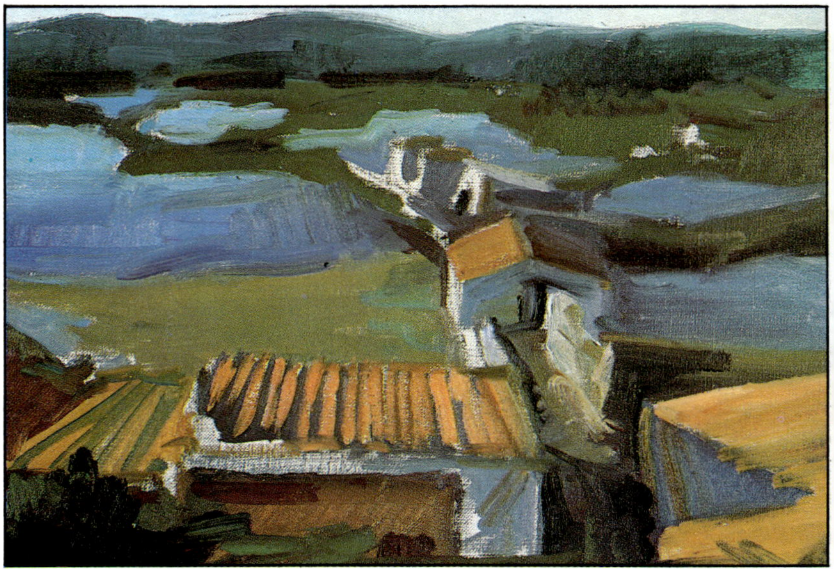

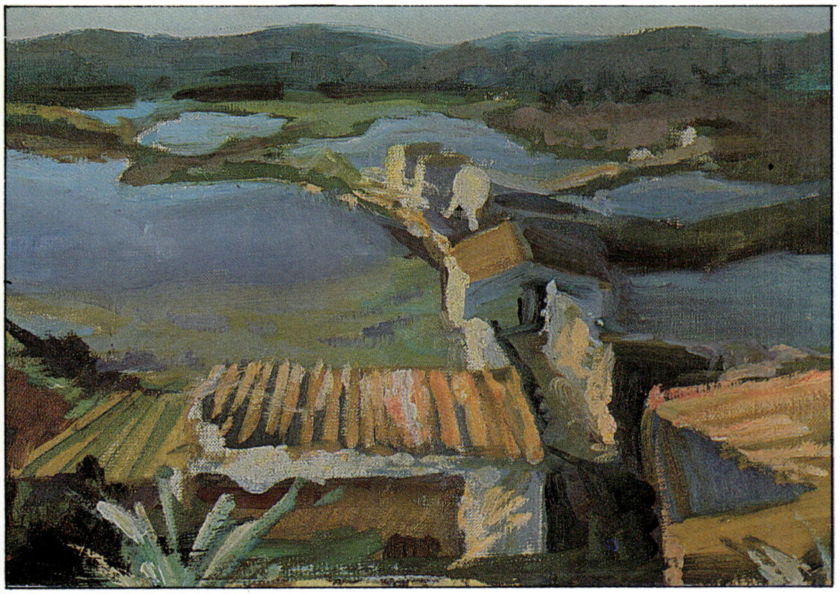

Fourth stage: Completing the picture

Finishing a painting is always a compromise between the artist and the work itself. It is difficult to pinpoint the moment when you feel that a particular brushstroke is one too many. In general, the last touches should merely accentuate a color or contrast in the foreground of the picture. Each artist has his own style and, in the case of our example, it is clear that the final, vigorous strokes have considerably enriched the foreground of this landscape.

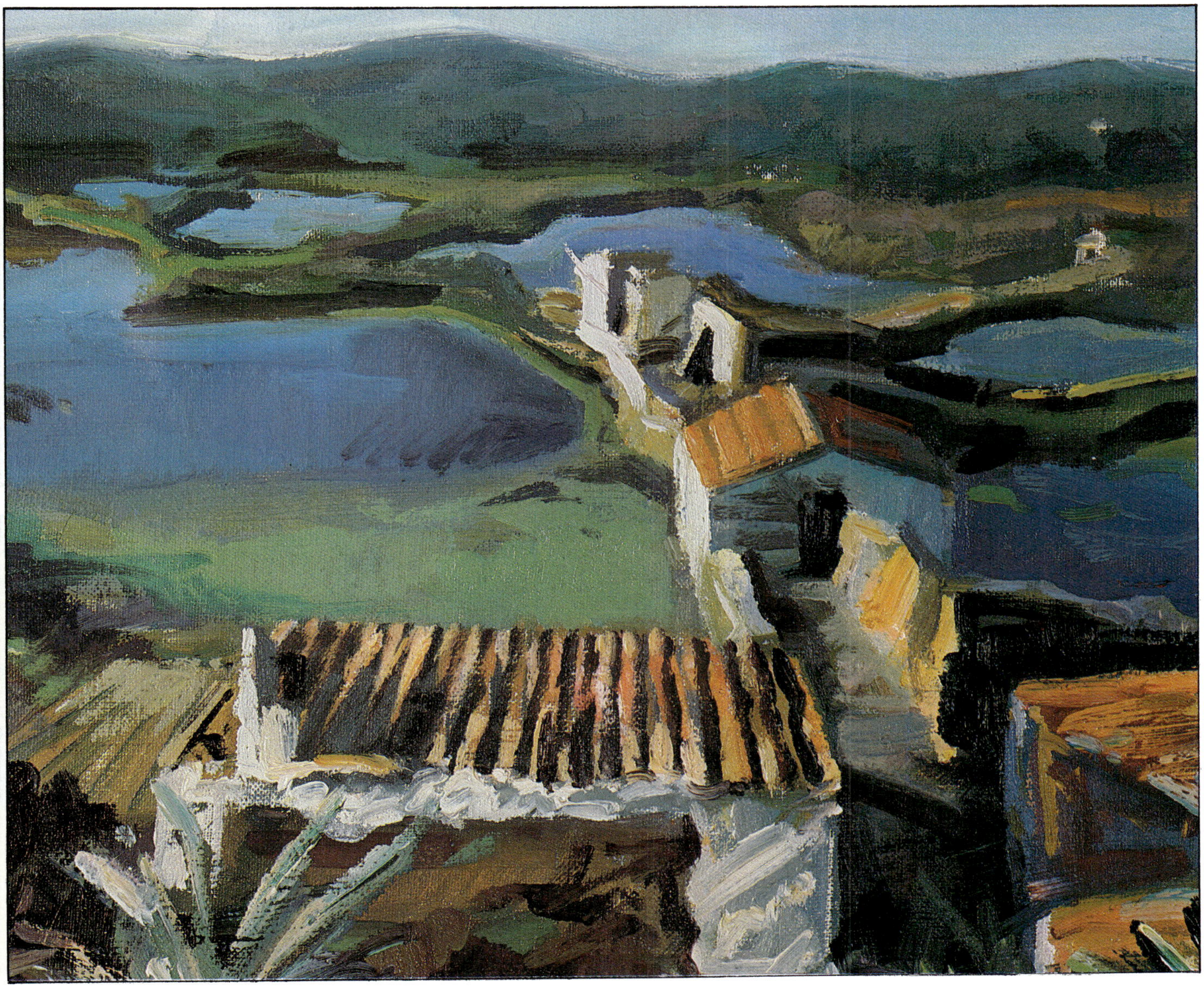

Study using the three primary colors

We have already discussed at length earlier in this book the potential of painting with just the three primary colors and black. Here we are going to explore the primary colors using oils, learning how to mix colors to create a specific shade. This particular lesson can only be learned by seeing, imagining, and then painting for yourself.

Let's consider the area of imagination. You have to try and imagine which colors are needed (in your palette) to reproduce the color of any object you see every day. Ask yourself, for instance, how you could produce the mahogany tone of your desk; or the yellow-red of the apple you are about to eat. Open the window and think about the colors of the buildings, about whether there is more white than blue in the sky, or perhaps a touch of crimson.

Later on, when you are ready to paint and have the model in front of you, the real value of this early apprenticeship will become apparent and you will be amazed to find that with one glance you can attempt an analysis of which colors to use for each part of your subject.

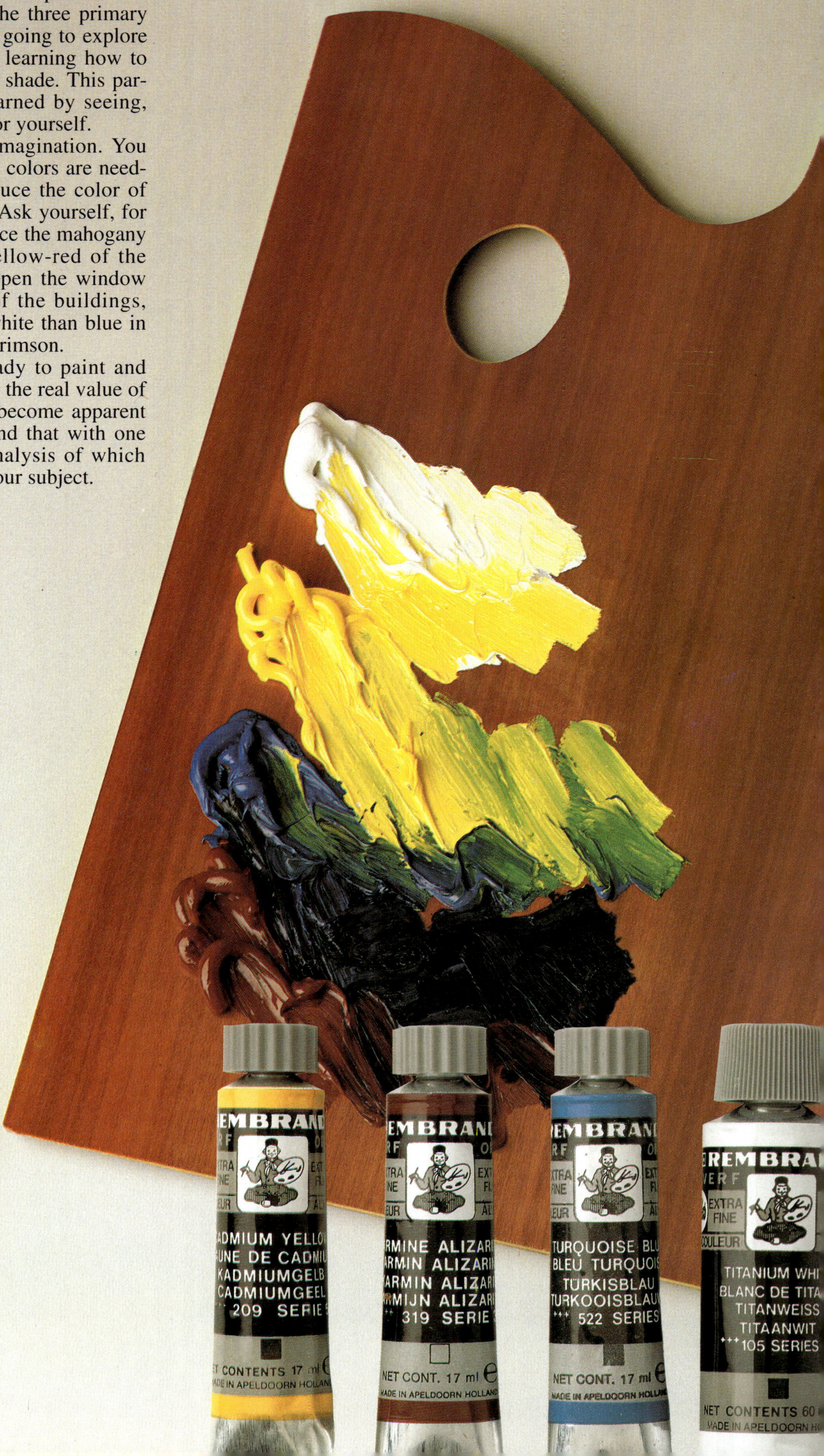

***Right.** The three primary colors with which we are going to get to know the medium and how to mix colors, as an introduction to oil painting. On the far right is a tube of white paint, indispensable when using the primary colors, cadmium yellow, crimson, and blue.*

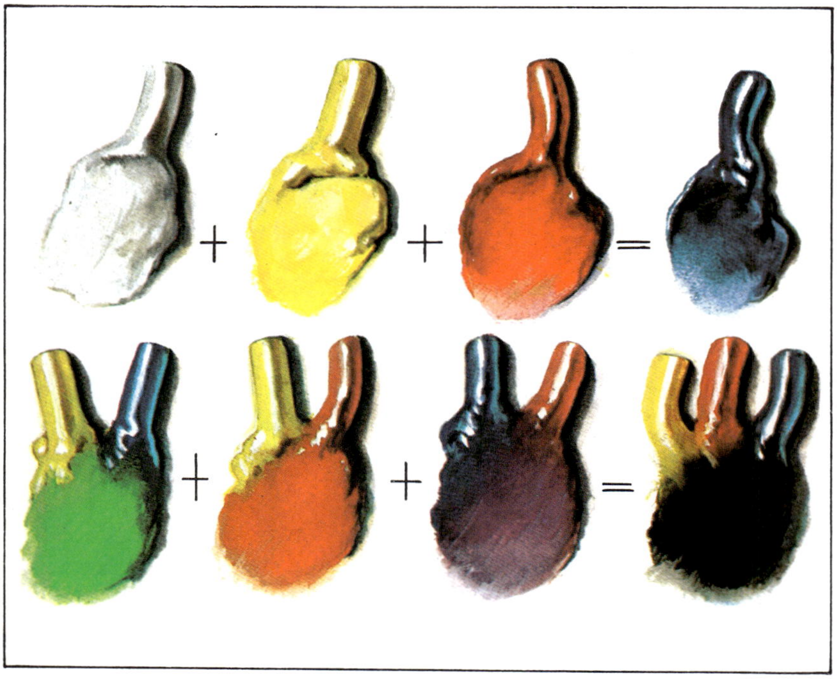

Through studying the theory of color, we know that the infinite number of colors in nature is the result of mixing, in varying proportions, the three primary colors that, in painting, are yellow, magenta or crimson, and blue. Specifically in oils, these primaries are:

Cadmium yellow medium
Alizarin crimson
Prussian blue

Experiment with these, mixing them first in pairs and then adding the third to each pair. Illustrated on the left are the three primaries and white, along with the secondary colors obtained by mixing pairs and finally black, which is made from a mixture of all three.

If you are still in any doubt about the possibility of painting any subject with just these pigments, bear with us through the next few pages.

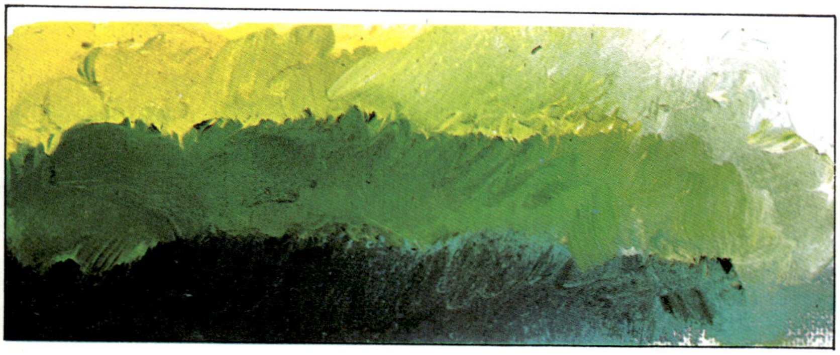

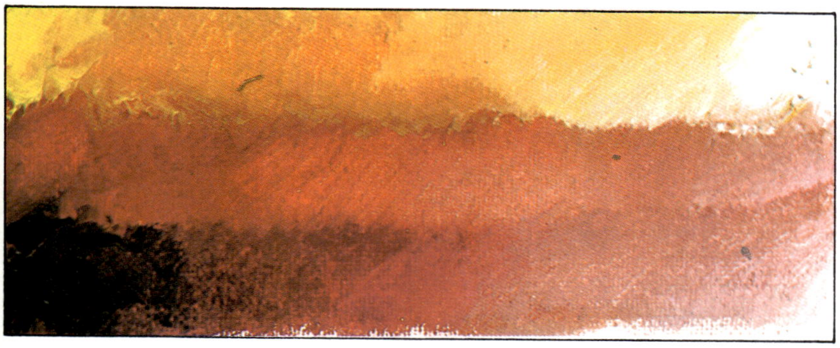

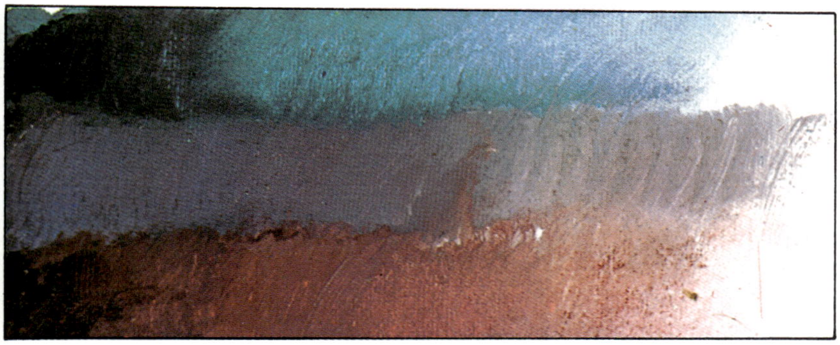

In these three illustrations (left) are shown, from top to bottom, three color scales: yellow-green, ochre-red, and violet-blue, demonstrating the principle that with the three primaries and white (when necessary), it is possible to create practically any color.

Although we have already explored this theme, it is worth reminding ourselves of the general principles of color theory.

For instance, the complementary colors are as follows:

Yellow complements **deep blue**
Cyan blue complements **bright red**
Magenta or **crimson** complements **green**
and vice versa.

The complements are useful for:

- Creating color contrasts.
- Painting shadows.
- Harmonizing color through a single color scheme, based on the subdued color scale.

On the subject of cyan blue, we should stress that there is no such color in oils. The term cyan blue is used in graphic art and color photography; in recent times it has been adopted in studies on the theory of color. Cyan is essentially a neutral blue, very like Prussian blue mixed with a hint of white.

Above. *The three primary colors.*

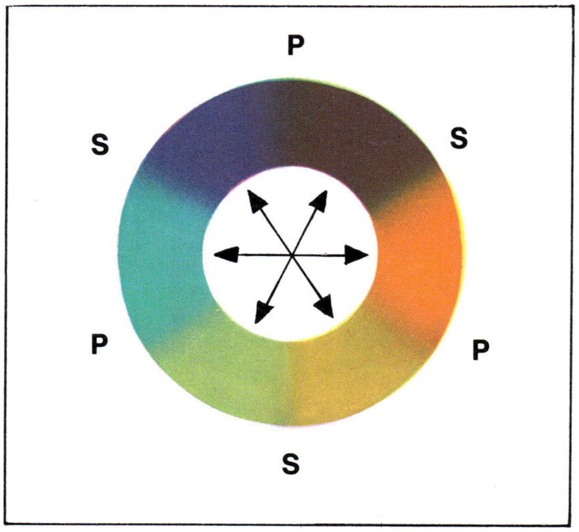

Right. *The chromatic circle limited to primary and secondary colors (arrows indicate complementary colors).*

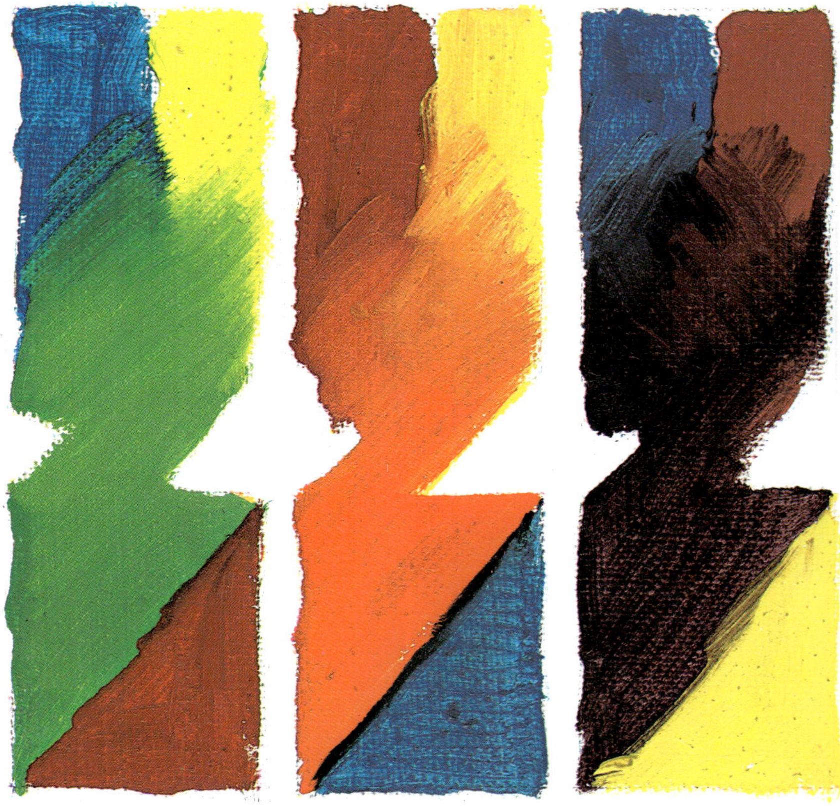

Right. *By mixing two of the primaries, you obtain the complement of the third. Blue and yellow make green, which is the complement of magenta or crimson. Magenta or crimson and yellow make bright red, complement of deep blue. Blue and crimson make violet, complement of yellow.*

The color of shadows

This is a very important subject, so much so that Rubens said, "It doesn't matter what color you paint the light, as long as you paint the shadow with the color that corresponds to the light." But, what is this color? What color should shadows be?

We propose a formula with which to achieve the "right" color for every shadow. We offer you the fruit of years of experience and training in the practicalities of painting. Briefly, the colors present in any shadow are:

A darker tone of the color of the object itself
The complement of that color
Blue, which is present in every shadow

If you follow the examples on this page, you will understand this principle more easily. Here are three rows of three spheres. The color of each sphere, darkened a little, added to its complementary color and then to blue, creates the color of the shadow. This formula is applied here to a yellow, a red, and a blue sphere.

It depends on the subject whether the blue to be added is a clean, neutral blue like cobalt blue, a greenish blue like phthalo blue, or a violet blue like ultramarine.

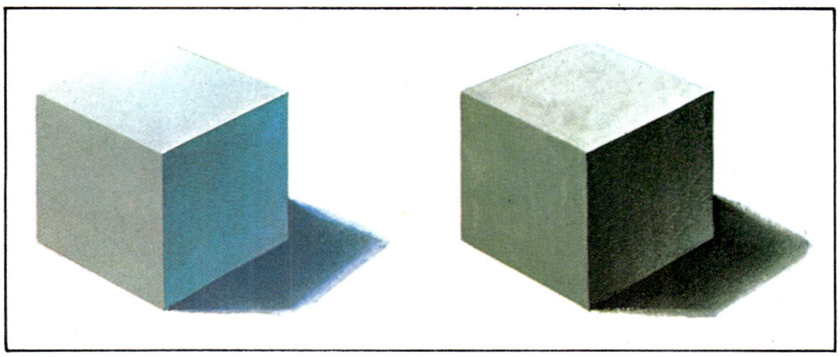

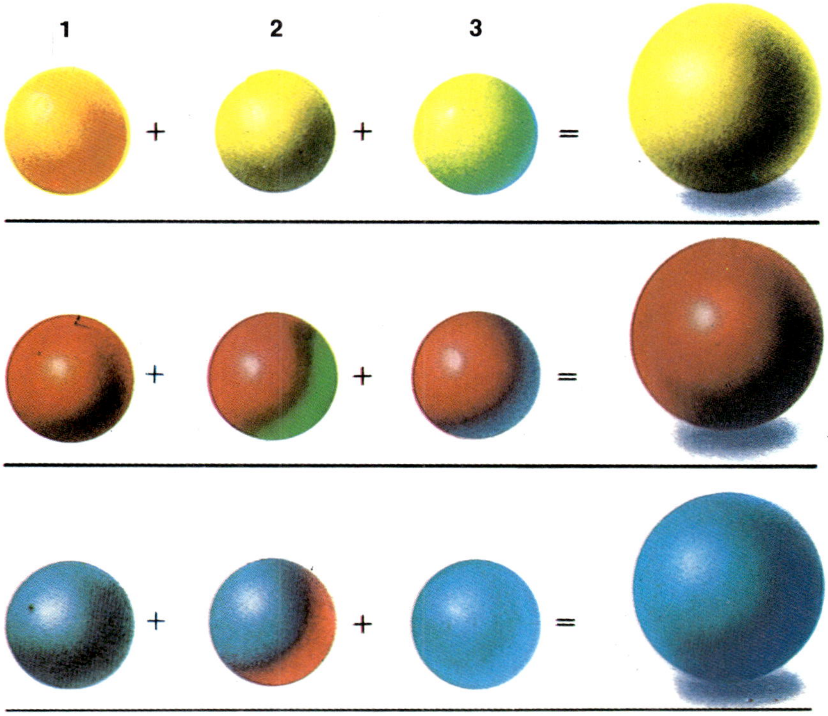

THE COLOR OF OBJECTS
Three factors determine the color of objects:
- **Local color** (their own color).
- **Tonal color** (light and shade).
- **Ambient color** (reflection of surrounding objects).

These three factors are in turn affected by:
- **The color of the light itself.**
- **The intensity of light.**
- **The atmospheric conditions.**

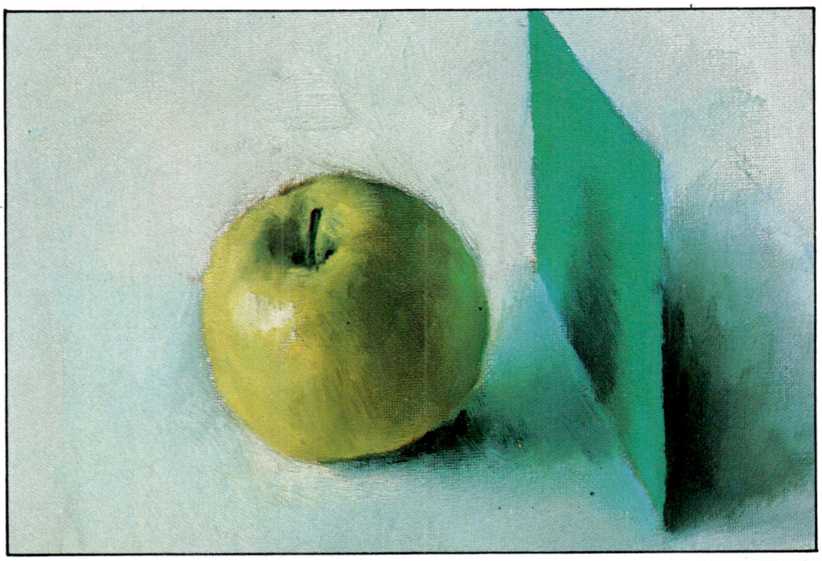

Exercise using the three primary colors

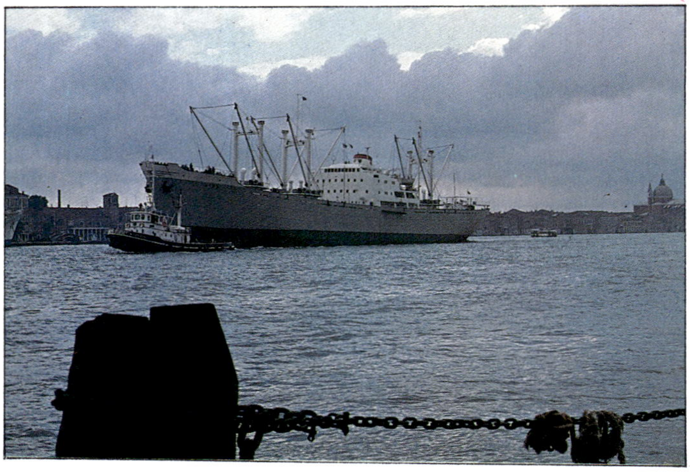

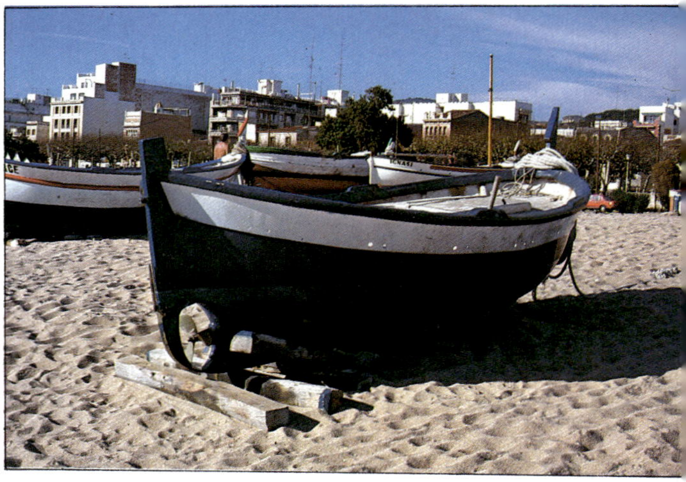

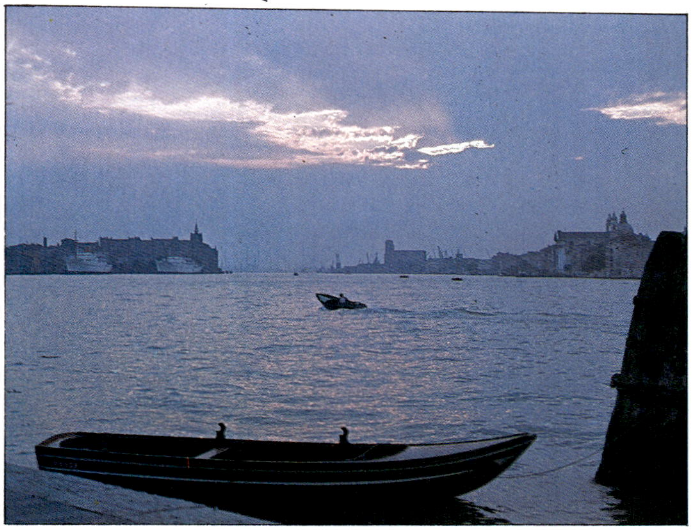

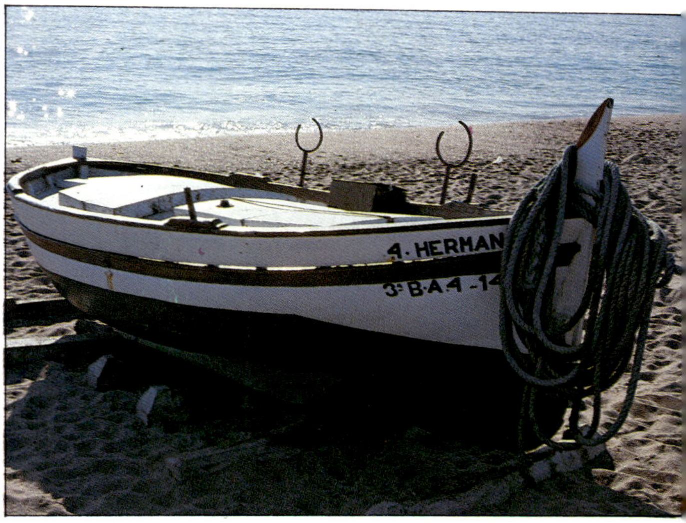

From the four subjects shown above, the artist has chosen the last, attracted by the luminous quality of a summer's evening and the constrasting colors and tones of the boat.

This exercise consists of making an oil painting using just three primary colors: alizarin crimson, cadmium yellow medium, and Prussian blue. We recommend that you work on a small canvas about 11 × 14 in. (35 × 27 cm), following the four stages we have demonstrated here.

First stage: Initial sketch

In this first stage we have sketched in the subject using the blue, because it is the dominant tone in our picture.

Notice that, while describing the outlines of the subject, we are using color diluted in a lot of turpentine so we can establish a feeling of depth even at this early stage.

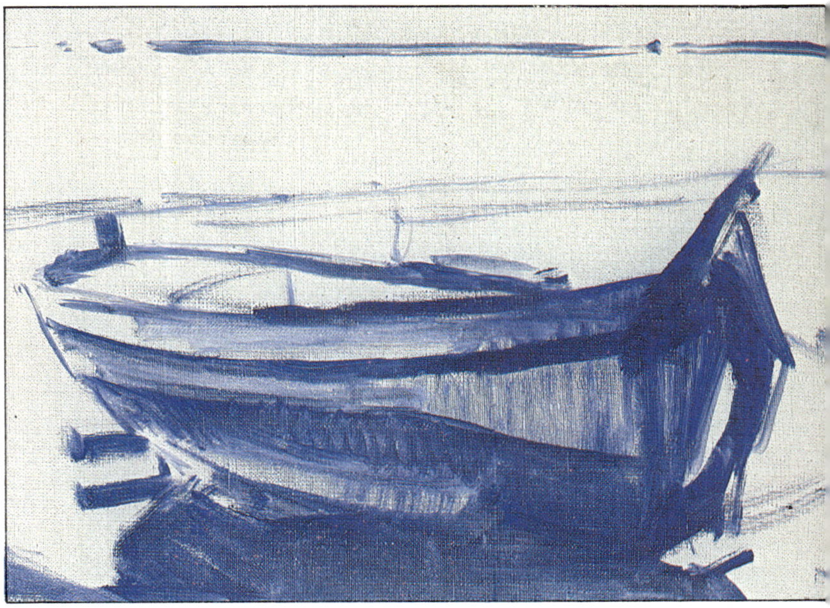

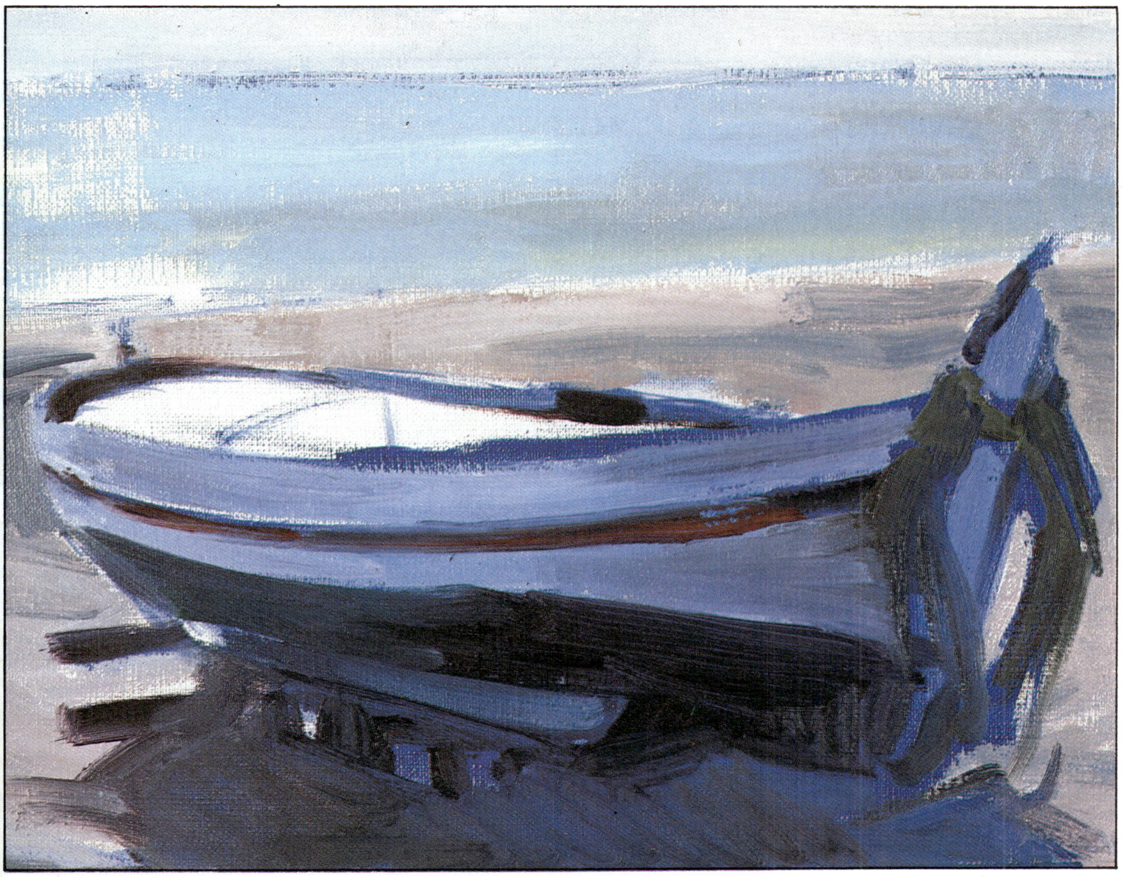

Second stage: Setting the tone

The whole picture area is blocked in with the colors of the elements as they appear to us.

See how the color of the sea has been created with white, blue, and a hint of yellow, producing the right shade of turquoise for the water.

Remember that the amount of each color added will contribute to the yellow, red, or bluish tendency of each tone. On page 13, when creating our 36-color chart, we experimented with this using colored pencils.

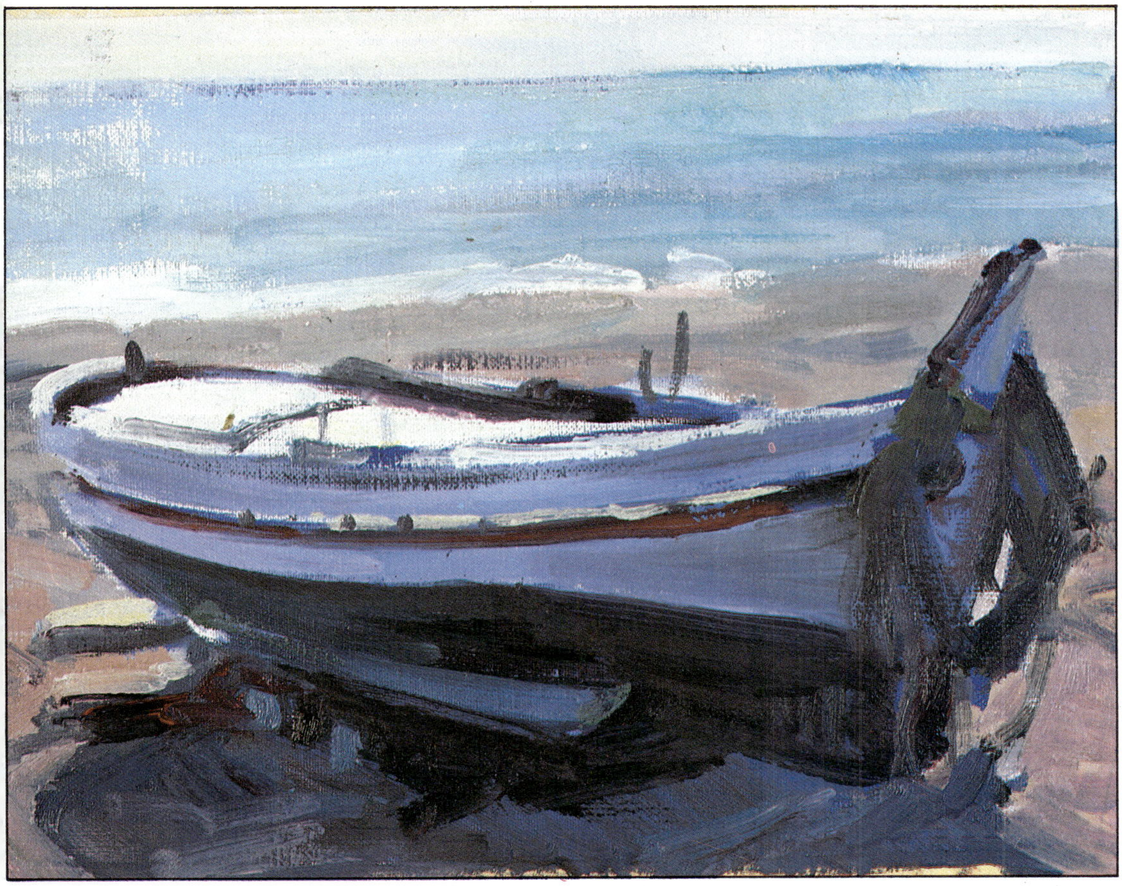

Third stage: Building up the color

The general coloring is now enriched, nuances of tone appearing as the picture is built up as a harmonious whole.

Don't hesitate to pause regularly, examining your painting through half-closed eyes; you will see that the creative process is not hampered in any way by these apparent hold-ups. From time to time it is valuable to just stop and reflect upon your work.

Fourth stage: Completing the picture

The work is completed without going into excessive detail, so that it retains a rather impressionistic atmosphere. If you paint from nature, remember that time is of the essence when capturing effects of light, which change as the day wears on.

In this last stage we have brought out a few minor details, adding spots of harmonious color with fresh, spontaneous brush-strokes.

Below is a selection of the color mixes prevalent is this painting, all of which were made from the three primaries plus white.

We feel that, as a complementary exercise (or perhaps, better still, as a preliminary study) it is worth your spending some time trying to create these colors on your palette so that, when you begin your painting, you can set off with confidence.

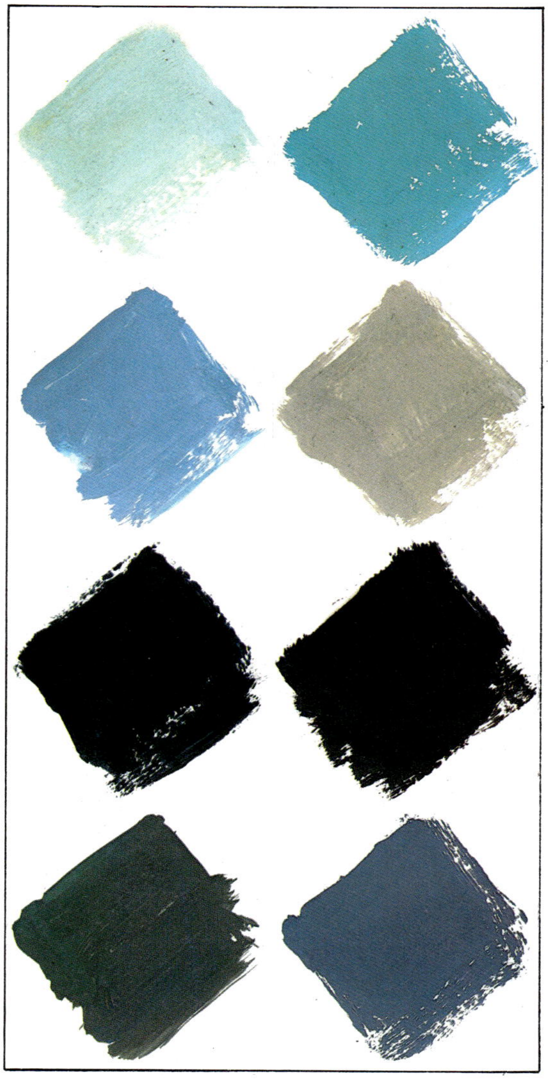

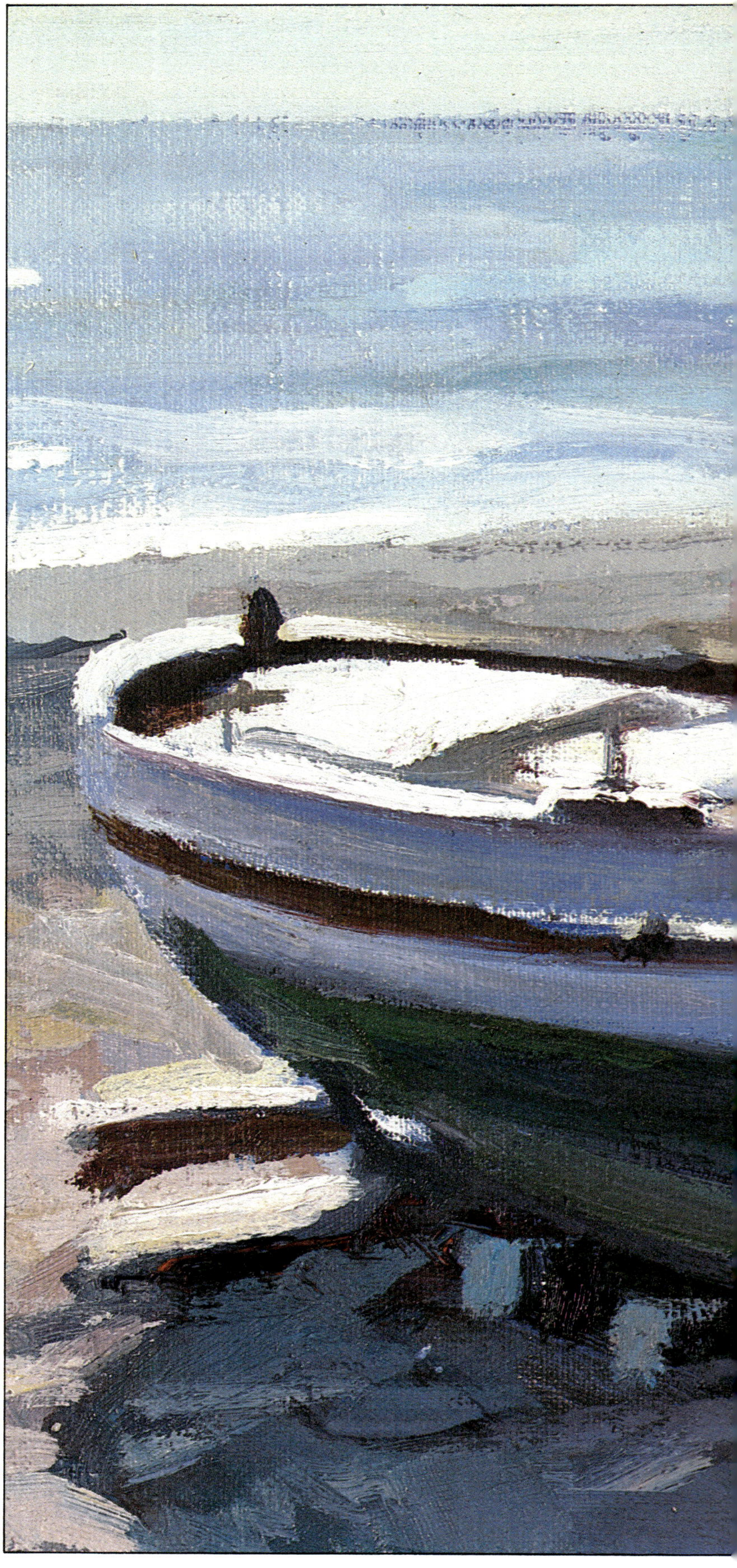

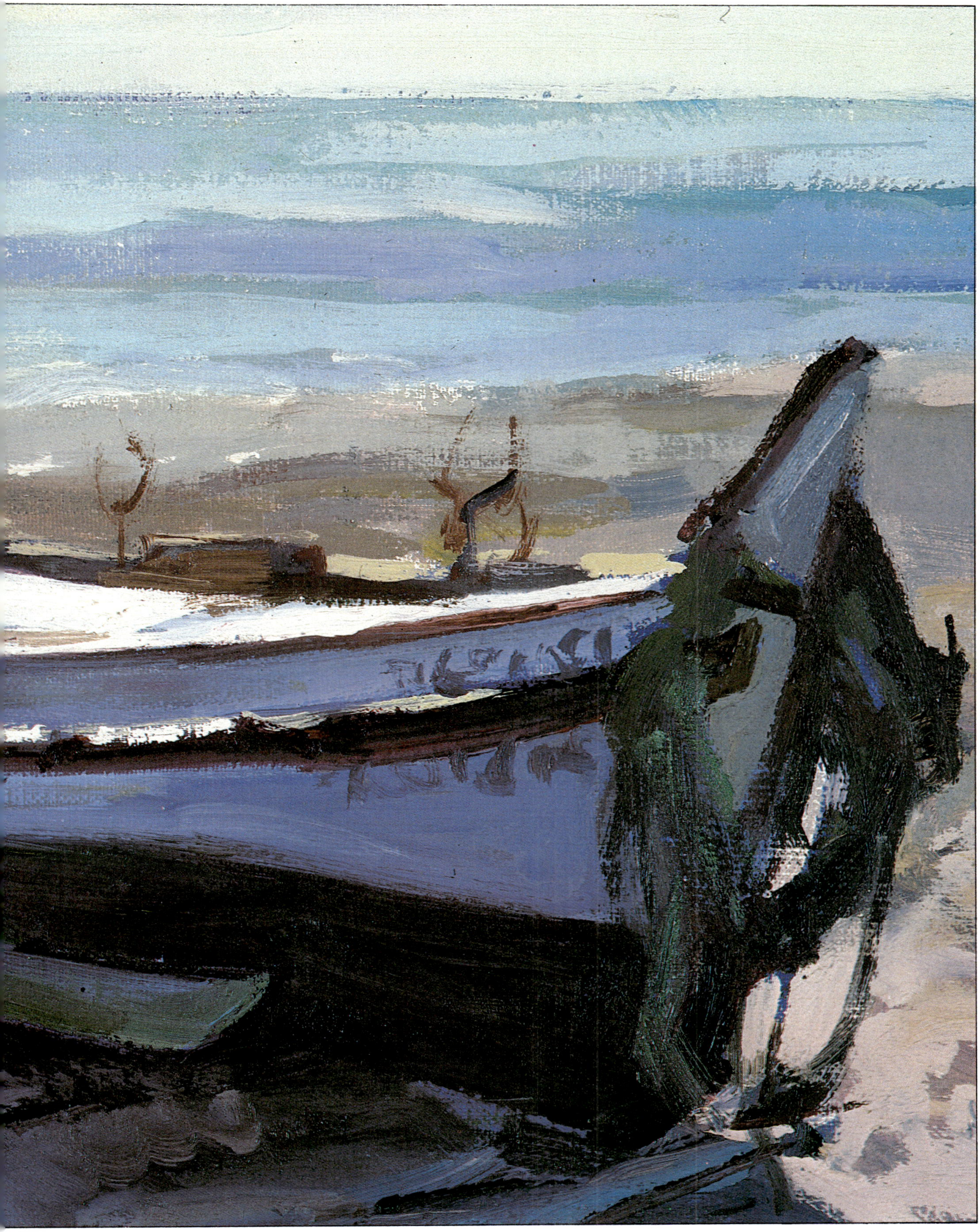

Oil painting

Probably one of the easiest questions about oil painting to answer relates to the usefulness of still life painting as part of the learning process. There are many excellent reasons why great painters through the ages, right up to and including the present, have chosen the still life over and over again as a theme for their works. Here are some of them:

- Van Gogh once described the still life as one of the best methods of learning and teaching the art of painting. Cézanne went further, describing it as an ideal vehicle for trying out various combinations and compositions of everyday things—fruit, comestibles, commonplace objects—using them to develop visual perception, an awareness of composition and of how to construct a painting as a harmonious whole.
- Painting a still life involves choosing the subject for oneself as well as the objects or elements contained within it.
- It also involves arranging those elements to form an agreeable and original composition, taking into account lighting, contrasts, harmony of tone (by varying the objects and their color and positioning), the intensity of the light, and so on.
- Painting at home, in the studio or workshop, without an audience and with all the creature comforts, allows the artist to concentrate and experiment, to look at all the effects and possibilities of form, color, style, and execution—in a word, to develop his potential.
- Once the artist has passed through this apprenticeship as a still life painter, he is able to take on any other subject with every likelihood of success.

***Below.** "Apples and oranges" by Paul Cézanne (1900). Cézanne was sixty-one when he painted this still life, one of the most famous of his many works.*

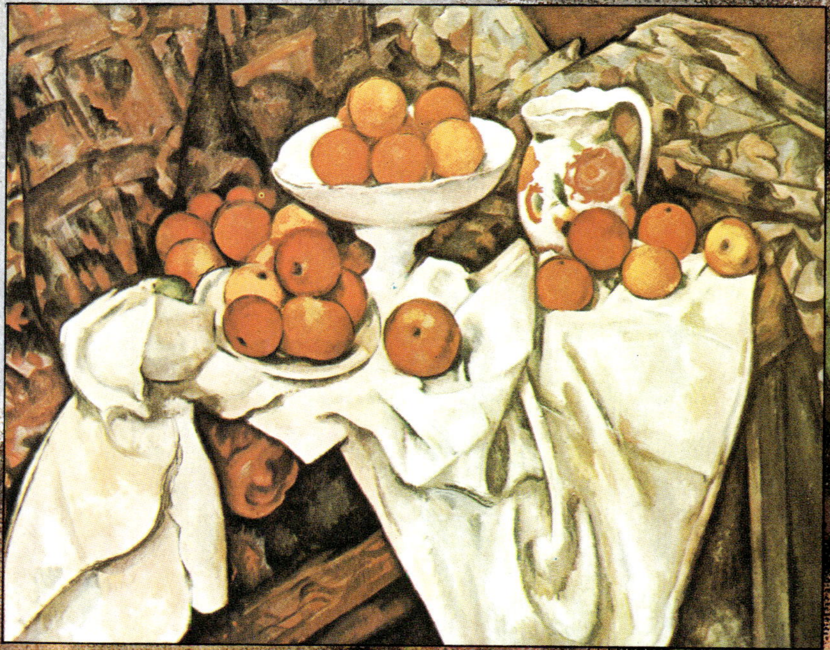

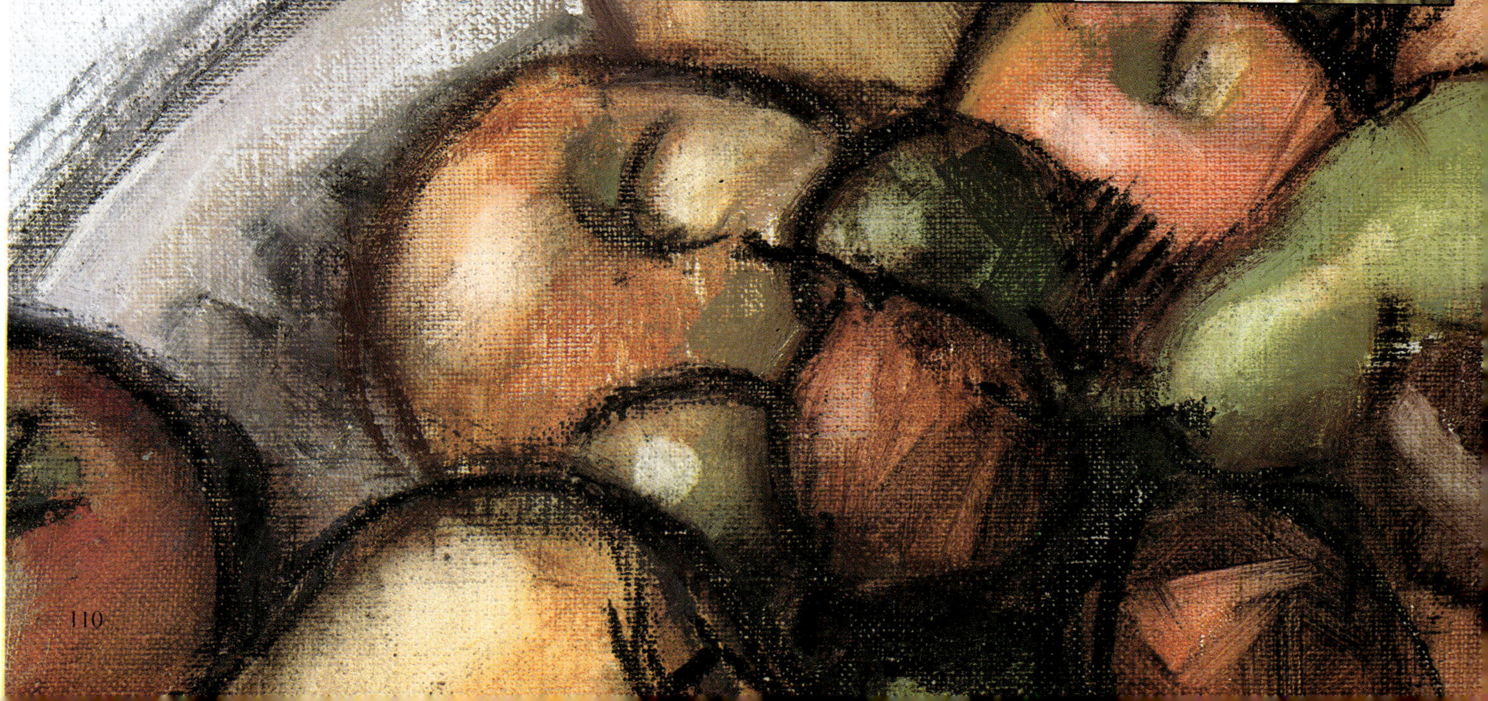

Caravaggio, father of the still life

It was the year 1596 when a twenty-three-year old Italian painter called Michelangelo Merisi "da Caravaggio" (his native village) arranged a few bunches of grapes, an apple past its best, some figs, some pears, and a peach in a wicker basket.

Caravaggio made history when he painted this subject: It was the first true still life recorded in the history of painting. After Caravaggio, the still life was frequently used as a theme by many great masters: Velasquez, Rembrandt, Rubens, Ribera, Zurbarán, Murillo, Chardin, Delacroix, Renoir, Van Gogh, Manet, Monet, Picasso, Dalí.

And Cézanne.

Cézanne deserves a separate mention; it is not without reason that he is considered the most important still life painter of modern times. It is worth making a long, almost religious study of Cézanne's still life paintings—any of them—to learn from the apparent disorder of the elements in each picture. It is only apparent disorder, for, in fact, Cézanne spent hours and hours of study on each work before he arrived at the perfect composition.

Cézanne and the Impressionists, just like Picasso, Velasquez, Murillo, and all the others, based their work on an idea hit upon in 1596 by the young "da Caravaggio" when he arranged a few pieces of fruit in a little wicker basket.

__"Basket of fruit"__ by Caravaggio (1573–1610), Pinacoteca Ambrosiana, Milan. This is the first recorded still life in the history of painting. There may have been other earlier attempts, but never with the intention of making the pieces of fruit themselves the theme or reason for the painting.

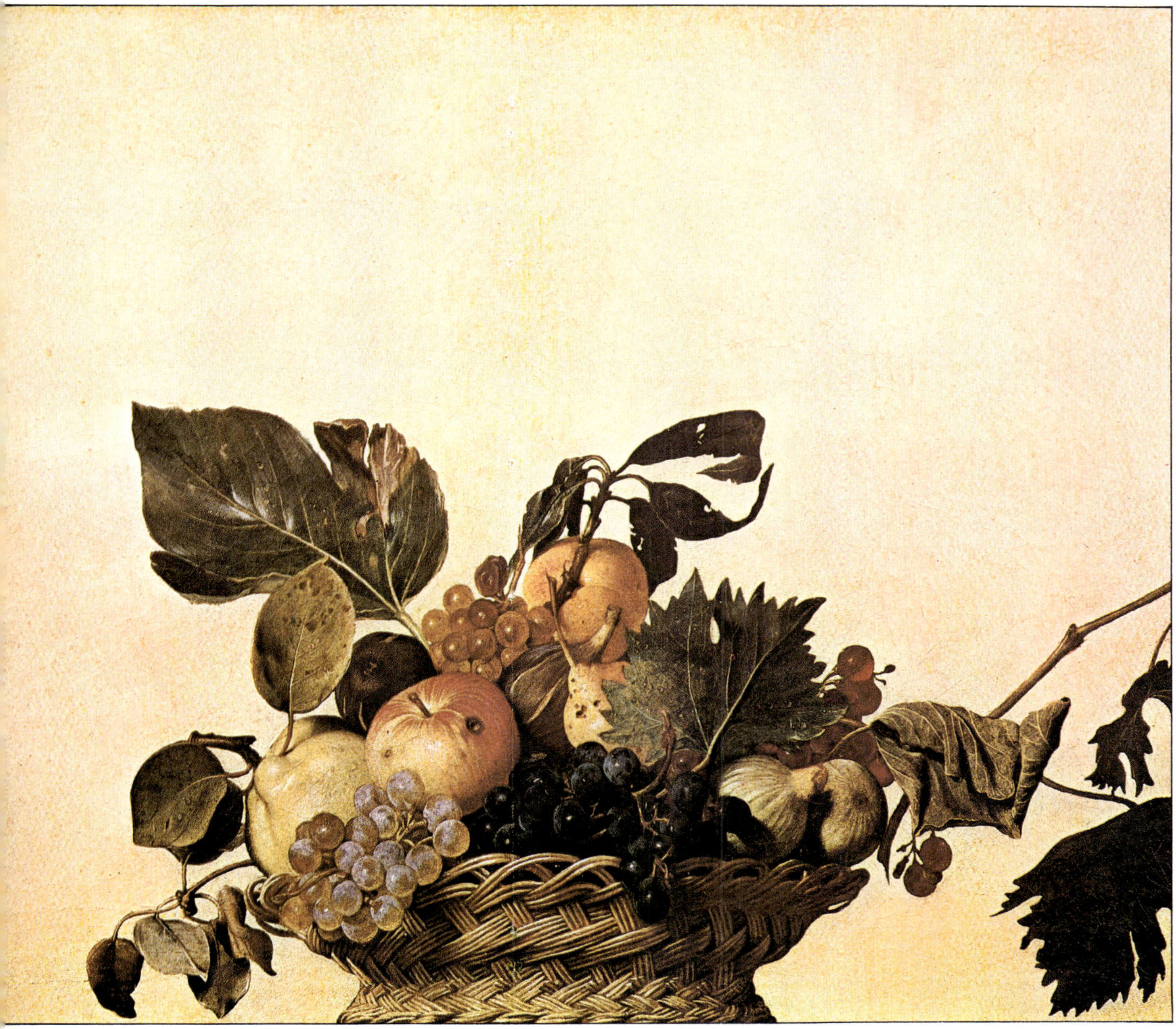

The still life. Preparatory steps

The construction of shapes

Be patient. The day will come when you are able to change and distort the laws of perspective, dispense with horizons, view-points, and vanishing points. Modern painting tolerates such bold moves; they are acceptable as long as the artist departs from a basis of proven and traditional experience. Then it is possible to start playing with the idea of a personal style, to get around the occasional rule.

But until that day arrives, keep asking yourself if you can draw a cube, a cylinder, or a sphere from memory. Do you think you can? Let's give it a try.

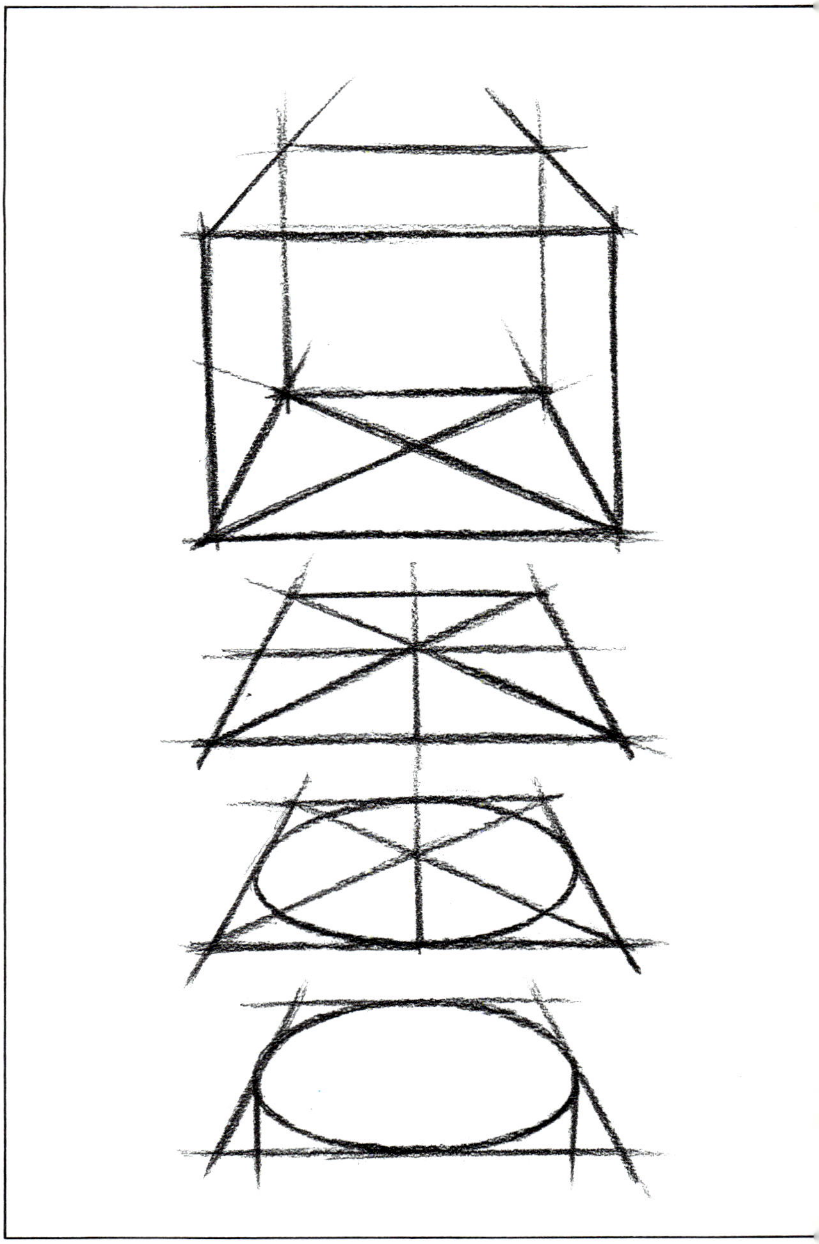

Right. *Try to draw from memory, freehand, without a ruler or set-square, diagrams similar to these. As you can see, they represent a cube, a square, and a circle.*

Bottom right. *Once you have learned to construct forms without difficulty, you can work confidently. Without diagrams or grids—even without an initial drawing—you can paint directly on to the canvas things such as this cup and saucer. That will be the moment when you have earned the option of bending the laws of perspective, drawing, and painting in any way you please.*

Bottom left. *If you are able to draw the previous figures freehand and from memory, you will now be able to draw the structure containing this cup and saucer. Don't be alarmed: You won't have to do this every time you draw something. We are doing it now to learn how to avoid mistakes of construction.*

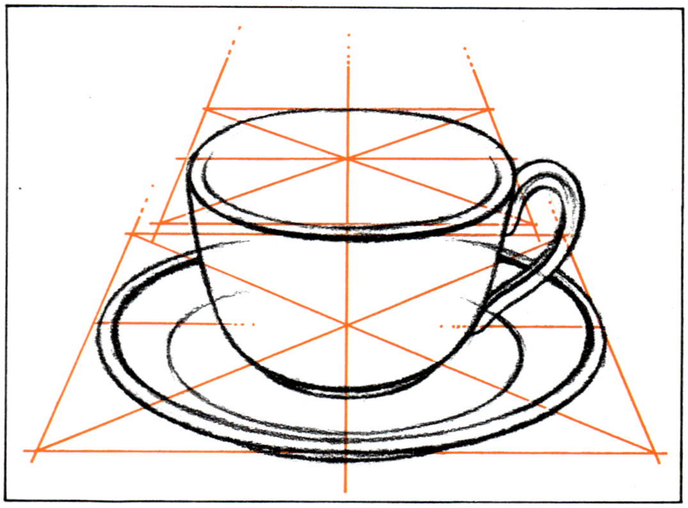

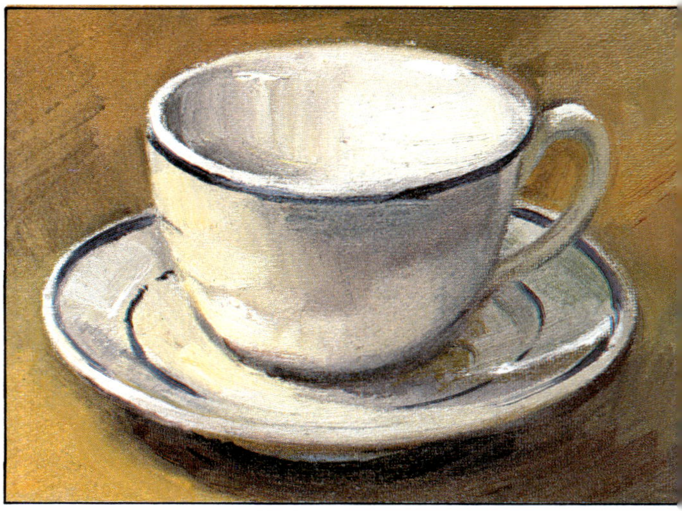

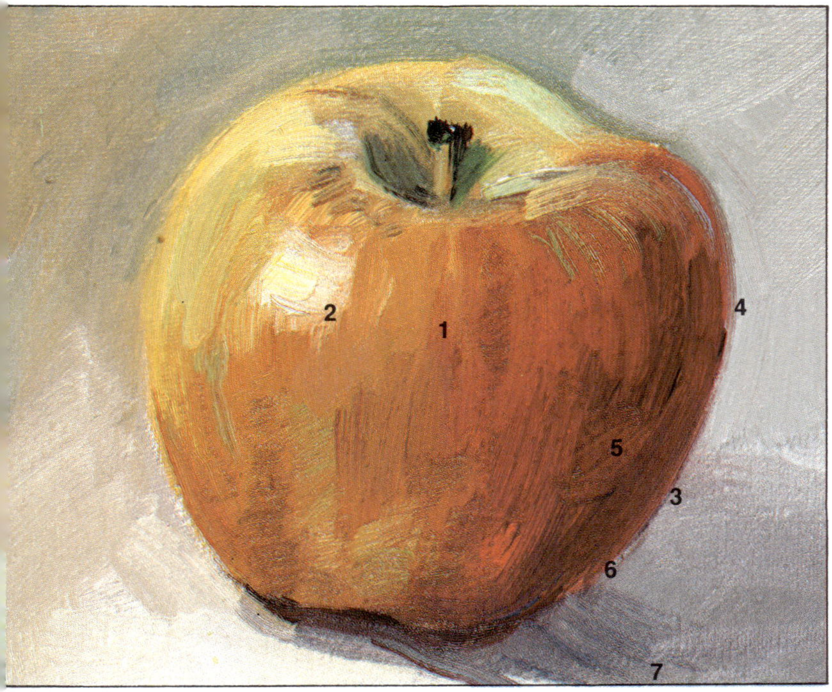

Evaluation of light and shade

We could describe light as drawing and painting objects, while shade explores their form and volume. To represent this volume, we draw or paint using color of varying tonal value and intensity. This evaluation is a fundamental part of drawing and painting.

The illustrations on this page may clarify these concepts. The objective is to see and understand, simply by observation and comparison, the different tonal qualities that make up any object. In fact, with just five shades of gray, plus black and white, it is possible to represent the entire tonal scale of our subject.

The depth or volume of any object is conveyed by a series of elements indicated in our illustration: 1. Light; 2. Reflections; 3. The "fade-out" of the shaded area; 4. Reflected light; 5. Half-light; 6. Shade on the object; 7. The projected shadow.

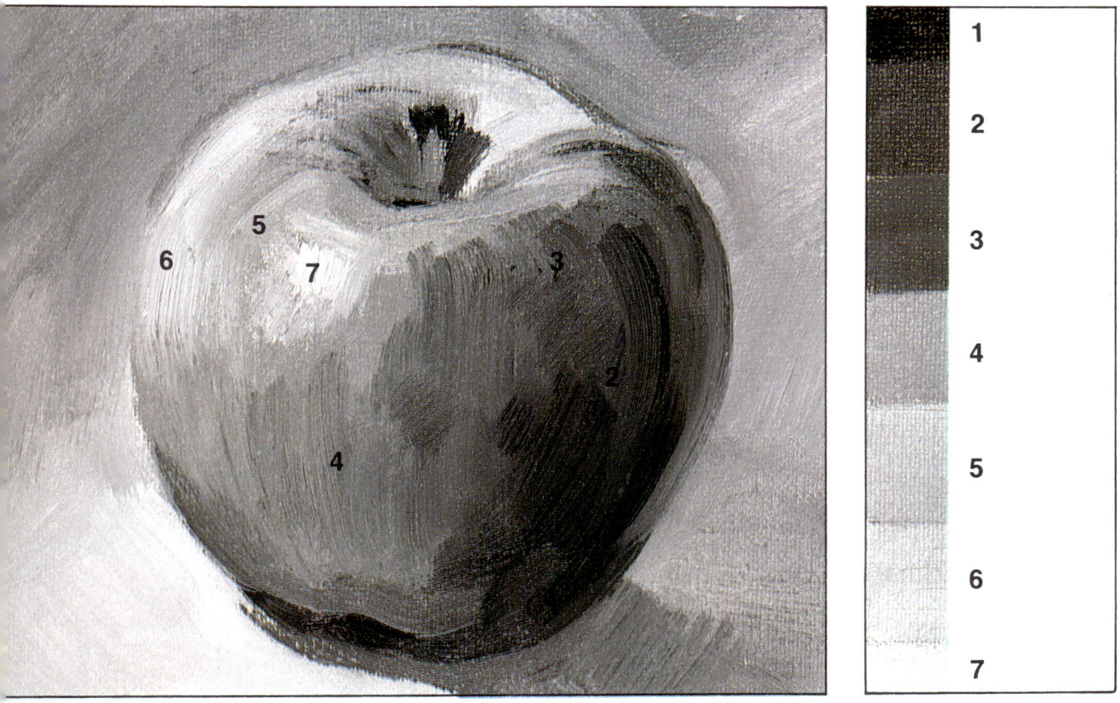

In this illustration you can see the variety of tones used to describe the volume of the object (look at the numbered scale). Try the same exercise using another subject, creating a tone scale similar to ours. Instead of an apple you could work with a different colored fruit, an orange, for example. It is likely that the darkest tone of an orange might correspond to number three on our apple.

The still life. Preliminary steps

Creating a pleasing composition that you are ready to paint requires nothing, in principle, other than undivided attention and a taste for hard work.

Composing a still life demands total dedication, trying out, looking at and comparing different combinations, arranging and rearranging until you are happy with the result.

Cézanne, for example, used to go back and forth from table to easel, looking at the model from every possible angle, moving elements from left to right, adding new ones, arranging folds in the backcloth, raising up objects in the central plane on boxes hidden beneath the drapery. This process could take hours, but when he finally decided he was ready to paint, nothing would induce him to change his composition.

We could learn a great deal from Cézanne's example.

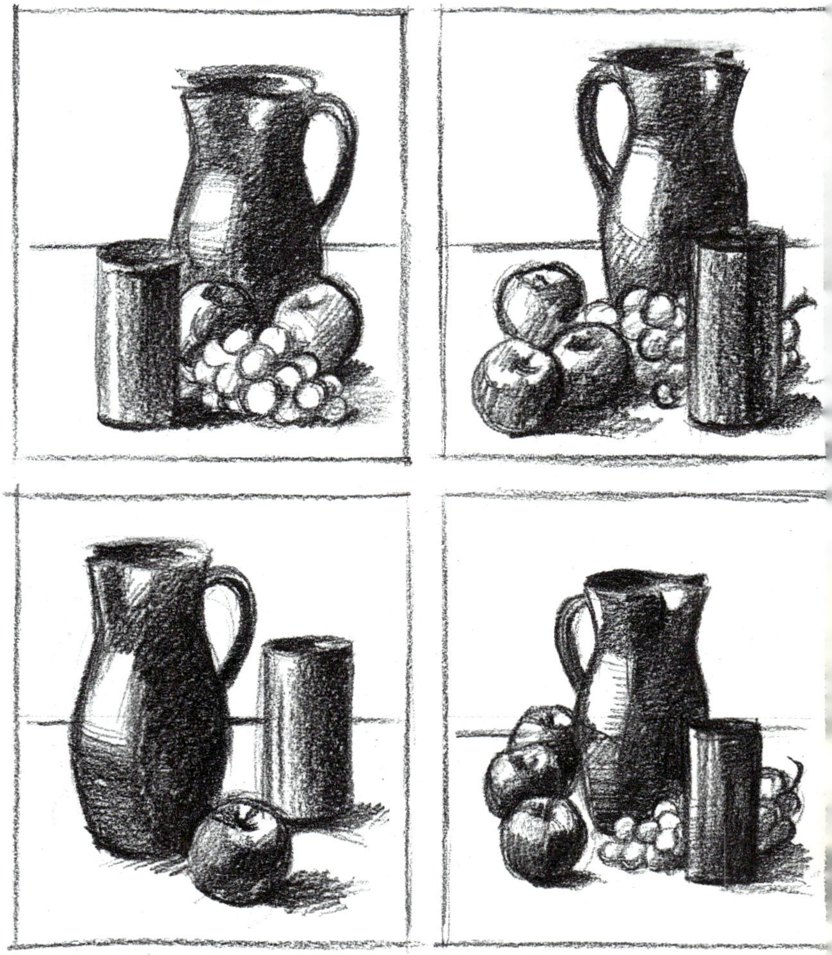

Above, left. *This first composition suffers from excessive uniformity (the elements are too close together).*

Above, right. *This time the jug is too far to the right and all the elements are too close to the edges of the picture.*

Below, left. *The third option is well-balanced, but too simple.*

Below, right. *Undoubtedly the best composition. It combines all the necessary qualities, providing interesting content while balancing effectively the rhythms of the composition and the volume of the objects.*

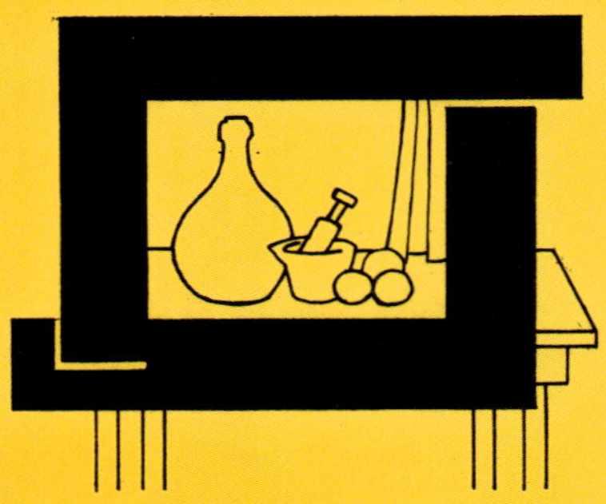

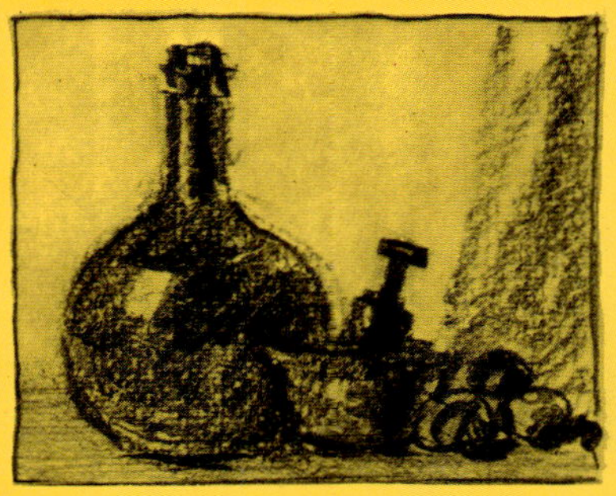

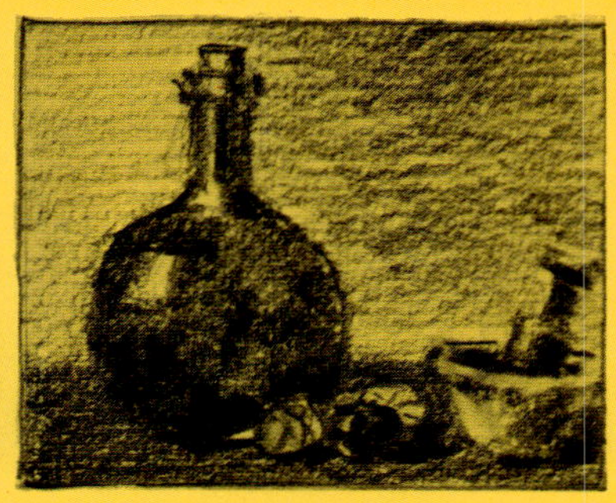

Using two set-squares made from black card, it is possible to frame and study the composition of your subject. It is also useful to make a couple of preliminary sketches in charcoal, sanguine crayon or with a soft, lead pencil (4 or 6B), working on paper of approximately 5 x 7 in. (12 x 17 cm).

In these sketches you can study the arrangement and proportion of the elements with respect to the picture area, the tone of the background, the light source, and so on.

Painting a still life in oils

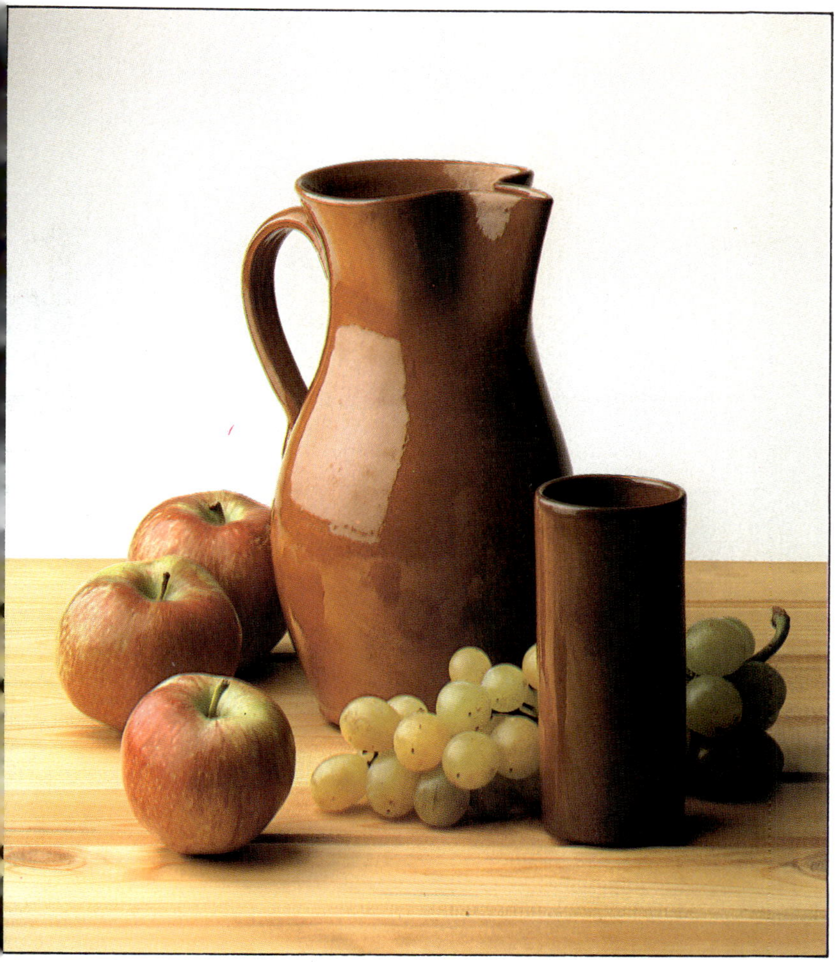

The moment has arrived to leave the learning process behind. Have your palette, your canvas, and your brushes at the ready. We are going to start painting! Here is a photograph of the composition we have set up and, as you can see, the light is coming from the left-hand side.

Now stop thinking about the subject and prepare to copy our exercise, which we will describe in four stages.

First stage: Initial sketch

This layout sketch is made in charcoal. It should be a quick, loose drawing, outlining the composition, the shapes and proportions. Once it is finished, the drawing should be fixed to prevent the black dust from dirtying the colored pigment.

Second stage: Background color

This subject does not offer a wide range of colors, with the result that depth and tone take priority. It is especially useful here to block in the first layer of color by means of the rapid application of complementary tones, diluted in a lot of turpentine; a few minutes later, and using slightly thicker paint, it will be possible to build up a light layer of tone all over the picture as shown in our photograph. This color brings life and vibrancy to the picture, at a stage in which we are experimenting with the tonal values which will be built upon later.

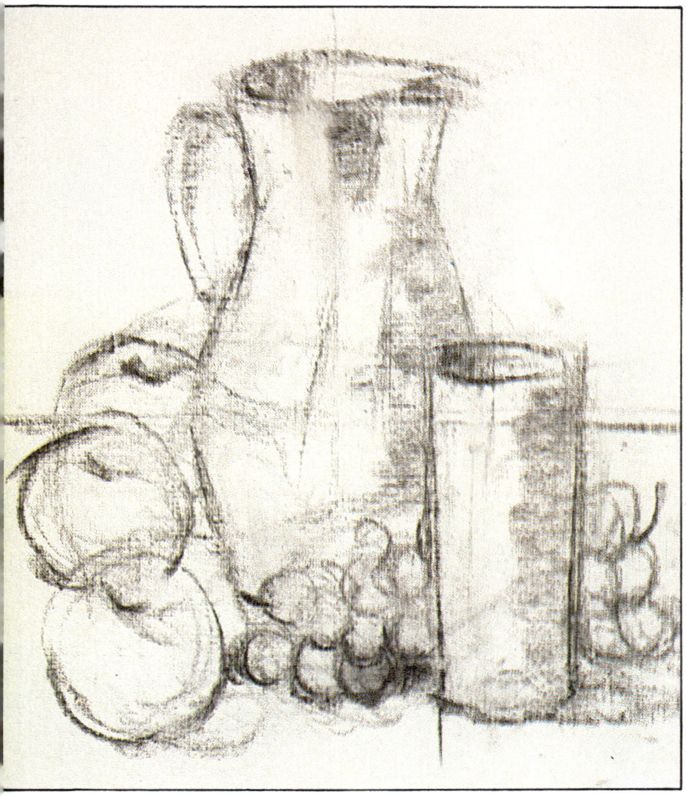

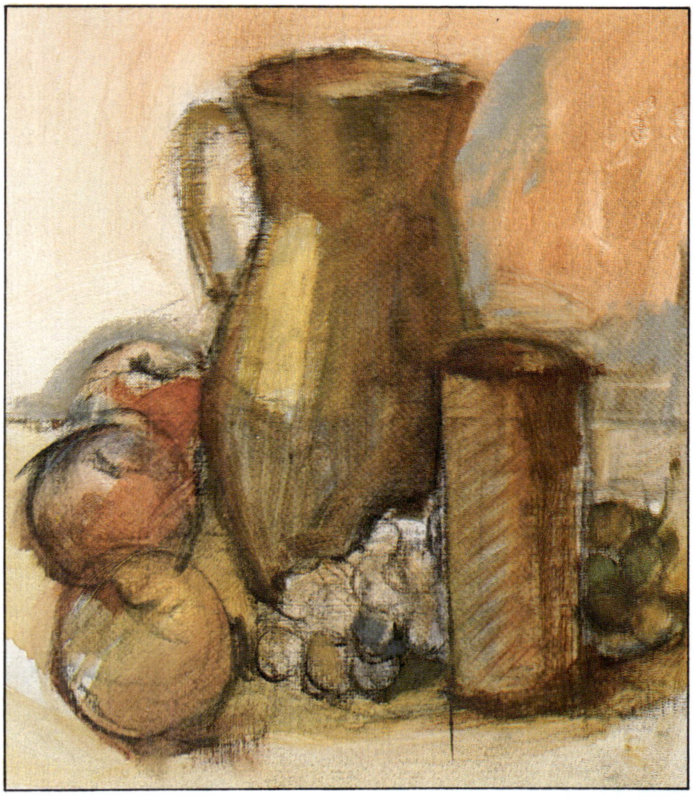

Third stage: Evaluation of light and color

By now the surface of the painting is totally covered with paint. Here we have attempted, without too many tonal variations and in a fresh and uninhibited way, to resolve color and tonal contrasts, emphasizing the sense of depth without detracting from the chromatic richness. Patches of almost pure color have been applied to the canvas, some mixed on the palette and some on the painting itself using light brushwork—see the apples, the bottom of the jug and the shading on the vase. In the close-up picture (below), you can see the contrast created by just a few touches of green and yellow on the reds, crimsons, pinks, and siennas of the apples. These touches also enhance the feeling of depth.

Fourth stage: Completing the picture

At this point it is important not to overdo the tonal variation or the general brushwork or the picture will end up looking contrived. During the third phase some parts of the painting were almost completed. Now, it is just a question of subtly refining outlines and the color of the background, the table and the fruit, making sure that no areas are left unpainted. Reflections are sharpened, some of the darker tones are strengthened, the harshness of the area of light on the jug is softened by making it pinker; finally, we take a look at the whole painting and decide that it is just right. We have achieved our objective.

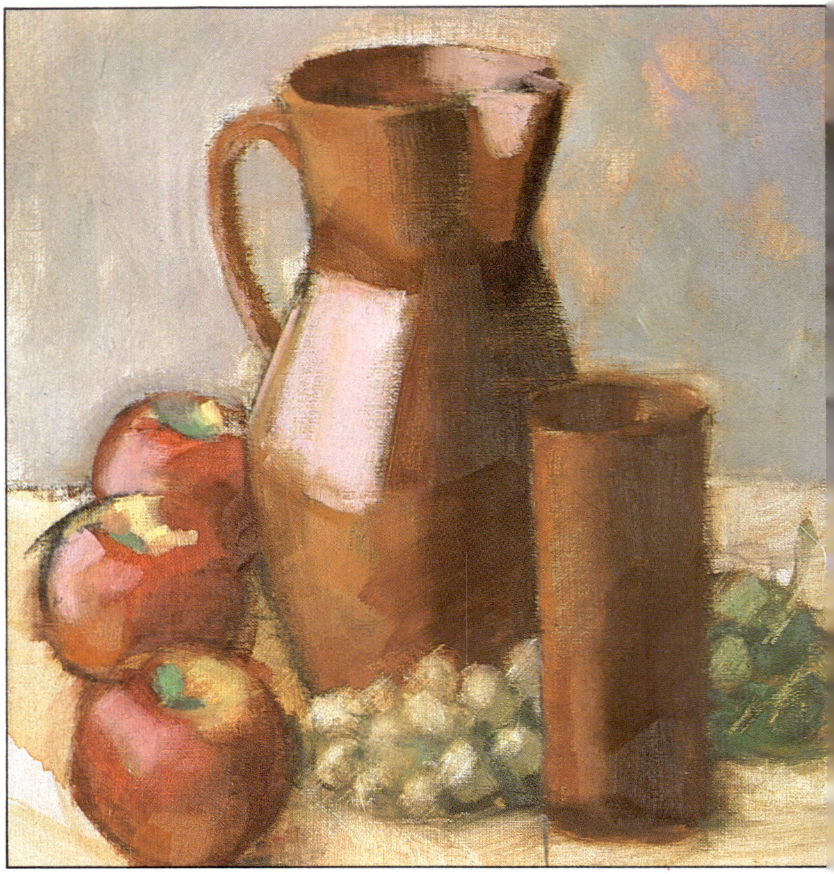

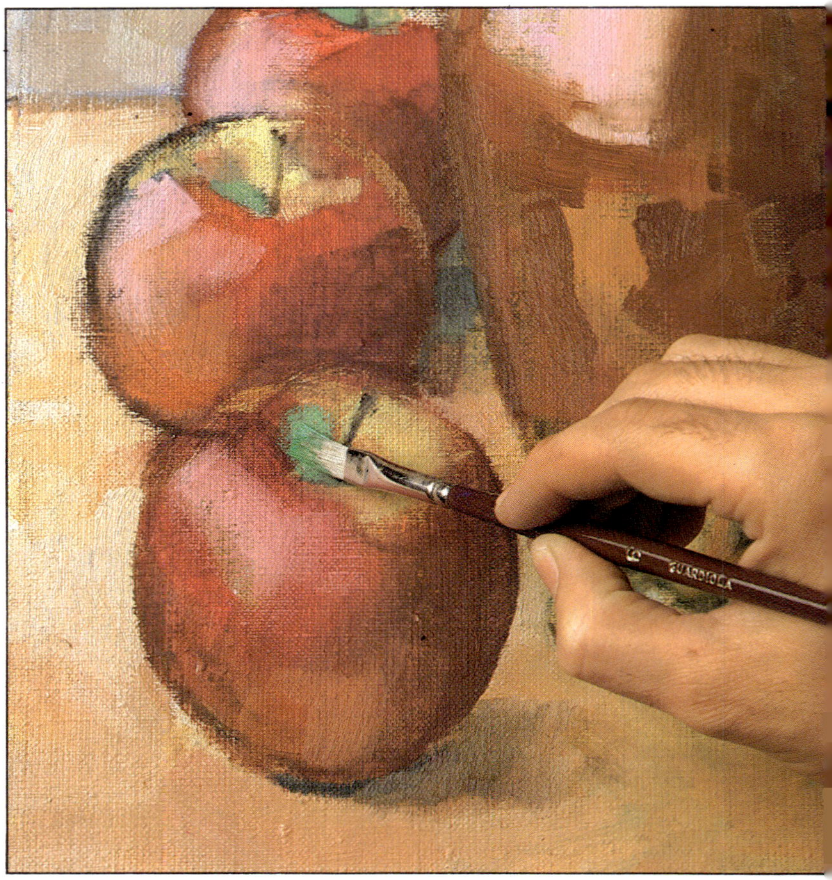

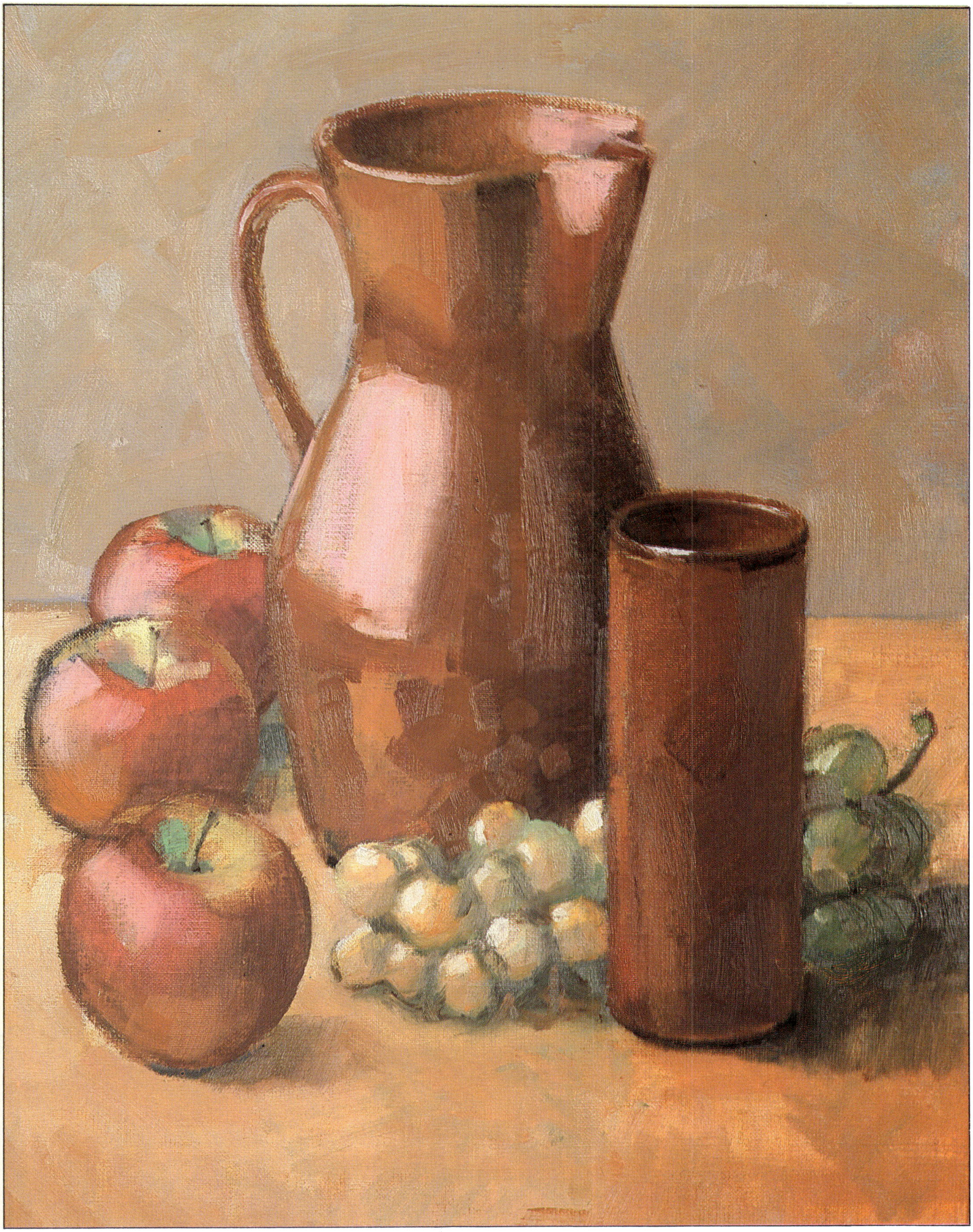

Landscape painting in oils

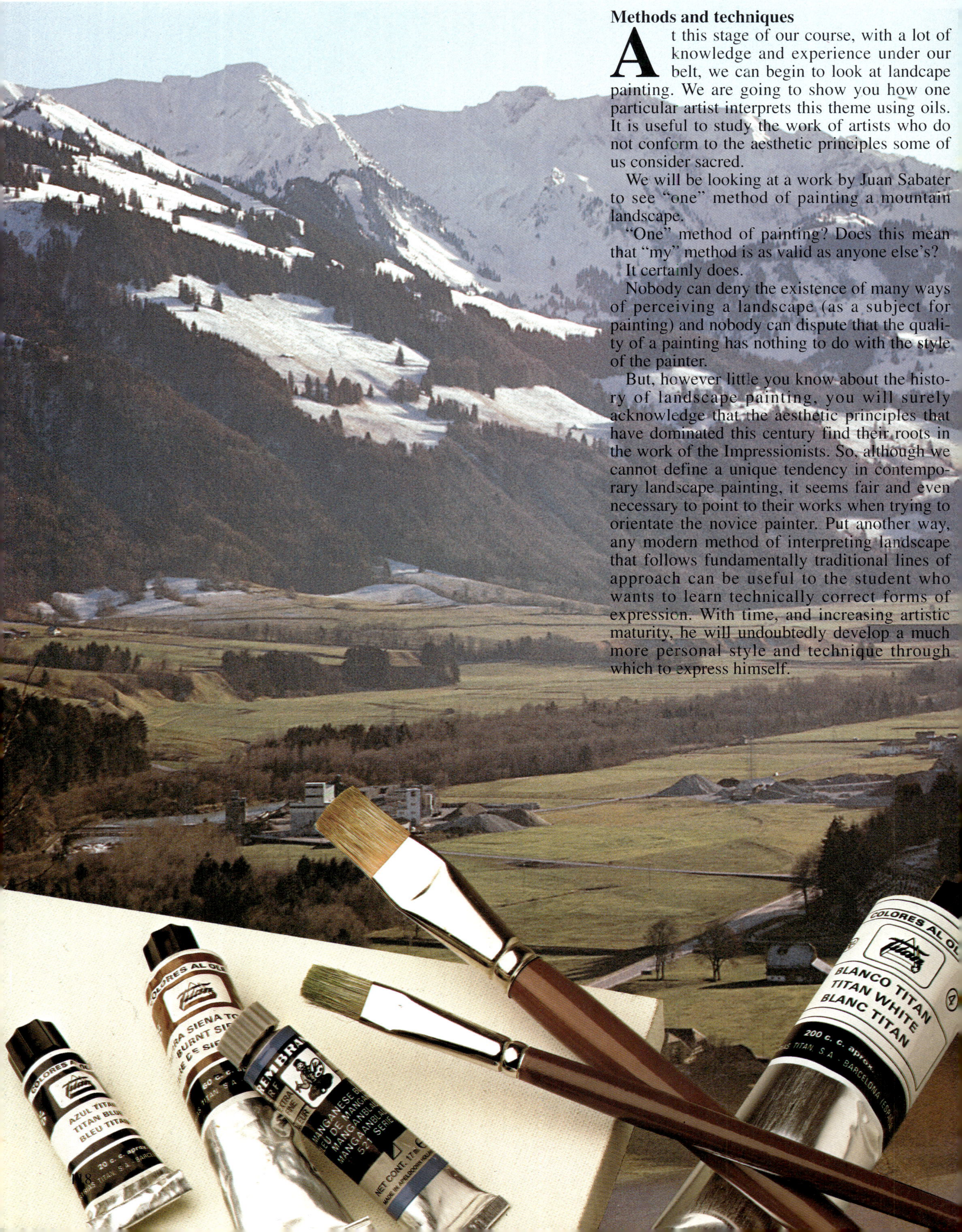

Methods and techniques

At this stage of our course, with a lot of knowledge and experience under our belt, we can begin to look at landcape painting. We are going to show you how one particular artist interprets this theme using oils. It is useful to study the work of artists who do not conform to the aesthetic principles some of us consider sacred.

We will be looking at a work by Juan Sabater to see "one" method of painting a mountain landscape.

"One" method of painting? Does this mean that "my" method is as valid as anyone else's?

It certainly does.

Nobody can deny the existence of many ways of perceiving a landscape (as a subject for painting) and nobody can dispute that the quality of a painting has nothing to do with the style of the painter.

But, however little you know about the history of landscape painting, you will surely acknowledge that the aesthetic principles that have dominated this century find their roots in the work of the Impressionists. So, although we cannot define a unique tendency in contemporary landscape painting, it seems fair and even necessary to point to their works when trying to orientate the novice painter. Put another way, any modern method of interpreting landscape that follows fundamentally traditional lines of approach can be useful to the student who wants to learn technically correct forms of expression. With time, and increasing artistic maturity, he will undoubtedly develop a much more personal style and technique through which to express himself.

Three examples from masters of the medium

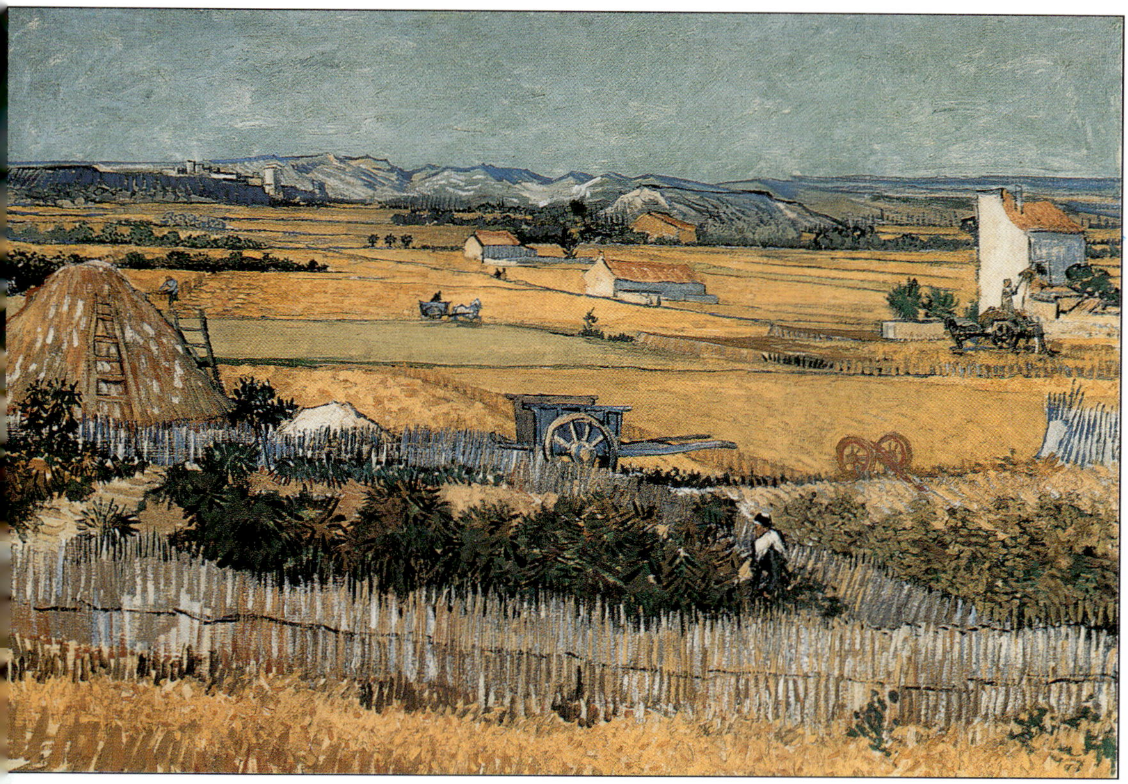

Three examples illustrate some of the techniques developed by 20th century landscape painters.

1. "Harvest at La Crau" *by Vincent van Gogh. Painted in 1888, this painting is considered a departure point for modern landscape painting.*

2. "The big pine tree" *by Paul Cézanne, painted around 1882. The shimmering pattern of superimposed brush-strokes remains a feature of contemporary landscape painting.*

3. "Lady in a wood" *by Giovanni Fattori, 1875. These "atmospheric" effects appeared in European landscape painting towards the end of the 19th Century.*

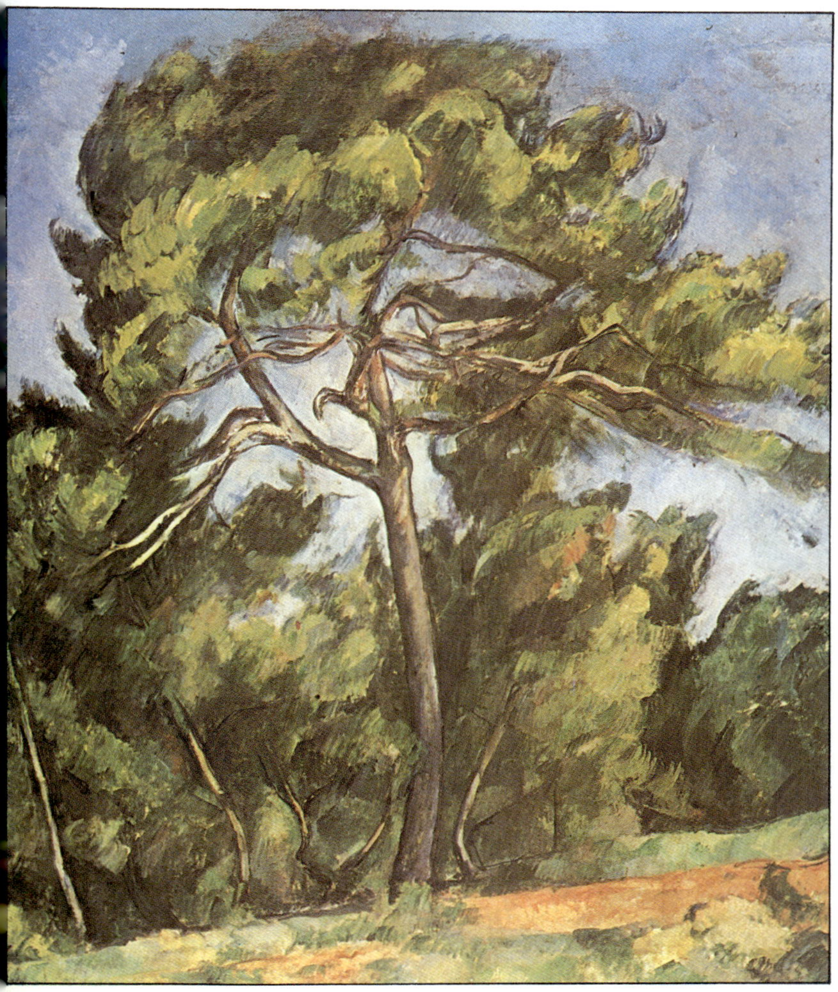

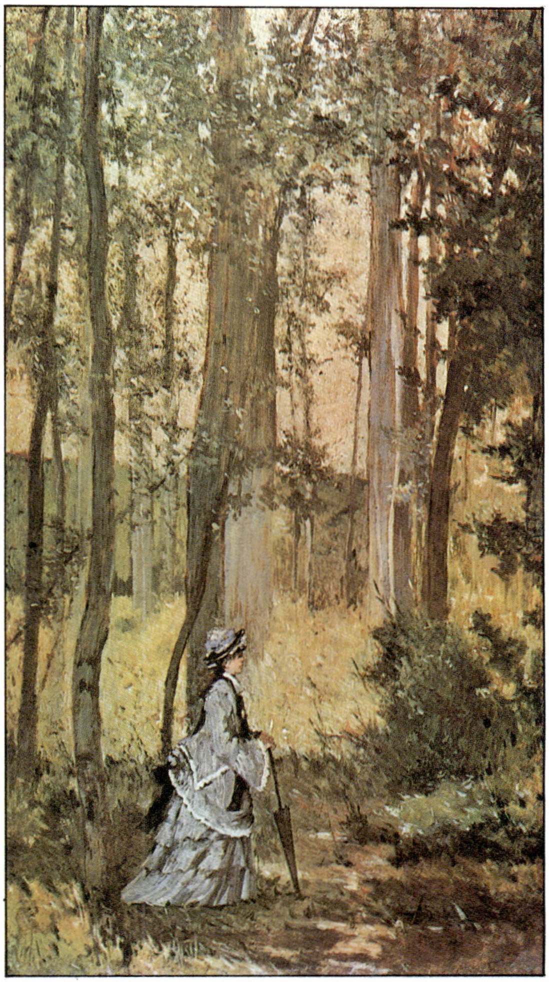

Landscape painting in oils. Study of trees

Pencil studies

In a landscape there are often trees and, frequently, one of them emerges as the focal point of the painting.

The problem for the inexperienced landscape painter lies not in painting *a* tree; it lies in painting *that* particular tree. As with all living things, no two trees are alike; this means that each one has its own personality, an individual character that the artist must be able to capture. The "personality" of a tree depends, basically, on its structure. It is the same with trees as with animals: There are certain characteristics common to each species, quite apart from which every individual has its own peculiarities that we must attempt to draw.

You will have to make dozens of pencil sketches like those on this page—or thousands, even, if you do not want to settle for mediocrity. Bare trees with intertwining branches, leafy trees with welcoming areas of shade, old, tortured trunks, and implausible root structures—you will need to study all of these and more.

Right. *In your sketches try to establish the overall structure of the tree. Analyze its branch formation, which will determine the logical distribution of the various leafy areas.*

Below. *An old Mediterranean pine, clinging to a rocky slope.*

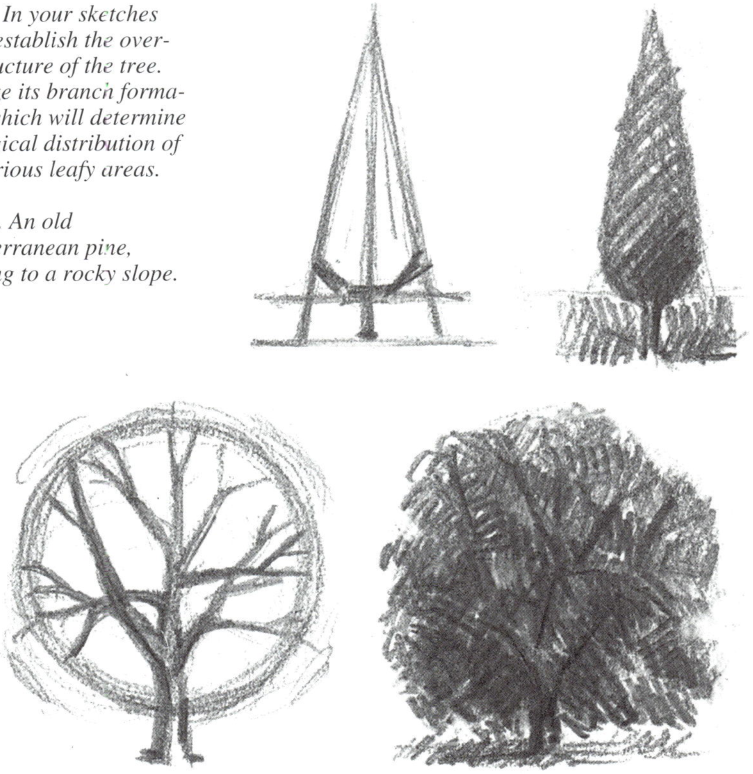

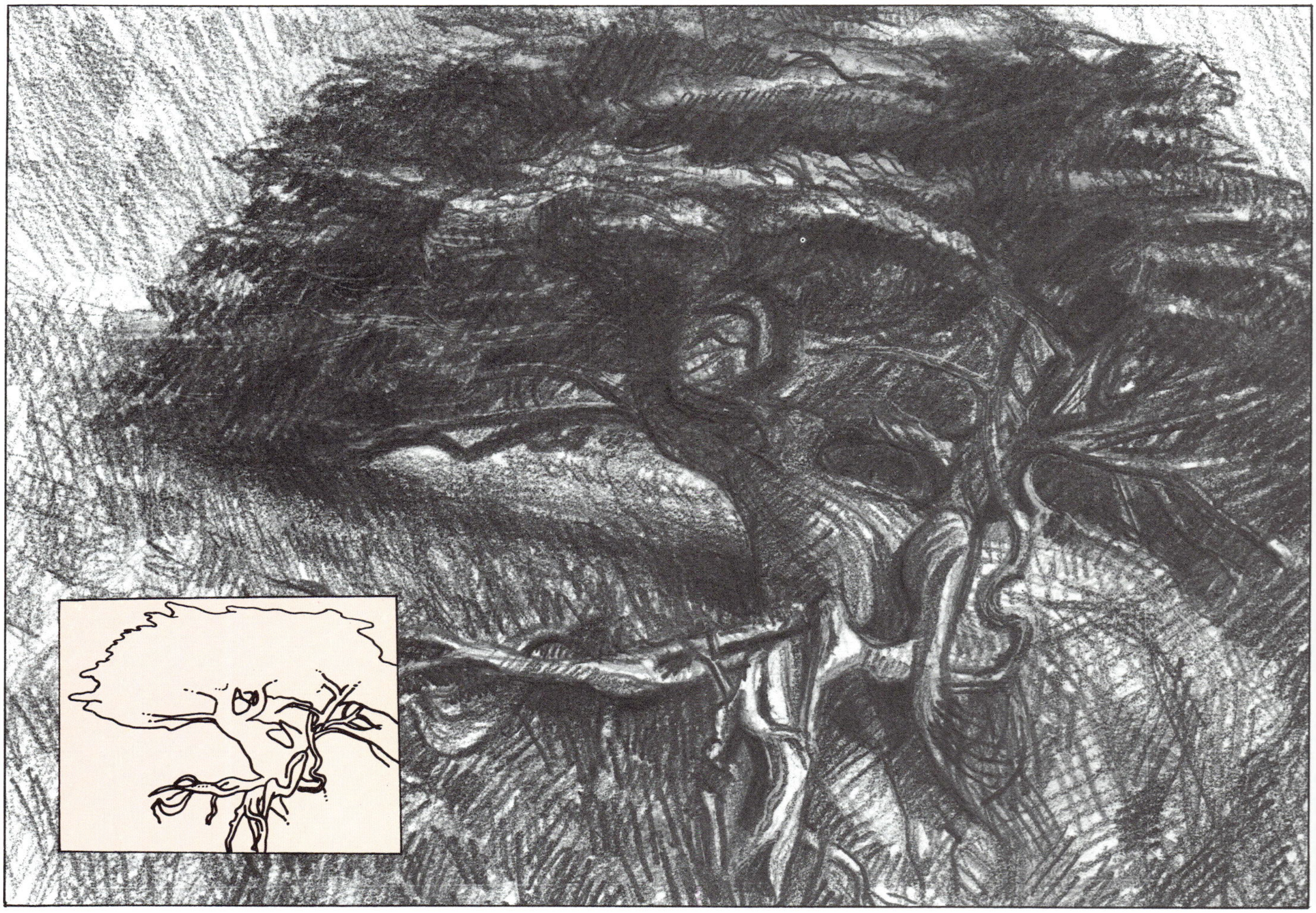

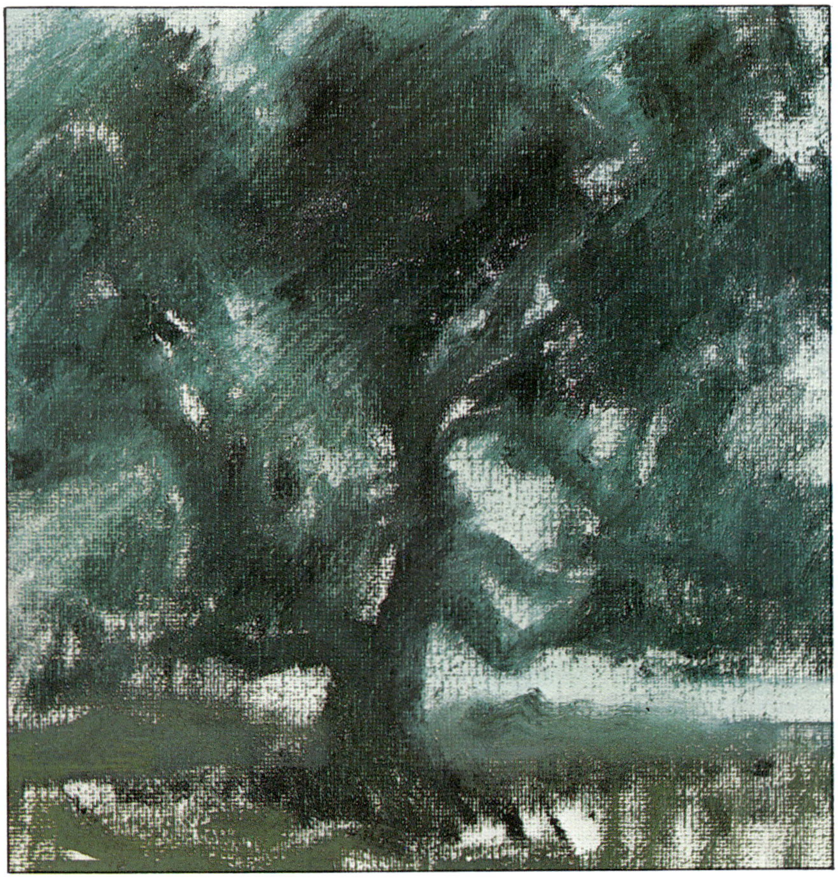

Oil study

Alternating with your practice of pencil studies, it is beneficial to use bits of canvas or cardboard covered with latex primer in order to make lots of oil studies of trees. The process is summarized in these illustrations.

1. Dark areas

Assuming you have first made a good outline drawing in charcoal, block in, using diluted paint, the areas corresponding to the different groups of leaves as well as the trunk and the branches. Leave a few blank spaces to allow the sky to "filter" through the leaves. Use a mixture of Prussian blue and burnt umber, which will give you a very dark green.

2. Finishing the picture

On top of the previous stage, once the paint is almost dry, fill in the sky areas with a mixture of ultramarine and white. By adding yellow and ochre to the dark green used for the first stage, you can create a scale of three new greens that will allow you to define the different areas of foliage.

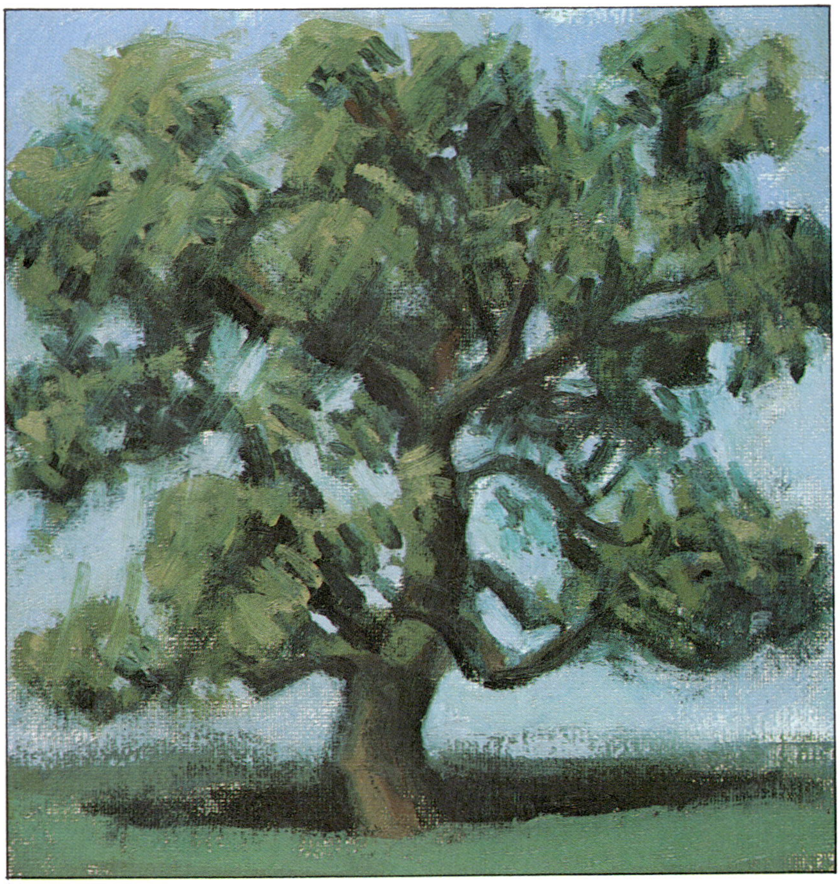

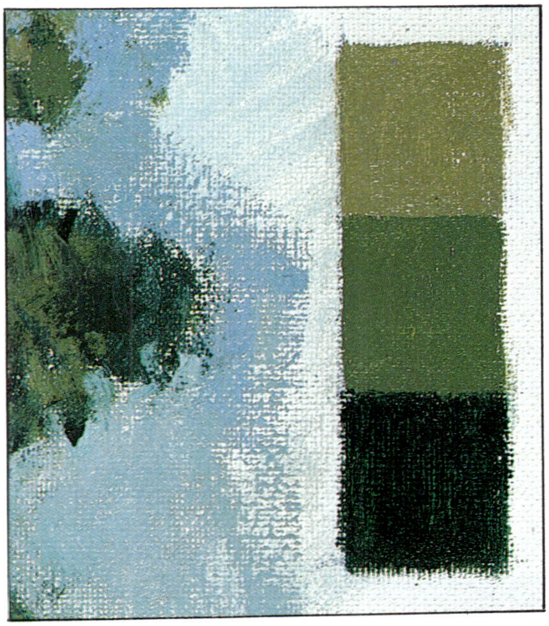

Left. *Study of a tree by Juan Sabater, following the process described.*

Above. *Scale of three greens made with Prussian blue, burnt umber, ochre, and yellow.*

Notice, in the close-up, the apparently carefree way of applying the brushstrokes—something the artist revels in. If you prefer a little more precision, that's fine too.

Painting a landscape in oils

An example to follow

Our intention with this exercise is to offer you the opportunity to study an individual approach to a subject. With this in mind, take a canvas no larger than 18 × 13 in. (46 × 33 cm) and follow the steps taken by Juan Sabater in creating his painting, which we will call "Winter Landscape."

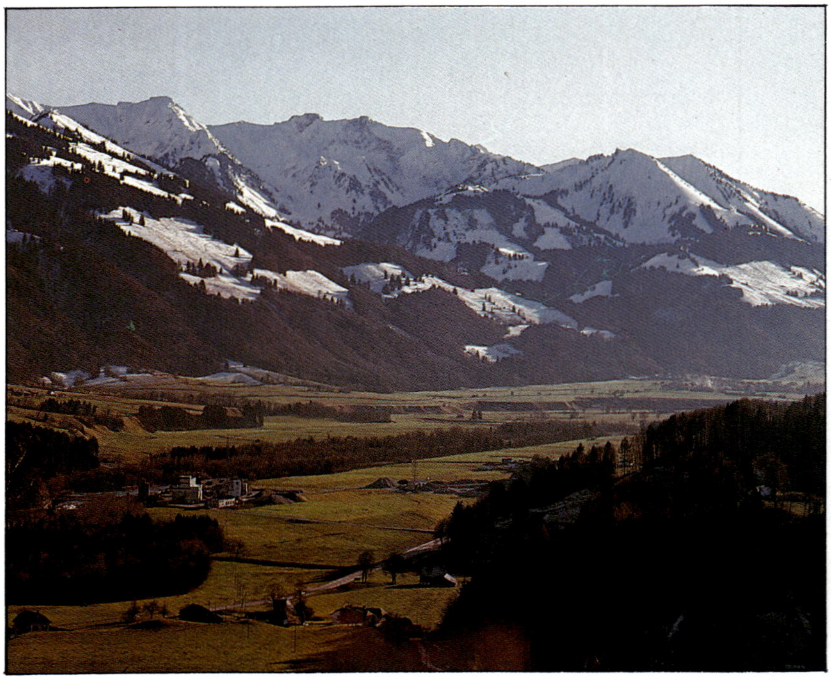

1. Layout drawing

With panoramic scenes in which there is no clearly-defined foregound, the initial sketch is, perhaps, more important than in other cases. Because there are no distinct forms, if the different areas of terrain are not mapped out at the very beginning it is easy to lose your way after a few brushstrokes. So trace out an initial charcoal drawing that will tell you, at any given moment, which area of the landscape you are working on. You can go over these lines with a fine brush using Prussian blue.

1

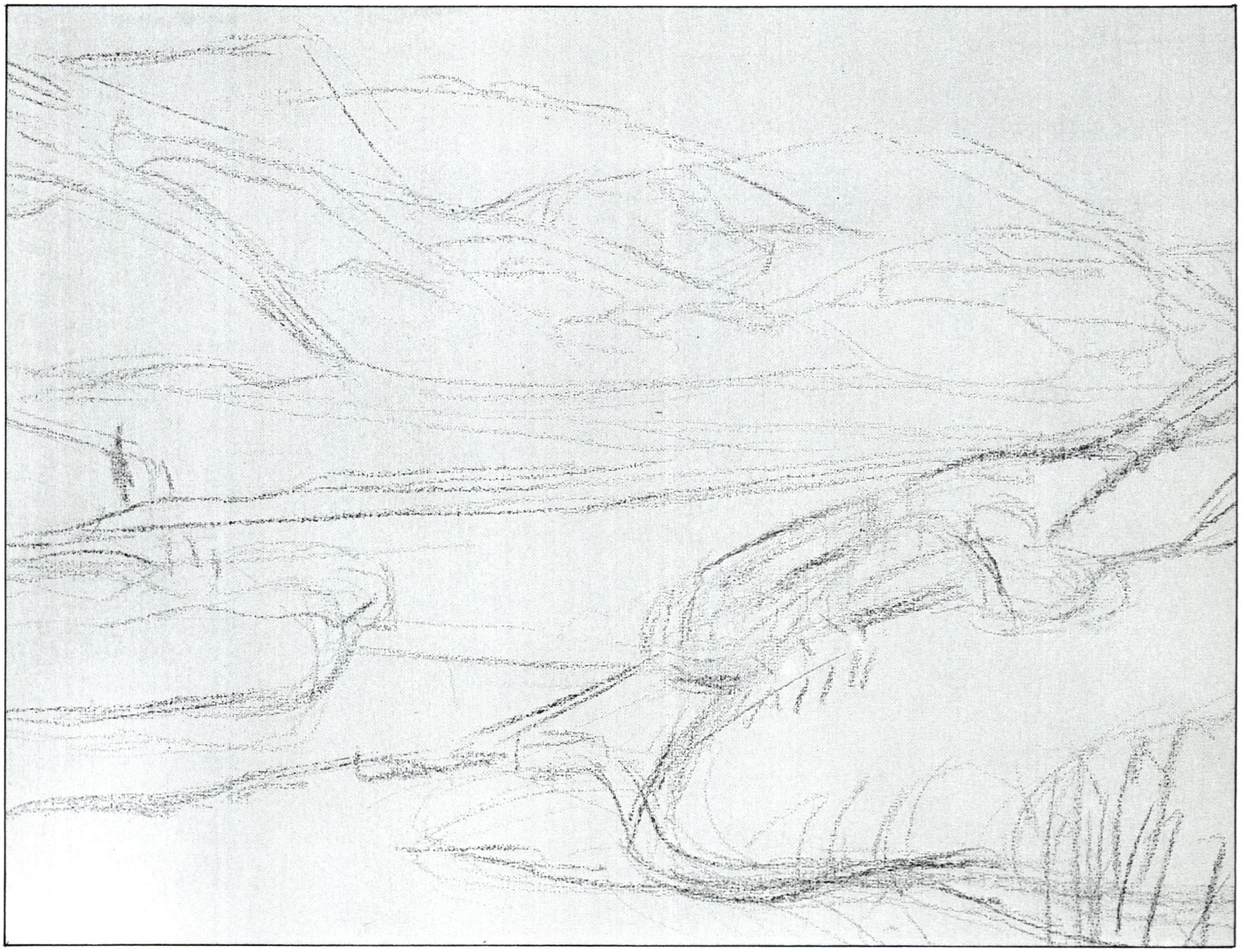

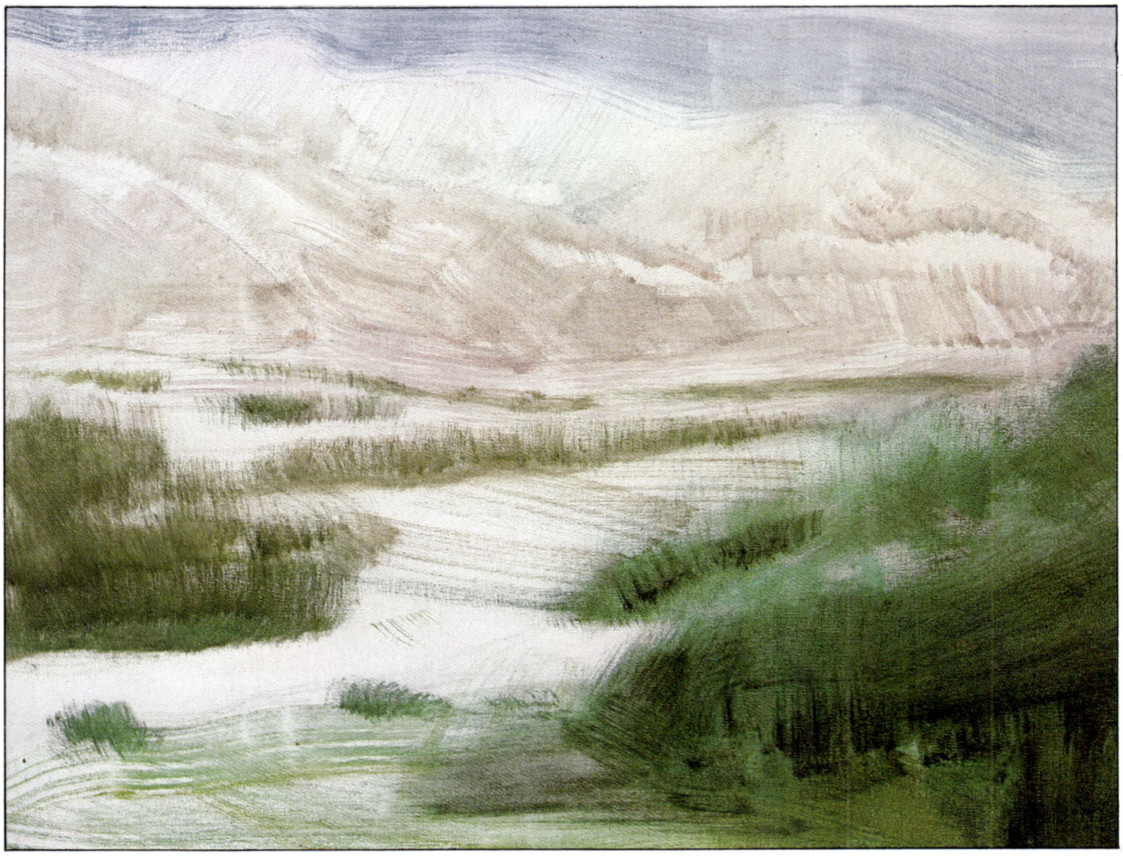

2. Initial color

Using a lot of turpentine and cool colors, begin, as Juan Sabater has done, to block in the darkest areas in the foreground. Although at this stage the exact color is not too important, you should try to maintain harmony of tone, more or less within the sap green or cinnabar green range, with traces of ochre and black. As for the mountains in the background, any muddy gray will do to suggest their initial structure.

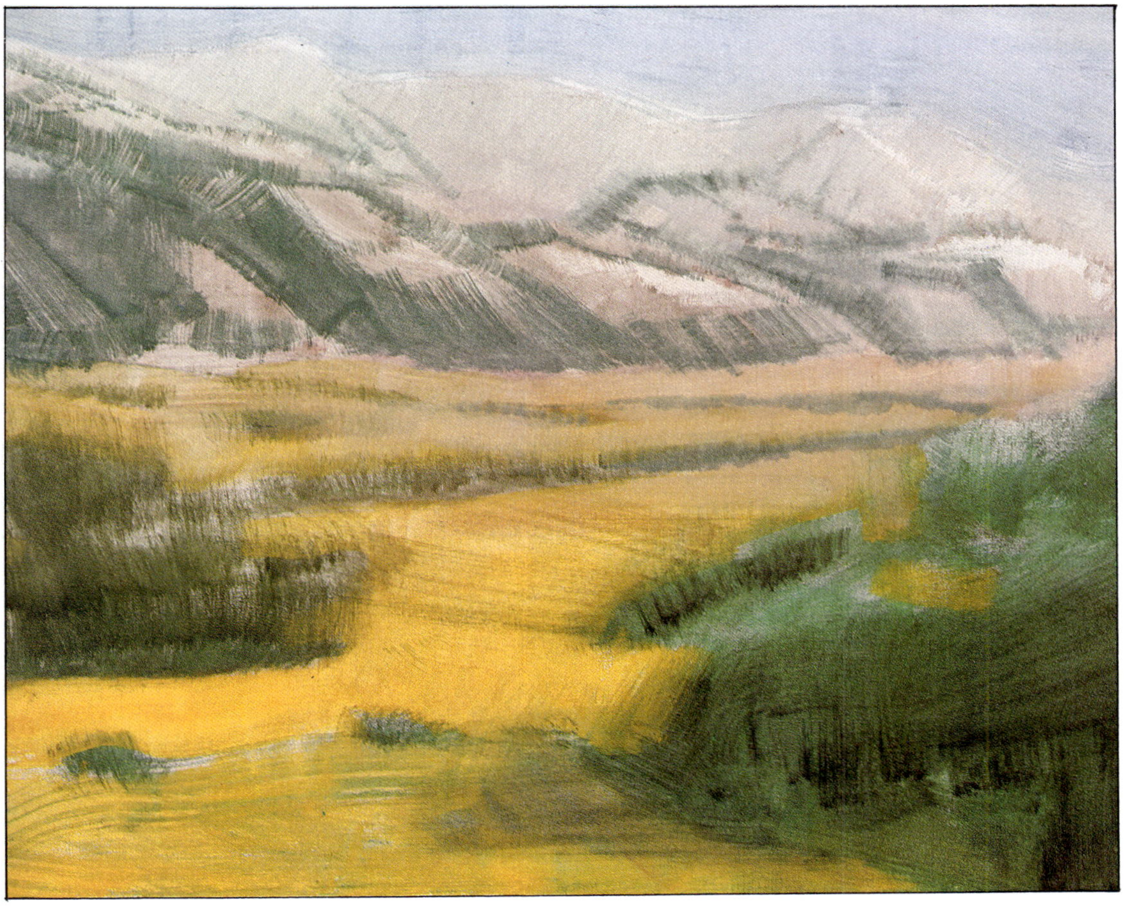

3. The first contrasts

On top of the previous stage, almost without touching the foreground areas, Sabater has introduced the warmer colors that provide the majority of chromatic contrasts in this winter landscape with its predominantly cool color scheme. Notice how atmospheric conditions begin to affect perspective: Cold tones become bluer as they recede from the foreground. The mountains, although without any clearly-defined color, have been described with a few structural brushstrokes, the direction of which is very important in Sabater's painting.

4. The build-up of color

Throughout this fourth stage, the color for each part of the picture has been mixed on the palette and transferred to the canvas with decisive brushstrokes. This part of the process has been divided into three close-ups and an overall view (following page). This is so you can see exactly how Sabater tones down the greens with black paint and, above all, the care he takes to ensure that each brushstroke follows the direction appropriate to the depth and form of the area he is working on.

4a. Close-up of the copse in the foreground, defined with dark, vertical brushstrokes, applied on top of the initial greens. See, to the left of the close-up, the diagram showing the proposed direction of the brushstrokes in each area.

4b. Now we move to the central foreground area. The trees continue to be painted with vertical brushstrokes, while the greenish ochres and other colors of the fields have been applied with horizontal strokes. Look at the diagram on the left of the illustration.

4c. The first undulations of the mountainous area, in which predominantly slanting brushstrokes are used (following the slopes of the hills). Notice how the colors become less and less intense as they fade into the distance.

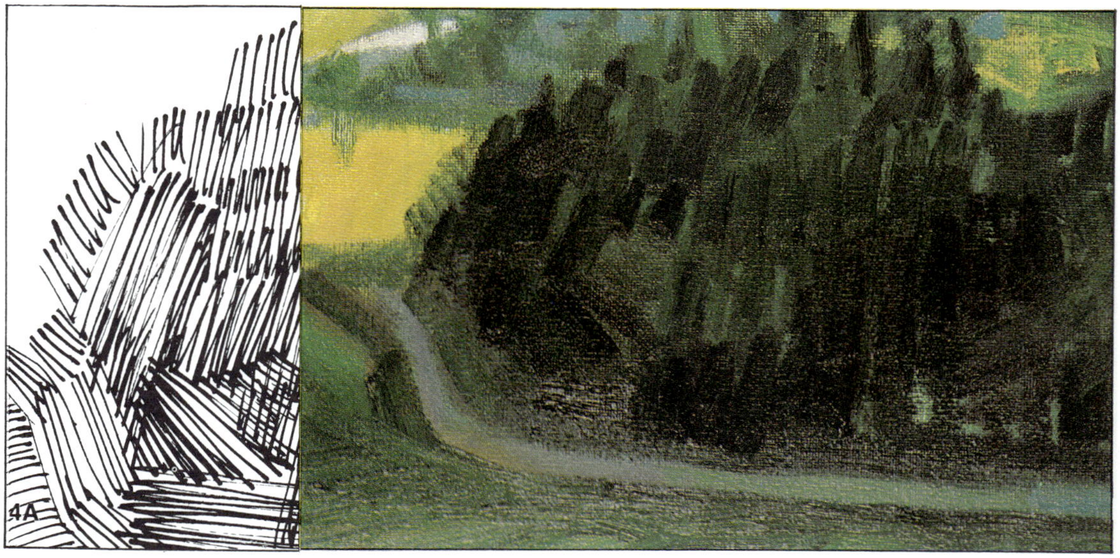

4A

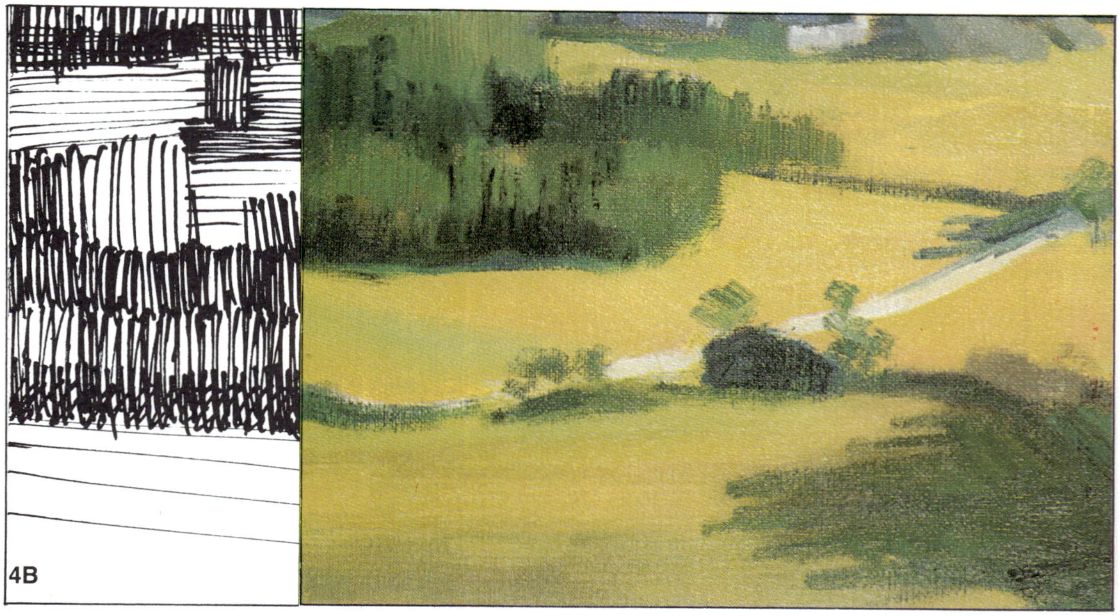

4B

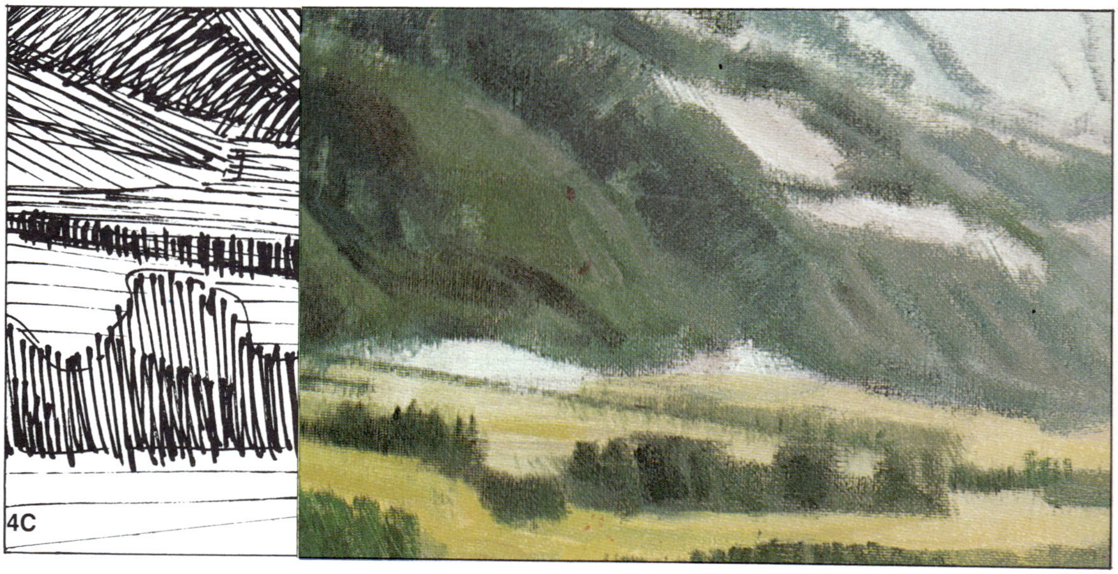

4C

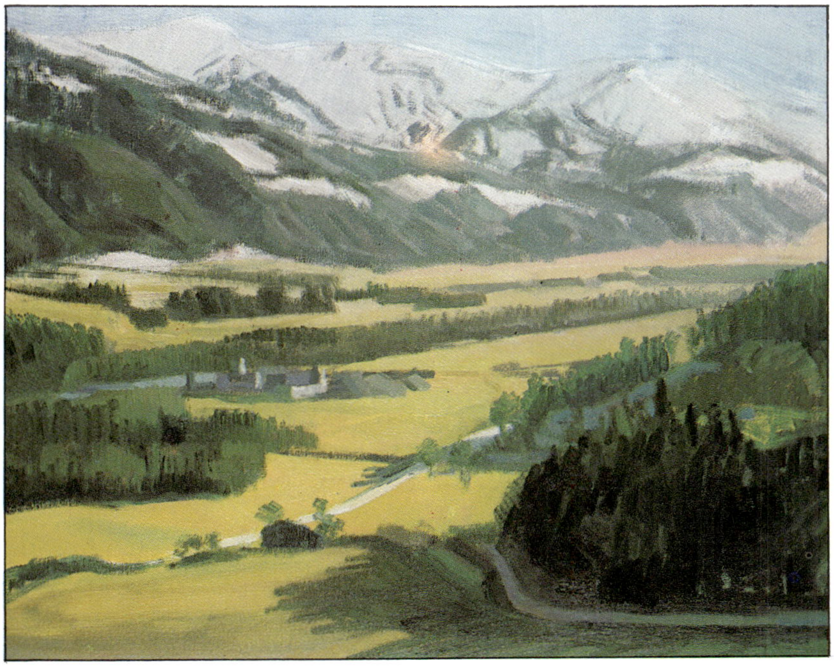

5. Final stage

If you compare the finished picture (below) with the smaller reproduction showing how it was left after the previous stage, you will find few, but significant, differences. Before allowing himself to feel completely satisfied with his picture, Sabater built up further layers of color on the brightest areas of the mountains to give a sense of depth; he also added a veil of cool color over the most distant meadows and, using white with a hint of blue, he brought out the sunlight sparkling on the snowy mountains.

Left.
Reproduction of Sabater's landscape before he decided to finish it off with a few touches to give it greater depth and luminosity.

Below.
The landscape completed to the personal satisfaction of our artist who is well-known for suggesting forms rather than going into minute detail.

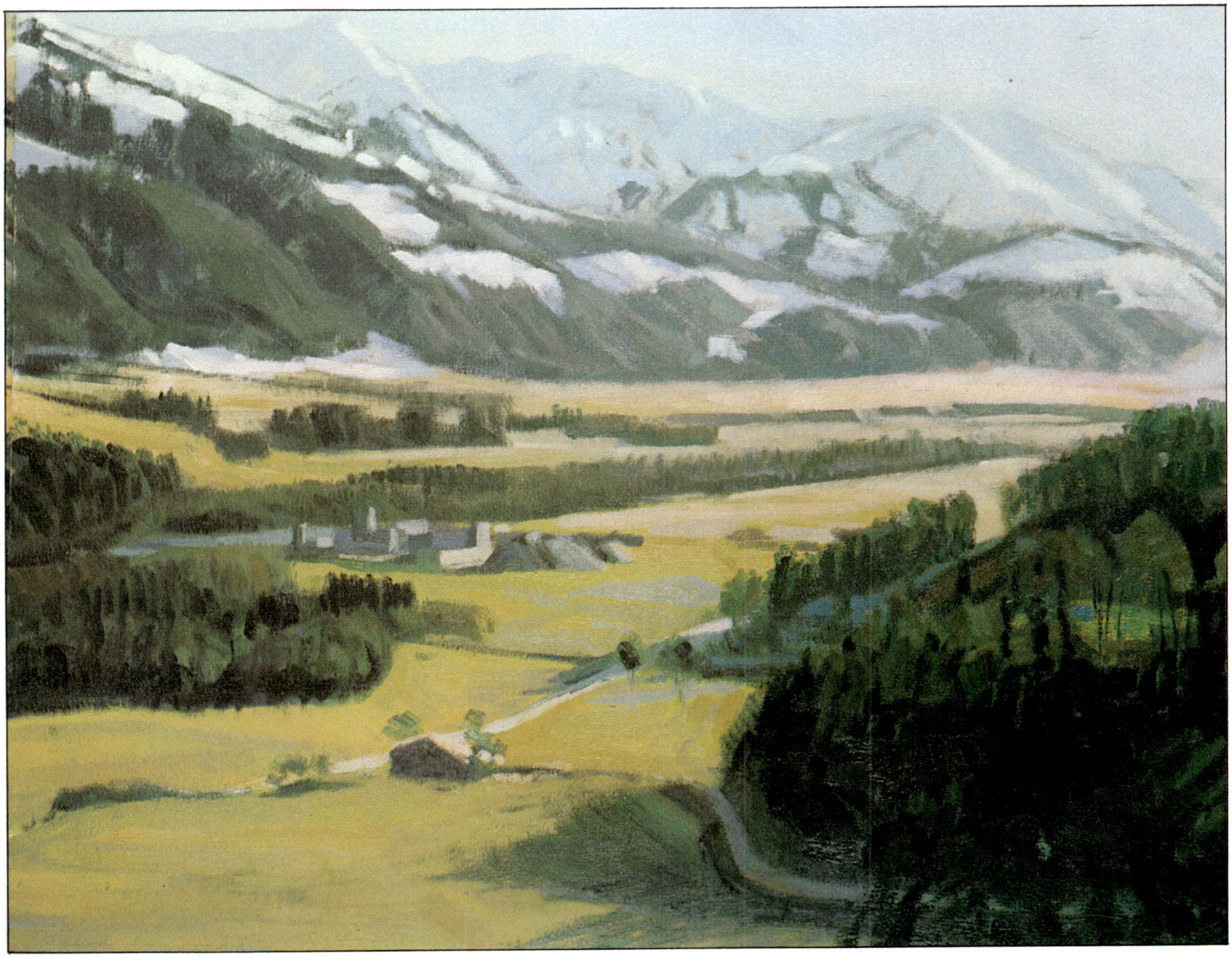